THE STORY
of the
CORONATION

A COLOURFUL IMPRESSION OF THE ABBEY CEREMONY

Expressly painted by E. C. Mansell and J. J. Boys

THE STORY

of the

CORONATION

KING GEORGE VI • QUEEN ELIZABETH

1937

Complete Historical
& Descriptive Record

*With 330 Illustrations and
Six Art Plates in Full Colour*

Edited by
SIR JOHN HAMMERTON

LONDON
THE AMALGAMATED PRESS LTD.

PRINTED IN ENGLAND
FOR
THE AMALGAMATED PRESS LTD.

TABLE OF CONTENTS

LIST OF COLOUR PLATES

FATHER AND SON

Glances Back and Glimpses Forward

by THE EDITOR

THOSE of us who can recall the pomp and circumstance of such gorgeously coloured landmarks of life as Queen Victoria's two Jubilees, the Silver Jubilee of King George V and the Coronations of King Edward VII and King George V, must have a certain envy of the younger generation who have witnessed for the first time in the Coronation of George VI a colossal display of national rejoicing. It is like one's first reading of "Robinson Crusoe" or "David Copperfield".

Do you think that we young Victorians who thrilled with national pride in 1887, and ten years later had the feeling that our Queen seemed destined to rule for ever, were in the least humbled by our young poet of those days who wrote "Recessional"?

> Lo, all our pomp of yesterday
> Is one with Nineveh and Tyre!

We were not. For, after all, every yester-day is one with Nineveh and Tyre, but every tomorrow is one with that City Beautiful to which we are all a-journeying. And, speaking for at least one of those Victorians, I found myself as joyously looking forward to King George's Coronation as, thirty-five years ago, I had looked forward to that of his grandfather.

Only two swift years ago I wrote as follows of the Silver Jubilee celebration of King George V:

"Apart entirely from the fact that of all the nations that went up to Armageddon from 1914 to 1918, Britain stands today, despite the hardships which she is still experiencing and the problems she has still to master, the envy of all in her economic strength, and her national energy in the pursuit of peace. In celebrating the Silver Jubilee of King George we are celebrating our hardly-bought but triumphant resistance to the greatest challenge which our history records to the supremacy and freedom of the British race. Victoria's Jubilee celebrated sixty years of scientific and industrial progress, and Imperial expansion, but in the present year of Jubilee we are celebrating our emergence from the gravest danger that ever threatened our national pride and independence, together with an advance in the social well-being of the nation which so recently as 1897 had seemed almost a Utopian dream. Let the Jeremiahs wail as they may, Britain's star is high and still in the ascendant."

The Hand of Destiny

With but slight modification these words might have been written for the new and even more noteworthy day of rejoicing which our King and Queen and all the peoples of the British Empire have just witnessed.

At the time of his birth, it is doubtful if anyone for a fleeting moment entertained the thought that some day here would be a future King of our realms, a future Emperor of India destined, perchance, to inaugurate a reign surpassing all those of his predecessors in prosperity and in happiness. The long and glorious reign of Queen

Photo] [*Vandyk*

OF BLESSED AND GLORIOUS MEMORY

Of no sovereign have the words "of blessed and glorious memory", by which a deceased sovereign is referred to in official documents, been more completely true than they are of King George V. With his wide human sympathy and his strong sense of duty went every other quality that can endear a monarch to his people.

Consort, and almost all the social duties of the head of the State were still sustained by the Prince of Wales and his beautiful Princess, afterwards to become King Edward VII and Queen Alexandra. They were surrounded by a brilliant Court circle, and both of them enjoyed to the full the round of gaiety which marked each recurring London season and the princely entertaining in the great country houses, as yet unshorn of any of their splendour, which took place in the autumn and winter.

Very different, however, was the part which the parents of the infant Prince played in the life of the country. To them fell many ceremonial duties, but their share in the purely social life of the Court was by comparison small. Both had simple tastes and both loved home life; they preferred, when their duties allowed them to do so, to live as an English country gentleman and his wife.

In this preference we see the outcome of the early life of both George V and Queen Mary. King Edward VII, bearing in mind his own rather unhappy childhood and youth, resolved that his own children should not at a tender age be obliged to take part in public functions, that they should not lead a life that was merely a long and arduous apprenticeship to the duties of the sons and daughters of the sovereign, that their childhood and boyhood should not be hedged about with all the restrictions that had circumscribed his own.

In consonance with this idea, Prince George, his second son, was put into the Navy. In the senior service he found a career dear to his heart, and one that he would dearly have loved to follow for many years to come. But the death of his elder brother, the Duke of Clarence, in January 1892 made him the second heir to

Victoria was still to last for another five years after the birth of the future King George VI, but age and increasing infirmity made the Queen less than ever inclined for public appearances or to play her part in state functions. Yet the decade during which our King of today was born was the grand climax of the Victorian era—a period of unexampled prosperity and social brilliance never since equalled.

The Queen was still living in seclusion, as she had done since the death of the Prince the throne, and brought to an end his active career in the Navy. But it did not, and could not, change those simple tastes, that love of home life, which are characteristic of the men of the "silent service".

Marked by equal simplicity were the tastes of our King's mother, afterwards to be Queen Mary. As the daughter of the Duke and Duchess of Teck she was remote from succession to the throne. Her childhood and youth were passed chiefly at White Lodge in Richmond Park, and her mother, the beloved Princess Mary of Cambridge, gave her an upbringing as simple as that of most children of middle-class parentage.

The life of King George V and Queen Mary was thus, from youth, as quiet and unostentatious as was possible in their exalted station. These things I mention because King George VI is in so many unexpected ways the son of his father—and mother. Our grateful memory of the father remains—and will remain—so vivid, and the example of the mother is so happily before us in the continuing stream of her admirable activities, that it is natural to recall the royal parents when our thoughts turn to their son and his Coronation.

One of the happiest auguries for the future unfolding of the reign which has just begun is the extraordinary resemblance it presents at the outset to that of George V. By a voluntary act of abdication King Edward VIII, who as Prince of Wales had attained in the hearts of his people a position of affection without parallel in the annals of royal princes, and whom the whole Empire had looked upon as its leader into the new era, made way for his younger brother, the Duke of York, to ascend the most glorious throne in the world, laying down an inheritance vaster than that which Diocletian, at the zenith of Rome's splendour, volun-

Photo]   *[Vandyk*

TRUE SON OF HIS FATHER

At the close of his speech after the passing of the Abdication Act the Prime Minister paid a striking tribute to King George VI in which he declared that "more than any other of his brothers he resembles in character and disposition of mind his father. . . . He will devote himself to his great task with the same devotion to duty."

tarily handed over to Constantius Chlorus and Galerius.

The circumstances of King Edward's abdication are still so vivid in the conscience of the world, and likely for ages to be remembered as one of history's most astounding romances, suffused with human sadness, that it is well to do no more than mention the fact that George VI has come to the throne by the withdrawal of his elder brother, and that George V also attained to the throne by the hand of fate, in more tragic manner, being laid upon his elder brother.

Father and son, moreover, had each the great good fortune to find for himself a wife endowed with the finest qualities of British womanhood worthy to be crowned beside her husband. Among his brothers, King George VI most nearly resembles, both in countenance and character, his revered father, and as his own earnest sense of responsibility in his great office is shared by Queen Elizabeth, the nation is justified in thinking that, so far as singleness of purpose and devotion to duty can command the rewards they deserve, the reign of George and Elizabeth will further strengthen the monarchy in the esteem and loyalty of the British peoples.

"Why do you crave for a daily glimpse of Queen Mary?" I asked an Eastbourne lady who had told me that on no day had she missed seeing our Queen Mother during the stay of the late King George and Queen Mary at Compton Place in the spring of 1935.

"Oh," she answered, "I suppose it is because she is so regal." To which I retorted that no adjective less appropriate could be applied to either of our much loved sovereigns of that day.

I shall say, indeed, that it is quite the stupidest epithet to use of any member of the Royal House of Windsor. If King George and Queen Mary had been "so regal", not a tithe of the stupendous enthusiasm with which the celebration of their Silver Jubilee was celebrated would have been forthcoming.

One with his People

The secret of their unique hold upon the affections of the British people was the fact that they were not at all "regal"—they were the veritable embodiment, in their persons and their private lives, of those qualities that make the ordinary folk of these lands examples of unpretentious domesticity to all the world.

Far from appearing "so regal" or trailing clouds of royal glory wherever they walked, King George and his most happily mated Queen seemed better to fit into our modern "middle-class" ways of life than into those of the Victorian aristocracy. They were British of the British, and the Britons are a "middle-class" nation.

The Family on the Throne

Is there anywhere a doubt that these endearing qualities which distinguished the reign of King George and Queen Mary and democratized British Royalty to an undreamt-of extent will suffer the least recession in the reign that has begun so encouragingly? Nowhere is there such a doubt in the public mind of the British people. For once more has the nation the felicity of witnessing "the family on the throne"—a token and symbol of that family life which is beyond all question the backbone of British national character.

The whole secret of Britain's marvellous recovery in the teeth of world depression lies in its democratic institutions, to which in the process of years the very throne has been added. The vast majority of the British people is composed of individuals who are neither serfs, wage-slaves, nor persons of wealth and leisure. And George V and Queen Mary, despite all the trappings of royalty to which they were born and which were necessarily preserved, achieved the miracle of adorning the highest position to which fate can call any human beings, and still remaining not merely human beings but ordinary simple folk, just like ourselves; indeed, nothing like so "regal" as some pompous neighbours most of us have known in our time!

And once more I ask my readers if this characteristic absence of "pomp and circumstance" which was so noteworthy in his parents is not even more noteworthy in King George VI himself, and in his lovely Queen, who, though boasting a lineage that goes back to Robert the Bruce, was brought up in an environment so far removed from regal splendour that her Coronation as Queen of England is the culmination of a veritable fairy tale. The letterpress and illustrations of this book will provide many an acceptable answer to this question.   *J. A. H.*

CROWN & MONARCHY

by A. D. INNES

*Author of "A History of the British
Nation", "England Under the Tudors"*

An Historical Account
of Those Vital Factors
in Our National Life

Photo]   *[Donald McLeish*

HISTORIC SEAT OF THE HOUSE OF WINDSOR

When on July 17th, 1917, King George V declared that henceforward his family would be known as "the House and Family of Windsor", he severed the last connexion of the Crown with a continental dynasty and linked it indissolubly with the great Castle which is an embodiment in stone of English history

CHAPTER 1

THE CROWN AND DEMOCRACY

Here it is clearly shown that the King of Great Britain and of the Overseas Dominions is actually the hereditary "First Citizen" of the Empire, and that none of his prerogatives clashes with true democracy

FROM remote antiquity, down to the time of the Great War of the twentieth century, which turned the world upside-down, the term monarchy has been commonly applied to describe every State-government in which there was an official head of the State who held that position actually or virtually by a hereditary title, without regard to the effective powers he enjoyed. The antithesis of a monarchy was a republic, a form of government in which, if there was any official head of the State at all, he was so not by any hereditary right but only by general consent, which might be expression of legal enactments (as in Rome) or of a military ascendancy, as with those rulers in the States of ancient Hellas from whom the name of "tyrant" is derived; whose counterpart we see in the dictators who have in post-War Europe so largely displaced the hereditary princes, even where king and dictator are standing side by side in the same State. The term monarchy in this sense has travelled a long way from its original meaning, which is "one-man rule". But it is in the original sense that there is an antithesis between monarchy and democracy, rule directed by the popular will. For in actual fact, although to students of political science monarchy is the rulership of one man as contrasted with the rulership either of a group (oligarchy or aristocracy) or of the majority (democracy), when we speak ordinarily of a monarch we are thinking of him not as a single person in whom all authority is vested and all

power concentrated, but as the hereditary head of the community, he may be no more than a figure-head without either authority or power, though he may bear the title of king or emperor. We do not necessarily assume even that he holds his office by hereditary right—many European crowns were held by election—but always on the assumption that the tenure is at least for life.

Autocratic Government

Monarchies, so named, range between those in which one-man rule predominates, where the monarch is in effect an "autocrat", and those in which his ruling or governmental powers are so limited that they almost or even completely disappear. When the War broke out, of the five effective military powers one was a republic; of the others, all monarchies, three were autocratic, the fourth limited or constitutional. When the Peace of Versailles was signed, the three autocracies had toppled to dust; parts of what had been their dominions became independent republics. Among the minor States, constitutional monarchy survived where it had been already established; but the old system of dynastic autocracies went overboard, apparently for ever, their place being taken either by constitutional monarchies or by republics.

The War had been fought, said President Wilson, to "make the world safe for democracy". Perhaps. For while a State under a constitutional monarchy may be as genuinely democratic, as genuinely directed and controlled by the will of the community at large as any republic, a republic may find itself subjected as completely to one-man control as under the most rigid of autocratic monarchies, while even in a constitutional monarchy it is possible for a dictator to assume autocratic functions. But this brings us to our main thesis, illustrated by our own history, that constitutional monarchy is not only consistent with democracy, but it is probably the system under which democratic ideals have their best hope of fulfilment.

For the most famous definition of democracy, by one of the greatest of democrats—"Government of the People for the People and by the People"—is true only if rightly interpreted: if "by the People" means by those in whom collectively the people as a whole reposes its trust and confidence. Government by the people is government *responsible to* the people. Government "by the people" as a whole, literally, is a sheer impossibility. There never has been, and never can be, any such thing. It was conceivable in the City States of ancient Greece where the "people", the entire adult male population of the State, could be assembled in a space not much bigger than, say, Trafalgar Square or St. James's Park: conceivable, but not practicable even there.

§—The Real Meaning of Democracy

IT is not the people, in the sense of the whole population, that can make laws, interpret them, administer them, or carry on the business of the State as a whole. The actual governing is done, can only be done, by a comparatively small number of persons —individuals or committees. Democracy means that the committees, the governors, the persons who do the governing, are answerable, responsible, to the people at large which has entrusted them with the governing powers ; which powers they hold only so long as the people at large chooses that they shall do so.

If the people chooses to entrust those powers to a committee of one, a dictator, the government is none the less democratic —provided always that the last clause is effective and he holds those powers only so long as the people so wills. The machinery by which the people expresses its will is another matter. But such one-man rule cannot take the form of constitutional monarchy for the simple reason that constitutional monarchy is not one-man rule at all ; because the constitutional monarch still at the most shares his rulership with others who do not derive their authority from him.

One other point remains. "The people" is a phrase which may very easily be, and often is, misused. The people means the whole people, including minorities. Now, the "will of the people" can only mean something upon which the majority of the whole—not merely of the largest section—are agreed. Minority opinions are swamped. Government *by* the people is government responsible to that majority.

Majority Rule

But government *for* the people is as meticulously careful of the welfare of minorities, of justice to minorities, as it is of the interests of majorities. In neither case does "the people" mean any section or group of sections, however large or influential. There are multitudes—democrats and anti-democrats—who argue as though "the people" meant only manual labourers. The whole mass of manual labourers forms a sectional majority of the people ; but by themselves they are not the people. A majority of them does not constitute a majority of the whole people : which includes not only hosts of wage-earners who are not manual labourers at all but even peers and capitalists. "Class consciousness" can never be the expression of the will of the people as a whole, being explicitly an assertion of sectional antagonisms. Your true democrat is he who recognizes that the will of the majority must be supreme, whether or not it coincides with his own will or with that of the majority of any particular section to which he may belong. Capitalists or engineers, parsons or dockers, landowners or railway-men, may each legitimately endeavour to get their own way; but unless and until their own way is also that favoured by a majority of the whole community, attempts to force it upon the majority are not democratic but anti-democratic. Democracy is government of the whole people, by governors responsible to the whole people, securing justice to, and in the interests of, the whole people.

Thus democracy may attain its most complete and adequate expression even while it recognizes a "First Citizen" for certain purposes; whether it calls him President, King or Emperor, and whether it calls itself a republic, or a commonwealth or a monarchy.

Democracy in any modern State—in any State at all which is more than a community numbering a population of a few thousands such as were the City States of ancient Greece or medieval Italy—is not a policy but a system of government; wherein the people are not themselves the governors, but the actual governors are responsible to the whole people, holding office or being removed from it at the will of the whole people, and bound to make the prosperity of the people as a whole the object of the policy they pursue.

Varieties of Republic

Thus monarchy is not in itself opposed to democracy, and, next, a republic is not in itself bound to democracy. There is no inherent connexion between democracy and those various types of government, collectively called republics, which have in common only one characteristic—a negative one: there is not in a republic a hereditary First Citizen. The system of

government under a republic may be aristocratic, exclusively in the hands of a few families who derive their privileges from descent; or oligarchical, in which the few derive their privileges from wealth or are admitted to the privileged circle only by the will of those who are already members of that circle. Of such types were the most famous and powerful republics of antiquity and of the Middle Ages—Rome and Venice. It may even be absolutist—autocratic—concentrating all power in the hands of a First Consul like Bonaparte, of a Lord Protector like Cromwell, or of some other dictator, an individual practically irresponsible. It may, of course, be democratic like Athens, the United States or France—but there is no necessary connexion between any one of the three systems and the republican form.

The First Citizen

A monarchy, then, in the modern acceptation of the term, is not a system of government at all, but a form or type, as is a republic, which may be found in an autocracy, in an aristocracy or oligarchy, or in a democracy. Wherever there is a First Citizen inheriting that position or claiming it as an inheritance for his descendants, or holding it presumably for life, and bearing the title of King or Emperor or Prince (which means no more than First Citizen), there modern phraseology recognizes monarchy, whether the powers and privileges of the monarch are unbounded or infinitesimal, indefinite or rigidly defined.

Nearly every democratic State has recognized an official First Citizen. If the democracy is republican in form, he is called a president and holds his office for a term of years by election at least nominally; if it is monarchical in form, he is called a king, and holds office for life—subject to deposition by general demand—by a title in which there is at least a hereditary element. That hereditary element is in itself neither democratic nor the reverse; it is simply a convenience, an expedient which in certain respects tends positively to increase the utility of the First Citizen, and in others to diminish negatively the drawbacks attaching to an elective First Citizen.

The difference between a monarchy and a republic lies not in their less or more democratic characters, but in the qualification for the position of First Citizen, a position which does not necessarily carry with it any governmental powers at all. Normally the monarch succeeds as a rule by a hereditary title, the president by a purely elective one. It is only in cases where the official First Citizen exercises actual governing powers that the question whether hereditary succession is anti-democratic arises, since it is with government that democracy is concerned.

Constitutional Monarchies

It is in this country that the form of constitutional monarchy has been worked out, and from this that other constitutional monarchies have been copied, with modifications. It is a form whereof the essence is that the official First Citizen, called the King, does not exercise governmental powers. It is arguable of course that it would be better if he did—as, for instance, the President of the United States actually does—but it is a simple matter of fact that he does not, and that so far as other constitutional monarchs do so they are departing from the British model. Hence on the question whether constitutional monarchy is a desirable institution, argument one way or other in the name of democracy is irrelevant. A hereditary right to governmental powers is no doubt inconsistent with pure democracy; a hereditary title to powers, functions, privileges, duties which are not governmental, is not.

"Well," it may be said, "if your First Citizen is to have no governmental functions, why have an official First Citizen at all, other than the actual working chief of the government itself?" The answer is : Because it is in many ways inadvisable that the working chief of the government should also discharge the functions of non-governmental First Citizen. In former times, a hereditary monarch discharged both sets of functions ; in some republics an elected president does so ; but it is by reason of the practical objections to such a combination that some republics have an elected president who is practically a non-governmental First Citizen ; while a constitutional monarchy has a hereditary king who is a non-governmental First Citizen.

The constitutionalist argument presents three stages. First, there are non-governmental functions for an official First Citizen to discharge. Second, it is better to separate those functions from the functions of the working chief of the government. Third, those functions can best be discharged by a hereditary rather than an elected First Citizen. The first proposition is hardly disputable. The second may be maintained on the democratic ground that the combination of functions tends to concentrate too much power in the hands of one citizen. The validity of the third depends upon the particular conditions, and upon the nature of the functions which the First Citizen is expected to discharge.

Functions of First Citizen

Put briefly : the First Citizen is to be the representative in the eyes of the public, foreigners as well as citizens, of the State as a whole, not of any section, group, class or party. With very rare exceptions—George Washington was one—an elected president is in actual practice chosen as the representative of a party. Again, where the whole State has the character of a union or federation of States, it is best that he should not be identified with one of those States more than with another. An elected president can hardly help being identified with his own State ; the king, whose ancestors have been from time immemorial kings of all the States concerned, fulfils our requirement and is identified with them all collectively but with no one of them in particular. The continuity of his race emphasizes the continuity and, therefore, the unity, of the whole State, whose king never dies ; no similar sense of continuity is suggested by the last of a series of presidents. The functions of the First Citizen demand, not indeed first-rate ability, but at least a high degree of special training ; the chances are altogether against an elected president having received such training, whatever his abilities may be, whereas the heir to a monarchy has probably had his eduction mainly directed to fitting him for the position to which in the natural course of things he will succeed. Such own lands : for nowhere else is there a long-established constitutionalist tradition. Elsewhere, the traditions of his House—if it be an old House—would suggest to every monarch, however limited his powers, inducements to use the constitutional monarchy as a stepping-stone, an instrument for restoring a monarchy not at all constitutional. For us (save for a single unfortunate experiment which broke down

THE KING GOES TO PARLIAMENT IN STATE

Only on the occasion of the opening of Parliament is there any public manifestation of the King's position as ruler of the realm. His Majesty then drives to Westminster in the state coach used after the coronation only for this purpose, with a bodyguard of medieval splendour. In the House of Lords he reads from the throne to the Lords and Commons the King's speech which is actually prepared for him by his Ministers.

arguments apply, indeed, mainly to a monarchy with traditions rooted in a sufficiently remote antiquity ; but those conditions are very precisely met by our own, the prototype of all constitutional monarchies.

Moreover, as concerns this country in particular, the Crown has one attribute which must not be overlooked. We Britons are apt not to note it, because to us it has become a matter of course. The peoples of other countries are apt to miss it, for the opposite reason, that it is an attribute of monarchy never realized in their in a dozen years), the sovereign for more than two centuries has taken his constitutional position for granted. A restoration in countries where a royal family has been discarded, the establishment of a borrowed dynasty in a newly constituted state, or the creation of a new dynasty would carry with them the possibility of the development of a reactionary activity on the part of the Crown, a menace to democracy from which the British constitutional monarchy of the House of Windsor is entirely free.

2

THE CROWN : AN HISTORICAL SURVEY

The story of the Crown in Britain traced from the far-off days when the King was chosen only as a doughty leader in battle down to the present time, with an explanation of the evolution of limited Monarchy

AMONG European peoples at least it may be taken as a definitely ascertained historical fact that the monarch came into being primarily as the war-leader of the community's armed forces. The need in battle of a single directing authority, whose orders were not to be questioned, presented itself at a very early stage. When men have become accustomed to yielding unquestioning obedience to a particular person in one field of activities, the habit extends itself to other fields ; and the war-leader's authority came gradually to be recognized in times of peace.

When the war-leader was incapacitated, it became natural that the successor chosen should be first the most efficient of his kinsmen—then a kinsman whose succession had been practically agreed upon beforehand—a son who would carry out for the new generation the functions which had been performed by the father—the eldest son unless there was strong reason to the contrary—finally, the eldest son in any case, in order to avoid the formation of factions and disputes, with internal dissensions in the community. Such in effect were the steps by which the elected or chosen captain developed into the monarch succeeding by the rule of primogeniture, the right of the first-born.

He was not at any of these stages a lawmaker : in primitive societies there was no law-making. There were recognized customs of the society—that was all. If an independent person ignored the customs or defied them, he paid the penalty at the hands of his outraged neighbours, who were supported by public opinion. Custom recognized individual rights of property within the community, varying in extent. Custom forbade one member of the community to injure another in person or property ; but those who were strong and could take care of themselves were not always scrupulously careful of their weaker neighbours' rights. If the weak were to be protected, or the strong kept from quarrelling, there must be in the community a judge, someone who could intervene, to whom appeal could be made, who could arbitrate, pronounce upon grievances submitted, and enforce his pronouncements.

Captain and Judge

In time of peace, the war-chief became in actual practice a sort of court of appeal, the judge whose decisions were final and would not be challenged. (So, as a familiar example, the "Judges" of Israel for the most part held their position because they had been successful captains.) When the functions of captain in war and judge in peace were united in one person who succeeded to the office by a recognized rule of heredity, monarchy—kingship—had definitely appeared. Incidentally, the king may also have acquired the functions of a chief priest, the interpreter of the will of the gods, the mediator through whom their goodwill to his people is procured and preserved, and their wrath appeased ; but this third function is by no means necessarily attached to the primitive monarchy—where it is so, and the monarchy, still primitive, encounters Christianity with its organized ecclesiastical system, it loses whatever there is of priesthood in it. But the monarch always remains, in theory, the supreme war-chief and the supreme judge. As the regions expand over which his sway extends, captains and judges must be multiplied ; but they are persons to whom he has delegated his authority, primarily appointed by him or with his sanction, and removable at his will. They are not rival but subordinate authorities.

Growth of Legislation

But increasing population and expanding territory involve something more—law-framing, legislation. The growth of local diversities of custom, diversities of individual interpretation on the part of judges, creates confusion, uncertainty as to what custom a man must act upon, what penalties he risks by breaking a rule intentionally or inadvertently. Legislation is primarily the codification of customs, defining and harmonizing them ; then revising them in accordance with the dictates of justice or uniformity ; then adding to them new rules for meeting circumstances of which the established customs have not taken account—for dealing with which there *are* no customs.

The judge has hitherto dealt with particular cases ; the law-giver is called in to formulate generalizations. The judge, as being, so to speak, the recognized official expert and interpreter of custom, becomes the formulator ; the monarch, already captain and judge, has added to his functions that of the law-giver. If then the armed forces of the community are entirely at his command, the subordinate captains all yielding him implicit obedience ; if he interprets custom as he pleases and can compel all to accept his interpretation ; if he can order the abolition of existing customs and the institution of

others at his own will ; if he is free in his own person to ignore inconvenient laws and authorize other persons to do so—then is the monarch absolute, an autocrat.

But in England the king never has been at any time anything of the kind in practice, even when in theory his powers have been most unlimited. Throughout the long period of history known to us as the Middle Ages, and for some time longer, the king of England was in fact the undisputed war-chief. It was not England that went to war with France or Scotland, but the king of England who went to war with his neighbour of Scotland or his cousin of France. He was the acting commander-in-chief of his own armies ; he led them in the field in his own person. But four hundred years have passed since Henry VIII played at commanding English troops on foreign soil ; and after Henry VIII the only kings of England who fought abroad in person were William III, who was commander-in-chief of Holland as well as King of England, and George II, whose horse bolted with him at Dettingen—whereupon he fought most valiantly on foot, since a horse might run away with him, but his own feet certainly would not.

Absolutism in Britain

The king has long ceased to command his own armies or to decide the issues of peace or war on his own responsibility. It is very much longer since he ceased to act as a judge in his own person. It is seven hundred years since King John set his seal to the Great Charter which surrendered every pretence on the part of the Crown to any royal right of personally overriding the law. And it does not appear that there was ever any time at all when a right on the king's part was acknowledged of making laws at his own will, or altering laws as seemed good to him.

England, in short, has never been ruled by a monarch who was an autocrat. Why then, do we hear, as we often do, of the "Tudor absolutism" and the "struggle with absolutism" under the Stuarts ? Simply because the English monarchy came nearer to being an autocracy under those dynasties than at any time before or since—unless we except the Commonwealth, when Britain was in form a republic, not a monarchy at all, or the era of the Norman Conquest, which was largely in the nature of a military occupation. Every Tudor monarch was careful always to act according to the forms of law. Every monarch, Plantagenet or Stuart, who claimed to override the law by prerogative, found his claim challenged, and challenged successfully, though it might be at the cost of civil war. Nearly every such conflict was followed by a restatement of the law which, in fact, carried with it a curtailment of powers hitherto exercised by the Crown ; in no case were the rights extended. The last formal conflict was decided by the revolution of 1688 ; and since that date royal powers which were not then even in dispute have fallen into disuse by force of circumstances and have become "unconstitutional" without formal abrogation.

In the familiar phrase, "the king reigns but does not govern". For many centuries he reigned and governed as well, but never as an autocrat—despite occasional attempts on his part to do so. The British conception of kingship has in these islands been established (still with gradual modifications) for more than two hundred years. Elsewhere it obtained no hold till almost within the last century. Its establishment in England was the outcome of a prolonged struggle ; and while that struggle was going on, a corresponding but in many respects dissimilar conflict was in progress in Europe which ended in a general establishment of autocracies, so that until the great cataclysm only here and there have other States had the chance of learning to understand what constitutional monarchy means —of appreciating the sense of a polity in which "the king reigns but does not govern".

Traditional Kingship

The traditional conception of a king is that of an autocrat or of one who at least aims at being an autocrat—one whose will is law and who is responsible to none. There seems to be no reality about the idea of a king who does not govern, and a king who does govern cannot be fitted into democracy. Monarchy, then, appears to be either a sham or something essentially undemocratic. It follows, then, that democracy is not to be found in a political system which includes the institution of kingship.

It is precisely this proposition to which our constitutional monarchy presents a flat contradiction in visible, tangible, concrete form. Our monarchy is neither a sham nor something opposed to democracy, but a real and valuable asset in a democratic State.

To realize that, the first step must be to understand how the constitutional monarchy has arrived, growing out of a monarchy always, indeed, "limited" but often nearer to absolutism than to constitutionalism.

§—Autocrats Within the Law

THE British constitution is rooted in the political system which was existent in England more than a thousand years ago. At the earliest stage of which we have positive knowledge there were several kings in England. It is rather more than one thousand years since Edward the Elder, son of Alfred the Great, was acknowledged as King of all England. The kingship of the House of Alfred was, like those which preceded it, a limited monarchy. The king was already supreme war-chief, judge and law-giver, succeeding by election in which hereditary title—not yet primogeniture—was a predominant but not the sole factor. Even as war-chief his authority was so far limited that the levies which made up the armed forces of the State could refuse to serve outside their own shires. As judge his pronouncements must be in accordance with the law ; and as law-giver he could not alter or add to the laws without the sanction of a council which probably every free man had a right to attend, though it was a right rarely exercised except by persons of importance, who could do so without inconvenience. His revenues were derived from his private estates. The only taxation was a land-tax, levied by consent of the Council, for the maintenance of forces to protect the country from the incursions of the Danes.

The Norman Conquest wrought a very substantial change. Theoretically, William of Normandy reigned as king of England by right of election, and ruled by the laws of England. But they were the laws of England as interpreted by Norman lawyers versed in a totally different system of law.

Mutual Obligations

According to the law thus interpreted, the king was the owner of every foot of land in the kingdom. Everyone who was possessed of land held it by grant from the Crown, or from someone to whom it had been granted by the Crown, and so on ; granted upon conditions of military or other services, and of fixed occasional payments, "feudal dues", carrying with them definite obligations which must be observed both by the Crown and the grantee, the vassal or baron. If the vassal broke them, he was liable to forfeiture of his estates. If the king broke them, the vassal could repudiate his allegiance and claim on his side freedom from the obligations. The king could claim just so much—and no more : the vassal had his counter-claims. The obligations were never all on one side ; they were mutual.

Thus the king could raise local forces for local action by summoning the shire levies in the Saxon fashion ; he could raise an army by calling upon his vassals or barons to join his standard with their vassals—but they were only bound to forty days' service. If he wanted more troops or longer service he must have a hired soldiery. If some of his vassals combined to defy him, he could only

suppress them through the loyalty of other vassals or of the shire levies. If he tried to ignore his own obligations, they would certainly combine to defy him, and loyal support for him would be lacking. In the event of a foreign war he could not enforce service long enough for an effective campaign. He could go to war with France or Scotland without leave of anyone—but without consent of the barons he would have no troops.

For he had not the revenue with which to hire forces. And he could not raise the necessary revenue. The feudal dues were fixed ; he could not levy taxes on the barons without their consent. Something he got by occasionally substituting for military service a payment called scutage. He could levy tolls on merchandise at the ports—afterwards known as "customs"— but that would not carry him very far in days when both imports and exports were small. Though the issues of war and peace were technically in his hands, practically he could not make war and carry it on upon foreign soil except by consent and goodwill of the barons.

The King's Judges

And it followed that he could not in practice make, alter or repudiate the laws without consent of the barons. In fact, it does not appear that any king except William Rufus, before King John, attempted to do so. The king as the fountain of justice delegated his powers to judges of his own appointment who supervised the local administration of justice and were, in fact, protectors of the weak, because it was not in the interest of the Crown that the strong should grow dangerously stronger by the administration of the law in their own interests. The wise kings, like Henry I and Henry II, were themselves the champions of law, and much too shrewd to aim at overriding it. If they wanted changes in the law, they took care to lay them first before the Council and make sure that the changes would be supported. So when King John arose and trampled upon the law, the barons—rather to their own surprise, perhaps—found themselves acting as champions of the law against the new despotism, and forced him to issue the Great Charter, which declared for ever that no one, king or baron or church-man, could resist the law with impunity ; and that the law could not be changed or additional dues be claimed, except by consent of the Council.

John's reign had another consequence of the first magnitude. He lost the greater part of the royal family's possessions in France (whence it had come), possessions held by the Plantagenets as barons of France. From that time developed the idea of English national unity. The last quarter of the thirteenth century saw this conception fully materialized under Edward I, and saw also the final shaping of the Council into a Parliament consisting of the greater barons and ecclesiastics summoned individually together with elected representatives of the Commons.

The king still governed. He appointed whom he would as administrators ; but the principle had during the last century been established that such appointments should not go to foreigners ; and no new taxes could be levied or changes be made in the laws without the consent of Parliament. On the other hand, the development of the national idea had this effect : that the king had become the visible, tangible incarnation of the idea of the State, England personified. As long as he was himself truly representative of the State, loyalty to England involved loyalty to the king—but only so long as he was himself loyal to England. He stood for national unity.

Parliamentary Control

But the time had now come when the king's revenues no longer sufficed to support the king's government even in time of peace—much less in time of war. In order to carry on, the king must have supplies ; he could only get them if Parliament was ready to grant them. King and Parliament both began to discover that the king could govern only by grace of Parliament ; if Parliament were dissatisfied,

seriously dissatisfied, with the government, it would not in set terms demand to take over the control, but it would refuse supplies, or at least curtail them and so paralyse the government's action. Thus, apart from the defining limitations of the Crown's legitimate powers, there were two checks upon its freedom of action—the power of the barons to appeal to arms, and the power of Parliament, which in this field very soon came to mean the Commons, to withhold supplies. Neither would be hastily brought into play, but the menace of either could not be ignored by the Crown.

End of Feudalism

After the Wars of the Roses the baronial check hardly survived into the sixteenth century. The old baronage had been largely displaced by a new nobility ; the old theory of land tenure by military service had perished ; the nobles could no longer summon hosts of fighting-men to their banners ; the last convulsive effort of the old order was crushed with the rebellion of the northern earls in Elizabeth's reign. During the century, the Tudor period, the Commons' power of the purse was hardly brought into play to restrain the Crown.

The ingenuity of Henry VII had enabled him to accumulate so much treasure that Henry VIII had been on the throne several years before he found it necessary to ask Parliament for money—and then he found it necessary to ask politely. But the revolution which he carried ' out was effected from first to last by Parliamentary sanction. Parliament, whether supported by public opinion or not, endorsed his policy, and allowed him to refill his depleted treasury with the spoils of the Church. Similarly, Parliament did, in fact, endorse the policy of Mary, and more emphatically that of Elizabeth, who never had any difficulty in obtaining from it all that she required. Hence the appearance of absolutism under the Tudors. They did not dictate to a cowed and powerless Parliament ; but they made sure that their policy—which was emphatically their own —would command Parliamentary support.

Even the legal powers of the Crown were extended for Henry VIII personally (not for his successors), so that he was actually all but absolute during his last years ; but by the deliberate act of Parliament itself, and not as rights inherent in the Crown. Everything that the Tudors did was done technically in accordance with the letter of the law, and without derogation from the powers of Parliament.

With the accession of the House of Stuart there came a change. Theoretical differences of opinion as to the powers of the Crown might have existed before, but they had been academic so long as neither Crown nor Parliament felt itself in opposition to the other on a practical question of material importance. But now the king of another country became king of England also ; a king who made open profession of the theory that there is no limitation at all to the powers of the Crown —all other powers being exercised by the king's grace while he himself is responsible only to the Almighty. The temper of antagonism was aroused at once—the suspicion that encroachments were coming. Parliament was conscious of a single weapon wherewith encroachments might be lawfully and successfully resisted—the power of the purse. The Crown must be most jealously prevented from increasing its income independently of Parliamentary grants.

But a new phenomenon appeared. The judges, appointed by the king, declared that new means of raising money by his own authority were within his legal powers ; revolutions in Parliament could not alter the law—no one had ever pretended that Parliament could alter the law without the king's consent, or denied that its final authoritative interpretation lay with the

CHARLES I WITH THE GREAT OFFICERS OF STATE

This picture of Charles I in the House of Lords illustrates a pamphlet entitled "Discours du bon et loial sujet" which appeared in 1648, the year before Charles's long defiance of Parliament brought him at last to the scaffold. Behind the King on the right stands the Chancellor. The Great Chamberlain carries the crown and the Constable the sword.

judges. Still, King James in action stopped short of the line the overstepping of which would threaten rebellion. But the hostile spirit was intensified as the King's policy proved more and more unacceptable and his choice of ministers more and more excited distrust and apprehension.

The King died; his son, Charles I, clung to the same theories and the same ministers —whose conduct of affairs was obviously deplorable. Parliament brought its one weapon into play, refusing to grant supplies until grievances were remedied and the obnoxious ministers dismissed. King and Parliament each professed to be claiming only legal rights, but each made on its own behalf unprecedented claims— the one to powers of raising revenue, the other to powers of controlling adminis- tration. The King found himself compelled to accept the "Petition of Right", which expressly abrogated some of the powers which he had already exercised; but he put his own interpretation upon it, and for eleven years succeeded in scraping together—by measures which public opinion condemned as illegal, while the judges pronounced them legal—enough to carry on the government without asking Parliament for more

Causes of the Civil War

But then there came a sudden need for more money—to meet an emergency, of the King's own creating, which had arisen in Scotland. The limit of unauthorized taxation had been reached, and Charles had no choice but once more to summon Parliament. And Parliament was in- exorable. Grievances must be remedied before supplies would be granted. Parlia- ment drove a merciless bargain—so long as it remained united. The remedying of grievances meant the formal surrender of the King on every point which had hitherto been in dispute. But one section of Parliament now demanded his surrender on two new points which had not been debated and would never have been thought of as debatable at an earlier date; the eccle- siastical system was to be reorganized at their dictation, and the control of the

armed forces was to pass from the Crown to Parliament. The other section of Parliament saw here a revolution which was not to their mind. There was a cleavage; the second section became inevitably a Royalist party, and no arbitrament but that of the sword was possible.

Civil war followed. It overturned the monarchy and set up a republic. But under the conditions of the revolution, order, the first necessity of the State, could only be restored and maintained by force. The republic resolved itself into a military dictatorship; the dictatorship collapsed with the death of the dictator. The man who might have succeeded to the dictator- ship if he had so willed preferred—as the whole nation undoubtedly preferred—a restoration of the monarchy.

The Power of the Purse

But it was a conditional restoration; a restoration which assumed that the claims surrendered by the Crown before the actual outbreak of the Civil War had been sur- rendered for good and all. It was to have no power at all of raising revenue for itself; instead of all the old sources of revenue, the king was to have a definite income granted him at the outset. If that was not enough he must come to Parliament for more. And Parliament was very soon able to insist that such moneys as it granted must be spent on those objects for which it had been granted. The "power of the purse" was indisputably and entirely vested in Parliament. So was the power of legislation, subject to the royal veto which would be exercised at the king's peril. Also in the course of the reign of Charles II it was established that though the king's right of directing policy and choosing ministers was undisputed, the ministers would be held accountable to Parliament for their actions, and could not be sheltered from the just resentment of Parliament by the royal authority and favour.

Charles II spent his life in providing himself with two weapons for securing the supremacy of the Crown: money which he inveigled into his own pockets out of those of the king of France ; and a standing army, paid with the French king's money, at his own disposal, just sufficient to stamp out any insurrection before it could make head. Both weapons crumbled in the hands of his successor. James II, imagining himself fully armed, set about acting on the assumption, and riding rough-shod over the law. But the French king's supplies failed him, and his army deserted as soon as there was someone to desert to. James took flight, and the crown was offered—on terms— to his son-in-law, William of Orange, who accepted it.

§—Monarchy as a Façade

THE Revolution of 1688 was the last phase of the old contest for ascendancy between Crown and Parliament. In form it was no more than the definite acceptance by the Crown of the Parliament's interpretation—differing from what had of late been the Crown's interpretation—of the existing law. But the application of the now accepted interpretation involved an actual revolution in the practical exercise of the powers of government.

In the first place, the Crown resigned all the claims put forward on its behalf which had been challenged during the past century. The theory of Divine Right was wiped out when the king's title to the throne depended on his acceptance of a formal agreement. He had no power whatever of raising revenue, or of applying it otherwise than as Parliament intended. He had no power whatever of making or changing laws, no power of suspending the operation of particular laws either generally or for the benefit of individuals. Arrested persons were automatically released unless brought to immediate trial. The king's ministers were accountable to Parliament for their actions, while all the king's official actions, being performed through ministers, were the ministers' actions. He could levy or maintain no troops without consent of Parliament. If he made treaties, they must be endorsed by Parliament ; in effect, he could not go to war without the approval of Parliament ; it was no longer, as hitherto, the

By permission of]   *[the Lord Chamberlain*

WILLIAM OF ORANGE LANDS AT BRIXHAM

In response to the request addressed to William of Orange, Stadtholder of Holland and husband of James II's eldest daughter, that he would come to England and "secure the infringed liberties of England", William landed at Brixham, Devon, on November 5th, 1688. The illustration is from a picture in Hampton Court Palace.

king who went to war, but England—or, after the Union of 1707, Great Britain.

Secondly, in the course of William's reign other limitations were imposed. He lost the power of removing judges, who thus became independent of royal favour when once they had been appointed. The annual meeting of Parliament was ensured by the practice of voting supplies for one year only, so that public opposition to the royal policy could find immediate expression.

Thirdly, as a consequence of these changes it became gradually obvious that the king's ministers must act upon lines acceptable to the majority in Parliament, and that the ministers themselves must be in general agreement; from which it followed that, although in theory his choice of ministers was free, it must in practice be limited to those who were personally acceptable to the Parliamentary majority for the time being. Theoretically, the

king continued to govern; actually the whole government had become responsible to the majority in Parliament for the time being, and must adapt itself to the will of that majority. Still, so long as the country felt that it could not afford to let the king go back to Holland, the majority also had to adapt its will to that of the king.

Hanoverian Succession

The coping-stone was set upon the reconstructed edifice by the Hanoverian succession. An Act of Parliament laid the succession, in 1714, upon a German great-grandson of James I. He occupied the throne merely in order that his Stuart cousin might be kept out of it. He and his new subjects took the least possible interest in each other. He was, to the country, not a necessity as William III had been, but merely a rather doubtful convenience. Active interference on his part would only have led to his permanent departure for Hanover. He left the ministers who had in the first instance been chosen for him to run the political machine, himself becoming a mere figure-head. One minister, who was able to command a majority in Parliament, presently controlled the whole government. From him the control passed to a family group, the second George having more but not much more voice in affairs than his father. By the time that the risk of a Stuart restoration was over, the system of government by ministers over whom the king had practically no control was firmly established; though no minister or ministers could govern without a majority of supporters in Parliament.

With the accession of George III came a renewed effort on the part of the Crown to recover the governing powers which it had lost. The method was new, and was attended with temporary success. There was no setting up the authority of the Crown against

Engraved by]   *[A. Fogg*

FIRST PRIME MINISTER

Sir Robert Walpole, who was head of the British Government from 1721 to 1742, is generally regarded as the first Prime Minister of Great Britain, though that position was not officially recognized until 1905. In the picture by Sir James Thornhill here reproduced he is shown in the House of Commons with Speaker Onslow.

the authority of Parliament; the young king took a leaf out of the book of the families who had captured the direction of Parliament. By strenuous and prolonged effort he attached to himself influential persons who among them could procure the election of more than half the members of the House of Commons. The king's ministers did whatever the king wished, and Parliament—the majority—supported whatever the ministers proposed to do. The result was the severance of the American colonies from the Mother Country, causing in turn the collapse of the king's party, which it had become impossible to reconstruct.

Thenceforth, though the king might succeed in rejecting ministers whom he disliked, he could not retain ministers who were solidly opposed by public opinion outside Parliament; nor, in fact, did he desire to do so—though in the single case where he found himself in flat opposition to Pitt he succeeded, disastrously enough, in carrying his point and refusing Catholic Emancipation. Twelve years after George III's death, the Reform Bill of 1832 finally did away with the personal control hitherto exercised over a great many constituencies, and Parliament became fully representative of a free electorate which was gradually rendered thoroughly democratic by successive extensions of the franchise.

The Reform Bill of 1832 made it for ever impossible to repeat George III's attempt to secure a Parliamentary majority subservient to the Crown by manipulating the constituencies, while more than two centuries have passed since the last attempt made by any British monarch to override the will of the people's representatives by any other method—a consummation ensured by the sixty-four years' reign of George III's granddaughter, Victoria. No minister can carry on the government in the face of a majority in the House of Commons which demands his resignation. Virtually, the Commons dictate the selection of the Prime Minister and limit without actually dictating the selection of other ministers. "The king reigns but does not govern"!

§—Crowned First Citizens

THE king reigns, but he is responsible to his people; that is, he will cease to reign if they, as a whole, will that he shall cease to reign. He is king on condition that he retains their goodwill. He does not govern. The government is carried on in the king's name; the ministers who carry it on are technically his ministers, but he can neither choose them nor dismiss them at his own will. They are responsible not to him but to the majority in the House of Commons. The House of Commons as a whole is responsible to the electorate as a whole; each individual member is responsible to his own constituency; and the constituency is more thoroughly democratic than anything hitherto known in the history of Mankind, since the franchise has been extended so that not only nearly all men but nearly all women also enjoy it. Obviously, then, a monarchy which is itself responsible to the people, which does not govern, and to which the government is not responsible, cannot prevent the government from being wholly democratic and preserving democratic ideals, in practice.

Even in theory the only point that can be urged against it on the plea of democracy is its partly hereditary character—partly hereditary but no more: for the power of changing the course of the succession has always been claimed and repeatedly exercised by Parliament; and the now reigning dynasty was set upon the throne to the deliberate exclusion of a prince whose purely hereditary right could only be challenged on the notoriously false pretence that he was a supposititious child. But while it might be claimed that succession by hereditary right to a position of political control is undemocratic, hereditary succession to a position of dignity is no more undemocratic than hereditary succession to a position of wealth. And it is hardly claimed as yet that the inheritance of wealth is in itself incompatible with democracy. It may be incompatible with socialism, but socialism is not democracy— is not a system of government, but a policy, and, fundamentally, an economic policy.

The Human Element

The Crown, the monarchy are in a sense abstractions—ideas impersonally symbolic of unity, thereby serving an extremely useful purpose. But the monarch is no abstraction; he is a living, active human being with an active part to play. He may simply abstain from playing it, leaving the Crown to its own personal function. He may go positively wrong, and adopt an inappropriate role outside the work of a constitutional monarch—though to say that a monarch may attempt to act unconstitutionally is no impugnment of the value of a constitutional monarchy. The chances are, however, first, that he will not attempt it, and, second, that if he does his action will be very promptly challenged; the occasionally pernicious activities of George III have become for him practically impossible. Any and every conceivable system is liable to abuse, but such abuse of constitutional monarchy has not for a century been an appreciable danger. On the other hand, the same king's indomitable courage and patriotism in the hour of the country's supreme peril provides an example of serviceable energy worthy of all emulation.

Thus if the king plays his part rightly he is an active unifying force within the realm, for in a constitutional monarchy "L'État, c'est moi" is true, but in a very different sense from that in which it was used by Louis XIV. To him it meant that the interests of his people did not count, and only interests personal to him were recognized as interests of the State. To the British monarch it means that he, as monarch, has no personal interests other than those of his people. The monarch is merged in his people, not the people in their monarch. The monarch is not the State to which the people are harnessed; State, monarch and people are One.

It was the work of Queen Victoria to identify the interests of the monarch with those of the State by making the interests of the State her own supreme personal interests, and her sole interests as monarch; and to show that this did not involve any attempt on her part to impose upon the State her individual view of its interests. When she came to the throne there was still a risk of the monarch attempting to assume a more active control—failing Victoria herself, her uncle the Duke of Cumberland, a bitter reactionary, would have become king. Hence the keenness of her zeal in public affairs was kept in the background, though well appreciated by those who were in touch with her, lest it should be misinterpreted. Later in life her shrewdness, experience and knowledge of men were often of no small value to the ministers, though the rarity of her public appearances diminished what may be called the spectacular importance of the Crown until its revival by the jubilee functions.

Victorian Jubilees

Pomp and pageantry may not command the respect of the stern rationalist; yet the imperial pageant of the jubilees did more than the wisest reasoning to rouse the popular imagination to a sense of the reality of the great British Commonwealth, while in form it was only the expression of the fact that a queen had been reigning for half a century.

Monarchists of the old type, however, have at various times talked and written as though the Crown's intervention in the conduct of policy and government would not only be legitimately within the letter of its rights but even in certain circumstances a positive duty. It was with that same honest conviction that George III declared that he would rather abdicate than sanction Catholic Emancipation.

Probably there is no intelligent person

today who has the shadow of a doubt that he thereby wrought irreparable harm. Since that time the Crown has never, as a matter of fact, adopted a similar attitude. Had George IV followed his father's example (as his brother, the Duke of Cumberland, desired), it is by no means impossible that he would have lost his throne. George IV's brother, William IV, once ventured upon the much milder step of dismissing a ministry, but that was only because of a mistaken conviction that ministers no longer had the country behind them. Even that experiment has never been repeated. Technically, the Crown has never been deprived by statute of its old unqualified power of veto; actually, in practice it is so long since that power has been exercised that it has become "unconstitutional". Its revival would obviously be anti-democratic, but those who would revive it are frankly anti-democratic, looking to it as a method of preventing from coming into force some popular decision to which they are opposed.

The constitutional principle is that the king acts only on the advice of his ministers. It is of course conceivable in a way that a

SIXTY YEARS A QUEEN—TWENTY YEARS AN EMPRESS

On the occasion of her Diamond Jubilee on June 22nd, 1897, Queen Victoria drove in state to a thanksgiving service held on the steps of St. Paul's Cathedral, and returned through South London. The great procession, here shown crossing London Bridge, impressed the Imperial idea upon the people, for representatives and troops of the Indian Empire and the Colonies took part in such a display for the first time. Throughout the long route the procession went at walking pace.

Bill might go through both Houses of Parliament in the teeth of the ministry, and that the ministry, instead of resigning or appealing to the electorate, might advise the Crown to veto the Bill; but in that case it would be the ministers who would act unconstitutionally. They would have already done so, by remaining in office after being defeated on a question of principle. What the vetoists mean, however, is that the king may legitimately act on his own judgement and veto a Bill presented by ministers for his assent. If he did so, he would cease *ipso facto* to be a constitutional monarch as the term is now understood, and we should have to reconsider our doctrine that the British monarchy is compatible with democracy, while a constitutional crisis would develop more acute than has been known since the accession of William III.

Personal Influence

The accepted principle has invariably been acted upon and has never been called in question by the monarch since the accession of Queen Victoria. The wishes and sympathies of the sovereign may indeed carry weight with the ministers in proportion to their confidence in his wisdom, knowledge and judgement. An able prince who has been for many years in touch with administrators and leaders of all parties at home and with foreign Courts also is in the position of a permanent official of exceptionally wide experience whose views and sentiments are always worth at least careful consideration, and all the more because, unlike a president, he has no possible connexion with, or dependence on, any political party; but his influence has no compelling force.

On more than one occasion, notably in the case of the Proclamation transferring the government of India to the Crown in 1858, the queen's personal influence proved of real value because the wisdom of her suggestions was convincing; but had it not been so they would not have been accepted. It remains, in short, a function of the Crown to exercise an influence proportionate to the confidence inspired by the monarch's personality; but there is no danger of the application of that influence in any but a perfectly legitimate and beneficial manner. And while it is thus exercised, it is in no possible sense undemocratic.

Nor can it be overlooked that the hereditary character of the First Citizenship carries with it advantages of a directly practical kind. The elected president is, in respect of non-governmental functions, an amateur, however naturally gifted he may be, and the qualities which secure his election are not those which fit a man peculiarly for the office. But the hereditary prince is a professional, who, whether naturally gifted or not, has been trained, in whole or at least in part, specifically for the position which must one day be his in the ordinary course of nature. In relation to the working government, the president, if he be also its working head, must be closely associated with party; even if he be not the working head, he is almost certainly elected as the nominee of a party, and cannot escape embarrassments if the government in power be not that of the party to which he owes his appointment.

Stability of Monarchy

The hereditary prince, associated with no party, unembarrassed by party ties, can stand always in the same relation to the government, however it may change and whatever party may be in power. There must always be a great circle of officialdom connected with the official head of a great State; with every newly elected president, experience proves that that circle is broken up and a new one formed, at least if the out-going and in-coming presidents have been nominees of opposing parties—very much to the detriment of public business. But when the hereditary prince succeeds his predecessor, he has every natural inducement to retain his predecessor's *entourage*, so far as it has proved itself competent, thereby at once avoiding all disturbance of public business, and securing for himself the personal advice and the personal services of trained experience.

CHAPTER 3

THE CROWN IN THE TWENTIETH CENTURY

Here is told the story of the Relations of King and People, of the testing of Crown and Constitution in the troublous days of the early part of the present Century

WE have traced down to the close of the nineteenth century the stages by which the British monarchy, once the mainspring of government, has ceased entirely to govern or to control government, the direction of which has in this country become more definitely democratic than any the world has hitherto known. What, then, is the function of monarchy in a democracy ? What value can it have ?

It has a function and a value in the first place, because human nature is an affair of sentiment and imagination as well as of hard reasoning, an affair in which symbols have more than a trivial importance. The crown is the symbol of unity ; it is the primary function of the monarchy to express and to strengthen that unity. And this is the more necessary because of the vast diversities whose unity it expresses.

If the monarch's hereditary title were indefeasible, the monarchy would be incompatible with democracy, because the king would not be responsible to his people. Not being in the last resort indefeasible, the fact that it is hereditary makes it a symbol of continuity and, therefore, of unity. For King George VI traces his descent through Stuart and Tudor, Plantagenet and Bruce, in continuous line for more than a thousand years not only to William the Conqueror and his Scots contemporary, Malcolm Canmore, but to Alfred the Great himself, the maker of a united England, centuries before Hapsburgs or Hohen-

zollerns were heard of, even before a Capet was king of France. Through the union of the Crowns of England and Scotland in the person of King George's ancestor James I came the unification of Great Britain, hitherto divided ; through the joint acceptance of the succession of George I, the unification attained its consummation, but only when all prospect of a re-severance of the Crowns had finally passed away. The Crown of Great Britain is the symbol at once of the age-long continuity of the English and Scottish nations, and of their unification after centuries of perpetual strife ; more than the symbol, since it was the actual link that brought them together, because by hereditary right, not by conquest, a king of Scotland became king of England.

Crown and Empire

For England and Scotland the Crown symbolizes a dual continuity merging in one ; for the British Empire (which would certainly be called Commonwealth instead of Empire but for the accidental association of the former term with a despotic military rule really appropriate to the latter), it typifies a continuous growth as of the proverbial grain of mustard-seed. The Empire is not an artificial linking-up of States which have no essential unity ; each one of them is not a new State but a new manifestation of the parent State. Australian, Canadian and New Zealander have an equal share with their specifically

English and Scottish brethren in the heritage of Alfred, Bruce and Elizabeth, of Wallace, Drake and Chatham, of Shakespeare, Milton and Burns. The Empire is not a league but a brotherhood ; a growth, not a combination. The fact is symbolized by the crown which belongs to them all, the crown which our King George inherits from his ancestor King Alfred ; the House of Windsor from the House of Wessex. There is no people on the face of the earth which can point to a like immemorial symbol of unity. It stamps the truth that we all have a common right in a common and splendid past pointing us to a common and splendid future. To other peoples who have no continuous historic national past, where a constitutional monarchy has but

recently been set up, it may be no more than an expedient of political utility, a piece of political machinery, the seal set upon a compact. If Canada or Australia were to separate herself from the British Commonwealth, she would not presumably set up a new dynasty of her own ; such a dynasty would symbolize nothing. Greece, freed after long centuries from the Turk, has no traditional bond with a foreign engrafted dynasty. But our monarchy, a thousand years old, is the visible certificate that we are all the sons of one mother. Even where the flag floats over those who are not of our own race—French in Canada or Dutch in South Africa—it signifies that we welcome them as "blood-brothers", adoptive sons of the same mother.

§—Emergence of the Imperial Idea

THIS is a function of the constitutional monarchy of the Empire which is, we may believe, destined to be of the first importance in the future, though it was only beginning to be realized when the nineteenth century ended. The reason for the failure is clear enough. The Imperial idea, the sense of the unity of the Empire, was not grasped either within the United Kingdom or in the oversea dominions.

Some can still remember the days when it was a practically universally accepted doctrine that every "Colony", as soon as it had developed sufficiently in population, wealth and political and economic organization to stand on its own feet, would inevitably demand complete separation and independence, which would as a matter of course be conceded with the parental blessing of the Mother Country. Such, it was assumed, was the natural law. There were dreamers who took a different view ; they held that the doctrine was based upon a misreading of history, assuming on the part of the Colonies a short-sighted devotion to particular material interests, a blindness to the dependence of those very interests upon wider considerations, and a complete

unconsciousness of the argument or the instinct which had recently driven the Federals in the United States of America to resist Secession at all costs. The accepted precedent was that of the secession of the American Colonies from the British Empire a century before—for it was the custom to ignore the essential fact that this was not the secession of free States from an equal union, but was the outcome of the doctrine and practice of subordinating the outlying regions of the Empire to its geographically central section. (Hence, in the eyes of the citizen of the United States, our monarchy is still the symbol of that doctrine of subordination.) But in the vision of the dreamers, that motive to separation was to disappear—not only, as it had already disappeared, in fact, but also in form. The future Empire was to be a union of free States, autonomous but united under one common, supreme authority which would no longer be that of a section but would be representative of the whole.

The vision has not yet perhaps been fully realized ; we are not yet clear as to the precise machinery by which it may be realized most perfectly. But it has become the common vision. The vision is well on the way towards certain realization. But it was not till the last quarter of the nineteenth century that it began to be looked upon as realizable ; and it was not till the twentieth that the Crown's part in it began even tentatively to come into play. The Crown, then, is a symbol for the great democracies of our own race united under it ; the symbol of their common share in a great past and of their unity in the present and in the future. All have in it, and it has in all, the same rights. It stands not for this or that section, but for the whole, not for this or that party, but for the united nation. No elective president could hold the same representative position. The democracies would have to provide presidents in rotation—an English, Scottish, Canadian, Australian president, and so on ; they would be presidential States in turn. Also the election of the president

would inevitably have in it at least a note of party. The chief of the whole would be the choice of a party in one State out of the many of which the whole is composed. But the hereditary monarch stands in the same relation to every one of the democracies ; he is a born member of all alike, not of one in particular ; he is no more and no less an Englishman or a Scot in the particularist sense than he is an Australian or a Canadian. And he has no association with any party, any class, any particular interest ; he belongs to the people.

For India, again, the Crown is a double symbol. European standards cannot be applied to Oriental peoples, for whom democracy as a working system has been called unthinkable, and autocracy or at least military rule belongs to the nature of things in the view of the masses. For us symbolism counts, though we are often unconscious of it ; for the Oriental it counts

INDIA'S RULING PRINCES PAY HOMAGE

King Edward VII was proclaimed Emperor of India at a Durbar at Delhi, but he was represented by the Duke of Connaught, and King George V was the first Emperor of India to attend the proclamation ceremony in person. King George, with Queen Mary, crowned and robed, is here seen on the dais receiving the homage of the ruling princes and chiefs.

infinitely more, and consciously. The Imperial Crown of India worn by a living Emperor has a meaning and can inspire a loyalty far more binding than any reasoned approval of the soundest political system. It is in the intelligible traditional order of things that the native princes of India should be the loyal dependants of a supreme monarch ; it requires no great degree of sympathetic imagination to realize how difficult it would be for them to assume the same attitude towards a supreme republic. The transfer of the government of India from "John Company" and its Governor-General to the Crown and its Viceroy in 1858 was not only a very valuable administrative change ; it was also a great step towards the creation of a sentiment of loyalty which would have no place in India if there were no British Crown.

The formal assumption by the Crown of the ancient Imperial dignity of the Moguls some twenty years later was another step in the same direction whose value was misunderstood in England simply because the Western mind does not readily appreciate the workings of the Eastern. To India the Crown symbolizes at once the legitimate continuity of the ancient authority of the Moguls and the dignity of the dynasty to which that authority has been transferred.

The Dominions, as we saw, have in the Crown precisely the same part as the Mother Country. The king is not the king of England ruling oversea dependencies : he is "His Britannic Majesty", king of Great Britain and Ireland and of the Britains oversea. No doubt there is a sense in which England has a more special claim upon him than other States of the Empire individually, just as in a sense she has a special claim upon each of them—because England is the birth-place of most of them, and the centre of the group. But the monarch ought to be hardly less at home in them than in England, and his person hardly less familiar to them. That ideal is in practice scarcely attainable ; in the reign of Queen Victoria and before it, it was not even an ideal. The Queen did not visit the Dominions ; the Crown was something remote from them.

King Edward VII, however, inaugurated his reign by sending the heir apparent in person to represent him at the inauguration of the Commonwealth of Australia, and the Prince, afterwards King George V, extended his visit to the other self-governing Dominions. A double purpose was served by thus bringing the future king in touch with his people ; each could realize the other,

AMBASSADOR OF EMPIRE

The Imperial tie was further strengthened during the reign of King Edward VII, who greatly gratified Australia by sending his son, then Duke of York, to open the first Commonwealth Parliament. He is here seen, with the Duchess, afterwards Queen Mary, landing at Melbourne on May 6th, 1901.

as had never before been the case. The voyage of the Ophir may be regarded as the first step on a course which, if rightly followed up in the future, should have a definitely cohesive influence ; though it was only a first step.

In the case of the visits to India, King Edward VII may be said to have taken the first step (though as heir apparent, not as Emperor ; for before King George V no crowned British monarch had set foot in India). Now, the appearance in India of the King-Emperor in person for the first time in history was an event of immense Imperial importance, strictly accordant with the position of the king of the British democracies as *Kaisar-i-Hind*. It can scarcely, indeed, be deemed advisable or desirable that such occasions should be of frequent recurrence—their effect would thereby be diminished ; rarity will make their impressiveness the greater. But it will be well that from time to time the personal link should make itself felt.

Edward VII when king did, as his mother had done, exercise an influence upon foreign relations ; but it was by reason not of any powers inherent in the Crown, but of his own personality. The Crown could not, and did not attempt to, commit the nation to alliances or to any policy whatever ; but the King could, and did, promote an atmosphere of goodwill. He could do so, because he was therein manifestly expressing the prevalent sentiment of his people. And it was the more effective because exercised at a time when the complex dynastic relationships in a Europe mainly under the political control of dynastic rulers had an importance almost obliterated in post-War Europe.

He seized an opportunity in an entirely constitutional manner, though without precedent ; but it was an opportunity which is not likely to recur under present-day conditions. It was upon his son and successor, King George V, that the tremendous task fell of raising the British constitutional monarchy to its highest value in an era of unprecedented strain and stress ; upon King George and upon the Queen and wife with whom he was so happily (in every sense) associated, through the five-and-twenty years of his reign.

§—The Buckingham Palace Conference

LIKE his father and his grandmother in their several ways, King George V from the time of his accession played consistently and loyally the part of a constitutional monarch on the lines to which his immediate predecessors had given first shape and then permanence. In spite of considerable pressure, he steadily withheld himself from anything in the nature of party politics. The public has no data even for guessing his personal views on the questions which before the War divided the State—such as tariff reform, Home Rule, the functions and constitution of the House of Lords. The one occasion when the King was, so to speak, called in, whether on his own motion or not, gave rise to some amount of criticism and comment, because the democracy is, rightly enough, suspicious of anything which might be made a precedent for unauthorized intervention by the Crown in the sphere of government ; but it was at once made clear that there was no ground for such suspicion. When in 1914 a highly critical situation had arisen in Ireland, the King intervened ; but the intervention was strictly in accordance with constitutional principles, not on behalf of one or another party, not to impose the King's wishes upon the government, but in the way of mediation, in the hope of reconciling the diversities, antagonisms, most of all the misunderstandings and mutual suspicions, which are the greatest obstacles to unity. Unity is the *raison d'être* of the Crown ; the object in view was precisely that for the sake of which the Crown exists.

The method was that of conference—not between the King and ministers or party leaders, but between the party chiefs themselves. The King summoned the conference to meet at Buckingham Palace, himself welcomed its members and urged upon them the vital necessity of the accord attainable by mutual trust and goodwill ; but he spoke not as the advocate of any sectional view, but as the voice of a whole people anxiously desiring a fair adjustment of a complicated and age-long problem. There was, indeed, no precedent for such action—there had been no precedent for the royal visit to India.   To create a precedent, however, is in no way unconstitutional, provided the precedent is in harmony with the workings of the constitution.   The action was not, unhappily, justified by success : but except in the eyes of pedants it did not require success for its justification.

James I as Mediator

Such intervention, in such exceptional circumstances, is entirely befitting.   Had the King taken upon himself the function of a dictatorial arbiter, he would have been transgressing his constitutional sphere. The difference between the two methods may be illustrated by the Hampton Court conference, called three centuries earlier by James I, a monarch whose faith was that, not of constitutionalism, but of Divine Right.   When the first Stuart had just ascended the throne of England, the country was torn by ecclesiastical differences.   Their adjustment was a matter of grave importance ; had it been successfully effected, there would perhaps have been no Great Rebellion. The need of adjustment was felt ; the method of conference was applied ; the Crown was to be the mediator. ? But mediation, according to James I, was the arbitrary insistence upon the unqualified acceptance of the views of the ecclesiastical party favoured by the Crown.   The Nonconformists wanted at least the option of dispensing with sundry ceremonial observances.   Some of them also desired the substitution of the Presbyterian

for the Episcopal system in the government of the Church.

His Majesty presided in person over the conference, discoursed freely, aired his very considerable knowledge of theological controversy, and snubbed the Nonconformists ; but when one of them ventured to introduce the word Presbyter, the royal wrath bubbled over.   "Presbytery agreeth with monarchy as well as God with the Devil !" quoth the monarch: and after that all chance of concessions to Nonconformity vanished.   Conferences initiated by the Crown on the Hampton Court model today would certainly be disastrous ! But the story itself reveals at once the immense distance we have travelled since the "wisest fool in Christendom" sat on the throne of England, and the sheer absurdity of dreaming that such days can ever return in this country.

George V—like two of his ancestors, each of them, though in quite different ways, a very notable figure in our history, Henry VIII and Charles I—was a younger son who succeeded to the crown through the earlier death of an elder brother. He came to the throne in the hour of a constitutional crisis of the first magnitude. Even then, though there were comparatively few people who realized the fact, a world crisis far more tremendous was impending: the Great War. For more than four years that war raged, to be succeeded by a peace and an attempt at reconstruction upon what was left of the shattered foundations of the political, social and economic structures of the past.

Father of his People

In that vast and still uncompleted task the British constitutional monarchy, and not least its head, had a principal part to play, and played it worthily ; so worthily, so modestly, so selflessly as concerned Their Majesties, so much as if it had all been mere matter of course, that it was only when the end was coming that King George became aware that he had won from the vast and diverse peoples over whom he reigned such a   profound   and   pervading   heart-felt affection and devotion as had been earned by no one of his predecessors since Alfred the Great, and from the world at large such universal respect as no other monarch has ever achieved, unless it were St. Louis.

We have referred above to the story of the Buckingham Palace conference because, in the first place, it was a characteristic example of legitimate intervention—not interference—on the part of the Crown as the supreme unifying element, not as a controller of policy, in a constitutional monarchy ; and, secondly, because its form made it conspicuous. But though there has been no other intervention of a like character, it is at least the general conviction that the royal influence made itself felt, even that it may have been the decisive factor, in extracting harmony out of a chaos of antagonisms, calming emotional hostilities, and evolving stability when

stability seemed most remote, but never with the shadow of a semblance of promoting the interests of any political party. If we are right in believing that such influence was exercised, it was always in discharge of the supreme function of the Crown as not only the symbol of unity but the agent of unification ; a function which can be discharged only by a head of the people who is entirely separated from parties and party warfare.

So also, in foreign relations, King George never assumed the traditional attitude of

British or other monarchs, the director of alliances, the maker of war and peace. This British conception was never intelligible to foreign potentates with an exclusively autocratic tradition behind them. But his own people always knew, whether in war or in peace, that their king was the embodiment of their own aim, their own ideals, the partner of their hopes, their cares, their self-sacrifice, their exemplar in his indomitable courage and unremitting toil.

King George, as we have already noted, also played no small part in developing the conception, which had hardly come into being before the fiftieth year of his grandmother's reign, of the Crown as the symbol of Imperial unity, and of the king in person as its very human embodiment ; not an abstraction, but as a man to be loved and honoured, a definite object of loyalty.

WHEN THE KING HELD CONFERENCE

The conference which King George V called at Buckingham Palace in 1914 to discuss the Irish question was attended by representatives of all parties. Above are Mr. Redmond and Mr. Dillon, and, right, Mr. Lloyd George and Mr. Asquith, then Prime Minister, on their way to the conference.

Queen Victoria's grandfather had in his time done perhaps more than any other single man to bring about the disruption of the Empire, to which, not quite a century after his death, George V succeeded. And what he did himself both before and after his accession he trained his sons to do —to make the Royal Family centres of a conscious loyalty throughout his wide-flung dominions, where before his own father no royal prince had ever set foot.

Just a hundred years have elapsed since the accession of Queen Victoria perhaps averted the fall of the monarchy by setting on the throne a young girl with high ideals, to the exclusion of a prince whose reactionary predilections would have been a serious menace to the constitution.

The throne at that time was not safe : never in its whole history was it more firmly established than it is today.

If we owe this fact largely to George V we owe it also to the unprecedented use of her position by his Queen Consort. England and Great Britain have known two queens regnant who take rank with the most successful rulers known to history ; but among all the queens consort, who that is not a student of history can name more than one or two in the whole period of a thousand years or so who added lustre to the Crown, or who, unless they were actively pernicious influences, were anything more than gracious, graceful partners of the royal dignity ? But Queen Mary has been something much more than this. The queen consort has no political powers, though George II's Queen Caroline exercised a personal influence over her husband which might have been dangerous if it had been less consistently judicious. But Queen Mary, seeking no political powers, made herself a power by embodying in herself the fundamental principle that in heart and sympathy the Crown and the people are one. With unwearying devotion, she never failed to share or to give a lead to the devotion of the women of the country through the years of anxiety. Wherever suffering was to be found, the Queen's sympathetic face and voice were to be seen and heard bringing cheer and consolation ; not as a "Lady Bountiful" but as the beloved mother of her people.

And now a new King and Queen are seated on the throne, a King and Queen in whom we have the best of reasons for a confident trust that they will prove worthy successors to a throne more than ever before securely established in the hearts of the people.

FATHER OF HIS PEOPLE

Every movement for the betterment of youth interested King George V and he is here seen at the opening of the new university college buildings at Nottingham in 1928. In the observance of his duties as a constitutional monarch his wide sympathy with his people found an outlet on such occasions as this.

OUR KINGS AND QUEENS

by THE EDITOR

From Edward the Confessor to Edward VIII:
A Biographical Review

KINGS AND QUEENS OF ENGLAND
FROM 1042 A.D. TO THE PRESENT DAY

Saxon

Edward the Confessor	(1042–1066)
Harold II	(1066)

Norman

William I	(1066–1087)
William II	(1087–1100)
Henry I	(1100–1135)
Stephen	(1135–1154)

Plantagenet

Henry II	(1154–1189)
Richard I	(1189–1199)
John	(1199–1216)
Henry III	(1216–1272)
Edward I	(1272–1307)
Edward II	(1307–1327)
Edward III	(1327–1377)
Richard II	(1377–1399)

Lancaster

Henry IV	(1399–1413)
Henry V	(1413–1422)
Henry VI	(1422–1461)

York

Edward IV	(1461–1483)
Edward V	(1483)
Richard III	(1483–1485)

Tudor

Henry VII	(1485–1509)
Henry VIII	(1509–1547)
Edward VI	(1547–1553)
Jane	(1553)
Mary I	(1553–1558)
Elizabeth	(1558–1603)

Stuart

James I	(1603–1625)
Charles I	(1625–1649)
[Commonwealth (1649–60)]	

Charles II	(1660–1685)
James II	(1685–1688)
William III and	
Mary II	(1689–1702)
Anne	(1702–1714)

Hanover

George I	(1714–1727)
George II	(1727–1760)
George III	(1760–1820)
George IV	(1820–1830)
William IV	(1830–1837)
Victoria	(1837–1901)

Saxe-Coburg

Edward VII	(1901–1910)

Windsor

George V	(1910–1936)
Edward VIII	(1936)
George VI	(1936–

RICHARD   1340–1405   1405–1603

1603–1689   WILLIAM III   1707–1714

1714–1801   1801–1837   VICTORIA

EVOLUTION OF THE ROYAL ARMS

In the course of seven hundred years there have been many changes in the Royal Arms.   Top left is the shield of Richard Cœur de Lion showing only three lions passant.   Edward III's arms (centre) were three lions in two quarters and the fleur-de-lis of France in the other two.   Henry IV, in accordance with the change in the French arms, reduced the fleur-de-lis to three.   The more elaborate arms under the Stuarts incorporated the lion of Scotland and the Irish harp, while William of Orange placed his paternal arms of Nassau in the centre of the shield.   After the Act of Union Scotland was given a larger display on the shield and under the Hanoverian kings from 1714 to 1801 the arms of Brunswick, Lunenburg and Westphalia appeared on it.   In 1801, in accordance with the treaty of Amiens, the fleur-de-lis were used no more and the Arms of Hanover appeared on an "escutcheon of pretence" in the centre of the shield.   Finally, as Queen Victoria could not succeed to the throne of Hanover, the arms of that kingdom were dropped and the shield took its present form

CHAPTER 4

OUR KINGS AND QUEENS
FROM EDWARD THE CONFESSOR TO EDWARD VIII

*Turning the pages of our island story, we see emerge therefrom
the colourful figures of those who, during the past nine hundred
years, have sat in the Coronation Chair at Westminster*

WHEN another page of our strange and eventful history is about to be turned—when a new coronation is toward and the names of a new but already well-loved King and Queen are about to be added to the long and illustrious roll of those who have worn our country's crown, it is natural and altogether fitting that our thoughts should revert to those who were the principal figures in the coronations of the past.

A picturesque motley of personalities do they present—men of strong will and of none, men whose names ring down the centuries and men whose fame hardly outlived their little day, men who displayed their conquering prowess on the battle-field and others whose power was in the subtleties of statecraft. From the Saxon sovereigns to those of the House of Windsor, they make a goodly showing, such as no other country can make its boast; and, moreover, what is most remarkable in this modern world where the only permanence is change, the age-continuing chain is

KING BEFORE THE CONQUEST
Edward the Confessor, depicted as above in the famous
Bayeux Tapestry, was the last but one of the Saxon kings
of England. He founded Westminster Abbey, and is
remembered as one who was Saint as well as King

forged throughout of royal links. In King George VI, Saxon and Norman, Plantagenet, Lancaster and York, Tudor, Stuart and Guelph find not only their heir but their descendant. The very crown that, in the most solemn moment of the coronation, is placed upon his brow, goes by the name of the royal saint who founded the Abbey in which over a period of nearly nine hundred years our sovereigns have been crowned.

St. Edward—the Confessor—makes a fitting first portrait in our gallery, for his passing was, in effect, the passing of the old dispensation that endured from the time England first became a nation.

Historians are somewhat scornful of his capacities and lack of achievement, yet when the martial triumphs of more vigorous kings have slipped into obscurity, Westminster perpetuates his love for the things that endure. The fierce rivalries of his reign are forgotten, but his tomb still stands in the church and city—a mere village then, set in a

Thameside marsh—that he loved so well.

He died, and Harold, "the last of the Saxons", succeeded to his State. With far greater gifts of leadership, with the fierce courage of his race, he yet was doomed to die in the hour of defeat, with the flower of the English nation around him.

William the Conqueror

THE Norman Conquest will ever remain the most indelible of our historical landmarks, and William I will always be regarded as the ruler who left most permanent evidence of his character and power on the country he had subjugated. A man of strong will and iron nerve, he was admirably fitted for the part he was to play.

William, who was the natural son of Robert, Duke of Normandy, was born in 1027, at Falaise, his mother being a tanner's daughter. William was in only the eighth year of his age when he succeeded to the dukedom, and if his country was peaceful during his minority he certainly lost no time when he came to manhood in waging war against his neighbouring barons and thus speedily achieved fame as a warrior.

On the death of Edward the Confessor, and the choice of Harold, son of Earl Godwin, as his successor, William of Normandy laid claim to the English throne, alleging that during a residence in Normandy Edward had sworn to recognize William as his successor.

With a large army and fleet, he set sail from St. Valery, on September 26th, 1066, landing two days later at Pevensey, on the coast of Sussex, "to assert his right".

It was early in the morning of October 14th that the fateful issue commenced. Harold had encamped on a range of hills opposite Senlac, and at first the Norman

cavalry charged in vain against the stern ranks of the men of Kent. But the tide of battle turned, and Harold and his two brave brothers were slain, the last of the Saxon kings was dead, and William was now able to claim the surname of "Conqueror". The Invader was crowned on Christmas Day of the same year, 1066, and one of his first acts as King of England was to build a convent at Senlac, to which he gave the name of Battle Abbey.

Five years after the battle of Senlac the Norman power was supreme throughout England, and the Saxons were, in every respect, a conquered people.

During the reign of the Conqueror was compiled that famous work known as the Doomsday Book, wherein a complete account of all the landed property of the country was set down. William made feudalism formidable in England by building a series of castles, garrisoned with his feudal army. The most famous of these is the Tower of London. William died at Rouen on September 9th, 1087.

WILLIAM THE CONQUEROR

A man of iron will, William I (centre) won England by force of arms and made his name feared throughout the country. Once victorious, however, he revealed himself as a statesman of the first order

William Rufus

CALLED Rufus or the Red King, William II was the second surviving son of William the Conqueror, who nominated him to the English succession. On September 26th, 1087, he was duly crowned at Westminster by the Archbishop.

But William had many a battle to fight in order to strengthen his position. On the death of Lanfranc, in 1089, Father Ralph became the chief adviser of the King and eventually Bishop of Durham, and once in this position of almost untrammelled power he caused the people to be cruelly oppressed and subjected to conditions which, in some respects, exceeded the severity of the Conqueror's reign.

Meanwhile, the King's brother, Robert, by his reckless extravagance, was ruining the dukedom of Normandy, which Rufus himself had long coveted, and Henry, who was certainly the wisest of the three brothers, had expended his patrimony in purchasing a third of his brother Robert's province of Cotentin.

In the hope of securing his own ends William had engineered a revolt of the citizens of Rouen, but Henry, on this occasion, supported Duke Robert's cause, and the revolt was speedily suppressed. Meanwhile, Henry's shrewd common sense was greatly increasing his power throughout Normandy, and we find William and Robert joining together in a siege of Mont St. Michel, Henry's stronghold, actuated by nothing else than jealousy of him.

In 1095 the strange movement initiated by Peter the Hermit began, and all over Europe knights and barons, together with the scum of the countries, were joining the ranks of the Crusaders. Amongst these was Robert, Duke of Normandy. Impecunious as usual, he had to turn to his brother William Rufus for financial assistance, which the latter readily secured from the public coffers on condition that Robert handed over the government of his Norman States to William.

On August 2nd, 1100, when at Mallwood Keep, in the New Forest, on a hunting expedition, he was killed by an arrow, generally believed to have been shot by Walter Tirel, the result of no accident, but designed to rid the kingdom of a ruler whose rapacity and profligacy had made his name a hateful one for ever.

Henry I

AMONG the hunting party in the New Forest on that fateful day was Prince Henry, the younger brother of William Rufus, and youngest son of William I. Hastening to London, he was at once proclaimed, and three days after his brother had fallen in the New Forest, Bishop Maurice, a willing time-server, crowned Henry King of England.

Knowing himself to be a usurper, Henry was anxious to conciliate the Saxons, who, though powerless to overthrow the Norman rule, were still sufficiently powerful to be of some account in the destinies of a king.

[British Museum

TWO NORMAN KINGS

William II, or William Rufus (seen on the left-hand coin), sought to increase his power by tyrannical means. On his death, England turned with relief to his brother, Henry I (right), who proved to be a great legislator.

The Pope was prevailed upon to canonize King Edward the Saxon as "Edward the Confessor" and a charter was granted to the Saxons, promulgating a code of laws to which the name of Edward was given. But his greatest concession was his marriage with the daughter of Malcolm of Scotland and Margaret, sister of Edgar Atheling, so uniting the Norman and the Saxon races.

In other ways he endeavoured to cultivate the goodwill of the Saxons, and it was well he did so, for on August 1st, 1101, his brother Robert landed at Portsmouth, and many Norman barons in England flocked to his standard. Although Henry advanced to meet him, he was too cunning to rush into battle, and a financial arrangement with the Duke settled the difficulty.

Later, however, taking into consideration the disturbed state of Normandy, the wily Henry considered that an excellent opportunity had arrived for possessing himself of that country. Crossing to Normandy with an army in 1106, Henry defeated Robert at the battle of Tinchebray and possessed himself of the duchy.

In 1118 Henry lost his good Queen Maud, after she had borne him two children, William and Matilda, or Maud. The former

was now called by the Saxon title of Atheling, and married at an early age the
daughter of Fulke, Earl of Anjou, who
soon after became King of Jerusalem.
Matilda married the Emperor Henry V of
Germany, but on his death she returned to
England and soon became affianced to
Geoffrey Plantagenet, eldest son of Fulke,
who had resigned his European States to
Geoffrey when he assumed his eastern
crown. The child of the marriage, Henry,
was fated to play an important part in the
history of England.

After the death of Maud, King Henry
had married Adelaide of Louvain. He had
also received at his Court the children of
his sister Adela, the wife of the Count of
Blois. The eldest son of Adela was
Stephen, Count of Boulogne, who had the
advantage of good looks and soon became
a favourite with all classes.

Prince William was drowned when returning from Normandy. Having himself gone
to that country to settle a dispute with
Geoffrey, King Henry was seized with
sickness, attributed to a surfeit of lampreys,
and died on December 1st, 1135.

Stephen

STEPHEN, the gallant Count of
Boulogne, attended the last moments
of the dying King, and then took his
departure and hastened towards the coast.
Arriving safely in England, he galloped fast
to the capital, and secured the assistance
of his brother Henry, Bishop of Winchester,
in proclaiming him King of England. The
Saxons were friendly towards him, as his
wife, Maud of Boulogne, was of their race ;
while the barons were reluctant to have a
woman rule them.

The nobles were promised privileges, the
people were to have protection and their
ancient laws restored, the clergy were to be
supported. Such was Stephen's programme,
and he ruled in some sort of a way without
opposition for three years. But already
his secret enemies were at work, Gloucester,
half-brother to the Empress Matilda,
among them. Mercenaries from the Conti-

nent were brought over by different chiefs
and garrisoned in their castles, and in
another direction the Pope was scheming
to bring England
under his control,
Stephen's brother, the
Bishop of Winches-
ter, having been in-
duced to become the
Pope's legate.

When Gloucester
had matured his
plans, David, King of
Scotland, marched at
his direction, at the
head of a formidable
army, into Yorkshire
in 1138. Archbishop
Thornton and Ralph, Bishop of Durham,
raised the signal summoning the barons of
the north in support of the English King,
and at Northallerton the Battle of the
Standards took place, the Scots and their
allies being heavily defeated.

USURPER

Stephen seized the throne
on the death of his uncle,
and his reign became a by-
word for lawlessness. From
a coin in the British Museum.

While Stephen was rejoicing over this
victory, the Empress Matilda landed and
proceeded by way of Arundel Castle to
Gloucester, the stronghold of its earl, her
half-brother. Here she set up her standard
and defied the power of Stephen, being now
supported by a considerable number of the
barons. In 1141 Stephen was defeated and
made prisoner by Gloucester, but before
the end of the year he was free again and the
civil war continued for about twelve years. It
was only on the death of the Earl of Gloucester that Matilda returned to Normandy.

Her son, Henry Plantagenet, had now
come to man's estate, and on the death of
his father Geoffrey, in 1151, he was acknowledged Duke of Normandy and also Earl
of Anjou, Touraine and Maine, marrying
shortly afterwards the divorced wife of
Louis, King of France, by whom he gained
the rich provinces of Guienne and Poitou.

Henry now raised a formidable army,
but when he invaded England the leaders
of both sides had grown weary of the
strife and a compromise was considered.
Stephen's son, Prince Eustace, had been
killed ; his brave and noble queen, Maud

of Boulogne, had died two years before. So he willingly agreed to a pacific settlement by which he was to retain the crown for his life and be succeeded by Henry, Duke of Normandy. In less than a year Stephen died, on October 25th, 1154.

Henry II

AT the time of Stephen's death Henry Plantagenet was in Normandy, and six weeks elapsed before he came to London to take possession of his new dominion. On December 19th, 1154, he was crowned at Westminster.

Henry set out on his reign with distinct promise of being an enlightened and successful ruler, guided as he was by an able grand justiciar in the Earl of Leicester. The foreign mercenaries who had made the doings of the robber-barons possible in the previous reign were expelled and the castles of the lawless chiefs demolished, while a distinct effort was made to establish something like justice in the treatment of the common people. Early in his career Henry also set his face against the pretensions of the Church of Rome and maintained the supremacy of the civil authority.

A great figure of Henry's reign was Becket, now Archdeacon of Canterbury, who soon became chancellor of the kingdom and the sovereign's most trusted adviser.

During the earlier years of Henry's reign the King's attention was devoted mainly to internal affairs, and in the course of his first decade he succeeded, so far as was possible at that time, in bringing his subjects under an equal law, though the clergy still ostensibly looked to the Pope as their only temporal sovereign. Trial by jury was now coming into general use, the population was increasing, and industry was being encouraged.

It was suggested to Henry that the recalcitrant clergy might be brought to acknowledge his authority if Becket were placed at their head, but the moment this clever schemer found himself Archbishop of Canterbury he became the leader of their resistance. For this the King deprived him of his temporal appointments, and, on Becket's refusal to accept the Constitutions of Clarendon, arraigned him as a traitor. Becket fled to France, where for some years he lived luxuriously under the protection of the Pope. Four years later the difficulty was so far patched up that Becket was again at Canterbury. Soon afterwards he was slain in the cathedral, supposedly at the instigation of the King. In 1173 he was canonized.

The conquest of Ireland was the greatest event of Henry's reign. He established his son John as lord of the country, but the prince proved so overbearing in his demeanour towards the Irish chiefs that he was soon recalled.

Henry's domestic relations were unhappy. He had quarrelled with his wife Eleanor, from whom he had separated, and the Queen, joining a conspiracy of his enemies, instigated their sons to rebel on different occasions and on varying pretexts. Henry had also to deal with many rebel barons, with the Earl of Flanders and with the Scottish King.

THE FIRST PLANTAGENETS

A new dynasty of English kings was ushered in with the accession of Henry II (left), a man of marked administrative ability but intolerant of opposition. The character of his famous successor, Richard I (right), is obvious from his appellation "The Lion Heart". He gave small attention, however, to governing his kingdom. Portraits from the tombs.

After some years of peace, his sons again took arms against him in Normandy, and at Rouen, while hostilities were still being maintained, Henry fell sick and signed a treaty of peace on his death-bed. He died on July 6th, 1189, leaving his kingdom greatly advanced in prosperity and the condition of the people much improved.

Richard I

RICHARD I, the eldest surviving son of Henry II, and a rebel against his father at the time of the latter's death, had no taste whatever for governing, but was at heart an adventurer. Henry had recently wrung from an unwilling people a considerable amount of treasure wherewith to join Philip Augustus of France on a third Crusade, and Richard possessed himself of this treasure and determined to carry out the project.

For something like nine months after his coronation Richard remained in England, making no effort whatever to govern, intent only on squeezing from the unfortunate inhabitants the utmost penny they could be forced to give by Longchamps, whom he had made Chancellor, to assist him in his Crusading undertaking. A fleet of one hundred ships was got ready and dispatched under William de Fortz, to proceed to Sicily. Richard had, in the meantime, arrived at Sicily by way of France, and was soon quarrelling with Philip, because the latter, at Messina, hoisted his standard on the ramparts as though he was sole leader of the Crusade.

After the capture of Acre, in June 1191, Richard alienated all his confederates, in spite of brilliant feats of arms, and so offended Philip that the latter returned home to intrigue with Prince John of England against him. Alarmed at news of these conspiracies, Richard concluded a three years' truce with Saladin and set sail for England. Driven by a storm into the Adriatic, he landed, and decided to travel by land disguised as Hugh the Merchant, but in Vienna he was captured and handed over to the Emperor, Henry VI, who held him prisoner until Longchamps, faithful to his royal master, succeeded in getting Henry to agree to a heavy ransom.

The despicable John had, meanwhile, raised an army and, declaring that Richard was dead, endeavoured to establish himself as king, but was opposed by the barons in both England and Normandy, the latter defeating his supporter, Philip of France, who invaded Richard's Norman provinces.

Longchamps having procured the ransom, the liberated Richard arrived in London on March 12th, 1194, meeting with a magnificent reception from the citizens. Instead of settling down to try his hand at the government of the people whom he had been called to rule over and who, for the most part, admired him personally, Richard, after being crowned a second time at the request of his barons, merely assented to further taxation of the over-burdened country, and returned to Normandy, where he was soon in arms against Philip.

For six years he continued the conflict, which was conducted with fearful barbarity on both sides, until, on April 7th, 1199, the Lion Heart was slain in an ignoble quarrel.

John

OF all the unworthy creatures upon whom the crown of England has rested, King John may be written down the worst. He has been aptly described as a "monster of tyranny, rapacity, cowardice, and injustice". The youngest son of Henry II, he was born on December 24th, 1167, and when twenty-two years of age had married Hadwisa, the daughter of the Earl of Gloucester. Ten years later, on May 27th, 1199, he was crowned, and in the same year he divorced Hadwisa in order to marry Isabel of Angoulême.

Tyranny of the most complete and relentless description was the keynote of King John's reign. Difficulty after difficulty arose between him and his barons, between him and the Church, between him and everybody with whom he came in contact. He was at war in Ireland, he fought in Wales, he attacked Scotland.

During his absence in an attack on France, for which he had allied himself with the Emperor and also with the Count of Flanders, the barons of England, together with the great prelates headed by Stephen Langton, the archbishop, took counsel together as to the best means whereby they might restrain his intolerable tyranny.

Thus began that great movement which was fated to exercise a powerful effect on the future of England, the first result of which was the granting of the epoch-making Magna Carta, signed on June 15th, 1215, at Runnymede, near Windsor.

Knowing too well the utterly base and treacherous character of their King, the barons occupied the city of London in pledge for the fulfilment of the agreement, and retained the power of levying war against the King should he violate his engagements. This was precisely the thing King John hoped to do. As soon as he had signed it, Gascony, Flanders and Brabant were called upon to supply an army of hired soldiers, and the arrival of these the King awaited at Dover.

The town of Rochester he took after a siege, and marched northward to punish the Scottish King for his support of the barons. The English nobles and clerics remained steadfast to their purpose, though they unwisely offered the crown to Louis, son of the King of France, who, having married Blanche, the niece of John, claimed a right to the throne. Arriving with an army, Louis recaptured Rochester and entered London.

John, meanwhile, having heard of Louis' invasion, hurried south to resist him, but on his way was seized with fever, and died at Newark, October 19th, 1216.

Henry III

ON the death of King John, his eldest son, Henry, was only nine years of age, having been born on October 1st, 1207, at Winchester. Louis, son of the King of France, had come to England in the hope of finding a sufficiently strong party to support him in an effort to secure the throne. But the barons now realized that in such a case the crown of England would become little better than a fief of France. Thus the measure of allegiance accorded to the young King Henry was practically representative of the entire country. He was crowned on October 28th, 1216.

In his sixteenth year Henry was declared of age. Three times during his minority the Charter had been renewed, and now de Burgh, who held the strings of government, altering it to the form which it bears today, compelled him to re-sign it. The barons had warned the King that in the event of a French invasion they would not supply him with the means of resistance if he did not ratify the Charter.

The condition of the people continued much as it had been for some generations. Though they were nominally assured of certain rights and privileges, the preference of the King for foreigners and his rapacity for tax-collecting were felt severely. In 1236 Henry married Eleanor of Provence. There had now come to the front in public affairs the figure of Simon de Montfort, Earl of Leicester, a Norman, who was destined

TWO KINGS OF THE THIRTEENTH CENTURY
Historians have had little good to say of John (left), and certainly his reign was marked by violence and civil war. His son Henry III (right), who ruled for fifty-six years, was similarly involved in warfare with his barons. Portraits from monuments.

to play an important part in the history of our country.

Henry's extravagance often brought him into financial straits, and eventually he summoned the great Council in order to obtain supplies, but was refused any grant until he again ratified the Great Charter preventing him from taxing the people without their consent. Meanwhile, the barons formed associations to redress the grievances of the country, and their next encounter with the King was when they met him in arms under the leadership of Simon de Montfort. On this occasion Henry was compelled to yield, and in 1258 the "Provisions of Oxford" were passed, by which the government passed virtually into the hands of the feudal lords, foreigners were to be expelled, expenditure reduced, and French claims renounced.

Henry soon obtained a dispensation from the Pope releasing him from his oath to observe these provisions. King Louis of France arbitrated between the Crown and the country, but on Louis awarding in favour of the Crown and the King soon afterwards breaking his oath, the barons took up arms, and a battle fought at Lewes resulted in the defeat of the King, who, with his son, Prince Edward, was captured by de Montfort. A treaty was agreed to, known as the "Mise of Lewes", whereby the objects of the barons were supposed to be secured, and de Montfort practically became ruler of the country.

Prince Edward, who was kept in free custody at Hereford, contrived to escape, and at the head of dissatisfied barons who had revolted, took up arms against de Montfort, who was defeated eventually in the hotly contested battle of Evesham.

After this there followed a period of comparative peace,

for Henry now allowed his son to be the real head of government. The King died, November 16th, 1272. The barons, on his death, took a voluntary oath of allegiance to Prince Edward, who had married in his youth Eleanor of Castile.

Edward I

IN Edward I England found a king of iron will and enterprise. Not only was he a capable ruler but an intelligent and determined legislator whose aim was to banish feudalism from political life and to consolidate his dominions.

Wales had so far maintained its rank as an independent principality, but the strong arm of Edward soon brought it into subjection, Llewelyn, Prince of Wales, being slain in 1282, and his brother David captured and executed the following year.

Edward's second son was born at Carnarvon in 1284 and, having become heir to the throne, was presented to the Welsh as Prince of Wales. This title thus became identified with the eldest son of the reigning King of England.

Edward next spent some years suppressing a revolt in his Gascon provinces, and also in interfering in the affairs of Sicily, but in 1290 he set his face towards the greatest undertaking of his reign. After the death of Alexander III the Scottish crown passed to his granddaughter, the "Maid of Norway". Edward had been successful in affiancing his son to her, but she died soon after landing at Orkney.

Her death was the signal for numerous claims to be put forward for the crown of Scotland, but of these only two had hope of recognition: John Baliol and Robert Bruce, both of whom were descended from David I

EDWARD I

Founder of England's Parliamentary system and "Hammer of the Scots". From a contemporary MS. in the British Museum.

of Scotland. Of these only two had any hope of recognition: John Baliol and Robert Bruce, both of whom were descended from David I of Scotland. Thanks to Edward, John Baliol was chosen King in 1292, and did homage to him. But Edward's policy was to bring about, if possible, the complete subjugation of Scotland, and to this end he treated Baliol as a mere tributary ruler, subjecting him and his country to so many indignities that Scotland threw off her allegiance, and in 1295 made an alliance with the French, with whom Edward had already become seriously embroiled.

Having abandoned Gascony and quelled a fresh revolt in Wales, Edward marched northward against the Scots, and won a decisive victory at Dunbar. But in 1297 a rising in the north was headed by Sir William Wallace. Douglas, Moray and other great nobles joined this patriot, whose followers drove the English entirely out of the country and followed them as far as the Tyne.

News of this reached Edward, then warring with the King of France, and he speedily made a truce with Philip and returned home, wreaking a terrible vengeance on the Scots at Falkirk. Wallace after this led the life of a fugitive and outlaw for years, but when Edward had taken himself south again, the Scots appointed Robert Bruce, son of the former claimant to the crown, together with Comyn, the nephew and heir of Baliol, regents. Edward threw himself against the Scots once more, and after the fall of Stirling Castle, Wallace, who still remained in arms, was captured and executed. Scotland was now incorporated with England, but England had scarcely begun to organize its government when revolt broke out once more. This time it was under Robert Bruce, grandson of the regent, who was warmly received by the Scottish barons as their leader. The English garrisons were driven from the land, and Bruce crowned at Scone as Robert I, on March 27th, 1306.

King Edward, now in the vale of years, took an oath to reconquer Scotland, but on the eve of a final attempt he died, July 7th, 1307.

Edward II

THE father had been a man of firm purpose and resolution, but the son who succeeded him was one of the weakest and most vacillating rulers England has ever known. He left Aymer de Valence to prosecute the war in Scotland, dismissed the ministers of the late King, and, recalling his former favourite, the banished Gaveston, he appointed him regent of the kingdom. Edward next went to France to marry Isabella, daughter of Philip le Bel, who was to become one of his bitterest enemies.

His coronation took place on February 25th, 1307, and Piers Gaveston occupied the place of honour at the ceremony, and so ostentatiously did the King display his favour for him that the barons demanded his banishment. To this Edward yielded, but Gaveston was later reinstated, until a rising of the barons under Thomas of Lancaster led to his execution.

Scotland still remained turbulent. The governor of Stirling had agreed to surrender the fortress to Robert Bruce unless relieved by June 24th, 1314, and Edward hastened from Berwick at the head of an army consisting of 100,000 footmen and 40,000 horse, only to encounter an overwhelming defeat at the hands of Robert the Bruce on the field of Bannockburn.

After this disaster Lancaster was in power for some years until a rival party arose and Hugh le Despenser, together with that nobleman's father, conducted the King's affairs. They speedily became hated by all the nobles of the country, and Parliament was compelled to pass a decree banishing the Despensers for life. Still, Edward was not without followers, and, marching to the west, he encountered the Lords Marchers, capturing one of the most powerful, Roger Mortimer. He next annulled the ordinances, recalled the Despensers, and in 1322 made yet another effort to defeat the Scots, only to encounter disaster once more. The following year he was glad to conclude a truce with Scotland.

Escaping to France in 1324, Roger Mortimer formed a liaison with Queen Isabella, who had long been estranged from her husband, and together they entered into a plot for the overthrow of Edward. The Queen affianced her son to Philippa, second daughter of the Count of Hainault, and with his assistance she raised an army and invaded England, accompanied by Mortimer. The Earl of Kent and other discontented nobles joined her, and the King fled with the Despensers to Wales. The latter were both put to death and Edward was captured and conveyed to Kenilworth Castle. Isabella had him deposed on January 7th, 1327, and he was finally lodged in Berkeley Castle, where he was put to death soon afterwards.

Edward III

EDWARD III, eldest son of the second Edward, was soon to show that he was not another weakling. The government remained for three years in the hands of Isabella and Mortimer, but in 1330 Edward threw off their domination. He captured Mortimer and had him executed, while Isabella retired into obscurity.

In 1332 Edward Baliol invaded Scotland with the support of some English barons and was crowned King during the minority of David Bruce, Edward III undertaking to assist the claimant on condition that, if successful, the crown of Scotland would be acknowledged as a fief of England. But the campaign was unsuccessful and the crown was restored to David, this time with the aid of Philip of Valois, King of France. Philip's interference gave Edward just the opportunity he wanted for declaring war against France, and he entered into alliance with the rulers of several foreign States.

His first efforts directed against Philip were crowned with failure, and he had to return to England for supplies, which were obtained only by extending important privileges both to peers and commons. The war dragged on for years, until on August 26th, 1346, Edward scored an important victory over the French and their Bohemian allies at the battle of Crécy.

But an enemy more subtle than any Edward could face followed him to England. In September 1349 the Black Plague was raging, and in parts of the country nearly two-thirds of the population fell before the destroyer.

In the succeeding year the death of Philip of Valois and the succession of his son John seemed to point towards a settlement of the war, but none was reached, and consequently the Black Prince, warlike son of a warrior father, landed in the south of France and ravaged the country, while Edward himself was devastating the lowlands of Scotland. The battle of Poitiers was a great victory for Prince Edward, and the King of France was brought captive to London. Another captive King, David Bruce of Scotland, was released

EDWARDS, DEFEATED AND VICTORIOUS

Edward II (left) was utterly unlike his great father, and was largely responsible for the loss of the campaign against the Scots. Edward III (right) was the father of medieval chivalry, and achieved notable victories (such as Crécy) for England on French soil. Portraits from the monuments.

shortly after, and as David Bruce and his rival Baliol both died childless, the crown of the northern kingdom devolved on Robert, the son of David's eldest sister, and the first of the Stuarts to mount the Scottish throne.

Before this, however, Edward had again invaded France, only to meet with reverses both on land and sea, and eventually he agreed to the Great Peace of Brétigny. Another disastrous war took place between England and France, when the people of Gascony rebelled against Edward's attempt to make them pay for his war in Spain.

In 1369 Queen Philippa died, and subsequently Edward III seems to have lost his old power of leadership. Female favourites at Court practically dictated the fortunes of the country after the death of the Black Prince in 1376, and on June 21st, 1377, Edward III lay dying.

Richard II

RICHARD II was the grandson of Edward III and son of the Black Prince. He succeeded to the throne at a somewhat critical and yet comparatively peaceful period in the history of the country, being only ten years of age at the time of his accession. The insurrection headed by Wat Tyler was one of the more exciting incidents of his minority, arising out of the popular opposition to the poll tax.

The great religious awakening, which in another hundred years was to give birth to the Reformation, was taking place steadily during the reign of Richard II. Parliament, too, thanks in large measure to the preposterous demands of previous kings, had now secured for itself a considerable degree of power. The growing opposition to the claims of Rome was becoming more general among the English clergy, while the untiring work of John Wycliffe and his colleagues was exercising a remarkable influence on the public mind. Literature was in a comparatively flourishing state, the poems of Chaucer and Gower, William Langland and John Barbour, achieving considerable popularity.

The material condition of the people was

likewise improving. Many serfs were now securing their freedom, and greater progress might have been made in this direction but for the ill-starred insurrection headed by Wat Tyler. And all this notwithstanding the fact that a feeble and

iN P G.

RICHARD OF BORDEAUX

A king whose later years of attempted revenge on his rivals have been the subject of tragic plays, both medieval and modern, succeeded Edward III on the throne. This was Richard II, who secured peace and prosperity for his country in spite of his own eventual failure.

vacillating king was on the throne and that the nobles were as busy as ever plotting and counter-plotting and quarrelling for power. At the outset Richard gave evidence of a well-meaning disposition, but became the dupe of his flatterers. He had married, in 1382, Anne of Bohemia, who proved a warm supporter of Wycliffe.

So unpopular did the King at last become, that Henry of Bolingbroke, grandson of Edward III and son of John of Gaunt, supported by powerful nobles, found no great difficulty in deposing him and inducing Parliament to bestow the crown upon himself in the year 1399. Richard was imprisoned in Pontefract Castle and died there within a year of his deposition.

Henry IV

ONCE again the throne of England was occupied by a usurper, and the accession of Henry IV was eventually the cause of the civil war between the houses of York and Lancaster which broke out in the reign of his grandson, Henry VI. Edmund Mortimer, the young Earl of March, and his brother were imprisoned by the usurper and kept in confinement, except for a brief period, till they died ; but it happened that a sister of Mortimer's survived and, as she married Richard of York, her descendants claimed precedence over those of John of Gaunt for the crown of England. It was thus that the rivalry of the two houses arose.

Henry had seized the crown, but the task of governing he found no easy one, beset as we was by plots and counter-plots which necessitated a liberal use of the axe. His policy happened to run counter to the wishes of the powerful Percys, who joined with Douglas and, securing the support of other influential nobles, marched towards Wales, to co-operate with Glendower, the Welsh prince, who was now practically independent. But Henry met them, July 21st, 1403, on the fiercely contested field of Shrewsbury, from which he emerged victorious, with Douglas and Worcester as his prisoners, and Harry Hotspur dead.

He did not, however, enjoy peace for long, and Glendower, Northumberland, Norfolk and Archbishop Scrope were soon causing him trouble once more, in an attempt to place the Earl of March on the throne. The King was successful in the field against them, though his execution of Scrope brought down on his head the thunders of Rome, this probably influencing him in the fierce persecution of Wycliffe's followers, which he soon after commenced. Glendower was eventually defeated in South Wales.

Henry IV, who died on March 20th, 1413, was the first English king who committed the infamy of burning his subjects for their religious opinions. The most that can be said in his favour was that during his reign the firm hand he kept on the affairs of the country tended greatly to increase the prosperity of the people.

An interesting representation of Henry's coronation is given in page 80

Henry V

HENRY of Monmouth, who ascended the throne in his twenty-sixth year, proved himself, according to his lights, an able ruler, whose bravery and perseverance won him the admiration of his people.

At home his chief rival was, of course, the Earl of March, whom he kept a close prisoner, as also the young King of Scotland, endeavouring to win their friends to his side by restoring to them their titles and estates. Like his father he sought to conciliate the Romish priests, who were becoming seriously alarmed for the prestige of their Church by the spread of the doctrines which Wycliffe was teaching. With Henry's complaisance the bloodthirsty Bishop of Arundel and his coadjutors were permitted to use the stake and faggot even more constantly than in the previous reign.

While these events were going forward, full of portent though they were to the future of his country, Henry was but little interested in them, his military activities and ambitions taking him to France, still torn asunder with internal strife. With 30,000 men he crossed to Harfleur and faced a French army six times as numerous as his own, with the result that at Agincourt he achieved one of the greatest victories in the annals of war.

The war was carried on into Normandy, the French, meanwhile, ravaging the English coasts ; until in 1417, with a still larger army at his command, Henry again took the field in person and, after capturing Caen, laid siege to Rouen, which fell after a protracted and brave resistance. Henry, now established as Duke of Normandy, still hankered after the crown of France, and when the Dauphin placed himself in opposition to the French King Charles VI, Henry, by marrying Catherine, the daughter of the latter, and joining forces with Charles, was recognized as his successor to the crown.

TWO KINGS OF THE LANCASTRIAN LINE

Henry IV (left), grandson of Edward III, owed his throne to Parliamentary support, and during his reign Parliament became almost paramount. His son, Henry V (right), revived the military glories of his ancestors, his great victory over the French at Agincourt representing one of the most stirring pages in our history. A sculpture in Westminster Abbey, representing the coronation of Henry V, is reproduced on page 220.

RIVALS OF THE WARS OF THE ROSES

The dispute which led to the protracted Wars of the Roses revolved largely around Henry VI (left), a gentle but weak-minded king, who was at times attacked by insanity. After many years of civil strife and open warfare, he was captured and secretly put to death by Edward of York (right), already acknowledged king as Edward IV. Under Edward's rule the land was at peace and the King encouraged trade and patronized such men as Caxton.

Returning to England with his queen and leaving his brother, the Duke of Clarence, as his lieutenant in Normandy, Henry had soon to take the field again, Clarence having been slain and his army cut to pieces in an attempt to invade Anjou. He went to raise the siege of Caen, but a fatal illness was upon him, and he died on August 31st, 1422.

Henry VI

THE throne of England now passed from the occupation of a stern, resourceful warrior to his infant son, who was only nine months of age when he became King, September 1st, 1422. The crown of France was also claimed on his behalf when, two months after his accession, his grandfather, Charles, the lunatic sovereign of that realm, died. The young King's uncle, the Dauphin, disputed the claim, and assumed the title of Charles VII. He was crowned at Poitiers, and soon established his authority over the southern provinces of France. The Duke of Bedford, an uncle of the child Henry, acted as regent in France, and carried on war with Charles VII, while the Duke of Gloucester, another uncle of the King's, was regent in England.

The young King, when he reached boyhood, was placed under the tutelage of the Earl of Warwick, and before long gave evidence of a weakness of character evidently inherited from his grandfather, the mad King of France.

Bedford was pressing Charles very closely in Orleans when there arose that most remarkable figure in the history of France, Joan of Arc, an ignorant peasant girl who, maddened probably by the deplorable condition into which the wars had brought her country, fancied she had received a divine command to fight for her fatherland. She was accepted by Charles VII and his leaders, who, whether or not they believed in the divine inspiration of the Maid of Orleans, at least saw the value of such a figure in an age of superstition. Her advent retrieved the fortunes of Charles, and so inspired his soldiers that the English,

despite superior numbers, were driven from Orleans, and Charles marched victorious to Rheims, where he was crowned. Joan was soon, however, made a prisoner by the French forces opposed to Charles, and after months of cruel treatment she was sold to the English, handed over to the Church, and burned at Rouen, after a mock trial, on May 13th, 1431, as a sorceress and a relapsed heretic.

Success now seemed to have completely deserted the English. Bedford died, the Earl of Shrewsbury was slain, and the Duke of Burgundy became an active ally of Charles. Fortress after fortress was surrendered to the French, until of all the territories won back by the prowess of Henry V, Calais alone remained.

Meanwhile, the weak-minded Henry was induced by his Council, led by Cardinal Beaufort, to marry Margaret, daughter of René of Anjou and Maine, and a particularly strong-minded woman. Gloucester and Beaufort were now at daggers drawn, and in 1447 the former was thrown into prison and murdered. The Cardinal, however, died six weeks after his nephew. During Beaufort's period of triumph the persecution of the Lollards was rigorously continued.

The condition of England was, indeed, deplorable at this time. Jack Cade's abortive rebellion was probably planned by some of the nobles who had their own ends in view, the most indefatigable of these being Richard, Duke of York, who claimed to have a better right to the crown than Henry, as he was descended from Lionel, second son of Edward III, while Henry was the great-grandson of John of Gaunt, Edward's third son. Soon after the birth of his son, the mind of Henry VI became quite deranged, and fear of a long minority with the hated Queen for regent induced many to side with the Duke of York against the House of Lancaster.

York was appointed Protector of the kingdom by the Commons. He was supported by the Nevilles, one of whom, Richard, Earl of Warwick, son of the Earl of Salisbury, became known as the "King-maker". The Dukes of Somerset,

Buckingham, Northumberland and Richmond were leaders of the Lancastrians.

The Wars of the Roses commenced at St. Albans, where the Duke of York met Somerset under arms on May 22nd, 1455. York was victorious, and Somerset, together with Northumberland, was killed, while the King was taken prisoner. Three years' peace followed, only to end with the Wars of the Roses resumed in terrible earnest. Warwick, on July 10th, 1460, inflicted a crushing defeat on the King's forces at Northampton, Henry being again taken captive. It was then agreed that he should retain the crown, but that his successor should be Edward, son of Richard, Duke of York. The latter was killed at Wakefield in 1460, and Edward marched to London, defeated Pembroke at Mortimer's Cross, February 2nd, 1461, and was joined by Warwick. Near St. Albans they were driven back by Queen Margaret, who had advanced with a large following from the north. But Edward drew off his forces and entered London, where, laying his claim to the throne before the Council of Peers, he was acknowledged King of England.

Edward IV

ALTHOUGH the luckless Henry had been deposed and Edward IV called to the throne by the voice of Parliament, the crown sat very insecurely on his head, and the Wars of the Roses were far from being at an end.

Queen Margaret gathered in the north a large force of English and Scots, not fewer than 60,000 in number, led by the Earls of Northumberland, Westmorland, Devonshire, and others, whose fathers had given their lives to the cause of King Henry. They advanced southward, while the young Edward proceeded northward, his forces increasing in number till they quite surpassed the Lancastrians.

On the eve of Palm Sunday, March 29th, 1461, these two great armies joined issue at Towton, with the result that the Lancastrians were put to flight, their leaders slain or captured to be speedily executed. Henry and Margaret fled to Scotland.

The victorious Edward was crowned in London, and his brothers George and Richard were created Dukes of Clarence and Gloucester.

In 1464 Margaret landed in Northumberland, where she was joined by Percy and Somerset, and on May 15th she encountered Warwick's brother, Lord Montacute, on Hedgeley Moor, near Hexham, where her hopes were finally shattered by the fall of Percy and the execution of Somerset. A year later Henry was imprisoned in the Tower.

To all appearances Edward had now firmly established himself on the throne, but his secret marriage with Elizabeth Woodville, widow of Sir John Grey, was to work the young King ill, as the favouritism naturally shown at Court to her relatives was little relished by Edward's strongest supporters, the Nevilles

Warwick, as an offset to the growing influence of the Queen's friends, privately instigated his tenantry and friends in the north to raise the standard of revolt. The royal army sent against them was defeated at Edgcott, July 26th, 1469, and Earl Rivers, the Queen's father, and her brother were beheaded. The "King-maker", having thus attained his object, induced Edward to confide in his loyalty and forthwith made him a prisoner, whereupon the Lancastrians, hoping to restore King Henry to the throne, took up arms again ; but Warwick, still a Yorkist, defeated them and liberated Edward. Later he changed sides, became reconciled with Margaret of Anjou, and landed on September 13th, 1470, at the head of an expedition.

King Edward fled to Holland, and his Queen to the sanctuary at Westminster, where, shortly afterwards, the ill-fated Edward V was born. Warwick entered London on October 6th ; Henry was released from the Tower, Parliament summoned, and Edward declared a usurper.

Fully conscious of his popularity in England, Edward did not remain long idle, and in 1471 he returned with an army and won battles at Barnet and Tewkesbury. Most of the Lancastrian leaders were captured and beheaded, but Pembroke, fleeing to Brittany, carried with him his young nephew, Henry Tudor, Earl of Richmond, who was to play an important part in English history at a later stage.

Secure now at home, Edward became fired with an ambition to win back the French provinces which had been lost during the minority of his predecessor, but his plans, both of conquest and of politically advantageous marriages of his daughters, went awry. He died on April 9th, 1483.

Edward V

THE boy who, in his thirteenth year, became Edward V, was then residing at Ludlow Castle, surrounded by relatives

EDWARD V

Like Edward VIII nearly five hundred years later, Edward V was an uncrowned King of England, although he wears a crown in the Canterbury royal window (above).

of his mother, among whom were the sagacious Earl Rivers, Sir Richard Grey, Sir Thomas Vaughan and Sir William Stanley. With these friends and a small retinue he set out for London on April 24th, 1483, arriving at Northampton the same day that Richard of Gloucester, brother of the late King, reached that town on a rapid progress to London. Gloucester, suspecting that the young King's friends intended to put an end to his own guardianship, caused them to be arrested and lodged in Pontefract Castle.

Thus it was that when young Edward made his state entry into London he was accompanied only by his direst foe, who played his cards sufficiently well to be appointed Protector of England and used the hapless Edward merely as a tool wherewith to sign decrees fraught with ruin to his own best friends. Within a short time the latter had all been done to death, and Gloucester had succeeded in withdrawing the Duke of York, younger brother of the King, from his mother's protection, and had placed him with the King in the Tower.

Richard III

IN the popular imagination, at least, Richard III may be written down the most picturesque scoundrel who has ever usurped the throne of England. Nevertheless, he had many elements that make for greatness, and in his brief and turbulent reign he wrote his character with a strong hand on the page of England's story.

As soon as he had the young princes safely shut in the Tower he declared that Edward IV's marriage had been invalid, and secured his proclamation as King. Together with his consort, Anne, daughter of the Earl of Warwick, he was crowned on July 6th, 1483, the preparations for the coronation of the ill-starred Edward coming in handy for Richard's own purpose. All who had supported him reaped rich rewards, and in order to win the good graces of the people Richard made a progress through the country, being crowned a second time at York.

By order of Richard the young King and his brother were smothered while

[N.P.G.

RICHARD III

Having obtained the Crown by usurpation, he kept it only two years, being slain on Bosworth Field.

they slept in the Tower. The new King, however, had many enemies. Even Buckingham, having some claim to the crown, being descended from the third Edward, rebelled against Richard and raised an army of Welshmen at his castle of Brecknock, but decided instead to support the claim of Henry Tudor, the youth with whom his uncle, the Earl of Pembroke, had escaped from the battle of Tewkesbury, and who had been carefully trained in France as a possible King of England.

Young Henry had received promises of support from the Lancastrian exiles, on condition that if he gained the crown he would marry Elizabeth of York, the late King's eldest daughter. From St. Malo, Henry, at the head of his army, sailed on October 12th, 1483, and a few days later was proclaimed by his adherents in England, but owing to a storm he was compelled to return, while Buckingham was beheaded.

But Henry renewed his plans for invasion, and on August 7th, 1485, he landed at Milford Haven at the head of a considerable army gathered in France, and on the 22nd Richard, deserted at the critical moment by professed supporters, was slain at the battle of Bosworth. Thus passed away, after a brief two years of troubled reign, the last of the Plantagenets.

Henry VII

THE first of the Tudor kings was as contemptible a specimen of the avaricious tyrant as any that had ever come to the throne of England. His one object in life seems to have been to wring the uttermost penny out of the country, to assist him in maintaining his royal dignity or in financing his own personal enterprises.

Henry claimed the throne as representing the House of Lancaster through the marriage of his father, Edmund Tudor, Earl of Richmond, to Margaret Beaufort, grand-granddaughter of John of Gaunt. The young Earl of Warwick, shut up in the Tower, had a better claim to the crown than Henry, while the Earl of Lincoln, son of Richard's sister,

[Victoria and Albert Museum

FIRST OF THE TUDORS

Henry VII was a man of strong character and artistic taste. The latter quality is exemplified by his endowment of the chapel in Westminster Abbey that bears his name.

the Duchess of Suffolk, had been named by the late King as his successor.

Henry soon had to deal with an unexpected pretender to the throne. A youth appeared in Ireland calling himself the Earl of Warwick, and as such was actually proclaimed Edward VI by the Lord-Deputy in Dublin, whereupon Henry brought forth the real Earl, and exhibited him to the people of London. This did not prevent Lord Lovell and other Yorkists from joining the pretender in an invasion from the Lancashire coast. The revolt was suppressed, and the pretender proved to be Lambert Simnel, son of an Oxford carpenter who had been trained by a priest to personate Warwick.

Another pretender to the crown was a youth who called himself Richard, Duke of York, and claimed to be the younger of the two princes murdered in the Tower. Like Simnel, he came to Ireland, but the fate that person met prevented the second pretender from gaining support. Returning to France, however, he was joined by some of the exiled Yorkists, and later went again to Ireland, and thence to Scotland, where he was received cordially by James IV, who gave him in marriage his own kinswoman, the beautiful Lady Catherine Gordon, daughter of the Earl of Huntly, and twice invaded England on his behalf, but had to retreat on both occasions.

Eventually, when Henry concluded peace with James, the pretender and his bride, with a small following, had to leave Scotland, but landed on the coast of Cornwall, where the Cornishmen flocked to his standard. At the head of 6000 men, the pretender marched on Exeter, where he was repulsed, and later on, at Taunton, he was deserted by his followers, and fled to the sanctuary of Beaulieu Abbey, whence, throwing himself on the King's mercy, he was taken to London and made open confession that he was an impostor, that his real name was Perkin Warbeck, son of the Comptroller of Tournai.

When Ferdinand of Spain refused, owing to these rivals to the succession, to allow his daughter Catherine to marry Henry's son Prince Arthur, both Warwick and Warbeck were executed.

Henry now betrothed Arthur to Catherine of Aragon, hoping to get his hands upon her splendid fortune. The prince dying soon after the marriage, Henry insisted on his second son and namesake, then eleven years of age, being betrothed to Catherine, six years his senior. His eldest daughter married James IV of Scotland, and through their descendants the two crowns were one day to be united. Henry died at Richmond Palace April 21st, 1509.

Henry VIII

YOUNG Henry VIII, handsome and debonair, came to the throne with every prospect of a happy and successful reign. Possessed of the enormous wealth hoarded by his father, he did not need immediately to risk unpopularity by applying the screw of taxation to the country. As soon as he succeeded to the throne he married Catherine of Aragon.

Henry's association with the wars of the notorious "Holy League" brought him neither honour abroad nor popularity at home, and while he was fighting on the Continent his brother-in-law, James IV of Scotland, renewed his alliance with France, to assist whom James invaded England, but at Flodden he met with defeat and death.

Almost as notable a figure as that of the King was the famous Wolsey, who had been recommended by Henry VII to his son as almoner, and rose to the position of greatest power next to the King himself. By birth the son of a small farmer, and sometime incumbent of Lymington,

Hampshire, in 1514 he became Dean of York, and the next year he received his cardinal's hat and the office of chancellor.

At the instigation of Wolsey, Henry put Buckingham to death, because he was nearly related to the royal line, and Henry, wishful to establish his power abroad, determined to be rid of every possible rival at home. De la Pole, the Duke of Suffolk, for a similar reason was also executed. Less effective were this ambitious King's literary attacks on the reformers, though they secured for him from Leo X the title of "Defender of the Faith", which still continues to be used by English monarchs, but with a very different significance.

Henry, from being as reckless in his expenditure as his father had been parsimonious, found himself in need of money to maintain his state, and Wolsey had to render himself still more unpopular by squeezing it from the people.

The domestic vagaries of the fickle King now commenced. He determined to be rid of Catherine and replace her with Anne Boleyn, a beautiful maid of honour, and although the Pope refused a dispensation for the divorce and Wolsey opposed the wishes of the King, which action brought about his final downfall, Henry was to receive assistance from a quarter he little suspected.

Thomas Cranmer, then a humble chaplain and a follower of Luther, suggested that the question of divorce should be judged by learned men on the authority of the Bible without reference to Pope or Cardinal. The Reformer Cromwell, who had lately become one of the King's councillors, also advised Henry to deny the authority of Rome, and in the end Parliament decreed the divorce between Catherine and Henry, and Anne Boleyn was married to the King. In 1534 Parliament passed an act declaring the King's Majesty to be Supreme Head upon earth of the Church of England. Sir Thomas More, who succeeded Cardinal Wolsey as chancellor, was executed for refusing to acknowledge the royal supremacy, and Cromwell now became paramount in the State after the King.

HENRY VIII AND HIS CHILDREN ON THE THRONE

Henry VIII, shown top left in a portrait attributed to Holbein, has lived in history as a man dominated by passion and self-interest. Nevertheless, at the time of the accession of his young son, Edward VI (top right), the prestige of England stood higher than ever before. His two daughters, Mary I (bottom left) and Elizabeth (bottom right), also came to the throne in due course, and their fame endures—the one as "Bloody Mary" and the other as "Good Queen Bess".

Still in want of money, Henry dissolved the minor monasteries, and their wealth went to replenish his coffers. The hapless Anne Boleyn was beheaded in the Tower on May 9th, 1536, Henry having accused her of infidelity, and the day following her execution Jane Seymour became his wife.

The country was becoming very uneasy, and risings took place, especially in the north, instigated by Rome. On October 12th, 1537, Queen Jane gave birth to a son, to the joy and satisfaction of the nation, but she herself died twelve days later. Henry now chose Anne, sister of the Duke of Cleves, whose portrait by Holbein had charmed him, but when she arrived he must have been disappointed, as a few months after their marriage he again induced Parliament to grant him a divorce, and Cromwell, who had been mainly instrumental in bringing about this union, was executed through the scheming of his Roman Catholic opponents. On the fall of Cromwell and the departure of Anne the Roman Catholics again secured ascendancy, and the King married Catherine Howard, niece of the Duke of Norfolk, whom he soon accused of profligacy and had executed in 1542. The following year he married Catherine Parr, the widow of Lord Latimer, a woman of strong character and courage, who survived him.

The last six years of the reign were marked by a desultory war with France, and by the overthrow of an invading Scots army at Solway Moss. Henry died on January 28th, 1547, after a reign of vital importance to English progress.

Edward VI

CURIOUSLY enough, one of the most restless periods in our history was that during which the gentle and enlightened youth Edward VI occupied the throne. He was the only son of Henry VIII, his mother having been Jane Seymour, and at the time of his father's death he was not quite ten years old. Carefully trained by Protestant tutors, the young prince had been brought up imbued with the principles to which his mother was attached, and had not his tutors too greatly strained a constitution naturally weak, Edward might have lived to a good age and spared his country years of suffering.

The Privy Council formed for the guidance of the King contained a nominal majority of Protestants, but its members were a very mixed lot, and plot and counter-plot made it inevitable that mischief would crop up. The Protector of the realm was the Duke of Somerset, uncle of the King, while Dudley, Lord Lisle, afterwards Earl of Warwick and Duke of Northumberland, was one of the strongest men on the Council and the most ambitious.

The Duke of Somerset, wishful to carry out the policy of the late King with respect to the union of the crowns of England and Scotland, through the marriage of Edward and Mary, used both diplomacy and arms in that direction, but without avail, and the hatred of the Scottish Romanists for the English Protestants was only intensified. Still the Reformation was progressing, and Parliament was favourable to Somerset's proposals for bringing the knowledge of the Scriptures to the common people. Acts for the Uniformity of Public Worship and a Book of Common Prayer were passed.

To add to the difficulties of governing at this time in different parts of the country, risings among the peasantry took place, and it is not always easy to distinguish between the religious difficulties and the agricultural question in assigning the cause of these disturbances. But the Earl of Warwick, whose plans were now ripening, suppressed an important revolt at Norwich, and the popularity following this exploit gave him the confidence necessary to stand forth as an opponent of Somerset, whose power was rapidly ebbing.

The Protector was seized and committed to the Tower, and Warwick, now created Duke of Northumberland, assumed the reins of government. He contrived to fill all the positions near to the throne with relatives of his own, and in betrothing his fourth son, Guilford Dudley, to the Lady Jane Grey, eldest daughter of the Duchess ot Suffolk and great-granddaughter ot Henry VII, he took the bold step of advising the invalid King to set aside the device of his father and settle the crown on the heirs of the Duchess, thus ensuring a Protestant succession. Twenty-two days afterwards Edward VI died of consumption

Lady Jane Grey

THERE are few characters in our national history so attractive as the ill-fated Lady Jane Grey. By the will of Henry VIII she was regarded as next in succession after his three children, but, as we have seen, the wily Northumberland had induced Edward VI to pass over his two half-sisters and recognize her as his successor. Brought up with her kinsman Edward, she had surpassed him in learning, and like him she was imbued with a sincere love of the Gospel.

Guilford Dudley, her husband, was a weak, characterless youth, but by this marriage, which took place on the eve of the King's death, his father hoped to bring the throne under his own power.

On a royal barge, amid gorgeous display, Lady Jane sailed to the Tower, but was received in London in dead silence, owing to the hatred of the populace for Northumberland.

Meanwhile Mary, daughter of Henry and Catherine of Aragon, had escaped and was soon at the head of 30,000 men. Northumberland, hastily raising an army, set forth to join issue with her, but the forces under his sons, who had hastened in pursuit of the princess, went over in large numbers to her side, while within the Tower itself there was treachery. Lady Jane had the mortification of seeing her councillors fall away one by one, and on the ninth day of her reign her father, the Duke of Suffolk, and Archbishop Cranmer alone remained faithful. Northumberland

[Contemporary Portrait

NINE DAYS' QUEEN

The beautiful and accomplished Lady Jane Grey, whose reign lasted nine days, was the victim of tragic circumstance.

himself, his troops deserting him, had fallen back on Cambridge, and acknowledged Mary as queen, while a hundred thousand men in her support were marching on London, where Mary was duly proclaimed at St. Paul's and Cheapside. Lady Jane's "reign" had lasted nine days.

She was soon in the hands ot Mary's minions, while the Tower filled up with prisoners, among whom were the dastardly Northumberland and his sons.

Mary, secure enough on the throne, might have spared her helpless and unwilling rival but that the ambassador of Charles of Spain, who wished to see the Protestant faith in England stamped out, determined that one so strong in it as Lady Jane Grey, who might be Queen of England some day, should die. Eventually Mary promised Charles's ambassador that her cousin should not live another forty-eight hours, and, attempts to convert her having been unavailing, on February 12th, 1554, Lady Jane, strong in her simple faith, went calmly forth to death.

Mary

APART trom her legitimate claim to the throne, Mary had the support of a great many Protestants, who, despite her known antipathies to the Reformation movement, did not credit her with possessing the vindictive and merciless nature which she was soon to reveal.

At the outset of her reign she had, indeed, protested that her subjects were to be allowed some measure of religious liberty, and the persecution of the Protestants was started so gradually that before the heaviest blows fell the influence of Rome in the country was again supreme.

The first object of the Queen's Romish advisers was to secure for her a husband, a task of some difficulty, for the unattractive person and character of Mary were notorious. When it eventually became known that she had accepted as her consort her cousin Philip, son of Charles of Spain, great indignation was aroused throughout the country. The men of Devon and Kent rebelled, so did the Welsh borderers, but the insurrection was soon put down and London prepared to welcome the Spanish prince. Mary's sister Elizabeth was supposed to have had a hand in the rising. She escaped execution, but was imprisoned first at Woodstock and then at Hatfield.

The royal marriage took place, July 19th, 1554, at Winchester, the Queen being then in her thirty-eighth year and her husband nine years younger, and the Spaniards overran the metropolis for some considerable time afterwards.

The work of re-establishing the dominion of the Pope in England commenced on December 1st, 1555. Throughout the country Protestants were arrested at worship, and it was ordered that all who failed to submit themselves to the Church before Easter Day should be proceeded against with the utmost severity.

So began one of the most appalling reigns of terror England had ever seen. Cranmer, Archbishop of Canterbury, Ridley, Bishop of London, and Latimer, Bishop of Worcester, soon went to the stake. Cardinal Pole became Archbishop of Canterbury and the persecution increased in fury.

The misguided Queen was soon to reap the reward of her folly. In the first place, Philip, finding there was no hope of Mary's having children, and being utterly without affection for her, left England a year after his marriage, while plots against the Queen arose on every hand, Elizabeth again being involved in one of these. Philip visited Mary again, and induced her to send an army of seven thousand men to assist him in his war with France. When the French eventually captured Calais, our last remaining stronghold on the other side of the Channel, the Queen, who lay dying, declared that the word "Calais" would be found written on her heart after her death.

Queen Mary died November 17th, 1558, just as peace had been concluded between France and England and Spain. She named Elizabeth as her successor, and thus all the schemes of the Romish prelates and nobles were undone.

Elizabeth

ELIZABETH'S creed was unknown. Though she had conformed to the Romish practices under the patronage of Mary, she was believed by every reformer to be at heart a Protestant ; and her first act on ascending the throne reassured even those who had their doubts, as she appointed Sir William Cecil, a strong Protestant, her chief adviser, and all persons imprisoned for religious opinions were set at liberty. Her coronation took place on January 15th, 1559. Rejecting an offer of marriage from Philip of Spain, she informed her Parliament, who humbly petitioned her to marry someone worthy to be her consort, that she preferred a single life, but promised to take their prayer into consideration. For twenty-five years she continued to play with the marriage proposals of many notable suitors, and at one time there were fears that she might marry her undesirable favourite, Robert Dudley, Earl of Leicester.

In her first Parliament, which opened on January 21st, 1559, an Act was passed separating for ever the Church of England from the Roman Church, and re-establishing the reformed service of Edward VI. Despite Elizabeth's dislike for Calvinism, an army was sent to aid the Scottish Covenanters against the regent, Mary of Guise, resulting in a settlement with France, which had been supporting Mary Queen of Scots, whereby the port of Calais was restored to England, the French troops withdrawn from Scotland, and Mary and the Dauphin renounced their claims to the English throne.

Under the sagacious chancellorship of Cecil every effort was made to improve the finances of the country and strengthen its resources against the possibility of an attack from the Spanish King, who was still bent on winning England for Rome. The agents of the Pope were abroad in the country, but carefully watched, while Mary Queen of Scots was now a prisoner at Sudbury Castle, her machinations against England having placed her in the power of Elizabeth.

Elizabeth's government was speedily increasing in strength, and this fact made Philip of Spain and the Romanists of France but the more anxious to break its power. Numerous plots against the Queen's life were brought to light by the vigilant Cecil, now created Lord Burghley. It was proved beyond doubt that Queen Mary of Scotland, now held in captivity at Coventry, had sanctioned Babington's conspiracy to assassinate Elizabeth, and, urged by her ministers, Elizabeth reluctantly consented to the execution of the Queen of Scots. This took place at Fotheringhay on February 8th, 1587.

Spain had been steadily preparing to attack England, and the two countries were now virtually at war. English cruisers scoured the seas and captured Spanish merchantmen, and Drake was dispatched with a fleet of thirty vessels to cripple the operations which Philip was making for sending what he arrogantly called "The Invincible Armada" against England. So successful was he that the Armada had to delay its departure for a whole year. It eventually approached our shores on July 20th, 1588. Under Drake, Frobisher and Hawkins, and other gallant commanders, the light and active ships of England sped forth from every port along the western shore to meet the vessels of the haughty Philip. Three days later Howard, with his whole fleet, came up with the Armada off Portland, and the fight raged day after day until the Spaniards anchored in the Calais Roads, where Hawkins, sending some fire-ships among them, burned many and scattered the rest.

During a furious gale many of the Spanish ships fell into the hands of Elizabeth's captains and their Dutch allies, or were driven ashore. Off Gravelines the rest of the Armada was riddled with shot. Attempting to escape around the north of Scotland, the Spaniards were again caught in a storm. A mere shattered remnant of the once proud Armada returned to Spain towards the end of September.

On the death of Lord Burghley, in his seventy-eighth year, he was succeeded by his son, Sir Robert Cecil, who became Elizabeth's adviser. There were difficulties now in Ireland, occasioned by a somewhat injudicious attempt to force the Reformation movement on the people, and the Earl of Essex, as Lord-Deputy of the country, was forthwith deprived of his office and forbidden the Court. He conceived the mad idea of raising London against the Cecils, an exploit which resulted in his being executed at the Tower on February 25th, 1601. His popularity with the people, however, led them to view Elizabeth's sanction of his execution with indignation, and this, together with the opposition of the Commons to her prerogative, her difficulties in the matter of succession, and the fact that old age and infirmities had crept upon her, preyed on her mind and her spirits, and she gradually pined away. On March 24th, 1603, she was found dead in her palace at Richmond.

Under Elizabeth's wise rule the country had reached a place of power which it had never before occupied among the nations of the world. English drama was born and a great flood of poetry burst forth. Arts and industries were encouraged and extended, and the way paved for England's future prosperity. Maritime supremacy was achieved and the establishment of colonies commenced ; the seed of the vast British Empire had taken root.

James I

ON the day of the aged Queen's death her Council, in order to anticipate the supporters of the other claimants to the crown, proclaimed James VI of Scotland, only son of Mary Queen of Scots and Henry Darnley, as England's King.

With the great majority of the people the succession of James I was hailed joyfully, as uniting the two kingdoms and thus lessening the chances of armed disputes about the throne. Nominally a

Protestant, he had the support of the Reformers, and, being the son of the Catholic Mary, the Papists hoped for his favour, as, indeed, they had been promised.

Small-minded, ignorant of English law, vain to a preposterous degree, James was soon blundering his way to London, having en route made knighthood a farce by dubbing 237 gentlemen in return for their courtesies. Utterly lacking in all personal graces, posing as a learned man and a patron of letters, he was destitute of any quality calculated to inspire the admiration of the people, and the cunning which he possessed, and which he mistook for sagacity, was exhibited in his endeavour to win the favour of Protestants and Papists alike. Financial straits, the result of extravagance, led him constantly to unscrupulous ways of raising money.

Peace at any price was his foreign policy, which led him to withdraw the support that Elizabeth had offered to the struggling Protestants on the Continent. Having none-too-kind recollections of his treatment at the hands of his Scottish Presbyterians, he endeavoured to force the Episcopalian system upon the country, even menacing the rights of Parliament, and asserting his claim to rule by divine right.

Plots became rife, the most important of these being the abortive conspiracy of Guy Fawkes, which had for its object the blowing up of both houses of Parliament when they assembled in October 1605.

James next carried out his plan of uniting the two kingdoms under the name of Great Britain, and the union tended greatly to increase the power of Parliament, despite which the King declared himself above the law and so free from its control. James brought to an end, in 1604, the long war with Spain, but by seeking to marry his son to the Infanta he succeeded in frightening his Protestant supporters. When Buckingham had secured control of foreign policy, James found himself dragged into the Thirty Years' War on behalf of his son-in-law, the Elector Palatine. This is said to have hastened his death, which occurred on March 27th, 1625

Charles I

UNLIKE his father, Charles I had some elements of dignity and seriousness in his nature, and sincerely desired to govern well, but the profligate Buckingham still retained his power as king's counsellor. Charles was married in 1625 to Henrietta Maria of France, and the Protestants were greatly disconcerted to find that the marriage treaty allowed for the early education of her children to be entrusted to the Queen, with the proviso that if they proved to be Romanists that was not to interfere with their right of succession.

Like his father, Charles set the laws and prerogatives of Parliament at defiance, but, unfortunately for him, the Commons had during the last twenty-five years so greatly increased in power that the result was very different. The King asked for a supply; Parliament demanded the redress of grievances. On August 12th, 1625, Charles dissolved Parliament, but assembled it again on February 6th, 1626, and from then until 1629 he was engaged in a ceaseless contest on three issues : the ascendancy of Buckingham, the repression of Puritanism by the High Church ecclesiastics, and the King's claim to raise money by royal prerogative without Parliamentary authority.

RULER OF TWO KINGDOMS
Son of Mary Queen of Scots, James VI, King of Scotland became James I, King of Great Britain. He had all the Stuart failings and few of their virtues, and his insistence on the "divine right of kings" had a bloody sequel. Portrait after Van Dyck

Soon after the prorogation of Charles's third Parliament Buckingham was murdered, and, aided by his unscrupulous ministers, Wentworth and Laud, the King now ruled the country with absolute despotism.

The nobles and gentry of Scotland entered into a national Covenant to abjure the rites and ceremonies and customs of the Romish Church, and to resist the introduction of prelacy into the Prayer Book.

Needing money to raise an army, the King was compelled to call a Parliament in the spring of 1640, but quickly dissolved it again. When news came that the Covenanters had crossed the Tweed, the King went north to engage them, but his forces were driven out of Newcastle on November 3rd. He called another Parliament, which, refusing to be dissolved at the royal pleasure, became known as the "Long Parliament".

By this Parliament Wentworth, now Lord Strafford, was impeached, and after a long trial was condemned to death as a traitor for attempting to overthrow the liberties of the country. Four years later the detested Laud met a similar fate.

Parliament now passed an Act which prolonged its existence until such time as its own vote should put an end thereto. The Star Chamber, High Commission Court, monopolies and other agencies of despotism were abrogated, and the King, realizing the growing strength of opposition to him, endeavoured to temporize.

But London had now risen against the tyrant, and from the home counties yeomen with the badges of Parliament in

THE "MARTYR KING"

By his death on the scaffold, Charles I is now often regarded as a martyr. There is little doubt, however, that though he possessed both charm and courage, he courted disaster by his own foolhardiness. From a miniature by M. Snelling, Victoria and Albert Museum.

their hats came trooping in. Train-bands mounted guard around Westminster Hall, and at the palace gates clamoured the mob. Charles, at length seriously alarmed, fled to Hampton Court, and his Queen to Holland, on February 16th, 1641. After futile negotiations the King hoisted his standard at Nottingham Castle on August 23rd, and civil war began.

Charles was joined at Nottingham by his nephew Prince Rupert, son of the Queen of Bohemia. On its part Parliament called out the militia, appointed the Earl of Essex to the command of the army, and Lord Northumberland to the navy. In Parliament itself a further change had taken place, for a new party had arisen, known as the Independents, who appealed to the Bible as the one authority on all religious matters and held that every Christian congregation should have supreme jurisdiction in things spiritual. Oliver Cromwell was the leading spirit of this party.

Until the Parliament's victory at Marston Moor, July 2nd, 1644, the balance of success lay with the Royalists. On October 27th another hotly contested day at Newbury went against the Royalists.

In the Scottish Highlands, Montrose was victorious over Argyll and thus raised the hopes of Charles, now at Oxford, around which the main army of the Parliament was lying inactive. But on June 5th, 1645, the King's military chances were annihilated. He tried to negotiate with the Scots, and, flying from Oxford, he surrendered to their army at Newark. They promptly handed him over to the

5

Parliament, and he was conveyed to Holmby House. The civil war ended.

Now commenced a struggle between the factions of the Parliament. The army, determined to get the King into their possession, refused to disband, on the pretence that eight weeks' pay was due, and five hundred horsemen under Cornet Joyce brought the King from Holmby to Hampton Court. Charles continued to play for time, entering into negotiations with the Scots, the Parliament and the army, all of whom were at variance with each other ; but his attempt to escape to France, Royalist insurrections in Wales and in the south-east of England, and invasion by the Scots in 1648 convinced the army of his faithlessness. The risings were put down, and Colonel Pride ejected from Parliament all the members who were not at one with the army.

The army now demanded that the King be tried publicly. On November 25th, 1648, this remnant of the "Long Parliament", known as the "Rump", declared by vote that, having made war against the Parliament, Charles was guilty of high treason. A high court, composed of a hundred-and-fifty commissioners, peers, members of the Commons and aldermen of London, was formed to try him, and on January 27th, 1649, he was condemned to death. Three days later Charles was beheaded on a scaffold erected in front of the palace at Whitehall.

Charles II

BY right of succession the eldest son of the dead King now became King in the opinion of a very considerable section of the English people, but on that fateful January 30th, 1649, it was announced by the Sergeant-at-Arms that whosoever proclaimed a king without the authority of Parliament would be deemed a traitor.

The young Charles was now at St. Germain, but to secure his throne he accepted the Covenant and landed in Scotland on June 16th, being received as a King.

Cromwell, at the head of his well-disciplined army, entered Scotland on July 22nd, and at Dunbar completely routed the

(N.P.G.

ENGLAND'S "MERRY MONARCH"
That there was a more serious side to Charles II's nature is shown by his foundation of the Royal Society and interest in the Navy. The king enjoyed both power and genuine popularity, and modern writers pay tribute to his outstanding abilities.

Scottish forces under Leslie. He took Edinburgh and marched on Perth, while Leslie with Charles at the head of eleven thousand men went south, whither Cromwell followed them. On September 2nd the irresistible general of the Commonwealth decimated the Scottish army at Worcester, and Charles was again a fugitive, eventually, after assuming many disguises, reaching Shoreham on October 15th, and thence gaining sanctuary in France.

Under Cromwell's rule many abuses were abolished, justice was administered with an exactness never before known, and religious liberty was accorded to all. His policy abroad was also wise and resolute, and added to the prestige of the growing empire. But the system he had founded could not last, since it rested almost entirely on his own personality. Soon after his death on September 3rd, 1658, the Protectorate came to an end.

A direct military government was now attempted, but proved a failure, and the

Rump was restored and, under pressure from General Monk, the excluded Presbyterian members were reinstated in Parliament. On May 1st, 1660, Sir John Grenville appeared with letters from the King, and both houses voted for the return of Charles, who entered London on his birthday, May 29th, welcomed by all who hoped that peace had now been established. Monk, for his services, was created Duke of Albemarle. Edward Hyde, afterwards Earl of Clarendon, became chief adviser.

Charles's promise of religious liberty took the shape of an Act of Uniformity passed in May 1662, whereby Episcopacy was to be forced upon Nonconformists as an alternative to the most heartless persecution. The Court degenerated into a condition of vice and corruption never yet equalled.

About the time of the war with Holland in 1664 the Great Plague broke out in London, carrying off over seventy thousand people, and in September 1666 came the Great Fire, at once a disaster and a mercy, for it swept away all the rookeries where the foulness of the plague still lingered.

Lack of money from these and other causes kept a considerable portion of the fleet out of commission, and the Dutch, seizing the opportunity, sailed up the Thames, burned several warships in the Medway and harried the coast. Peace was concluded with them, England retaining the State of New Netherlands in America, which was rechristened New York.

Charles's younger brother James had now become an avowed Papist, and on his advice the King also professed himself a Romanist to Louis of France, from whom he was receiving financial assistance, and from whom he wished help to renew his attacks on the Dutch. In 1667 Clarendon, who had made himself unpopular with both King and Parliament, was forced to resign and flee the country.

Charles, still unable to get enough money from Parliament, concluded, in return for a large sum, the secret Treaty of Dover with France, but also formed an alliance with William of Orange, giving to him in marriage Mary, the eldest daughter of his brother James, she having been brought up a Protestant.

The next notable feature of this reign was the excitement occasioned by Titus Oates and his alleged discovery of a plot to re-establish Popery. The King's scandalous dealings with France were exposed in Parliament, a Bill brought in to exclude James from the crown, and in 1679 the Habeas Corpus Act was passed.

The Covenanters of Scotland were meanwhile suffering great persecution, and the severest measures taken against them were mainly prompted by the Papist James. It was now that the terms Tory and Whig came into use, the one being applied to all who supported the Stuarts, and the other to those who championed liberty. Numerous political clubs in London were gaining a power which alarmed the King, who proposed to Parliament, assembled in Oxford in 1681, that James should be deprived of royal authority but should be recognized as King. The Commons would not have this arrangement, and the exclusion Bill was revived, but the King dissolved Parliament and revenged himself on the London politicians by securing the forfeiture of the city's charter in June 1683. The Whigs, now desperate, conceived the mad Rye House plot to shoot the King, but it was discovered and many conspirators were put to death.

During his last four years Charles reigned without a Parliament, and the country, free from foreign or civil wars, achieved a large measure of prosperity. Charles died February 6th, 1685.

James II

HAVING succeeded his brother as King, James, an avowed Papist, swore before the Council to preserve the government in Church and State as by law established, repeating the same oath in Parliament. A revenue of nearly two millions was voted to him, though he was already a paid pensionary of the French King.

In every way within his power his Romanist friends and supporters were rewarded from the moment he exercised his authority as King, and Protestants were placed under serious disabilities. The Duke of Argyll headed a rebellion in the west of Scotland, and was executed. Monmouth rebelled, but at Sedgemoor disaster overtook him. In the wake of this came the Bloody Assize, when Judge Jeffreys wreaked vengeance on all who had risen to the cry of "Monmouth and Protestantism!"

Papists were appointed to important offices in every sphere, while the Church was placed under the control of a High Commission Court, of which the nefarious Jeffreys, become Lord Chancellor, was head.

In 1687, by the Declaration of Indulgence, suspending all laws against Romanists and Dissenters alike, James merely succeeded in alienating the whole of the nation, and the acquittal of seven bishops in 1688, after their trial for refusing to subscribe to the Declaration, was the signal of a great popular outburst against the King. The birth of his son (afterwards known as the Pretender) ensured a Catholic succession. Public feeling would stand no more, and William of Orange, grandson of Charles I and husband of James's daughter Mary, was invited by a number of English nobles to come over to England in support of the Protestant cause. On November 5th, 1688, William landed at Torbay and marched towards Exeter.

From all parts of the country came news of risings, and the King's Jesuit advisers took flight. At Reading William defeated some Irish troops sent against him. James fled to France, whence he organized ineffectual plots against William.

JAMES THE CATHOLIC

It was his rôle as an over-zealous Roman Catholic that more particularly alienated James II from his people. He was a king sadly lacking in political ability, and the employment of such men as the notorious Judge Jeffreys only led to his eventual downfall. Painting by J. Riley in the National Portrait Gallery.

On December 19th the Prince of Orange was holding his Court at St. James's, and it was ultimately settled that he and Mary should be declared King and Queen of England, the royal authority being exercised by him alone ; that on their death the children of Mary should succeed, and in default of these those of Princess Anne and her heirs, before those of the Prince of Orange by any subsequent wife. This Act of Settlement was prefaced by the famous Declaration of Rights, which set out the respective powers of King and Parliament.

William III and Mary

WILLIAM, as far as was humanly possible, selected the best men from all parties for his Privy Council, though at the outset of his reign his chief difficulty was to find men whose intentions were honest. He reserved to himself, and wisely, the control of foreign affairs, but, confiding in none, he stood practically alone in handling the difficulties of his position.

He proved his liberal views and also his political wisdom in the Toleration Act and in the Act of Grace and Indemnity, 1690, both of which won him many adherents.

The convention which William finally agreed to between England and Scotland provided for the establishment of the Presbtyerian form of worship in the northern kingdom. Energetic measures were taken against the clans loyal to the Stuarts, all of which were required to swear allegiance to William before a certain date. That this had not been done was the excuse given for the Massacre of Glencoe in 1692.

[N.P.G.

TWO SOVEREIGNS ON ONE THRONE

William III, Prince of Orange (left), and his wife Mary II (right), came to the throne as joint sovereigns following the flight of the latter's father, James II. The supreme motive in William's career was rivalry of France, and he succeeded in involving England in the Continental quarrel. Portraits after W. Wissing.

the Jacobite plots took the form of conspiracies against the life of the Protestant King, in several of which the fugitive James was concerned.

On December 28th, 1694, to the great grief of her husband and the British people, Queen Mary, who died childless, succumbed to smallpox.

Weary of war, France concluded a peace at Ryswick in September 1697, and when William returned to England after that event the enthusiasm with which the people welcomed him showed that for all his Dutch coldness of manner he had won his way to their hearts by his devotion to their country's cause.

By the Act of Settlement of 1701 the succession passed, after Anne, who had no surviving children, to Sophia, wife of the Elector of Hanover, and granddaughter of James I. William died as the result of a riding accident, on March 8th, 1702.

Ireland had declared for James in 1689, and a serious situation soon developed. James, financed by Louis, landed in Ireland with French troops. But William acted with energy. At the head of 6000 men, English, French Protestants and Danes, he came within sight of James on July 1st, 1690, and defeated him at the battle of the Boyne. James, after accusing his Irish troops of cowardice, hastened to Kinsale, and thence crossed to France, never to return. But Ireland had not been entirely conquered by the battle of the Boyne, and it required a further expedition under Marlborough to bring it under the rule of William.

William now crossed to Holland to hasten the equipment of the Dutch fleet, Mary being left to conduct the affairs of the kingdom with courage and ability. The situation seemed critical, as Louis was preparing his expedition to invade the country and re-place James on the throne. The English fleet, one of the most powerful the country had ever raised, joined that of Holland at St. Helens in the second week of May 1692, and the French were decisively defeated at La Hogue.

On land, where William was engaged with the French forces, although he scored few victories, he successfully defended England from invasion, and henceforth

Anne

"GOOD QUEEN ANNE", who succeeded her brother-in-law William, was amiable and virtuous rather than intellectually gifted, but she made an excellent queen. Her husband was little more than a nonentity, but Anne was a devoted wife and also a sorrowing mother, for only one of her children survived infancy, and he died at the age of ten.

The most influential man in England was now Marlborough, who owed his preferment not merely to his own prowess as a general, but to the fascination of his wife, formerly the beautiful Sarah Jennings, who gained great influence over Anne. William had foreseen the important part Marlborough would have to play in the war of the Spanish succession, and appointed him to the command of the troops of the States-General.

With this war on hand the country might have been forced into something like solidarity, but, instead of that, political factions were quarrelling bitterly, and in Anne's first Parliament, Harley, chosen Speaker, was a man of strong Jacobite tendencies. In religious affairs the High Church was again all-powerful, standing strong for government by divine right. Little by little customs which had been so characteristic of the Restoration seemed to be creeping in again.

On the banks of the Danube, joined by Prince Eugene and now in command of 50,000 men, Marlborough was engaged in one of his most important campaigns. On August 13th, 1704, he fought the famous battle of Blenheim, completely defeating the French and Bavarian forces. The decisive victory of Ramillies was won by Marlborough on May 23rd, 1706.

Although the crowns of England and Scotland had been united, not so the two countries, but after much discussion and negotiation the Act of Union was passed on March 6th, 1707, and the first Parliament of Great Britain met on October 23rd.

In 1708 the Spanish Netherlands revolted against the Dutch domination which had resulted from the victory of Ramillies, but the situation was saved by Marlborough's great victory at Oudenarde.

In 1709 he was again successfully commanding the allied armies in Flanders. At home, however, he was losing influence. Charged by Harley in 1711 with misappropriating public moneys, Marlborough was deprived of all his offices and retired abroad.

Harley, who had been created Earl of Oxford and Lord High Treasurer, and St. John, Viscount Bolingbroke, actuated by mutual jealousy, now accused each other of intriguing with the

QUEEN ANNE

[N.P.G.

Anne was a woman of personality rather than intellect, but she exercised a considerable influence on contemporary life. Her reign was a Golden Age of literature and military glory.

Jacobites, and this led to Oxford's downfall, whereupon Marlborough hastened over from Antwerp, while the Whigs set themselves to oppose the schemes of Bolingbroke and his confederates.

On May 28th, 1714, the Princess Sophia had died in her eighty-fourth year, leaving her son, the Elector of Hanover, heir to the British crown. Queen Anne died the same year, on August 1st.

Anne's reign saw the inauguration of the present system of party government, directed by a cabinet, the members of which all profess the same political creed.

George I

ON the death of Anne, the Elector of Hanover, great-grandson of James I, was proclaimed in the three capitals of Great Britain and Ireland as George I, to the bitter disappointment of the Jacobites, whose leader, Bolingbroke, fled the country and joined the Pretender across the water.

The new King arrived at Greenwich, accompanied by his eldest son, on September 18th, 1714, and set himself to rule his new country honestly and with genuine regard to its welfare. Since he spoke no English he had to entrust the conduct of affairs to his ministers.

The Jacobite intriguers still continued active, and many of those in high places were suspected of trafficking with the Pretender, Marlborough himself being among them. Oxford and Ormonde were both impeached for high treason, the one being committed to the Tower and the other escaping. On September 6th, 1715, the Earl of Mar raised the standard of rebellion at Braemar on behalf of the Pretender, and the fiery cross was sent throughout the Highlands, while a border rising, headed by Forster and Derwentwater, took place. The death of Louis XIV, however, was a serious blow to the prospects of the Jacobites.

The Pretender arrived at Dundee, and, proceeding to Scone, he assumed the condition of royalty, even fixing a day for his coronation. But he inspired no enthusiasm among those with whom he came in contact, and at the approach of Argyll he was seized with panic, and retreated to Montrose on February 4th, 1716, escaping soon after, along with the Earl of Mar, to his native land.

The succeeding year was signalized by the alliance between Germany, England, France and Holland against Spain, in consequence of which the Pretender had to quit France for Rome, and soon afterwards married the granddaughter of John Sobieski, King of Poland. The Spanish opposition to England was mainly dictated by Cardinal Alberoni in the vain hope of restoring the Stuart dynasty and the Romish faith, but Philip of Spain, finding the alliance too much for him, eventually became a member of it himself, and peace was restored to Europe.

Great distress was caused to thousands of people in England by the failure of the Mississippi Company in 1719, and in the following year the South Sea Company came to a similar end, creating a public panic and a great political upheaval. Walpole now came into power and used his financial ability to restore order after the crash. His influence grew from year to year until he was able to create for himself

KING FROM HANOVER

George I was born and died a German and never managed even to speak the tongue of his adopted country. He relied for government on his ministers, chief among whom was Walpole, England's first Premier. Portrait after Kneller London Guildhall.

the post of Prime Minister and virtually to rule the country.

The last years of King George, who died on June 11th, 1727, were embittered by incessant quarrels with the son who was to succeed him and who, meanwhile, led the opposition against him and his ministers.

George II

BORN on October 30th, 1683, the eldest son of George I was forty-four years of age when he ascended the throne. Twenty-two years earlier he had married Caroline of Anspach, and had a family of three sons and five daughters.

It cannot be said that he was in any sense a more regal figure than his father, but he possessed a genuine love of justice and undoubted personal courage, while his wife was a woman of great capacity and shrewd judgement, whose advice on difficult questions he was wise enough to take.

In 1729 peace was concluded between England and Spain at the request of the latter, the Spaniards abandoning their claims to Gibraltar. For twelve years now, under the wise guidance of Walpole, the country enjoyed peace, and made rapid strides in commercial prosperity.

In 1737 a quarrel arose between the King and his eldest son, Frederick, and the latter, being turned out of Court, joined the opposition led by William Pitt.

Walpole had striven strenuously for peace, but after Caroline's death in 1737 his power declined, and he was unable to prevent a renewal of the war with Spain. He resigned office and was succeeded by the Earl of Granville and then by the Pelhams.

The country was also drawn into a general European war at this time, and an army was sent under the incapable Earl of Stair to support the cause of Maria Theresa in her claim to the Austrian dominions of her father, Charles VI. King George himself, accompanied by his second son, the Duke of Cumberland, went out to take personal part in the war. Both of the royal soldiers displayed great courage at the battle of Dettingen, June 27th, 1743, when they inflicted defeat on the French. This was the last battle in which a British sovereign led his troops in person.

Encouraged by France and Spain, the Young Pretender, Charles Edward Stuart, then twenty-four years of age, embarked at Dunkirk with a French force of 15,000. But the elements warred against him ; his fleet, sorely crippled, had to return to Dunkirk, and France gave up efforts on his behalf. The following year, however, with only seven attendants, he gallantly made the attempt, and raised his standard at Glenfinnan, a few Highland chiefs rallying to his support. By way of Perth he reached Edinburgh and was proclaimed James VIII at Holyrood.

Eventually he came as far south as Derby, but by December 24th he had fallen back on Glasgow, won a victory at Falkirk, and had then to retreat towards Inverness, owing to defections in his ranks. At Culloden, on April 16th, 1746, the cause of the Stuarts went under for ever.

Jacobitism effectively stamped out, the country now settled down to peace so far as internal politics were concerned, and in 1746 Chesterfield became Prime Minister. Frederick, Prince of Wales, died on March 20th, 1751, leaving nine children. The great statesman William Pitt, afterwards Earl of Chatham, was steadily building up his reputation, and Henry Fox, afterwards Lord Holland, was also now taking a leading part in politics. The King developed a strong dislike for Pitt, and his last years were marked by the struggle between monarch and minister. Apart from this, George was content to reign as a constitutional sovereign.

In 1757 the Seven Years' War commenced over the partition of Prussia, and into this England was drawn. The King did not live to see its end, as he died in his seventy-seventh year, on October 25th, 1760, having reigned for thirty-three years.

George III

GEORGE III, eldest son of the Prince of Wales, was twenty-two years of age when the death of his grandfather called him to the throne.

The young King's determination to wield power was apparent from the day of his succession. Within a year he had dismissed Pitt and replaced him by Bute. By means of bribery and intimidation he forced the Commons to agree to the preliminaries of the Peace of Paris, 1762, and by 1770 he had formed his own party, the "King's friends", with North as Premier. For twelve years George directed, through him, the affairs of the country ; but the Commons' vote for a reduction of his power, 1780, and the folly of his policy in regard to the American War of Independence proved that autocratic rule was doomed to failure in Britain.

[N.P.G.

CONSTITUTIONAL KING

George II was one of the first kings to undergo the limitations of constitutional monarchy. Like his father, he was more closely attached to Hanover than to his kingdom of Great Britain and Ireland.
Portrait after Thomas Hudson.

While the War of Independence had been proceeding in America, England was also warring with France, Spain and Holland, and Russia, Sweden and Denmark formed an armed neutrality, ready to deliver a fatal blow if the contest had gone against our country. On January 20th, 1783, peace was secured by the Treaty of Versailles.

This year, at the early age of twenty-three, William Pitt, second son of Lord Chatham, became Prime Minister, and to his lot fell the guidance of the country through one of the most eventful periods of European history. His sane and masterly policy in dealing with domestic affairs preserved the peace of England during those terrible years 1789 to 1795, when revolution raged in France and the Bourbon monarchy came to the guillotine. In 1793 the extraordinary spectacle of revolutionary France at war with England, Holland, Spain, Austria, Prussia and five smaller States was presented to the world, and this condition obtained for twenty-two years.

An ill-conceived rebellion of the Irish, prompted by the French Revolution, was speedily suppressed, and following thereon Pitt carried a Bill on June 7th, 1800, for the Union of Great Britain and Ireland, since which Irish peers and burgesses have sat in the British Parliament. In the succeeding year, and again in 1804, the King's fits of temporary insanity, which first manifested itself in 1788, returned, and at such periods the affairs of the country were under Pitt's sole direction.

Breaking down under the strain of office held under circumstances of peculiar difficulty, Pitt died on January 23rd, 1806, and was succeeded by his able opponent, Fox, who, however, died soon afterwards.

KING FOR SIXTY YEARS

First English-born sovereign for nearly sixty years. George III was determined to be a "real king"— a resolve which resulted in due course in the loss of the American colonies. His last years were clouded by insanity. Portrait after Sir T. Lawrence.

The aged King was again showing signs of insanity, which so developed, together with subsequent loss of sight, that in February 1811 Parliament conferred the regency upon the Prince of Wales, and Lord Liverpool became Prime Minister.

Queen Charlotte died in November 1818, and on January 9th, 1820, King George, now eighty-two years of age, expired in the sixtieth year of his reign. During his later years he enjoyed greater popularity. This was due, in part, to sympathy with his illness, but more to his blameless private life and his homely ways, which appealed to the growing middle class.

George IV

AS the eldest son of the late King had acted as regent for ten years, the accession of George IV to the throne made little or no change in public affairs, though it was a period of much anxiety.

As a youth he was handsome and cultured, but his profligacy and unbridled extravagance outraged popular opinion. His scandalous treatment of both his morganatic wife, Mrs. Fitzherbert, and of his wife Caroline brought him into still worse odour. Immediately after his coronation ceremonies, from which Caroline was

GEORGE IV

The "First Gentleman in Europe" hardly lived up to his designation, either as Regent or King.

excluded, the King paid a visit to Ireland in the hope of helping to pacify that long-distressed portion of his dominions, and he next crossed to his German domains, where he was again crowned as King of Hanover. His success in Ireland was by no means conspicuous, but in Scotland, where he held a levee at Holyrood and appeared in Highland costume, he certainly increased his popularity.

Politically, the reign was a victory for Parliament, at the head of which was Canning. George resisted reform as long and as strongly as he could, but was compelled to assent to measures for the relief of Nonconformists and Catholics.

The King had long been an invalid, spending most of his time at Windsor, and on June 26th, 1830, he succumbed to gout and dropsy.

SAILOR KING

William IV had only a short reign, but he had already seized the popular fancy as England's sailor prince. He was of a conservative and unassuming nature, and kept within strictly constitutional limits. From an engraving by J. Cochran after Henry Dawe.

William IV

HENRY, Duke of Clarence, the popular sailor prince, third son of George III, now came to the throne as William IV, being at the time of his accession in his sixty-fifth year.

He was fortunate in his domestic affairs, and deservedly so. Simple-hearted and unassuming, he had no taste for pageantry, and in his wife, Adelaide, he was peculiarly happy. She was crowned with him on September 8th, 1831.

William IV set out with the firm intention of ruling as a constitutional monarch, and fortunately for the country and himself, at a time of great European unrest, he was faithful to his trust. So afraid of encouraging any change in politics, which

might pave the way to more revolutionary measures, were the Duke of Wellington and other Conservative leaders of the time, that the Duke's house at Hyde Park corner was attacked, and even the King had to be careful of his movements. Earl Grey, however, came in at the head of a reform ministry after Wellington's power had waned, and England was saved from any violence such as had taken place on the Continent, though to English minds the disturbances were grave enough, when, on October 3rd, 1831, the Reform Bill was rejected by the Lords. Serious riots occurred at Derby and Bristol, and at Nottingham the mob burned down the historic castle.

At the end of 1831 a new Reform Bill was introduced by Lord John Russell, and the King, in his speech, recommended a speedy and satisfactory settlement of the question. The opposition to the Bill came from the House of Lords, and so determined were the people that it should pass as law that the government, rather than lose the Bill, had decided to urge the King to create as many new peers as would be necessary to counterbalance the opposition ; but to this William would not agree, and the ministers accordingly resigned office. Wellington was unable to form a new ministry, and Earl Grey had to be recalled. But, meanwhile, the populace had spoken in no uncertain voice, and eventually the Bill was carried and the crisis brought to an end.

With the exception of his dismissal of Melbourne in favour of Sir Robert Peel, 1834, William took no further active part in politics. He died on June 20th, 1837, sincerely mourned by his people.

During the reign of William greater attention was devoted by statesmen and politicians to the condition of our industrial classes, and from this time onwards there has been a deepening of interest in all kinds of social work. The prosperity of the country was increasing steadily. Reduction of the newspaper stamp from fourpence to one penny greatly increased the power of the Press ; other minor reforms were helping to ease and improve the condition of the people.

Victoria

AT five o'clock in the morning of June 20th, 1837, the Archbishop of Canterbury and the Lord Chamberlain arrived in haste at Kensington Palace to inform the young Princess Victoria, then residing there with her mother, the Duchess of Kent, that by the death of her uncle she had become Queen of Great Britain and Ireland. She had attained her eighteenth birthday only on May 24th, but on this historic occasion it is chronicled that she comported herself with that dignity and true queenliness for which her character was ever noteworthy.

Her coronation, which took place on June 28th, 1838, is described in pp. 135 to 142. Among those attending it were the Duke of Saxe-Coburg-Gotha and his son, Prince Albert, who in less than three years was to become Prince Consort, Her Majesty announcing at the opening of Parliament on January 16th, 1840, that she intended to ally herself in marriage with the Prince, and adding, "I humbly implore that the Divine blessing may prosper this union and render it conducive to the interests of my people, as well as to my own domestic happiness." This prayer was abundantly fulfilled. The marriage took place on February 10th, 1840, and on November 21st of the same year the Princess Royal was born at Buckingham Palace.

QUEEN-EMPRESS

Few English sovereigns have enjoyed such universal popularity as did Queen Victoria in the closing years of her sixty-three-year reign. Her death seemed a personal loss to every one of her sorrowing subjects.

Such was Victoria's devotion to her husband, and such his quiet good sense, that a difficult position was turned into an ideal relationship. She remained the head of her country, but Albert, after the first year, though always in the background, inspired her every action. He preferred Peel where she had preferred Melbourne, and after the latter's defeat in 1841 she learned to trust and even to like the former. The Court became a little dull, and the visits to Osborne and Balmoral, which grew longer as she grew older, commenced. Quarrels with her ministers were frequent, anyone, and in particular Palmerston, who disagreed with the Prince Consort getting short shrift.

The death of the Prince Consort in 1861 was a blow from which Victoria never recovered. She retired into a more or less strict seclusion, but her participation in the affairs of government was continuous. She refused, indeed, to delegate any of her political duties to the Prince of Wales and was apt to be high-handed with her ministers. Palmerston died in 1865, and for the next twenty years the political stage was held by Disraeli and Gladstone.

It was to Disraeli alone, if we except the gillie, John Brown, that she gave her affection after the death of her husband. She warmly approved his imperialistic policy, and his idea that she should style herself Empress of India, which she did in 1877. It is impossible to attempt anything like a sketch of Queen Victoria's reign in a page or two of this book ; moreover, in its general bearings it is familiar to the present generation. Of the life and character of the Queen it was well written : "She has bequeathed to her people, as an imperishable, priceless gift, the incomparable influence of a personality that cannot but have a widening effect on the future of the great nation to whose well-being she devoted her constant energies through more than sixty years ; a nation which developed under her beneficent sway from less than 165,000,000 to about 400,000,000 inhabitants, and which, from occupying an area of less than 8,000,000 square miles, now counts within its borders over 11,000,000 square miles.''

Edward VII

EDWARD VII was born at Buckingham Palace on November 9th, 1841, and in the succeeding month was created Prince of Wales.

In 1859 he studied for a time at Edinburgh, and then went to Oxford (Christ Church), visiting Canada and America in the following year. In 1861 he was studying at Cambridge (Trinity College) and receiving military training at the Curragh. His marriage to Princess Alexandra of Denmark took place on March 10th, 1863.

Good-looking, good-humoured, frank and open, with an untiring zest for life, and of cosmopolitan tastes, by his marriage Edward greatly increased the popularity which he already enjoyed. For very many years he performed with tact and assiduity the representative functions which Queen Victoria felt herself unable to face.

There is no doubt that he gained much from the freedom with which he consorted with his future subjects. His public appearances were never perfunctory : he mixed easily and freely with people. As time went on his knowledge of social and political movements became extensive.

Edward's political knowledge was acquired under considerable difficulties. Not until he was turned fifty was Queen Victoria's assent obtained to his receiving

Photo, Stuart

THE PEACE-MAKER

Edward VII was an international diplomatist of great insight, and by personal meetings with foreign rulers did much to preserve the peace not only of Europe but of the world.

copies of important dispatches : but foreign politics fascinated him, and from middle life to the close of his short reign he was profoundly interested in international affairs. The record of his "ambassadorial" travels is exceptional even for the princes of democratic Britain, and was continued after he came to the throne. But the extent to which he concerned himself with social affairs was equally marked.

Edward became king in his sixtieth year. His scrupulous avoidance of any party attachments in politics and his exemplary performance of his public duties consolidated the position of constitutional monarchy in England. It remained for him as a king to popularize the kingship amongst his democratic subjects. Edward succeeded. His Court became brilliant, and the continuance of the sporting habits of his earlier years increased his popularity.

In the realm of diplomacy, within the wider scope that his sovereign position now permitted, he used the abilities he had already shown with admirable judgement. His influence was devoted to the task of strengthening England's position in Europe, and the successive visits he made abroad contributed materially to this end.

King Edward succumbed to an attack of bronchitis, May 6th, 1910.

George V

THE future King George V was born at Marlborough House, London, June 3rd, 1865. He was the second son of the Prince of Wales, afterwards King Edward VII, and his wife Alexandra.

Prince George entered the Navy on June 5th, 1877, joining the Britannia at Dartmouth with his elder brother, Prince Albert. They voyaged in the Bacchante to the West Indies, and in 1880 went on a cruise round the world. On his return home he passed his examination for sub-lieutenant at the Royal Naval College, Greenwich, obtaining a first class in seamanship. Promoted commander in 1891, he was given H.M.S. Melanthus, but the sudden death of his brother in 1892 made him heir, after his father, to the throne and curtailed his naval career. He was created Duke of York and took his seat in the House of Lords, June 17th, 1892. On July 6th, 1893, he married Victoria Mary, daughter of the Duke and Duchess of Teck.

The Duke undertook in the next few years many public duties, and the death of Queen Victoria, January 22nd, 1901, and his father's accession to the throne increased his responsibilities. As Duke of Cornwall and York, he fulfilled a previously planned tour of the British Dominions, leaving England with the Duchess on the Ophir, March 16th, 1901. He opened the first Parliament of the Australian Commonwealth ; visited New Zealand, meeting the chiefs of Maori tribes ; and was welcomed warmly at the Cape and in Canada.

On his return home, November 1901, the Duke was created Prince of Wales, and on December 5th he delivered a notable speech in the London Guildhall, urging an increased alertness on the country's part in order to meet competition. With the Princess of Wales he made a tour of India, 1905–06, being present at a magnificent Durbar ; and in 1908 the royal couple visited Canada.

King Edward died after a very brief illness, May 6th, 1910, and the Prince ascended the throne as George V.

The following years were ones of tension at home, in Ireland and abroad. The outbreak of the Great War in August, however, overshadowed all other perplexities in the next four years, and by his actions and bearing the King won the loyalty and affection of all who came in contact with him. He went to France on several occasions to encourage his army, and also visited the grand fleet ; and he paid frequent visits to munition and other factories at home. In addition, he and the Queen set a practical example of economy in the conduct of their homes. In 1917, by royal decree, the name of the Royal House was changed from Guelph to Windsor. The King and Queen were indefatigable in visiting the sick and wounded and in their philanthropic and other efforts.

The King opened the new Parliament of Northern Ireland at Belfast, June 1921, and in a notable speech appealed for co-operation between Irishmen. With the Queen he made a state visit to Brussels, May 1922, subsequently visiting the war graves of France and Belgium.

In the national crisis that arose in 1931 the King played an unobtrusive but extremely valuable part in persuading the leaders of the three parties to combine in order successfully to meet the emergency, thereby well illustrating the value of constitutional monarchy ; and, in addition, he set an example of sacrifice by giving up a large portion of his civil list.

King George had the directness of a sailor in his public and private speech ; his wide travels and his excellent memory enabled him to grasp problems with alertness and insight. Fond of open-air life, an exceptionally good shot, a keen yachtsman, and, like his father, a patron of the Turf, he would have been happy in the occupations of a country gentleman. On his own estates he did much to improve the breed of British cattle. His genuine and wide interest in all forms of sport was shown by his frequent appearances at Lord's, at the tennis championships at Wimbledon,

[Photo, Russell

FIRST OF WINDSOR LINE
In George V, Britain and the Empire found the perfect expression of constitutional monarchy combined with selfless nobility of character.

and at Rugby and Association football matches. His exertions in every direction, together with his close attention to affairs of state, were unrivalled in the history of kingship.

King George died, after a short illness, on January 20th, 1936.

Edward VIII

ON his father's death the Prince of Wales ascended the throne, to the accompaniment of whole-hearted and widespread expressions of popular affection and esteem.

Born on June 23rd, 1894, he served when a boy as a naval cadet at Osborne and Dartmouth and in 1913 entered Magdalen College, Oxford. On the outbreak of the Great War he was gazetted to the Grenadier Guards and appointed A.D.C. to Sir John French, and later he saw service in Egypt and on the Italian Front.

After the War he became the "Ambassador of Empire", visiting Newfoundland and Canada in 1919, Australia and New Zealand in 1920, and India in 1921–22. Three years later he was in West and South Africa, and then, and again in 1931, he visited the Argentine. Canada gave him a royal welcome on his return visit of 1927. He was in East Africa in 1928, and South Africa saw him again in 1930, but from then on he gave most of his attention to affairs nearer home. His interest in social service in general and better housing in particular was most marked.

His modern outlook grew more apparent when he became king. He continued to make use of his aeroplane—he was the first British king to fly—and instituted many changes in

[Photo, Hugh Cecil

KING FOR 1936

A reign begun with high promise in January 1936, ended eleven months later with the voluntary abdication of Edward VIII, known henceforward as the Duke of Windsor.

the management of the royal estates and he ceremonial of the Court.

In March 1936, when inspecting the just-built Queen Mary at Clydebank, he insisted on seeing the shame of Glasgow's slums as well as the glories of her shipyards. "How do you reconcile this with what we have just seen?" he is reported to have asked.

His interest in his old comrades of the Great War was evinced afresh when he unveiled the Canadian National War Memorial on Vimy Ridge in July, and on Armistice Day laid his wreath on the Cenotaph. In this, the last month of his reign, he inspected the Home Fleet at Portland, and also paid a visit to the "distressed area" of South Wales. His determination to go behind the scenes, followed by his promise to the mining folk, stricken by poverty and unemployment, that "something shall be done", appealed to the public conscience with tremendous force.

Never had his influence been so great, his fatherly interest in his people more manifest. Yet it was then that the storm-clouds broke. Rumour had been busy with his name for months past— rumour that linked him with an American lady. The possibility of a morganatic marriage having been ruled out, and the fact made clear that none of the governments of the Empire was prepared to accept his choice of a queen, King Edward decided on the bitter alternative.

On December 10th, 1936, he signed the formal act of abdication, and so the shortest reign in English history since that of Edward V, 453 years before, came to an end by a tragic act of renunciation.

THE EVOLUTION OF THE CORONATION

by E. ROYSTON PIKE

Associate Editor
"The Encyclopedia of Modern Knowledge"
"The New Popular Educator", etc.

Its Symbolism and Significance Popularly Explained

CHAPTER 5
The Call of the Coronation

CHAPTER 6
Crowns and the Crowning

CHAPTER 7
Symbolism of the Ceremony

CROWNING THE KING: A MEDIEVAL PICTURE

CORONATIONS are colourful landmarks in our history, but it is seldom that the contemporary artist enables us to visualize the pageantry of the crowning of long-passed centuries. This picture, however, of the crowning of Henry IV in Westminster Abbey on October 13th, 1399, is reproduced from a miniature in the fine Froissart MS. in the British Museum. Judging from the expression on the King's face one may suspect that already he anticipates what Shakespeare makes him experience, that "uneasy lies the head that wears a crown". An interesting feature in this picture is the raised platform or scaffold on which the chief participants in the ceremony are placed.

CHAPTER 5

THE CALL OF THE CORONATION

*As the "Home Country", Britain makes at all times a tremendous appeal
to the overseas visitor, but in Coronation Year the motives that draw
the multitude from all parts of the Empire are immensely strengthened*

FOR weeks and months past the feet of a vast multitude—vast beyond men's counting—have been turned towards the ancient Thames-side city of Westminster.

They have come from every corner of the Empire and beyond. Winter still reigned in England when some of them set out on the many thousand miles' journey. In the burning blaze of the tropic sun they packed their bags, and the monsoon rains slithered off their topees and the naked bronze of their bearers' backs. A train snorted and puffed into a wayside station in the Australian Bush, and an "Aussie" stepped aboard, on the way back to the land he had last seen during days of convalescence in wartime. Up the gangways at Sydney and Melbourne marched a host to whom England was only a name—but a name that drew them across twelve thousand miles of intervening ocean. Still farther "down under" Anzac veterans marshalled the families that had not been called into being when they last sailed from Britain. And in far-away, infinitely remote islands of the South Seas, white-skinned traders shut their shops and tramped down the coralline path to the waiting launch.

Right across the world Canadian ranchers said laconic farewells to their neighbours, packed the wife in the buggy and trotted off to the nearest station on the great line that runs across a continent. At every stop from Vancouver to Montreal fresh pilgrims joined the train, and the passenger lists of the boats that left the harbour bore names drawn from all the provinces of Canada, from her great cities and little townships, from the Arctic wastes and the American borderland. In the Atlantic, far from sight of land, they were hailed by another floating hotel, packed to the boat-deck with British folk—from the West Indies, or the English "colonies" in South America, or perhaps from New Zealand.

The Orient Moves West

In India mighty rajahs set out attended by a host of gorgeously-garbed retainers, and the natives of a thousand villages learnt with awe of their lord's great adventure into the lands beyond the mountains and the unbelievable sea. In Burmese temples and Hindu shrines, in Moslem mosques and the Christian churches of Southern India, prayers were said for those near and dear, or remote but powerful, who were setting out. Some said good-bye in a club in China ; some had a final whisky in a Singapore bar. Nigerian tribesmen salaamed their chieftains as they took the trail to the coast, and far south of the line Zulu spears flashed in a farewell salute. At the Cape, Boer and Briton, old hates and rivalries all forgotten, clamoured for berths on the English-bound liners ; and a little later a host of Britons by birth, and many more by descent, stormed the booking-offices that were the gateway to the trip across the "herring-pond".

White men—white with the pallor of city life or bronzed by days and nights spent in the fields trod by the herds or crunched by tractors' "caterpillars"; brown men—aristocrats of India's highest castes and denizens of Malaya's trading coast; yellow men—from the quays of Shanghai and Hong Kong; black men—black with the ebony induced by Africa's sun on the naked bodies of a thousand generations: whatever the colour, whatever the tinge, it was represented in that motley host, drawn from the four winds, but converging on one small island set in the cold, grey waters of the northern sea.

At first the stream was a trickle, hardly that. Here, far removed from London in time and place, a solitary bearer of the white man's burden succeeded in temporarily shifting the load; there a little party was formed to undertake the journey of many moons and miles. But as the year grew older, so the trickles became a stream, and the stream a river, and the river a torrent, and the torrent a broad and swift-moving sea. All the ocean track-ways that led to Britain were threshed by the turbines of the world's greatest ships; every railway speeded load upon load to the ports; every aerodrome received and dispatched a long succession of 'planes all bound the same Britain-ward way. Looking down from an empyrean vantage-point, the observer would see the smoke of fleets of tiny vessels, puffing their way into Liverpool or Glasgow, Plymouth or Southampton, or up the long and winding channel to London; at night he would glimpse a multitude of creeping scintillations, Man's million lights reduced to the pattern of Nature's glittering glow-worms.

Analysing the Appeal

What is the call that has sounded to such effect in all the corners of the earth? What is the motive that inspires the marching millions? What is the impulse that makes an army leave the lands that gave them birth, the friends and more than friends that centre about their homes—that makes them incur the expense, face the discomforts, and in many cases the dangers, of a trip across the lands and oceans that separate them from Britain's shores?

We know the answer, of course; but when we have said "the Coronation" have we reached the bottom of the matter? What is there in the Coronation that men—and women—should come to see it, not only from every part of the Empire, the British Commonwealth of Nations, but from many parts of the world without the Imperial bounds?

Three main reasons may be distinguished, and of these three the first to be mentioned is not necessarily the most potent in its drawing power, though it may be the first to spring to mind.

Pageantry Beyond Compare

The Coronation is a pageant on a colossal scale, one that dwarfs into insignificance any and all of the spectacular achievements of recent years. When Their Majesties went to their crowning in Westminster Abbey they were accompanied by an unexampled concourse of the great and rich and beautiful. Peers with a lineage reaching back through many centuries, whose arms are history in epitome; peeresses whose natural charms are enhanced by jewels of priceless worth; statesmen whose fame has gone out to all the nations; solemn dignitaries of the Christian Church; soldiers loaded with decorations won on the field and sailors whose flag has flown on all the Seven Seas; troops in glittering uniforms, gold and silver, scarlet and blue and yellow. Streets gay with flags and bunting, bands crashing out the strains of martial music, bells clanging from grey old towers and steeples; magnificent processions, gorgeous ceremonies, the intoxicating atmosphere of excited movement, full-throated cheers, swift-moving spectacle of the panoply of Imperial power arrayed as never before to demonstrate and impress.

Some say that there is far less colour in Man's world nowadays than in those infinitely remote days of "before the War". Many a gilded throne crashed into irretrievable ruin when the "cease fire" sounded; and the republics, even the dictatorships, that succeeded to the collapsed royalties were, in comparison, conceived in monotone. Beyond the Continent, in the "new" countries of America and the Antipodes, political expression has always been a colourless affair, a matter of logical simplicity, not a dazzling pageantry. The ceremony with which a president of the United States or the French Republic is installed or a Prince becomes King of the Belgians, with which the Governor-General of the Canadian Federation or the Australian Commonwealth or the Union of South Africa takes office—all these are imposing in their solemn formality, but they are as nothing in the eyes of the observer compared with the pomp and show that in accordance with the ancient practice attends the crowning of Britain's monarch, the Empire's head.

Here, indeed, is a very compelling urge. The spectacle of a generation, the finest pageant that the ingenuity and artistry of men can provide to charm the eyes and ears of a mighty multitude.

Loyalty Made Manifest

But next we have something deeper. The Coronation is not only a colourful spectacle—it is a tribute to a great personality. The portrait of King George VI looks down from the walls of mansion and cottage, planter's home and rancher's shack, miner's cabin and seaman's berth; wherever the British flag flies, there, we may be sure, a picture of the King-Emperor is present too. The King is the best-known individual in the whole of the British dominions. From birth he lives ever in the public eye. Millions have followed the story of his babyhood and boyhood, of his gradual growth and development into manhood, of his career of service on the sea, at home and abroad. The romance of his love-match thrilled a multitude of female bosoms, and all the mothers of the Empire have glowed with maternal joy over the photographs of the little Princesses. Though he has not received the education for the immediate kingship such as was his elder brother's lot, King George has, nevertheless, been brought before his people by the camera and printed word and has, indeed, been actually seen in the flesh by a great host of his present subjects both in Britain and overseas.

Royalty in the Picture

His Queen, too, since her wedding-day has been acclaimed as the "Second Lady in the Empire" and, as such, has been regarded with the utmost interest—nay, more, affection. Her famous smile has exercised its captivating influence wherever she has gone, in the Home Country, in Australia and East Africa and all the outposts of British rule at which the barques of the royal voyagers have touched. There can surely be no more popular photograph in the whole of the Empire than one showing the new sovereigns forming a family group with their two little daughters—an ensemble so like those to be found in the photograph album of a million families and, as such, all the more welcome and delightful.

To see the King and Queen, then, is a very natural desire in the hearts of their subjects, wherever they may be, and of whatever race and class and station. Londoners who see Royalty in the day's march, as it were, may seem a trifle blasé over the event, but when a Royal Jubilee is proclaimed or a Coronation goes on its magnificent way through the streets of the metropolis, the Cockney world pours out in its vociferous millions to cheer the King on his way. Those from whom Royalty is removed by thousands of miles are stirred by the same desires and impulses. Raiding their hardly-contrived bank balances and nest-eggs, they make the long journey. They hope to see a picture of fairyland come true; and such is the glory of the Coronation pageant that of a surety they are not disappointed.

We must remember, too, that the King is not merely a great personality, the most famous personage in the Empire. He is the symbol of Imperial unity, the living expression and embodiment of what we call the Crown. He is the inheritor of what his father was the first to exemplify. In him we and the world see the only link that now binds each of the great Dominions to the Mother Country and to one another. There is no Imperial constitution, no parliament of the Commonwealth, no cabinet directing the policy of the United Kingdom, and Canada, Australia, New Zealand and South Africa.

By the Statute of Westminster of 1931 the last of the legal bonds was definitely removed. Each Dominion is now supreme in its own house ; it makes its own laws, levies its own taxes, undertakes its own local defence. Only one thing have they in common with Britain—allegiance to the common sovereign. And, be it noted, in the choice of this sovereign they have a voice ; when Edward VIII abdicated in the close of 1936, the accession of his successor was the subject of preliminary consultation with the cabinet of each of the Dominions.

Imperial as Never Before

When our fellow citizens from across the seas come to the Coronation, then, they are coming in honour of the man who is their sovereign, by their own election and selection. They will remember, and we should do well never to forget, that King George is King of Canada, of Australia, of New Zealand and of South Africa. This Coronation was bound of necessity to be far more *Imperial* than any which have gone before. George VI is King in a wider and different sense than was George V when he ascended the throne made vacant by the passing of Edward the Peacemaker. The Coronation is no mere British pageant ; it is the occasion for the solemn declaration and recognition of the fact that it is the King who symbolizes in his person the unity of the Imperial Commonwealth of Free Peoples.

A spectacle of old-world magnificence attuned to modern needs, a tribute of world-wide loyalty to the British Crown ; is the Coronation something more ? For the answer we must look at the history of our country and of our race.

More than a thousand years have passed since the first king ruled over all England, the ancestor of our present sovereign. Nearly nine hundred years ago they were crowning a king in Westminster Abbey. Long before America was discovered, when the Antipodes were thought to be the fantasy of a disordered imagination, when Asia existed but in the realm of legend, and Africa was sunk in the darkest night ; when the oceans were unsailed wastes of water and a journey to the next village was the talk of a lifetime—even then England was an ordered State and the solemn crowning of her kings marked chapters in her aging story.

Turning a Page of History

We are the children of no parvenu amongst the nations. Our patriotism is not born of frenzied demagoguery on the platform or in the Press. More than five centuries ago one of our statesmen, inspired by true love of country, could be supposed to speak of "this royal throne of kings, this sceptred isle" as :

> This other Eden, demi-paradise ;
> This fortress built by Nature for herself
> Against infection and the hand of war ;
> This happy breed of men, this little world,
> This precious stone set in the silver sea,
> Which serves it in the office of a wall . . .
> This blessed plot, this earth, this realm, this
>   England . . .

John of Gaunt, in whose mouth Shakespeare puts these famous words, and the poet himself, both walked the stones of the Abbey that are now covered with the Coronation carpet, both stood beneath the pointed arches that gave back the cheers that greeted the crowning of the latest heir of the Confessor.

Go into the little village church, ivied and lichened, grey with years. History stares at you from the escutcheon nailed above the door ; the stone seats beside the entrance have provided rest for generations of tired folk. The bells whose ropes dangle yonder from the misty rafters of the tower have rung for a dozen Coronations ; perchance they gave warning of the Spaniards' coming in the Channel. The recess beside the altar speaks eloquently of a primitive rite, a more ancient Church. The brasses upon the chancel floor show knights embattled in armour such as the Crusaders wore, and dames in stately steeple-hats, Upon the walls a Tudor squire and his lady, beruffed in starched magnificence, kneel to pray surrounded by a goodly quiverful of boys and girls they had given to the State. From this pulpit all the winds of theological opinion have blown since the days of the Reformation, and where now the square pews stand were ranged the medieval worshippers. As for the churchyard, the bones of the village fathers lie deep, pressed heavily in layer upon layer, in one rich mould of human soil. They sleep in their hundreds beneath the boughs of the trees which sheltered them when they came with their bows for archery practice after service, within hail—but they are beyond sight and sound—of the green over which they danced as blithe youngsters when time-honoured revelry greeted the return of May.

In the Celtic Fringe

What is true of England is true too, of course, of Scotland and Wales and Ireland. Each has its long history of slow but unceasing development, of gradual growth in civilization and culture. There were kings in Scotland almost as early as there were in the southern kingdom, and in Ireland perhaps before. Wales for centuries had its native princes.

By a long-established and entirely understandable process the growth of our nation's story is marked by the names of the sovereigns called to reign over us. True, the date we record and recall is that of the monarch's accession, but it is the Coronation that is made the occasion for the ceremonial acknowledgment of his high estate.

The Coronation, then, should remind us —those of us that need the reminder— that we are the legatees of an ancient history, the trustees of a mighty inheritance that it is our bounden duty to hand on to those that shall come after—hand on unimpaired and, if the fates so will, enhanced. The crowning of yet another of the long line of kings indicates the opening of another chapter in our "rough island story".

Co-heirs in the Colonies

Some may think that this aspect of the Coronation concerns but the denizens of Britain. It is true, of course, that overseas, where now the Union Jack is the emblem of Empire, of loyal fellowship, there were only a few generations ago unpeopled wastes, vast prairies untouched by the delving hand of Man, limitless expanses where the only humans were naked and savage aborigines. Today great cities stand where the kangaroo leaped before the Bushman and the Red Indian sought his fleeting prey. Millions of acres of ploughland and plantation testify to the untiring industry of our emigrant farmers. But what have the Sydney or Winnipeg suburbans, the ranchers of Alberta, the fruit-farmers of Tasmania, the sheep-kings of New Zealand, to do with the pageantry at Westminster ?

Nothing ? If that is our answer, then we have forgotten for the nonce the magic of kinsmanship. The Canadians who swept over the ridge at Vimy, the "Aussies" who made sure that "Australia would be there" in the shell-pocked soil of the Somme, the "Anzacs" who hung on like grim death to the stricken rocks of Gallipoli—would you tell *them* that they had no part in Britain's legacy of glory and of sacrifice, that the traditions handed down by forty generations had no meaning, no message for them ? Shakespeare and Milton, Henry V and Cromwell, Cœur de Lion and Elizabeth, commanded the reverence of these men's fathers as they did of ours, who live in the womb from whence the Dominions sprang. Our fellow citizens across the sea are bone of our bone, flesh of our flesh, blood of our blood. The genes that—we are not sure how—convey from one generation to the next the characteristics that make us

Britons, did not emerge out of nothingness in America or the Antipodes or Africa, but are links in a great unbroken and unbreakable chain of life that joins us all and carries us back to the very beginnings of our race.

When the King goes by, then, the colonials (as we used to call them) have as good a right as the home-born Britons to cheer him on his way. The Coronation is a landmark in the history of the Dominions, just as it is in that of the United Kingdom.

Here, then, we have surely more than sufficient reasons for the setting in motion of the vast host of Imperial pilgrims, drawn from every village and town of the "Old Country", from every State and corner of the overseas dominions of the Crown. A pageant such as no other country can attempt to rival ; an occasion for the display of loyalty to a Person and a Principle, the King and the Crown ; an historic stage in the path trodden by the members of our race, at home and abroad. No wonder the pavements of the capital are packed with a motley multitude, and that their cheers punctuate the rumbles of the royal coach on the road to Westminster.

CHAPTER 6

CROWNS AND THE CROWNING

For thousands of years Crowns have been the symbols of Royal rule, and the elaborate ceremonial of the Coronation links our present time with the ages before History began

TREMENDOUSLY striking and infrequent as they are in a world from which much of the colour of pageantry has departed, Coronations are in a sense *usual*.

Many years elapse, at least in the ordinary course of events, between one Coronation and the next, but, looking back on our history as a nation, we see the Coronations of our sovereigns sparkling at intervals in the night of almost forgotten things. There are so many of them, they have occurred so often, that we have lost in part the wonder which they must originally have inspired. We take the Coronation as a thing that naturally occurs a short time after a new King or Queen ascends the throne. The sublime pomp and ceremonial comes within the accepted order of things. We marvel at them, but we see the marvellous in the trappings rather than in the inner core.

Why should there be a Coronation, the formal placing of a *crown* upon the new sovereign's head ? Why should the ceremony take place in a most sacred place ? Why should not the public revelation of the monarch be made in some other fashion, in this way or in that ? For an answer to these questionings we must go far outside our own country, far back beyond the beginnings of our own recorded history.

The word "coronation" comes from the Latin *corona*, a crown—not such a crown as the King wears, however, but a circular ornament or badge of office or distinction, made of metal, flowers or leaves. Crown, diadem, coronet, garland, and fillet all mean very much the same thing and may hardly be distinguished from one another.

It is impossible to say when the custom of crowning a leader or national hero or victorious competitor first arose. When the nations of antiquity swim into our ken the custom is both general and frequent.

The Greeks crowned the victors in the public games with wreaths of laurel. The Romans rewarded the valour of their warriors with crowns of varied material and design, appropriate to the field in which the bravery had been displayed or the nature of the deed of heroism it was desired to reward. Thus there was a crown of grass and wild flowers for the general who relieved a beleaguered garrison, and a garland of oak leaves for the soldier who saved the life of a fellow citizen in battle; a gold circlet ornamented with ships' beaks was given to successful naval commanders, and a castellated circlet was the prize of the first to scale the ramparts of a besieged city. There were crowns for conquering generals, and crowns for newly-married couples; crowns for popular bards and crowns worn by priests engaged in the holy rites beside the altar. Guests rollicking in the festive chamber wore floral fillets, and so, too, did those who assembled to honour the memory of the dead.

Amongst the Israelites, too, there were crowns, although only one Coronation is mentioned in the Scriptures, viz. that of Jehoash, King of Judah (2 Kings, xi, 12), on whom, we are told, the High Priest placed a crown, though the Hebrew word signifies possibly nothing more than a fillet. Saul apparently possessed a similar emblem, and some authorities assert that Solomon was the first Jewish king to be crowned in formal fashion; if this be so, it is somewhat surprising that we are told nothing about his crown in the inventory of his palace equipment. Certain of the later kings undoubtedly wore fillets about their brows, and crowns or garlands were donned by brides and bridegrooms in the Jewish kingdoms.

In some of the pagan mystery cults, crowns or garlands were worn by the sacrificial victims, and the brows of the men who personated the Mexican supreme deity —personated him to the extent of dying by the obsidian knife in his place on the pyramid steps—were similarly adorned.

The pharaohs of ancient Egypt had crowns—of two shapes, one for the Upper Country and one for the Lower; the "Great Kings" of Assyria . . . But enough has been said to show that there have been crowns of a sort and coronations, formal and informal, in every age and stage of civilization and culture. We find them if we step right back across the shadowy line that separates history from pre-history — so far back, indeed, that the why and wherefore of the ornament and the use are alike sunk in everlasting and unfathomable night. We shall never know what petty ruler, what local chieftain, it was who first managed to invest the metal circlet with a mystic meaning, a regal significance.

We do know, however, that the crowns of antiquity, whatever their purport, whoever their wearer, had little resemblance beyond their shape to the magnificent

[Munich Glyptothek

ORIGIN OF WORD "CORONATION"
The emperors of ancient Rome wore crowns—"corona," hence "coronation". They were made not of gold, however, but of oak leaves. Here we see Octavian—the great Augustus—wearing his simple diadem.

objects that are brought from behind the bars of the Jewel House in the Tower of London to the great pageant in Westminster Abbey. In olden times, as we have seen, crowns were made of flowers or leaves as well as gold and silver. The Roman Emperors wore wreaths of leaves, but amongst the oriental sovereigns a band or fillet of silk or linen was very general. The band became in the course of time a golden diadem, and the diadem, gradually growing in richness and magnificence, became transformed into the crown we know and see today. By comparing the portraits of our English kings it is easy to trace the development of the royal emblem, from a mere circlet to the glittering creation of gold, pearls and precious stones.

The details have been preserved of the Coronations of the sovereigns of old, but in all—whether of the Eastern Empire, whose capital was Constantinople, or the Western, that had its nominal seat in Rome ; in France or England, Spain or Scotland— the really vital part of the ceremony was not the placing of the crown upon the king's head but his anointing by the presiding bishop or archbishop.

Significance of Anointing

Old as is the act of crowning, it can be but a new-comer on the stage of ceremony compared with the rite of anointing. Readers of the Old Testament will remember with what frequency kings and priests and prophets, the sick, the wounded and the dying, and even inanimate objects— sacred stones and pillars and the like— were anointed with oil.

Scholars cannot agree as to the original meaning or the exact significance of the rite. From time immemorial anointing the body with olive oil, to which aromatic spices are often added, has been part of the toilet ritual of Eastern peoples, regarded very much in the same way as we look upon our daily baths. To omit the process was a sign of mourning ; to resume it a sign that joy had once again become permissible. Some authorities extend this conception of cleansing by the application of

oil to the religious sphere, suggesting that the Hebrews who anointed persons and stones did so as signifying that, figuratively speaking, these were clean and sweet-smelling, agreeable in the sight of Jehovah as in that of men. Others are of the view that the oil was a substitute for animal fat, which, as one of the great seats of life, was peculiarly fitted for the food of the gods. But another conception of anointing seems to have been that, in some mystic, little-understood way, it symbolized the outpouring of the divine spirit.

Preliminary Consecration

On this view, when a king of Israel was anointed, he was regarded as receiving thereby some portion of divinity : he was no longer man, mere man, but a man called to the highest office and endowed with the more than human attributes required to perform its duties to the full. Similarly, when a king of England or of France was led to his crowning, he was always anointed just before, in order that he might be in the sacred condition requisite for his office. Consecration, in other words, preceded the crowning.

This brings us to a consideration of the essentially *religious* nature of the Coronation ceremony.

To the man in the street—and still more, perhaps, to the woman—the Coronation is primarily a magnificent pageant. Indeed, most people are hardly aware of the fact that it is anything else. To them the King is always associated with colourful and gorgeous display, and what more fitting, then, that the public demonstration of his kingship should be made the occasion for old-world pageantry on the most lavish scale ? Hence they pack the streets and stands and cheer the King and those who go in procession with him with whole-hearted loyalty, never troubling themselves about the why and where and how of the great ceremony.

A few moments' thought, however, should suffice to show that more is intended than a show, awe-inspiring and brilliant though it may be. The scene of the Coronation is always set in West-minster Abbey, and the crown is placed on the King's head by the Primate.

If you were to ask a member of the assembled multitude why a church—for the Abbey, despite its fame as a show-place, as the pantheon of the British race, is first and foremost a place of Christian worship—had been chosen for the cere-mony, he would perhaps be nonplussed, and he would be in a similar fix if you inquired why the Archbishop of Canter-bury was the chief officiant. It may be that after some moments of reflection he would suggest that the one fact and the other were due to the operation of the principle of use and wont—or, as he would probably put it, "It always has been so."

A Religious Service

Possibly, however, the man you button-holed would be a church-goer, and he would be able to inform you that there was a service as well as a crowning and a pro-cession. If he was a chapel-goer he might add a remark to the effect that he thought it very unfair that only Church of England clergy and ritual should be employed in the Coronation of one who numbered as many Free Churchmen amongst his sub-jects as Anglicans.

Here, then, we have discovered a fact of the very first importance. The Coronation is a religious rite, a Christian, a Church of England, service. If we bear this in mind, it is not surprising that it should have for its setting the most historic church in His Majesty's dominions, and that the priest to perform the actual act of Coronation is the spiritual head of the Established Church, the Church of which the King is, by law, the supreme Head.

In the days before Christianity the king was proclaimed as such by some spec-tacular demonstration. The Anglo-Saxons, for instance, lifted their chosen ruler upon their close-locked shields and paid him homage by bending the knee and raising their swords, to the accompaniment of tumultuous cries. With the triumph of

Christianity, however, a new sense of dig-nity and responsibility was introduced. The king was still acclaimed as the most worthy of all who might claim to rule, his worthiness proved by his prowess on the battlefield, by his wisdom in the council chamber and justice on the judgement seat. But he was now recognized as something more. He was the chosen of men, but he was the chosen of God too.

We have little time nowadays for the theory of divine right of kings. The phrase has an old-world sound, reminding us of the furies of a debate which has long since passed into the history of controversy, although in the seventeenth century and even later the theory was held with pas-sionate zeal by a majority of the nation, and it was responsible in large measure for plunging the country into the great struggle of the Civil War and the Revolu-tion of 1688. To the simple folk of the early age of our history the very fact that a man had evinced such high gifts of leader-ship, had proved himself possessed of such a high degree of bravery and wealth of wisdom, was proof beyond the doubting that the power of the divine was within him—that he was the favoured of the Almighty. In those days the fittest to rule was acknowledged to have the right to rule ; the votes of men merely confirmed the choice of God.

Hallowing the Election

That there should be no manner of doubt concerning the man upon whom that choice had fallen, the Church soon con-trived that the lay election should be confirmed as soon as possible by the ecclesiastical power. We follow the prac-tice of centuries in that the Coronation does not take place until some months, perhaps as much as a year, after the day of accession. A sense of fitness precludes the crowning of a sovereign while the corpse of his prede-cessor is hardly cold, and has not yet been laid in the ground. No such scruples troubled the kings of an earlier day. A king was not a king until he had been solemnly crowned by the Church, and hence the Coronation was pushed on with what we should regard as indecent haste. William II, for instance, was crowned within three weeks of his father's demise, and Henry IV but a fortnight after his predecessor's abdication. In those times delay was dangerous. The accession almost synchronized with the Coronation, and what the people lost by way of long-prepared pageantry the nation gained in the security that a speedy succession gave.

We have no records of the earliest Coronations in these islands, but it is certain that they have occurred for more than thirteen hundred years. The first of which we are told by the chroniclers is that of one Aidan, a British kinglet who was consecrated —not, apparently, crowned—at Iona by St. Columba about A.D. 600. After England was Christianized her kings were crowned at Kingston-on-Thames— where a "Coronation Stone" of more than dubious authenticity is preserved—or Winchester, but since 1066 they have as a rule been crowned in Westminster Abbey. Here, again, the religious element is apparent,

for though the Abbey was not the cathedral of the metropolis—indeed, for many centuries it was the church of a Benedictine community—it was the most "sacred"

British Museum]   [Cotton MSS., Nero D.i

A SAXON CROWNING

Kingship was well ingrained in the Anglo-Saxons. This drawing by the thirteenth-century St. Albans monk, Matthew Paris, shows two pre-Conquest Anglian monarchs—Wemund, wearing his crown, and his son Offa.

building in the country. In the same way, it may be remarked, French kings were crowned not at Paris but at Rheims ; those of Scotland at Scone, not at Edinburgh ; those of Spain at Toledo, and not Madrid ; and the Tsars at Moscow, and not St. Petersburg. The importance of religious associations outweighed the political advantages that would arise from the choice of the capital for the solemn event.

Different though they be in many particulars, the earliest English Coronation services, or "Orders", of which we have any record, and that used in 1937 have much in common. Through them all runs the unmistakable thread of religion. The ceremony is a service of Christian communion and worship. A Coronation is a public function hallowed by the Church —a drama, if you like, performed in a church with high ecclesiastical dignitaries

CROWNS OF MEDIEVAL PATTERN

Crowns were part of the necessary furniture of the medieval monarchs, but they varied greatly in design. Of these two statues at Rheims, the one on the left is reputed to represent St. Louis—Louis IX, King of France from 1226 to 1270. On the right is another member of the *galerie des rois*, wearing a more ornate type of crown.

included in the cast and acting the part of stage managers. Another link with the age-old past is the fact that it is the Established Church under whose auspices the ceremony is performed. True, centuries ago the Church was Roman and now it is Anglican, but all through the centuries it has been held to be Catholic. Before England was a nation, her kings were crowned by bishops of the Church that was even then national—bishops whose spiritual descendants are the archbishops and bishops on the episcopal bench today.

There are four principal English Coronation "Orders": the Anglo-Saxon, which was probably used at the Coronation of Edgar, first king of all England, in 973, and of Harold II and his successful rival, William the Conqueror; a twelfth-century form, with which Richard I was probably crowned; the "Liber Regalis", dating from the fourteenth century and existing in manuscript form in the archives of the Dean of Westminster; and the "English" Order of 1689, devised for the Coronation of William III and Mary II by Compton, Bishop of London (after the unsettling experience of crowning a Catholic king—James II— in a Protestant church), and since adopted in more or less the same form for all subsequent Coronations right up to this present year. Taken as a whole, then, the Orders cover a period of nearly a thousand years; they constitute a striking illustration of the unbroken continuity of our national history, and of the permanence of certain conceptions and institutions in our midst.

Through them all runs, as was said above, the thread of religion. They are all designed for a religious service held in a building consecrated for Christian worship. All contemplate a Christian priest as the presiding officer. In all

there is a formal entrance into the sacred edifice, prayers of consecration, act of anointing, benedictory prayers, and blessing. These features are general; most of the Orders have in addition other religious incidents which are not universally reproduced, though they may be paralleled. For instance, the "Liber Regalis" provides for Mass, whereas, in conformity with the change in the nation's religious allegiance, the English Order, and all those that have been subsequently based upon it, include a service of Holy Communion and the presentation to the sovereign of a Holy Bible.

CROWNED IN HOLY RHEIMS

One of the manuscripts of Froissart's *Chronicles* contains this illustration of the crowning of Charles V, King of France from 1364 to 1380. From 1179 until the Revolution the French sovereigns were solemnly consecrated in the cathedral with the sacred oil supposed to have been brought from heaven to St. Remy by a dove.

CHAPTER 7

SYMBOLISM OF THE CEREMONY

No single hand or brain has been responsible for the ritual that attends the Coronation of Britain's King. Rather is it the result of an age-old process of development and adaptation to changing needs.

BEARING in mind its evolution through the centuries, we cannot be surprised that the Coronation Service abounds in archaic survivals of word and deed. Yet the archaisms are not mere senseless relics of a bygone time. Rather, each is still endowed with the vitality of a symbol whose meaning is no whit exhausted. Let us, then, consider the principal elements in the service, paying particular attention to the symbolism of which they are the expression.

Religion strikes the first note, as the royal procession moves up the church to the strains of the anthem. Then comes the "Recognition", the solitary survival of the election by bishops and people which marked the Anglo-Saxon rule. From his place in the "theatre" (i.e., to quote the "Liber Regalis", on the "stage somewhat raised between the high altar and the choir of the church of St. Peter at Westminster near the four high pillars in the cross of the said church") the Archbishop of Canterbury proceeds with the Lord Chancellor, Lord Great Chamberlain, Lord High Constable and Earl Marshal to the four sides of the stage, and at each one makes the declaration and appeal: "Sirs, I here present unto you King *George*, the undoubted King of this Realm: Wherefore, all you who are come this day to do your homage and service, Are you willing to do the same?"

As the words are spoken, the King stands up before his Chair and turns and shows himself to the congregation at each of the four sides. "The people signify their willingness and joy, by loud and repeated acclamations, all with one voice crying out, 'God save King GEORGE.'"

So, led by the boys of Westminster School, the cheers ring out and the trumpets blare. In 1937 as a thousand years ago; in the Coronation rite of today lies embedded a custom going back to the days when England was still pagan, when she was not yet a kingdom, when her kings were called to rule by the vociferous vote of their chieftains and followers.

Now the Litany is sung by two bishops, the choir singing the responses, and then Holy Communion marks the beginning of the Coronation Service proper. The Epistle and Gospel are read, the Apostles' Creed sung, and the sermon preached.

The Royal Oath

Next the Oath is administered—the promise ancient in substance but redrafted in form in 1937—sworn by the sovereign to govern all the Peoples of the Empire according to their respective laws and customs; to "cause Law and Justice, in Mercy, to be executed" in all his judgements; to "maintain the laws of God and the true profession of the Gospel"; to "maintain in the United Kingdom the Protestant Reformed Religion established by law", and to "maintain and preserve inviolably the settlement of the Church of England . . . ." "All this I promise to do." Then the King kisses the Bible and signs the Oath.

The Oath is not a symbol, but rather a hard, ineluctable fact. One of the first acts of a new king is the declaration in the House of Lords that he is a "faithful Protestant", and at his Coronation he repeats the avowal with all the weight that solemn ritual and asseveration can impart. He must, too, be an orthodox Christian, as is implied by his recitation of the Creed.

Now we come to what is the most striking of the successive stages of the service. The anointing occupies the place of honour in all the "Orders" that have been preserved, although it is true that in earlier ages the King was anointed on shoulders and elbows as well as head, breast and hands as now. Earlier still, in Saxon times, the head only seems to have been anointed.

As the preliminary to the solemn act, the choir sings the hymn "Veni, Creator Spiritus".

Then the Archbishop: "O Lord, Holy Father, who by anointing with oil didst of old make and consecrate kings, priests and prophets, to teach and govern thy people Israel: Bless and sanctify thy chosen servant GEORGE, who by our office and ministry is now to be anointed with this Oil, and consecrated King of this Realm."

Threefold Anointing

Putting off his crimson robes, the King seats himself in St. Edward's Chair—the "Coronation Chair"—and is anointed by the Archbishop on the crown of the head, the breast and the palms of both hands with holy oil poured into a spoon from the ampulla—i.e. a vessel shaped like an

"I HERE PRESENT UNTO YOU KING GEORGE"

For more than a thousand years the formal presentation of the new monarch to his assembled subjects, for them to signify their approval of his elevation to the throne, has been an essential part of the Coronation procedure. This illustration shows the fourth of our six Georges being presented in Westminster Abbey on the occasion of his coronation in 1821. This part of the ceremony is known as the Recognition.

eagle. "As Solomon was anointed king by Zadok . . . so be you anointed, blessed, and consecrated King over this People. . . ."

As we saw in an earlier page, the original meaning of anointing is lost in the depths of the past, but the words of the Coronation Service leave us in little doubt as to the reason for its present use. Because the kings of Israel were anointed as evidence of their Divine selection and election, so the seal of the Almighty is set on the sovereigns of Britain. Our Anglo-Saxon forefathers used a horn for the anointing, as in the days of Samuel and Saul, but for many centuries the Archbishop at Westminster has dipped his fingers in oil poured from the ampulla into a spoon.

Having been anointed, the sovereign is now in a fit condition to receive the various items constituting the Regalia.

Here we have another break in the symbolic pattern. Religion hallows the entrance into the church, but the voice of the priest is subordinate when the cheers of the assembled congregation—the representatives of the populace —hail the man the Archbishop introduces as the sovereign of their choice. Again religion supervenes, with the rite of Holy Communion and the solemn mysticism of the anointing. And now the emblems of temporal power are brought to the fore. The priestly gives place to the knightly.

First, the spurs. Taken off the altar by the Dean of Westminster, they are handed by him to the Lord Great Chamberlain, who, kneeling down, touches His Majesty's heels with them ; after which they are returned to the altar. The symbolism is obvious. The King is the head of his

Bibliothèque Nationale, Paris]   [*Photo, Giraudon*

CROWNED BY CHRIST

That kings rule by God's will is illustrated by this ivory carving of a Byzantine emperor and empress receiving their diadems from the hands of Our Lord.

country's chivalry and thus receives the time-honoured chivalric appanages and emblems.

Next, the State Sword is handed by the Archbishop to the King with the words : "With this Sword do justice, stop the growth of iniquity, protect the holy Church of God, help and defend widows and orphans, restore the things that are gone to decay, maintain the things that are restored, punish and reform what is amiss, and confirm what is in good order. . . ."

So the symbol of royal justice and of the fact that the King is the head of the Army is girt about him by the Lord Great Chamberlain, and then by the King himself is laid on the altar. One of the most curious of the many curious incidents of the service follows at this point : the sword is "redeemed" by a certain peer for a hundred new shillings, and throughout the remainder of the ceremony is borne naked before the King.

Now come emblems of truly regal significance. First the King dons the Imperial Robe—a magnificent garment of rich cloth-of-gold, embroidered in purple silk and stiff with silver coronets, fleurs-de-lis, Tudor roses, shamrocks, thistles and eagles. Its clasp or morse contains the figure of an eagle—the symbol of Imperial domination. The robe, indeed, is the Imperial mantle, such as was worn by the emperors of Byzantium and was earlier still the cloak of the Imperial commander. We must remember that even before 1066 our Kings were proudly acclaimed as emperor, or basileus, of the islands of Britain. Four-square in shape, the Imperial Robe is supposed to symbolize in its corners the four corners of the world,

Photo]   [A. Schroll, Vienna

ROMAN ORB

Above is the jewelled orb that was included in Charlemagne's imperial regalia.

all subject to the power of God.

The same conception is repeated in the next offering to the King—that of the "Orb with the Cross". "And when you see this Orb thus set under the Cross," says the Archbishop, "remember that the whole world is subject to the Power and Empire of Christ our Redeemer." Thus we have the Orb, the symbol of the monarchy of this world, associated with, but subordinate to, the symbol of Divine kingship.

For hundreds of years our sovereigns have been pictured with orbs in their hands. The Bayeux Tapestry shows King Harold holding one at his Coronation. In Byzantium the same emblem was put in the hands of the emperors, and in pagan Rome, too, the emperors were pictured with orbs—without, of course, the cross.

Next the King is invested with the anulus or ring, "the ensign of kingly dignity, and of defence of the Catholic Faith." This ring is sometimes called the "wedding-ring of England", and it is placed on the fourth finger of the right hand.

After the presentation of the ring comes that of the royal sceptre or baculum —the Sceptre with a Cross as it is termed —and the Sceptre

with a Dove. The one is "the ensign of kingly power and justice"; the other, the "Rod of equity and mercy". Just before receiving these impressive emblems into his right and left hands respectively, the King dons a glove presented by the Lord of the Manor of Worksop, "who now may support His Majesty's right arm".

Climax of the Ceremony

The putting on of the crown follows. This is *the* ceremony so far as most people are concerned. Very naturally it is presumed that the *crowning* is the most vital feature of the *Coronation*. Yet it has been argued that it is of quite secondary importance, on a level with the gifts of the orb and sceptres; the Coronation is primarily a *religious* ceremony, and in it the really vital feature is the anointing—the consecration of the King, whereby he assumes the dignity of God's Chosen.

Such a view may be that which prevailed up to the last century, but to us it has a distinctly medieval flavour. To those assembled in the Abbey the greatest moment of the great series of events is the placing of the crown—St. Edward's Crown —on the King's head. This is the signal for tremendous cheers. The words "God Save the King!" echo amongst the pillars of the Abbey as they have echoed on similar occasions for hundreds of years past. The peers assume their coronets; the trumpets ring out; and in the distance may be heard the rumble of the guns of the Tower.

Immediately afterwards the sacred reappears, in the presentation of the Bible to the newly crowned sovereign, and his benediction by the Archbishop.

ENTHRONEMENT OF HAROLD

From the Bayeux Tapestry executed by the Norman ladies after the Conquest of 1066 is taken this representation of Harold II, the "last of the Saxons", holding the orb at his crowning at Westminster by Archbishop Stigand.

From the anointing to the benediction the King sits in the Coronation or King Edward's Chair—itself surrounded by a wealth of ancient legend. Now, having received all the ensigns of Royalty, having been proclaimed and acclaimed as the indubitable king of this realm, he is "lifted up" into the throne by the archbishops, bishops and peers ; and to him, regally placed, come, after the Archbishop's exhortation, all the princes and peers present to do their homage.

"Lifted Up"

How the ancient phrase "lifted up" takes us back through the ages to the days of the Heptarchy and beyond, to when England had not yet been invaded by Saxon feet but in the swamps and forests of Germany they elected their kings by lifting them upon their shields ! Tacitus tells us that this was the way of royal election beyond the Rhine, and the Roman soldiery, when they became emperor-makers, used the method they had copied from the Teutons.

"Lifted up !" In a moment we are carried back in imagination to the days of barbarian Britain. Centuries have passed, the old world has been transformed under the touch of mechanical invention and non-human power. Countries our forefathers never heard of have been brought within the realm of the crowned. Yet the old conception, the old formula, the old ritual, persist—and will persist.

The illusion of time-dispelled is not banished by what follows. Saxon king-making makes way for medieval chivalry. Archbishop and bishops performing their homage on bended knees,

swearing to be "faithful and true" in acknowledgment of "the service of the lands which I claim to hold of you, as in right of the Church". Peers temporal, too, princes of the blood royal, dukes, marquesses, earls, viscounts, barons—each and all of the nobility present in the ancient building on that great day pledges himself to "become your liege man of life and limb, and of earthly worship ; and faith and truth I will bear unto you, to live and die, against all manner of folks". Then the first of each "Order" slowly ascends the throne, stretches forth his hand, touches the crown and kisses the King's cheek.

Rumble of drums, blare of trumpets, deep-throated cheers interspersed with the schoolboys' shrill treble. A King has been chosen, crowned, acclaimed. Another page has been turned in the massive and un-closing volume of our national story.

In an age when crowns and empires have toppled in the dust and the most naked and violent innovation stalks the political stage, Britain retains the stately pageantry hallowed by the practice of centuries. With us the past is not dead. Rather it is the vital soil in which we and ours have our roots. Like the mighty oak that we love to regard as the symbol of our race, we reach far down into the layers of history, seeking and finding there the nutriment we need.

Not a pageant merely is the Coronation ; not entirely a religious ritual nor merely a political form. Not one of these, yet all combined. Our history compressed within the compass of a few hours, our genius for conservative adaptation made manifest, our national continuity expressed in a parade of symbolism marking another mile-stone on our Imperial way.

REPUTED CROWN OF CHARLEMAGNE

This imperial crown, preserved at Vienna, is composed of eight plates of gold, four embellished with enamelled figures and four studded with jewels. From a jewelled cross in front an arch extends to the hindermost plaque.

FLAGS AND EMBLEMS OF THE BRITISH EMPIRE

THE
VICTORIAN FAMILY ALBUM

Groups and Portraits
of Queen Victoria and
Her Descendants down
to the Present Day

CHAPTER 8

The Victorian Family Album
With Comprehensive Genealogies

7

THE BEGINNING OF THE STORY

One of the most charming of Winterhalter's many charming paintings is that which shows Queen Victoria with the Prince Consort and their youthful progeny in 1847, when the baby in the picture was Princess Helena, known to history as the Princess Christian. The Queen is in the maturity of her charm ; her husband is revealed as a very handsome and dignified Victorian *paterfamilias*.

Beside the Queen stands the Prince of Wales—fifty years and more are to pass before he becomes King Edward VII. He married Princess Alexandra of Denmark in 1863 and had five children, the second of whom was George V of happy memory.

The little toddler on the left of Winterhalter's picture is Prince Alfred, Duke of Edinburgh, who was born in 1844 and married in 1874 the only daughter of Tsar Alexander II of Russia. In 1893 he succeeded as Duke of Saxe-Coburg and Gotha and died in 1900. One of his daughters is Dowager Queen Marie of Rumania, who is the mother of King Carol of Rumania, Elizabeth Queen of the Hellenes, and Marie Queen of Yugoslavia.

THE VICTORIAN FAMILY ALBUM

Pictures of the Royal Family are possessed of a never-failing appeal, and here in these pages, taking as our starting-point Winterhalter's famous painting of Victoria and Albert and their children, we meet again the princely offspring unto the third or fourth generation of that auspicious union

AMONGST the many good things that have come down to us from the Victorian era is the practice of keeping an album of family portraits—a little picture-gallery, as it were, of the intimate circle of the home.

True, the album of our grandparents' fancy was a much more substantial affair than the dainty little book we purchase so inexpensively at the stationer's, and the photographs of the Victorians are far more formal than the "snaps" in which we delight. But the underlying interest is the same, whether the photographed is in a crinoline or a bathing-dress, standing against canvas scenery in a photographer's salon or reclining in a garden hammock.

Usually the interest is confined to members of the family. Uncles and aunts, to say nothing of cousins, are distressingly unattractive to those who are without the pleasure of their acquaintance. But when the photographs are of royalty, then the interest is multiplied ten-thousandfold. We all like to see portraits and "snaps" of the King and Queen, Queen Mary and the little Princesses, the uncles and aunts and other members of the royal circle.

·We start with Queen Victoria and the Prince Consort, for the very good reason that they were, in effect, the founders of the Royal Family as we know it today. When, just a hundred years ago, Victoria ascended the throne as a girl of eighteen, the Royal Family had dwindled almost into nothingness, and this in spite of the fact that the

Queen's grandfather, George III, had had fifteen children. Her marriage with her cousin, Prince Albert of Saxe-Coburg-Gotha, was blessed by four sons and five daughters, and the number of her descendants is legion.

Those were the days of thriving trade and vast overseas expansion, and the families of Britain may be said to have kept pace with her economic and political progress. From 1841 to 1857 the royal children entered the world in quick succession—nine in sixteen years—and in thousands of households loyal subjects copied their sovereign in this as in many other things. Nowadays families are smaller (though many more children survive to adulthood), and we find the houses the Victorians lived in—high, somewhat gloomy structures, with basements and attics and flight after flight of stairs—far too large and uncomfortable for our tastes and needs.

The next photograph in our album was taken forty years later. The Queen is no longer a buxom wife but an aging widow, somewhat portly but still very obviously a queen. Albert has been dead many years, and she has never recovered completely from his loss. For long she has been in practical retirement. Now, however, it is Jubilee year, and the reappearance of Her Majesty has given rise to world-wide expressions of devotion.

We turn the page, and now we see the Queen, widowed but surrounded by her grown-up sons and daughters. The date is

GENEALOGIES

VICTORIA *m.* ALBERT OF SAXE-COBURG-GOTHA

Her children, genealogies of whose descendants are given below, were nine in number:

(1) **Victoria** (Princess Royal) 1840–1901; *m.* Frederick William, afterwards Frederick III, King of Prussia and German Emperor.

(2) **Edward VII,** 1841–1910; *m.* Alexandra, d. of Christian IX, King of Denmark.

(3) **Alice,** 1843–1878; *m.* Louis, Grand Duke of Hesse-Darmstadt.

(4) **Alfred,** Duke of Edinburgh, 1844–1900; *m.* Marie, d. of Alexander II, Emperor of Russia.

(5) **Helena,** 1846–1903; *m.* Prince Christian of Schleswig-Holstein.

(6) **Louise,** b. 1848; *m.* Duke of Argyll.

(7) **Arthur,** Duke of Connaught, b. 1850; *m.* Louise, d. of Prince Frederick Charles of Prussia.

(8) **Leopold,** 1853–1884; *m.* Helen, d. of the Prince of Waldeck-Pyrmont.

(9) **Beatrice,** b. 1857; *m.* Prince Henry of Battenberg.

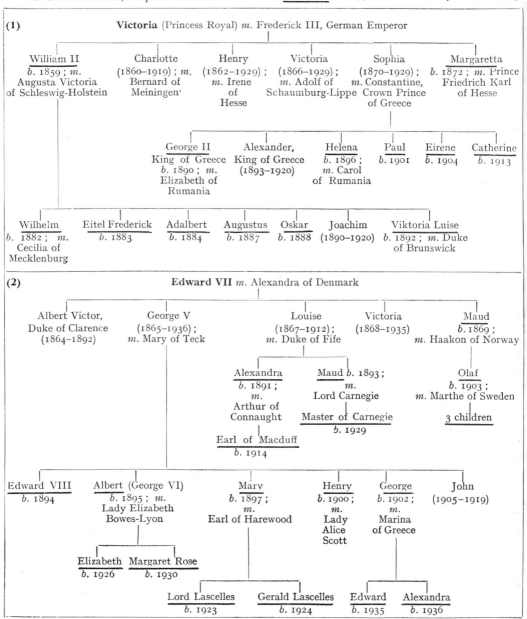

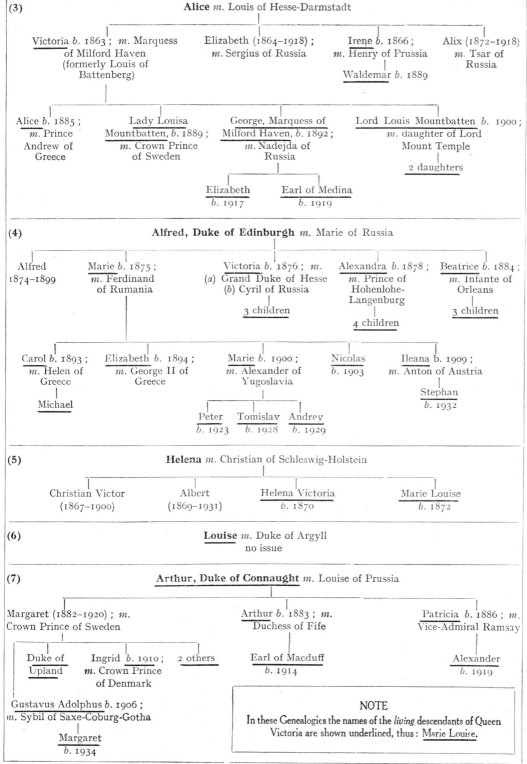

(3)   **Alice** *m.* Louis of Hesse-Darmstadt

Victoria *b.* 1863 ; *m.* Marquess
of Milford Haven
(formerly Louis of
Battenberg)

Elizabeth (1864–1918) ;
m. Sergius of Russia

Irene *b.* 1866 ;
m. Henry of Prussia

Waldemar *b.* 1889

Alix (1872–1918)
m. Tsar of
Russia

Alice *b.* 1885 ;
m. Prince
Andrew of
Greece

Lady Louisa
Mountbatten, *b.* 1889 ;
m. Crown Prince
of Sweden

George, Marquess of
Milford Haven, *b.* 1892 ;
m. Nadejda of
Russia

Lord Louis Mountbatten *b.* 1900 ;
m. daughter of Lord
Mount Temple

2 daughters

Elizabeth
b. 1917

Earl of Medina
b. 1919

(4)   **Alfred, Duke of Edinburgh** *m.* Marie of Russia

Alfred
1874–1899

Marie *b.* 1875 ;
m. Ferdinand
of Rumania

Victoria *b.* 1876 ; *m.*
(*a*) Grand Duke of Hesse
(*b*) Cyril of Russia

3 children

Alexandra *b.* 1878 ;
m. Prince of
Hohenlohe-
Langenburg

4 children

Beatrice *b.* 1884 ;
m. Infante of
Orleans

3 children

Carol *b.* 1893 ;
m. Helen of
Greece

Michael

Elizabeth *b.* 1894 ;
m. George II of
Greece

Marie *b.* 1900 ;
m. Alexander of
Yugoslavia

Peter
b. 1923

Tomislav
b. 1928

Andrev
b. 1929

Nicolas
b. 1903

Ileana *b.* 1909 ;
m. Anton of Austria

Stephan
b. 1932

(5)   **Helena** *m.* Christian of Schleswig-Holstein

Christian Victor
(1867–1900)

Albert
(1869–1931)

Helena Victoria
b. 1870

Marie Louise
b. 1872

(6)   **Louise** *m.* Duke of Argyll
no issue

(7)   **Arthur, Duke of Connaught** *m.* Louise of Prussia

Margaret (1882–1920) ; *m.*
Crown Prince of Sweden

Duke of
Upland

Ingrid *b.* 1910 ;
m. Crown Prince
of Denmark

2 others

Gustavus Adolphus *b.* 1906 ;
m. Sybil of Saxe-Coburg-Gotha

Margaret
b. 1934

Arthur *b.* 1883 ; *m.*
Duchess of Fife

Earl of Macduff
b. 1914

Patricia *b.* 1886 ; *m.*
Vice-Admiral Ramsay

Alexander
b. 1919

NOTE

In these Genealogies the names of the *living* descendants of Queen
Victoria are shown underlined, thus : Marie Louise.

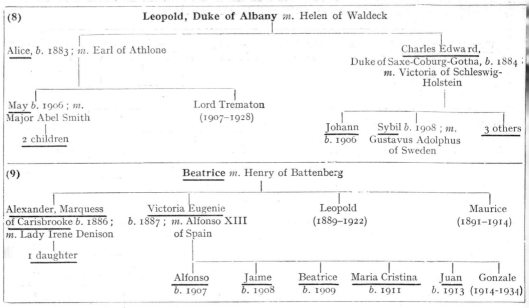

(8)   **Leopold, Duke of Albany** *m.* Helen of Waldeck

Alice, *b.* 1883; *m.* Earl of Athlone

Charles Edward, Duke of Saxe-Coburg-Gotha, *b.* 1884; *m.* Victoria of Schleswig-Holstein

May *b.* 1906; *m.* Major Abel Smith — 2 children

Lord Trematon (1907–1928)

Johann *b.* 1906   Sybil *b.* 1908; *m.* Gustavus Adolphus of Sweden   3 others

(9)   **Beatrice** *m.* Henry of Battenberg

Alexander, Marquess of Carisbrooke *b.* 1886; *m.* Lady Irene Denison — 1 daughter

Victoria Eugenie *b.* 1887; *m.* Alfonso XIII of Spain

Leopold (1889–1922)

Maurice (1891–1914)

Alfonso *b.* 1907   Jaime *b.* 1908   Beatrice *b.* 1909   Maria Cristina *b.* 1911   Juan *b.* 1913   Gonzale (1914-1934)

the late eighteen-sixties, when Britain is at the height of the Free Trade period. It was a serious age, and it is interesting to note that the Prince of Wales, shown standing in the centre of the picture, was at the time a young man of twenty-six; his beard added years to his appearance, and his whole air is that of a middle-aged gentleman. His wife and sisters, too, in their voluminous crinolines, have little of the youthful charm that we associate nowadays with girls, married and unmarried, in their twenties. Theirs is the serious deportment of Victorian womanhood, and the four daughters look very little older in their photographs in the opposite page, taken twenty years later.

Another page or two is turned and we have a series of charming family groups—growing larger with the passing of time, until in 1894 we have a truly Victorian gathering at the wedding of Victoria's grandson, the Grand Duke of Hesse. His mother was the Princess Alice, who died in 1878 from diphtheria caught while nursing her youngest child—a supreme instance of maternal self-sacrifice that deeply moved the home-loving Victorians.

Already we have made the acquaintance of the Duke of York, as King George V was called for many years, and now Princess May—the Queen Mary who is still happily with us—comes to join the family circle. Ere long another generation of princes and princesses comes on the scene, and we feel that now we are moving amongst familiar faces. We see the royal children in infancy, as boys and girls, as adolescents, and in the full bloom of their youth.

Then they, too, marry and the great public delights to see the smiling faces of the lady whom our tongues still call the Duchess of York, of Marina of Greece and the Duchess of Gloucester. The last two are shown in this series, but the reader is referred to pp. 169 to 212 for portraits of the family on the throne.

So far we have been concerned with the main branch of the Victorian royalty. But Queen Victoria is the ancestress of numerous royalties found in well-nigh every country of Europe. Her descendants sit, or have sat, upon almost every throne on the Continent.

In page 100 there is printed a list of the nine children of Queen Victoria. Immediately following are nine genealogical tables, numbered in order, showing the chief descendants of each of the nine sons and daughters. The ramifications and the extent to which they spread over the whole of Europe are indeed remarkable.

Photo]   *[J. Russell & Sons, Southsea*

QUEEN VICTORIA IN HER JUBILEE YEAR

Victoria, daughter of the Duke of Kent, was born in 1819, and succeeded William IV on the throne in 1837. Three years later she married Prince Albert of Saxe-Coburg-Gotha, who exercised a profound influence until his untimely death in 1861. Extraordinary scenes of enthusiasm marked the celebration of Victoria's Jubilee in 1887, at which time this photograph was taken. The Queen died in 1901 after the longest reign of any British monarch.

THE ROYAL FAMILY IN THE LATE SIXTIES

The upper photograph, taken in 1867, shows Queen Victoria with, from left to right, the Duke of Albany, the Princess Royal, Princesses Helena and Alice, the Duke of Connaught, the Prince and Princess of Wales, Princesses Beatrice and Louise, and the Duke of Edinburgh.   Below, with Queen Victoria at Osborne House, about two years later, are Queen Louise of Denmark, Prince "Eddy", Prince George of Denmark, Prince George, Princess Dagmar who afterwards married the Tsar Alexander III, Princess Louise of Wales, and her mother, the Princess of Wales.   (*See Genealogy No. 2, p. 100.*)

QUEEN VICTORIA'S DAUGHTERS AT THE JUBILEE

Queen Victoria had five daughters, all of whom married ; but at the time of her Jubilee in 1887 one, Princess Alice, had died.   Those living were (top left) Princess Beatrice, who married Prince Henry of Battenberg ; (top right) Princess Louise, Duchess of Argyll ; (bottom left) the Princess Royal, who married the Crown Prince of Prussia and was the mother of the last German Emperor, William II ; and (bottom right) Princess Helena, wife of Prince Christian of Schleswig-Holstein.

Photo (bottom right)]   [*Bassano*

ANOTHER QUARTETTE OF QUEEN VICTORIA'S CHILDREN

In this page are illustrated four more of Queen Victoria's children. Top left, Princess Alice, who became the Grand Duchess of Hesse ; top right, Alfred, Duke of Edinburgh, who adopted a naval career and eventually succeeded to the Duchy of Saxe-Coburg-Gotha. Of the lower photographs that on the left shows Leopold, Duke of Albany ; and on the right Arthur, Duke of Connaught, who now, fifty years after this photograph was taken, is the only son of Queen Victoria still living.

IN SUCCESSION TO THE THRONE

On March 10th, 1863, Edward, Prince of Wales, second child of Queen Victoria, married Princess Alexandra of Denmark, who was then only eighteen years of age. They are here seen with their first son, Albert Victor, later Duke of Clarence, but known in the royal circles as Prince "Eddy". In 1901, the Prince and Princess of Wales came to the throne as King Edward VII and Queen Alexandra. The Queen survived her husband by fifteen years.

A ROYAL GROUP IN SCOTTISH GARB

Edward and Alexandra, when Prince and Princess of Wales, had five children who survived infancy, of whom the four eldest are seen above with their parents, the year being 1868. These are Prince "Eddy", then aged four, Prince George, three—this was the future monarch's first appearance in Scottish national costume—Princess Louise, aged one, and Princess Victoria, an infant in arms.
(*See* Genealogy No. 2, p. 100.)

ALEXANDRA, PRINCESS OF WALES, AND HER CHILDREN

From 1877 to 1879, the two royal Princes, Albert Victor and George, began their naval service on the training-ship Britannia. This photograph, showing the Princes at home with their mother, Queen Alexandra, and their sisters, Princesses Louise, Victoria and Maud, was taken before their embarkation on H.M.S. Bacchante for a world cruise, which lasted, with only one short break, for three years. (*See* Genealogy No. 2, p. 100.)

Photos]   *[Ralph Downey*

FAMILY GROUPS OF THE NINETIES

The upper group shows the Prince and Princess of Wales with their family—from left to right standing, Prince George, Princess Victoria, the Duke of Clarence and Princess Maud. Sitting between her mother and father is the Princess Royal (Louise). The lower photograph includes the Prince and Princess of Wales, the Duke of York (the title conferred on Prince George after the death of the Duke of Clarence), his wife (later Queen Mary) and their first child, afterwards Edward VIII.

Photo]   [*W. S. Stuart, Richmond*

MEETING OF EUROPE'S ROYAL HOUSES

The central figure in this historic photograph, taken at the wedding of the Grand Duke of Hesse at Coburg in 1894, is Queen Victoria, then aged 75. On her right is the Kaiser William II, while on her left is the Empress Frederick, the Kaiser's mother and former Princess Royal. Also in the group, on the left, are the Tsar Nicholas II, the Tsaritsa and the Prince of Wales.

(J. Russell & Sons, Southsea

WITH HER GRANDSON AND HIS BRIDE

Princess May, daughter of the Duke and Duchess of Teck (Queen Victoria's cousin), was betrothed in 1891 to the Duke of Clarence, then second in succession to the throne. In the following year, however, the Duke died. The Princess subsequently married his younger brother, George, who had been created Duke of York. The union was fully approved by the Queen.

QUEEN VICTORIA AS GREAT-GRANDMOTHER

The Duke and Duchess of York (the future King George V and Queen Mary) had six children, of whom four were born before the death of Queen Victoria in 1901. The great Queen is here seen in the last year of her life holding Prince Henry in her arms. The other three children are the eldest, Prince Edward (then aged six), Prince Albert (sitting) and Princess Mary (by the chair).

[Photo] [J. Russell & Sons, Southsea

HOUSE-PARTY AT OSBORNE, QUEEN VICTORIA'S FAVOURITE RESIDENCE

After the death of the Prince Consort, and with the gradual approach of old age, Queen Victoria made fewer public appearances, passing much of her time at Osborne House in the Isle of Wight. There her life was brightened on occasion by visits of the younger generation, and here we see a family party on the lawn. The Duke and Duchess of York are present with their three eldest children, and also in the group, with their children, are the Duchess of Fife, the eldest sister of the Duke of York, and Princess Henry of Battenberg, better known to most people as Princess Beatrice.

Upper photo]   [Debenham

KING EDWARD VII WITH THE YOUNGER GENERATION

Queen Victoria died at Osborne on Jan. 22nd, 1901, and was succeeded by the Prince of Wales, who took the title of Edward VII. Above are the King and Queen with the Russian royal family, including the ill-fated Tsar Nicholas and his wife (Victoria's grand-daughter). Below are King Edward and Queen Alexandra with their grandchildren, left in their care during the absence on an Empire tour of the Duke and Duchess of York in 1901.

KING GEORGE V'S CHILDREN IN HIS CORONATION YEAR

This photograph shows the six children of King George V and Queen Mary at the time of the Coronation in 1911. They are, from left to right behind, Prince Albert, Princess Mary, and Prince Edward, who was invested as Prince of Wales in the same year. In front are Prince John (who died in 1919), Prince Henry, and Prince George.

Photos] *[Downey ; Sport & General*

DURING AND AFTER THE WORLD WAR

The upper photograph was taken on the Silver-Wedding anniversary of King George and Queen Mary in 1918. Four of their children are with them ; the Prince of Wales was on active service in France at the time. Below is a group on the balcony of Buckingham Palace after the wedding of Princess Mary to Viscount Lascelles in 1922. It includes the King, the bridal pair, Alexandra the Queen Mother and Queen Mary.

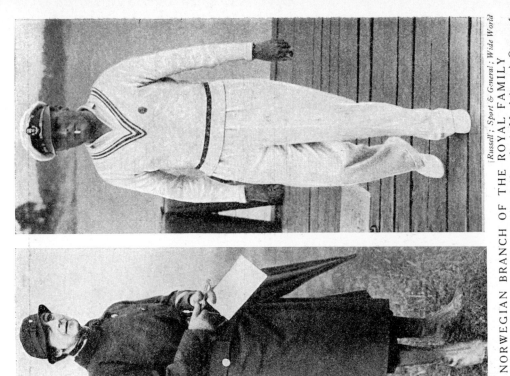

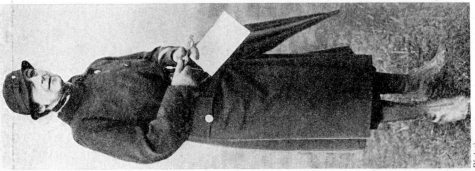

[*Russell ; Sport & General ; Wide World Photos*]

NORWEGIAN BRANCH OF THE ROYAL FAMILY

The youngest of the children of Edward VII and Alexandra is Maud (centre), Queen of Norway on the accession of her husband as Haakon VII in 1905. She has one son, Prince Olaf, seen (left) with his grandmother in 1910, and (right) after winning a yacht race in 1936.

EX-KING AND QUEEN OF SPAIN

Princess Victoria Eugénie, only daughter of Princess Beatrice and Prince Henry of Pattenberg, was married in 1906 (when this picture was taken) to Alfonso XIII, King of Spain from his birth in 1886 to his exile in 1931. King Alfonso and Queen Ena (as she is usually called) have five children—three sons and two daughters ; another son died in 1934. (*See* Genealogy No. 9, p, 102.)

THE CARNEGIE FAMILY

In 1923, Princess Maud, younger daughter of the Duchess of Fife, married Lord Carnegie, heir to the ancient Scottish earldom of Southesk. Lady Maud Carnegie is seen left on her wedding-day, and right, with her son, the Master of Carnegie, born in 1929. (See Genealogy No. 2, p. 100.)

LAST SURVIVORS OF QUEEN VICTORIA'S CHILDREN

There are now only three surviving children of Queen Victoria's family of nine. The youngest is Princess Beatrice (left), Governor of the Isle of Wight. She married Prince Henry of Battenberg in 1885, and had three sons and a daughter. The other survivors, seen together on the right, are the Duke of Connaught and Strathearn and Princess Louise, Duchess of Argyll, who is now nearly ninety years of age. Another photograph of the latter is given in page 105. Her husband died without issue in 1914.

QUEEN MARY'S BROTHER AND HIS FAMILY

The Duke of Albany, youngest son of Queen Victoria, had two children, the elder of whom is Princess Alice, Countess of Athlone.
Her husband is the youngest son of the Duke of Teck ; he was created Earl of Athlone during the War, when he adopted the family
name of Cambridge They are seen above with their daughter, Lady May, and Major Abel Smith, whom the latter married in 1931.
Lady May now has two children. (*See* Genealogy No. 8, p. 102.)

Princesses Helena Victoria and Marie Louise (above) are grandchildren of Queen Victoria, being the daughters of Princess Helena and Prince Christian of Schleswig-Holstein. Of their brothers, the eldest, Prince Christian Victor, died on active service during the South African War in 1900 and Prince Albert in 1931. (*See* Genealogy No. 5, p. 101.)

THIRD AND FOURTH GENERATIONS

Above are illustrated three direct descendants of Queen Victoria by the Duke of Connaught, her surviving son. His grand-daughter, Ingrid, who married the Crown Prince of Denmark, is shown in the foreground of the left photo with Sir Alexander Ramsay, who is followed by his wife, Lady Patricia ("Princess Pat"), the Duke of Connaught's surviving daughter. On the right is Lady Patricia Ramsay again with her son Alexander, who is a cousin of Princess Ingrid. (*See* Genealogy No. 7, p. 101.)

Photos]   [Keystone ; Sport & General ; Topical

PRINCE AND PRINCESS ARTHUR AND THEIR SON

Prince Arthur of Connaught, seen (top) with his wife, who is Duchess of Fife in her own right and sister of Lady Maud Carnegie (*see* page 120), is the only son of the veteran Field-Marshal, the Duke of Connaught, and himself followed a military career until 1920. His son, the Earl of Macduff, with whom he is seen (below left) at the latter's coming of age in 1935, has joined the same regiment, the Royal Scots Greys, in the uniform of which he is seen on the right. (*See* Genealogies, Nos. 2 and 7, pp. 100, 101.)

Photos]   *[Sport & General : Fox Photos*

DESCENDANTS OF QUEEN VICTORIA'S THIRD CHILD

The third child of Queen Victoria, Princess Alice, married the Grand Duke of Hesse. She had six children, the eldest of whom married Prince Louis of Battenberg, afterwards Marquess of Milford Haven. They had two sons and two daughters: the present Marquess seen above with his wife; Alice, Princess Andrew of Greece; Princess Louisa, second wife of the Crown Prince of Sweden (below left); and Lord Louis Mountbatten (below right). (*See* Genealogy No 3 p. 101.)

YUGOSLAVIA'S ROYAL FAMILY

In 1934 King Alexander of Yugoslavia was assassinated, and was succeeded on the throne by his eldest son, Peter II, great-great-grandson of Queen Victoria through her son the Duke of Edinburgh.   Below is the young King with his brother, Prince Tomislav, on his way to attend a memorial service.   The upper photograph shows Marie, the Queen-Mother (daughter of Ferdinand and Marie of Rumania), with her three children—Peter, Tomislav and Andrei.   (*See* Genealogy No. 4, p. 101.)

QUEEN VICTORIA'S DESCENDANTS IN RUMANIA

Queen Elisabeth (top left), former wife of King George II of Greece, is a great-grand-daughter of Queen Victoria, being descended through the Duke of Edinburgh and his daughter Marie, Dowager Queen of Rumania.   Queen Marie is seen below with her daughter Ileana, the latter's husband, Archduke Anton of Austria, and their three young children.   King Carol II of Rumania (shown top right with his son, Crown Prince Michael), is Queen Marie's eldest child.   (*See* Geneaology No. 4, p. 101.)

THE PRINCESS ROYAL AND HER SONS

Princess Mary (right), created Princess Royal in 1932, is the third child and only daughter of the late King George V and Queen Mary. In 1922 she married Viscount Lascelles, later Earl of Harewood. Above are their two sons, the Hon. Gerald Lascelles and the present Viscount, at a meet in Yorkshire, where are the family estates.

Camera portrait by E. O. Hoppé

KING GEORGE VI AND QUEEN ELIZABETH

This portrait was taken in 1926, when Their Majesties were Duke and Duchess of York

To face page 128

[Imperial War Museum ; Photopress ; L.N.A.

'hotos]

DAYS IN THE PRINCE OF WALES'S LIFE OF SERVICE

s King George's eldest son, the Prince of Wales had to take his part early in the life of the nation.   The year 1918 found him
·ith the troops on the Italian Front (top left).   He was President of the Wembley Exhibition in 1924–5, and (top right) he is seen
with Sir Robert Baden-Powell at a scouts' inspection.   Below, the Prince on a visit to a Church Army lodging-house.

DUKE OF KENT AND HIS BRIDE FROM GREECE

Prince George, youngest surviving son of King George V, was created Duke of Kent in October, 1934. In the following month he married Princess Marina of Greece and Denmark, who is a daughter of Prince Nicolas of Greece, and a cousin of George II, King of the Hellenes. They have two children—Prince Edward of Kent, born in 1935, and Princess Alexandra, born on Christmas Day, 1936.

[Photo]
[Fox Photos

THE DUKE AND DUCHESS OF GLOUCESTER

In 1935, the engagement was announced of Prince Henry, Duke of Gloucester, to Lady Alice Montagu-Douglas-Scott, third
daughter of the Duke and Duchess of Buccleuch. Their wedding, although somewhat overshadowed by the death of Princess
Victoria, was an occasion for great rejoicing, for both are extremely popular. The Duke followed an Army career until the accession
of his brother as George VI.

Photo]   *E. O. Hoppe*

KING AND QUEEN FOR TWENTY-FIVE YEARS

No King of England has ever commanded more loyal devotion than King George V, who reigned from May 6th, 1910, to January 20th, 1936. Always by his side was his consort, Queen Mary, who was the King's second cousin and a generation nearer to their common ancestor, King George III. Above, the royal pair are seen at the opening of the new Science Museum at South Kensington in 1928.

A CENTURY OF CORONATIONS

by

THE MARQUESS OF LORNE, K.T.
Author of "V.R.I."

SIR RICHARD HOLMES, K.C.V.O.
Editor "Edward VII : His Life and Times"

F. A. MACKENZIE
Author of "King George V in his Own Words"

Contemporary Accounts of the Three Crownings of British Monarchs in the Hundred Years 1837–1936

QUEEN VICTORIA
IN CORONATION ROBES

*From the painting
by Sir George Hayter*

THE present work is, by a remarkable succession of events, in direct association with "V.R.I.", the popular account of Queen Victoria's life published in 1897, the year of her Diamond Jubilee. That work was a very brilliant piece of literary expression by a nobleman long known to letters as the Marquess of Lorne and as son-in-law of Queen Victoria, his widow, Princess Louise, happily still surviving.

When, in the late years of King Edward VII's reign, the present Editor was charged with the task of arranging a record of His Majesty's life and times, he approached King Edward with the suggestion that the Marquess of Lorne (who had then become ninth Duke of Argyll) might supervise the work and collaborate in its writing. His Majesty expressed his wish that another Editor be chosen, as he considered the Duke to be too closely connected by ties of family to be an impartial judge, and eventually gave his consent to Sir Richard Holmes, who from 1870 to 1906 had been Librarian at Windsor Castle and by reason of his long association with the Royal Family was better equipped than anyone else to write about the private and public lives of King Edward VII, Queen Alexandra and the Royal Family. Hence, "Edward VII : His Life and Times", which bore Sir Richard's name as Editor, was essentially an authorized biography ; but, unhappily, that Editor did not many weeks survive the inauguration of the work, and it fell to the lot of the present Editor to carry it through. At a later day it became this Editor's privilege to compile "Our King and Queen" as a three-volume record of the lives and reign of George V and Queen Mary, and later still to produce a special Silver Jubilee Edition of it in one volume.

It seems appropriate to turn to these well-known and widely circulated publications today—all of them issued by the same publishing house—and extract therefrom (a) the Marquess of Lorne's vivid description of Queen Victoria's Coronation, including the eye-witness account of the Duchess of Cleveland, (b) the colourful chronicle of King Edward VII's coronation from Sir Richard Holmes's "Edward VII," and (c) F. A. Mackenzie's description of George V's coronation from "Our King and Queen." To be able to read these contemporary records of the preceding coronations of one hundred years in conjunction with that of George VI seems to me an entirely acceptable experience.

CHAPTER 9

THE CORONATION OF QUEEN VICTORIA

Queen Victoria's coronation in 1838 struck a note of solemn dignity and magnificence that had been markedly absent from the crownings of her two uncles. This account was written by her son-in-law, then Marquess of Lorne, K.T., later Duke of Argyll.

THE young Queen's crowning took place on Thursday, June 28th, 1838. It was remarked that it was the first time that the British people had had occasion to crown a young and pretty woman. Queen Anne had suffered from gout and had become middle-aged, so that at the time of her crowning she could neither walk far nor stand long. Queen Elizabeth was also a deal older when she succeeded.

It was resolved that befitting pomp should accompany so novel a situation; but the Government had had a considerable deficit in their annual budget, and so they intended to make the ceremony as brief as possible. Lord Fitzwilliam, in the House of Lords, made a speech in which he implied that a great deal of show on such an occasion was only fit for a barbarous age. But he found no response in the assembly he addressed. Nevertheless, Lord Melbourne was persuaded to forgo some of those observances which had been carried out when George IV became King, such as the walking procession of all the Estates of the Realm, and the great banquet in Westminster Hall. It was remembered that, at the last feast, as soon as the chief personages had quitted their seats, a rush had been made by the well-dressed people in the stands and galleries to despoil the tables of some of the small plate, which was carried away as souvenirs.

The tradesmen remonstrated at the proposed curtailment, but were assured there would be sufficient ceremony to attract crowds and to make the purchase of costumes necessary. The famous Marshal Soult, who had opposed our troops so vigorously in the Peninsula, was sent as ambassador from the King of France, and brought over with him a state carriage that had been used by the Prince of Condé.

Soult's was not the only remarkable carriage in the Coronation procession, for the Duke of Devonshire had a gorgeous vehicle which had been built when he went as Envoy Extraordinary to St. Petersburg.

Order of the Procession

The procession formed near Buckingham Palace and started at 10 a.m., with trumpeters and a squadron of the Household Brigade. Then followed foreign ambassadors and ministers, bands, more cavalry, and the carriages of the Duchesses of Kent and Gloucester, the Duke and Duchess of Cambridge, and the Duke of Sussex, more mounted bands, and the Queen's barge-master and nearly fifty watermen, these preceding twelve royal carriages conveying the household. Then more cavalry and more music, and the Staff and distinguished officers; the Royal Huntsmen, the Yeoman Prickers and Foresters, the Yeomen of the Guard and their officers. Then, in her state carriage, drawn by eight cream-coloured horses, the Queen. She was followed by the Captain of the Royal Archer Guard of Scotland, and by an escort of cavalry.

Proceeding along Constitution Hill, Piccadilly, down St. James's Street to Pall Mall and Charing Cross, the procession wended its way to Whitehall and Parliament Street, and thence to the west door of Westminster Abbey. Galleries had been raised to hold four hundred persons—a small provision compared with that of the Jubilee time. A temporary organ and orchestra had been placed at the west end of the choir. Upon an open colonnade of pointed arches another gallery, at the east end beyond the altar, was arranged for six hundred persons, and reserved for the Commons.

Pomp and Majesty

Two more galleries above St. Edward's Chapel provided space, amongst others, for the trumpeters. Above the sacrarium were boxes for the sovereign, the Earl Marshal, the ambassadors and the Lord Chamberlain. The peeresses were in the north transept, the peers in the south, the judges and Knights of the Bath and aldermen in the choir, the bishops on the floor to the north with the clergy of Westminster, and the Royal Family opposite. The royal box was filled with relatives from abroad.

The clergy headed the procession, followed by heralds and household officers, then prelates and officers of state, then the Duchess of Cambridge, wearing a robe of purple velvet, her train borne by a lady. After her the Duchess of Kent. Both these Royal Duchesses wore a circlet on their heads, having their coronets borne before them. Of the Regalia, the St. Edward's Staff was carried by the Duke of Roxburghe, the Golden Spurs by Lord Byron, the Sceptre with the Cross by the Duke of Cleveland, a third sword by the Marquess of Westminster, the Curtana by the Duke of Devonshire, and the second sword by the Duke of Sutherland. The coronets of these noblemen were carried by pages. After the Black Rod, the Deputy Garter and the Lord Great Chamberlain of England came the Duke of Cambridge in his robes of state, with his baton of Field-Marshal, his coronet borne by the

Marquess of Granby, his train by General Sir William Gomm. The Duke of Sussex in his robes of state followed, his coronet borne by Viscount Anson, his train by Edward Gore and Lord Coke. Then came the Duke of Leinster as High Constable of Ireland, the Earl of Errol as High Constable of Scotland, the Duke of Norfolk as Earl Marshal, with his baton, and the Duke of Wellington as Lord High Constable of England, with his staff and Field-Marshal's baton. The Sword of State was borne by Viscount Melbourne, and the Sceptre with the Dove by the Duke of Richmond; St. Edward's Crown by the Duke of Hamilton, the Orb by the Duke of Somerset, the Patina by the Bishop of Bangor, the Bible by the Bishop of Winchester, and the Chalice by the Bishop of Lincoln. They preceded the Queen, who wore a royal robe of crimson velvet, furred with ermine and bordered with gold lace, the collars of the Orders of the Garter, Thistle, Bath and St. Patrick, and a circlet of gold.

Attendants on the Queen

Her Majesty was supported on either side by the Bishops of Bath and Wells and Durham. Her train was borne by the Ladies Adelaide Paget, Frances Cowper, Anne Fitzwilliam, Mary Grimston, Caroline Lennox, Mary Talbot, Wilhelmina Stanhope, and Louisa Jenkinson, assisted by the Lord Chamberlain, Lord Conyngham, followed by the Groom of the Robes, Captain Francis Seymour, with ten Gentlemen-at-Arms on either side, with their Lieutenant, Standard-Bearer, Clerk of the Cheque and Harbinger. After these came the Duchess of Sutherland, Mistress of the Robes; Lady Lansdowne, First Lady of the Bedchamber; the other Ladies of the Bedchamber—Ladies Normanby, Tavistock, Charlemont, Lyttelton, Barham and Portman; the Maids of Honour—the Hon. Margaret Dillon, Harriet Pitt, Caroline Cox, Matilda Paget, and the Misses Murray, Cavendish, Spring Rice and Lister; the Women of the Bedchamber— Ladies Forbes, Digby, Clive, Barrington, Copley and Gardiner, and the Hon.

Mesdames Campbell and Brand. Then came the Gold Stick of the Life Guards, Field-Marshal Combermere ; Master of the Horse the Earl of Albemarle ; Captain-General of the Royal Archer Guard of Scotland, Captains of the Yeomen of the Guard, Gentlemen-at-Arms, Lords in Waiting, and a number of others.

§—The Scene in the Abbey in 1838

THE sight in the Abbey was brilliant in the extreme. Galleries had been erected in the aisles, and above ten thousand of the greatest and most famous people in the land were present. The array of fine dresses and of jewels is said to have been dazzling in the extreme. The Austrian Minister seems to have surpassed everyone else in magnificence, and was literally covered with jewels down to the heels of his boots. A lady who was present wrote that he looked "as though he had been snowed upon with pearls, and had also been caught out in a rain of diamonds" !

As the Queen entered the Abbey, preceded by the officers of state bearing the Regalia, the anthem, "I was glad when they said unto me, Let us go into the house of the Lord", rang through the long arches, and echoed back from the distant roof, while the booming of cannon could be faintly heard from without. Next came the National Anthem, and then a deep hush as the Queen knelt before the altar for a few moments in silent prayer. When she rose, the boys of Westminster School, acting upon ancient right, chanted "Victoria, Victoria, Vivat Victoria Regina !" and then came the Recognition. This was a very striking ceremony. The Queen and the Archbishop of Canterbury turned to the four quarters of the compass, and the prelate called out in each direction, "Sirs, I here present unto you Queen Victoria, the undoubted Queen of this Realm ; wherefore, all you who are come this day to do your homage, are you willing to do the same ?" To each of these challenges the people addressed made answer, "God save Queen Victoria."

After the Recognition, the Queen went with her attendants to the altar, and, kneeling upon the steps, offered a golden altar-cloth and an ingot of gold of a pound weight. Then followed the Litany and the first part of the Communion Service, the sermon being preached by the Bishop of London, after which came the elaborate ceremonies of the Coronation Service.

The Archbishop of Canterbury, addressing the Queen, asked, "Is your Majesty willing to take the oath ?" to which she replied, "I am willing."

"Will you solemnly promise and swear", asked the prelate, "to govern the people of this United Kingdom of Great Britain and Ireland, and the dominions thereto belonging, according to the statutes in Parliament agreed on, and the respective laws and customs of the same ?"

"I solemnly promise so to do," answered the Queen.

"Will you, to the utmost of your power, cause law and justice, in mercy, to be executed in all your judgements ?"

"I will."

"Will you, to the utmost of your power, maintain the laws of God, the true profession of the Gospel, and the Protestant Reformed religion established by law ? And will you maintain and preserve inviolable the settlement of the United Church of England and Ireland, and the doctrine, worship, discipline, and government thereof, as by law established within England and Ireland, and the territories thereunto belonging ? And will you preserve unto the bishops and clergy of England and Ireland, and to the churches there committed to their charge, all such rights and privileges as by law do or shall appertain to them or any of them ?"

The Queen replied, "All this I promise to do" ; after which she went to the altar and, laying her right hand upon the Book of the Gospels, said, "The things which I have heretofore promised, I will perform and keep. So help me, God." Then, kissing the Book, she signed the oath, and knelt in prayer while the choir sang the hymn, "Come, Holy Ghost, our souls inspire".

Symbolism of the Anointing

Next came the ceremony of the Anointing. The Queen took her seat in St. Edward's Chair, and a canopy of cloth-of-gold was held over her while the Archbishop anointed her with oil on the head and hands, saying:

"Be thou anointed with holy oil as kings, priests, and prophets were anointed. And as Solomon was anointed king by Zadok the priest and Nathan the prophet, so be thou anointed, blessed, and consecrated Queen over this people, whom the Lord thy God hath given thee to rule and govern. In the name of the Father and of the Son and of the Holy Ghost. Amen."

The Archbishop then pronounced a blessing on the Queen; and the various insignia of royalty, the sceptres, orb, spurs, etc., having all their civil or ecclesiastical significance, were handed to her with appropriate exhortations. The words used by the prelate as he placed the Sword of State in the monarch's hands were so significant that we quote them in full: "Receive this kingly sword, brought now from the altar of God, and delivered to you by the hands of us, the servants and bishops of God, though unworthy. With this sword do justice, stop the growth of iniquity, protect the Holy Church of God, help and defend widows and orphans, restore the things that are gone to decay, maintain the things that are restored, punish and reform what is amiss, and confirm what is in good order; that doing these things you may be glorious in all virtue, and so faithfully serve our Lord Jesus Christ in this life that you may reign for ever with Him in the life which is to come. Amen."

The Imperial Mantle of cloth-of-gold was then placed upon the Queen's shoulders, and the ruby ring upon her finger. Unfortunately the ring was rather small, and she suffered considerable discomfort in the process.

Next came the most important act of all. The Archbishop, having first offered prayer, took the Imperial Crown from the altar and placed it on the Queen's head. Instantly all the great crowd of peers and peeresses assumed their glittering coronets, and the Abbey rang with the shouts of "God save the Queen!" The crowd outside caught up the shout, the church bells were set ringing, and a signal from Whitehall set the guns firing, not only in London, but at all the chief ports and garrison towns. The crowds in the streets waved hats and handkerchiefs and cheered themselves hoarse.

After this ceremony there followed the presentation of a Bible to the Queen, and the singing of the Te Deum, and then she was conducted to a throne placed in the centre of the church, where all could see the next part of the proceedings.

The Peers Pay Homage

This was the act of homage, performed by the Lords Spiritual kneeling around the Queen, pronouncing the words of homage, and kissing Her Majesty's hand. The Princes of the Blood Royal ascended the steps of the throne, took off their coronets, knelt, pronounced the words of homage, touched the crown upon Her Majesty's head, and kissed her left cheek. The Duke of Norfolk and sixteen other dukes present did the same, with the exception of kissing the hand of the Queen instead of the cheek.

Their example was followed by twenty-one marquesses, ninety-three earls, nineteen viscounts, and ninety-one barons. Lord Rolle, who was very infirm, on ascending the throne slipped, when the Queen rose and extended her hand, expressing a hope that he was not hurt. The words used in doing homage were these: "I do become your liege man of life and limb, and of earthly worship, and faith and truth I will bear unto you to live and die against all

GOD SAVE QUEEN VICTORIA!

The concluding stage of the Coronation of Queen Victoria is shown here in a reproduction of a portion of the painting by Sir George Hayter. The Queen is seated on the throne in the centre of the Abbey, wearing the crown and holding the sceptre, with the cross in her right hand. In her left hand she holds another sceptre with a dove.

139

manner of folk, so help me God.'' The Duke of Wellington was much cheered when performing his homage, and when this part of the ceremony was concluded the members of the House of Commons gave nine hearty cheers, accompanied with frequent cries of "God save Queen Victoria", which were repeated throughout the building by the congregation. The peers present were in number 245 ; the peeresses 158.

The crown which had been made for George IV weighed more than seven pounds, and was considered too heavy for the Queen's use. A new one was, therefore, made for the occasion. It weighed considerably less, and was formed of hoops of gold covered with precious stones over a cap of rich blue velvet, surmounted by a ball, in which were small diamonds, having on the top a Maltese cross of brilliants, a splendid sapphire in the centre, and a cluster of brilliants and fleurs-de-lys and Maltese crosses around the centre of the crown. The large heart-shaped ruby worn by the Black Prince was in front of it, a large oblong sapphire below it, and clusters of dropped pearls, with emeralds, rubies, sapphires, and other gems in a circlet.

VICTORIA'S CROWN

In the front of Queen Victoria's Crown shone the Black Prince's Ruby, and about the magnificent stone glittered 75 diamonds.

During the homage the Earl of Surrey, Lord Treasurer of the Household, threw to the occupants of the choir and the lower galleries the Coronation medals, which were scrambled for with great eagerness. The Queen was divested of the symbols of sovereignty and received the Holy Sacrament, after which, again resuming her crown and holding the Sceptre, she took her seat. After the blessing had been pronounced the service was concluded by the singing of the Hallelujah Chorus.

§—A Personal Account by The Duchess of Cleveland

THE Sovereign, still with the crown on her head, and holding the sceptre, now rose and went to the west door, where she mounted a state carriage in which she could be seen well by the people. Among these was one who wrote : "When she returned, looking pale and tremulous, crowned, and holding her sceptre in a manner and attitude which said, 'I have it, and none shall wrest it from me' ; even Carlyle, who was standing near me, uttered, with emotion, a blessing on her head."

The Duchess of Cleveland, who, as Lady Wilhelmina Stanhope, was one of the train-bearers, contributes the following recollections :

"The Queen looked very well, and was perfectly composed. She wore a circlet of splendid diamonds, and was dressed in gold tissue, over which was fastened a crimson velvet mantle, bordered with gold lace, and lined with ermine, with a long ermine cape, which very ponderous appendage we were to support.

"As train-bearers we stood according to our rank, as follows : Lady Caroline Lennox and Lady Adelaide Paget ; Lady Mary Talbot and Lady Fanny Cowper ; Lady Anne Fitzwilliam and myself ; Lady Louisa Jenkinson and last, not least, Lady Mary Grimston.

"We were all dressed alike in white and silver. The effect was not, I think, brilliant enough in so dazzling an assembly, and our little trains were serious annoyances, for it was impossible to avoid treading upon them. We ought never to have had them ; and there certainly should have been some previous rehearsing, for we carried the Queen's train very jerkily and badly, never keeping step properly; and it must have been very difficult for her to walk, as she did, evenly and steadily, and with much grace and dignity, the whole length of the Abbey.

"The Abbey itself was a beautiful *coup d'œil*, as we marched up amidst thunders of applause and handkerchiefs and scarves waving everywhere. The Queen acknowledged her reception very graciously.

"I think her heart fluttered a little as we reached the throne; at least, the colour mounted to her cheeks, brow, and even neck, and her breath came quickly. However, the slight emotion she showed was very transient, and she stood perfectly motionless while the Archbishop, in an almost inaudible voice, proclaimed her our undoubted Sovereign and Liege Lady. After this she took the oaths, the Litany and Communion Service were read, and the Bishop of London gave us a very good sermon,

EYE-WITNESS

Lady Wilhelmina Stanhope, later Duchess of Cleveland, left a vivid account of Victoria's crowning.

though we, who were standing the whole time, thought it somewhat of the longest.

"The ceremonies that followed were minute and rather tedious. Before the anointing we accompanied the Queen into St. Edward's Chapel—as unlike a chapel to all appearances as possible—where she was robed in a sort of white muslin wrapper, trimmed with very fine Brussels lace, and the dalmatic, a robe of cloth-of-gold, worked with the rose, shamrock, and thistle in colours, and lined with crimson. The diamond circlet was taken off, and the mantle (to our great relief), and she reappeared in the Abbey bare-headed and simply wearing the dalmatic.

"As she knelt before the altar, with clasped hands and bowed head, with her loose robe of gold brocade hanging from her shoulders, she looked exactly like the representation, in some old picture, of a fair young devotee in the costume of the Middle Ages.

ADMINISTERING THE SACRAMENT TO THE NEWLY CROWNED QUEEN

After the homage, the Queen was divested of all the symbols of royalty and took the sacrament. The bread was administered by the Archbishop of Canterbury, and the cup handed her by the Dean of Westminster. Only about six others of those present took the sacrament with the Queen. This illustration is from a painting by C. R. Leslie, R.A.

"She was assisted into St. Edward's Chair by the old Archbishop, and there solemnly crowned and anointed Queen. The burst of applause in the Abbey, when the crown was placed on her head, and the sight of all the peers and peeresses crowning themselves at the same moment, was really most impressive ; and in the midst of the cheering Handel's magnificent anthem, 'The Queen shall rejoice !' thundered in.

"After this the Queen was enthroned and we took up our station on the steps of the throne during the homage, and amused ourselves with watching Lord Surrey, the Treasurer of the Household, dispensing medals in the midst of a most desperate scramble, and nearly torn to pieces in the universal excitement. The pages were particularly active, and some of them collected ten or twelve medals apiece. The train-bearers wrung out one each from Lord Surrey, whose temper was entirely gone, and who looked as red and voluble as a turkey-cock. I had another given to me by one of the pages.

HOMAGE TO HER MAJESTY

Queen Victoria, in this painting by Sir W. J. Newton, is seen at her coronation receiving the homage of the peers. Behind her are the ladies in attendance and the great officers of the Royal Household.

"I saw little of the homage. The Duke of Wellington was prodigiously cheered. Lord Rolle fell down, and was carried away by two strong peers ; and a great deal more of the same sort may have happened, but I saw none of it. I merely had the advantage of seeing them put on their coronets again after the ceremony was over, Lord Wilton fitting on his being in itself a study.

"After the homage we returned with the Queen to the chapel, where her mantle— now a purple one—was fastened on, and we waited for three-quarters of an hour for the procession to form in the same manner as on entering the Abbey.

"The Queen complained of a headache, from having her crown very unceremoniously *knocked* by most of the peers— one actually clutched hold of it ; but she said she had guarded herself from any accident or misadventure by having it made to fit her head tightly. She had besides to bear the heavy orb and sceptre across the Abbey ; but when she reached the robing-room she disembarrassed herself of them, unclasped her mantle, took off her crown, and, having got rid of all her royalty, sat down on the sofa and amused herself. We, too, were allowed to sit down for the first time."

But the Queen's day of fatigue was not yet over, for she had to entertain 100 at dinner in the Palace. The Duke of Wellington had a great hall at Apsley House. Cabinet Ministers gave state dinners. Illuminations, fireworks, a fair in Hyde Park, and free admission to the theatres were provided for the gratification of Her Majesty's subjects in London. There was no accident of any importance, except in one case where a balloon made a bad descent. The House of Commons voted £70,000 on account of the Coronation, a very small sum compared with the large amounts given for similar ceremonies abroad. A number of peers were created or raised a step in the peerage, among these being the father of General Lord Methuen ; and twenty-nine baronets, amongst them Lytton Bulwer and William Herschell.

CHAPTER 10

THE CROWNING OF EDWARD VII
AND HIS QUEEN

*After a lapse of more than sixty years, the Coronation of King Edward was bound
to arouse immense interest and enthusiasm ; but its postponement, due to the
King's illness, made it an occasion for thanksgiving as well as for rejoicing*

SO deep were the love and loyalty given to King Edward by his people that his sudden illness and almost unhoped-for recovery changed the character of the nation. The Coronation ceremony, which had been fixed for June 26th, 1902, had had to be postponed, for only two days previous to that great event the King was taken ill with perityphlitis. An operation was so successfully performed by Sir Frederick Treves that the King made a remarkably speedy recovery, and after a short period of repose, spent on his yacht in the waters of the Solent, he was able to announce that the Coronation would take place as early as August 9th.

It is certain that never in the history of Christian kingship was the religious importance of the ritual of Coronation so clearly manifested as it was on Saturday, August 9th, 1902. This effect was produced by the concurrence of three extraordinary circumstances. It was the greatest Imperial event in English history, for King Edward was the first English Emperor to assume the crown. It was a festival of peace, marking the conclusion of the most terrible war in which the nation had engaged since the Napoleonic era. And finally, following as it did immediately on the illness of the King, the Coronation closed and consecrated a period of trial and suspense unprecedented in the annals of the British people and its rulers.

Though, owing to his illness, the procession had to be shorn of some of its splendour by the departure of many of the princely representatives of the reigning families of the world, it still retained many features that were new in the history of the British monarchy and the British race. King Edward was the first of our kings to be attended at his crowning by an illustrious group of statesmen from our self-governing Colonies. He was the first to be accompanied by a glittering throng of the great tributary potentates of India. He was the first to be escorted by detachments of troops from our great democracies oversea, and from our Asiatic, African and American dependencies.

The Postponement

Only in one respect was the Coronation deprived of any of its pomp by reason of its postponement. The special missions sent by foreign Powers to represent their governments at Westminster Abbey were compelled to depart without waiting for the King's recovery. Some of the special ambassadors had come from the ends of the earth to pay respect to King Edward, and their absence could no longer be extended. Others from less distant countries had pressing duties waiting them at home.

The postponement of the Coronation had at least one happy result. It enabled our oversea democracies to take a more intimate share in the ceremony in August than

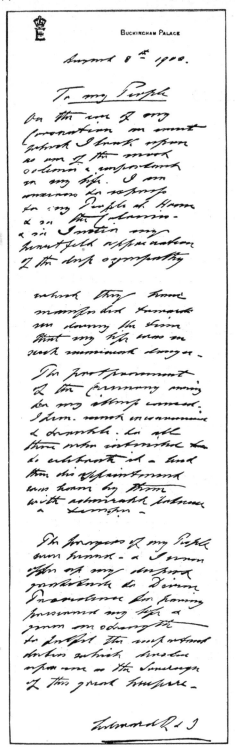

KING EDWARD'S LETTER TO THE NATION

they would have been able to do in June. From Canada alone, 5000 visitors had come to London, while from the more distant dominions of Australia, New Zealand, and South Africa, many a shipload had sailed.

The soldiers of the Colonial forces who came to London for the Coronation were regarded with deep interest. The contingent sent by Canada, numbering 660, was representative of all the composite population of Canada.

Every State in the Commonwealth of Australia was also represented at the Coronation, while New Zealand sent with its white settlers a body of loyal Maori warriors. Cape Colony and Natal, ravaged by the war, dispatched some of their defenders. The Imperial Light Horse, Thorneycroft's Mounted Infantry, the South African Light Horse were represented; and so were Remington's Tigers, the Scottish Horse, and Kitchener's Fighting Scouts.

The Maoris of New Zealand were not the only soldiers of native origin. From North Borneo came a little band of Dyaks. The Sultan of Perak brought from the Straits his bodyguard of Malays. Ceylon sent its white-clad, sinuous Sinhalese; Fiji its bronze-tinted giants, clothed in crimson, white and blue. Many a branch of the great Bantu family was seen on the London pavement: Nigerians and Haussas from West Africa; Sudanese and Swahilis from the centre and east, wearing the uniform of the King's African Rifles. The red tarboosh marked the Mahomedan guardians of Cyprus, and the yellow Mongol features of the Hong Kong police told of England's outpost in the Far East.

One of the parks around London was peopled with an imposing contingent of the native troops of the Indian Army, recruited from Kashmir to Cape Comorin, and from the Afghan hills to the delta of the Godavery. There were Tamils, Telugus, Mahrattas, Brahmin-Jats and Rajputs, Gurkhas, Sikhs, Afridis and other Pathans,

KING EDWARD ON HIS WAY DOWN WHITEHALL

Although the Coronation of King Edward VII took place in a month in which, before the War, London was said to be "empty", huge crowds began to assemble in the streets and parks in the small hours of August 9th, 1902. This photograph shows the scene in Whitehall with dense crowds on the pavements and every stand and window packed with spectators.

Hazaras from Afghanistan, and Mussulmans of diverse origin and locality.

It was with feelings similar to those aroused when the Prince of Wales went forth to give thanks for his recovery from grave illness in 1872 that the people of London gathered at daybreak on August 9th, 1902, to watch him ride out to be anointed and crowned. Many of the spectators still felt doubtful whether their beloved ruler would ever live to wear the diadem of Empire. They were apprehensive of news arriving at any moment that King Edward had had a relapse, and that the ceremony would again have to be postponed.

The Royal Procession

Not until the stupendous thunder of the massed cannon rolled through London and announced that the King had left his Palace did they believe that all was well with him. Some of them were dozing on the kerb along the line of route when the gleam of dawn began to appear in the sky, and for many long hours they waited on, all animated by one desire, to see King Edward go forth to be crowned, and to see him return with his beautiful Queen.

The gorgeous procession moved slowly through London, a broad stream of scarlet and gold. Headed by the band of the First Life Guards in their glittering state uniforms came the cavalcade of Royal Horse Guards, with the King's barge-master and twelve watermen. This advance-guard of the sovereign's escort was followed by the pages, maids of honour, and officers of the King's household. After them rode the brilliant and distinguished throng of the aides-de-camp of King Edward. Among them were three Indian princes: the young Maharajah of Gwalior from Central India, the Maharajah of Cooch-Behar, and Sir Pertab Singh, the Maharajah of Idar and leader of the Imperial Service troops. In this part of the procession about one hundred officers took part, and, with their many-coloured uniforms, made a fine and a stirring spectacle. The aides-de-camp were followed by the three officers who had recently commanded British forces successfully in the far ends of the earth: Lord Kitchener, Admiral Sir Edward Seymour and Sir Alfred Gaselee. These three conquerors were accompanied by the Headquarters Staff of the Army, and the rear of this brilliant military display was brought up by the veteran Lord Roberts.

Then came His Majesty's Marshalmen, twenty-five Yeomen of the Guard, clad in the glorious attire of the Tudor period. Another band of brilliant soldiers intervened; these were the equerries to the King, and among them were Prince Albert and Prince Christian of Schleswig-Holstein, and Prince Charles of Denmark. They were followed by an escort of Colonial mounted troops and an escort of Indian cavalry.

But when at last the King appeared in his coach, clad in a crimson robe and wearing on his head the Cap of State, there was a storm of cheers in deafening unison. In a scene of the wildest enthusiasm ever seen in England, King Edward rode down Whitehall to the minster where for thirteen centuries the sovereigns of England have been anointed and crowned.

Inside the Abbey

At about half-past nine on the morning of August 9th, 1902, eight thousand persons assembled in the ancient minster, forming in their glittering and many-coloured costumes a vast jewelled cross in the nave and the transepts. The scene was incomparable in its picturesqueness and magnificent pomp. Through the old windows, subdued by the gem-like colouring of the stained glass, filtered a faint light, which infused into everything a sense of dignity.

In the arches were galleries filled with spectators in gorgeous attire, but so high and distant that they were blurred into a confused mass of colour. Prelates and priests in cloth of gold; peers and peeresses in ermine and crimson; courtiers and soldiers in scarlet and yellow; knights in the medieval dress of the orders of chivalry. The blue and old gold of the carpets and hangings blended with the grey hues of the ancient stones, and framed the rich mosaic of colours.

Although, as has been seen, the special embassies sent by foreign countries to the Coronation of Edward the Peacemaker were compelled by the illness of the King to depart without fulfilling their mission, a considerable number of members of the reigning houses of Europe came back to see him crowned. They were all of near kindred to the King and Queen. Although it is not customary for sovereign rulers to attend Coronations, one reigning prince sat in the choir of Westminster Abbey. He was the Grand Duke of Hesse, the eldest son of Princess Alice. Next him was seated the heir of Greece, representing his father, King George of the Hellenes, brother of Queen Alexandra. By the Duke of Sparta was his uncle, the Crown Prince of Denmark.

PASSING UP THE CHOIR

King Edward VII and Queen Alexandra are here seen just after entering the Abbey. The King is wearing the royal crimson robe and the Cap of State. Queen Alexandra, later to be crowned, alone of the ladies present wears no hair ornament.

On the other side of the choir were Prince and Princess Henry of Prussia, both grandchildren of Queen Victoria. Beside them was the Crown Prince of Rumania with his wife, a princess of Saxe-Coburg, but born a maid of Kent when her father was Duke of Edinburgh.

In the absence of the special envoys, the ambassadors accredited to the Court of St. James's represented their governments at the Coronation. One special mission, however, remained. The Ras Makunen from Abyssinia stood for the line descended from the Queen of Sheba. At some distance from him, among famous diplomatists of Europe, was the representative of our new ally, Japan. He, unfortunately, had discarded the flowing flowery robe of the Land of the Rising Sun for the less picturesque costume of the Western world. But ranged against the screen in the places of highest honour was a line of Indian feudatory princes, whose jewels rivalled in splendour those of the Regalia about to be assumed by their Imperial suzerain.

Statesmen of the Empire

Not far from the Indian potentates sat the Prime Minister of the Dominion of Canada, in his knightly robes of blue—Sir Wilfrid Laurier, of French race, descended from the countrymen of Montcalm, from whom Wolfe won Quebec. Close to him was the Prime Minister of New Zealand, Mr. Richard Seddon. On the north side of the choir sat Sir Edmund Barton, the Prime Minister of the new Commonwealth of Australia, while Sir Robert Bond, the Prime Minister of the oldest British Colony, Newfoundland, was seated above the black chief of the Barotses, who came from the newest territory acquired by English pioneers, Rhodesia, named after that empire-builder who had died but five months before the Coronation. South Africa was represented by the minister of loyal Natal, Sir Albert Hine, and two governors of the Crown Colonies, Sir West Ridgeway and Sir Walter Sendall, graced the ceremony.

Among the British statesmen in the

choir were two political opponents who had more in common with one another than with many of the men of their own party. Sir Michael Hicks-Beach, wearing for the last time the robes of the Chancellor of the Exchequer, and Sir William Vernon Harcourt, his predecessor at the Treasury. Both these statesmen stood for the great tradition of English Parliamentary life. Of the new type of political leader created by the new era, Mr. Joseph Chamberlain was the most remarkable example present.

All the traditions of English feudalism conserved in the glowing verse of Shakespeare were vivified that day in the ancient Abbey. Even before the sovereigns arrived with their sumptuous escort, the centre of the minster was a scene of splendour. Great galleries with dim blue hangings concealed the transept containing the tombs and monuments of statesmen who had laid the foundations of Empire, and hid the little corner in which reposed the great poets and prose-writers whose genius had carried the English language to the ends of the earth. On the right hand sat the peers in their white-caped robes of crimson and their coronets ; on the left were four hundred peeresses in velvet and minever.

Beginning of the Ceremony

On August 9th, 1902, the ceremony began at ten o'clock by the procession of the Regalia. They were brought by the Chapter of Westminster from the Jerusalem Chamber, where they had lain overnight, to the Chapel of Edward the Confessor behind the high altar. The King's scholars of Westminster, the choirs of the Abbey and of the Chapel Royal, and the canons and minor canons of Westminster formed the procession.

When the Litany had been sung and the oil in the Ampulla had been hallowed, the Regalia were taken in procession through the crowded Abbey to the western porch and left with the peers appointed to bring them to the sanctuary. Some time afterwards the first of the royal processions entered, led by the daughters of the King. The

Duchess of Fife, the Princess Victoria and Princess Maud passed slowly through the admiring ranks of their father's subjects, followed by their aunts, Princess Helena, the Duchess of Argyll and Princess Beatrice. Two aged forms in the procession of the Royal Family represented a generation older than that of King Edward. Leaning on his staff was the Duke of Cambridge, and close to him was his sister, the venerable Grand Duchess of Mecklenburg-Strelitz ; both of them had come to the Abbey sixty-four years before at the Coronation of Queen Victoria.

The Heir Apparent

The procession of the Prince and Princess of Wales came behind the glittering retinue of the princely representatives of many of the reigning houses of Europe. Clad in their robes of State, the royal couple paced along the nave amid the expectant crowd.

By this time the King's procession had arrived at the Abbey. King Edward and his Queen entered their retiring-rooms, and, having put on their robes, they advanced up the nave into the choir. No statelier pageant was ever seen in England than the proceeding of Their Majesties to the west door of the Abbey. Nothing marred the solemn beauty of the scene. The tiers of eight thousand spectators in robes of State formed on either hand towering banks of rich colouring for the regal pageant to pass through. The procession itself was a vision of unsurpassed splendour and dignity. First came the Chaplains in Ordinary, then the Prebendaries of Westminster in red copes embroidered with gold. Behind them were five pursuivants in tabards of figured silk damask, and the officers of the orders of knighthood. Mr. Dymoke, the King's Champion, carried the Standard of England ; the O'Conor Don bore the Standard of Ireland ; Mr. Wedderburn held by hereditary right the Standard of Scotland, and the Duke of Wellington bore the Union Standard. Four Knights of the Garter, Lords Rosebery, Derby, Spencer and Cadogan, were appointed to hold the canopy over the King during the anointing.

Behind the blue-mantled Knights of the Garter came two other ministers, the Duke of Devonshire and Mr. Balfour. It was not, however, as Prime Minister of the United Kingdom that Mr. Balfour took an active part in the Coronation, but only as Lord Keeper of the King's Privy Seal. It is a strange fact that until 1905 the Prime Minister of the Mother of Parliaments was a personage unknown in constitutional law and state ceremonial, and consequently no place was reserved for him at national festivals. This was due to the comparatively recent origin of his office. The Lord Chancellors of England and Ireland, who followed Mr. Balfour, represented offices of far more ancient dignity ; and still more ancient than theirs was the office of the aged man who walked behind them. For Dr. Temple, the venerable Archbishop of Canterbury, was on this day next to the King and Queen in importance. It was from him, the holder of a position established in England by a Christian missionary in the sixth century, that the monarch was to receive his crown.

The Coming of the Queen

The Primate was followed by a herald and two pursuivants ; and then, preceded by high officers of State bearing her Regalia, Queen Alexandra crossed the threshold of the Abbey, and the joyful music of the march to which her procession moved was drowned by the conclamation of "Vivat Regina, Alexandra ! Vivat, vivat, vivat !"

Unlike all the other ladies present, she wore no ornaments in her hair, for a diadem with the blazing Koh-i-noor set in it was soon to be placed on her brow. She was dressed in white, and yet, by reason of her immense and sumptuous purple train, her attire was of a regal magnificence. Broidered with gold and stamped with Imperial crowns, the train was borne by eight pages in brilliant scarlet, and the end of it was carried by the Mistress of the Robes, the Duchess of Buccleuch. Two

bishops in their vestments, and ten gentlemen-at-arms in brave attire walked by the side of the Queen. Four duchesses—the Duchess of Marlborough, the Duchess of Montrose, the Duchess of Portland and the Duchess of Sutherland—were appointed to hold over the Queen a rich pall of cloth-of-gold at her anointing. The whole group moved with the Queen, as she took her way by the north of her throne to her seat in the south of the sanctuary. The Dean and canons passed before her to the further corner, and there the bearers of her Regalia handed over the royal emblems to one of the ecclesiastics, to lay upon the high altar.

The King's Regalia

In the meantime, the Archbishop of Canterbury, with the Lord Chancellor, the Lord Great Chamberlain, the Lord High Constable, with the Earl Marshal on his right hand, and a King of Arms, stood at the entrance to the sanctuary waiting for King Edward. The music grew more triumphant, the silver trumpets sounded a loud and long acclaim, and the King's procession, in its heraldic splendours, came in a broad stream of glowing colours up the nave. At the head of the Regalia the Sceptre of the Cross was borne by the Duke of Argyll. Lord Carrington carried Saint Edward's Staff, and Lord Grey de Ruthyn and Lord Loudoun the Golden Spurs. Two famous field-marshals, Lord Roberts and Lord Wolseley, carried, sharp and naked, the Sword of Spiritual Justice and the Sword of Temporal Justice. Between them was the pointless Sword of Mercy, in the hands of the Duke of Grafton. Then, divided from the field-marshals by the blazoned tabards of a row of heralds, was an ornate cluster of high officials and nobles who by long tradition walked in front of the sovereign. Here was the Lord Mayor of London exercising the ancient privilege of bearing the City Mace in this place of honour. The Sword of State was borne by Lord Londonderry, and to the Duke of Marlborough fell the distinction of carrying the most significant symbol in

SUPREME MOMENT OF KING EDWARD'S CORONATION

King Edward VII was crowned by the aged Archbishop of Canterbury, Dr. Temple. Seated on the lower left of the illustration is Queen Alexandra. On the King's right hand are the Duke of Grafton, bearing the blunted Sword of Mercy, Lord Roberts bearing the second sword and Lord Wolseley the third. To the right of the Archbishop of Canterbury is the Archbishop of York, and at the extreme right is the Dean of Westminster, who has just handed the crown to the Archbishop.

the Regalia—the Imperial Crown. Then, clad in his royal crimson robe of State, with the Cap of State on his head, and with his purple train upheld by eight pages, came the King. "Vivat Rex Edwardus! Vivat Rex Edwardus! Vivat, vivat, vivat!" came the shout, taken up by the choir.

As King Edward moved up the choir, a silence fell upon the multitude. In the half-light which filtered in through the painted glass, King Edward seemed for a second only the dusky shadow of a king. Then one saw that, though pale with emotion, he walked firmly and straight; his step was as secure as if he had known no infirmity. Kneeling at the faldstool by his chair, he said a short prayer, and the Coronation Service opened with the Recognition.

Presentation of King Edward

King Edward stood up and showed himself to the multitude. By his side was the venerable Primate of England, who presented him to the people, saying; "Sirs, I here present unto you King Edward, the undoubted King of this Realm; Wherefore all you who are come this day to do your homage, are you willing to do the same?" From every arch of the ancient Abbey rang the answering shout: "God save King Edward!" Then, after the silver trumpets had sounded, the calm voices of two bishops were heard in the opening of the Communion Service.

The Epistle and Gospel were read by two bishops, and the Creed recited, and the King placed on his head a Cap of State, and prepared to make the covenant with his people, the substance of which dates from at least the earliest days of the Anglo-Saxon monarchy. The Archbishop of Canterbury advanced and said:

"Sir, is your Majesty willing to take the oath?"

"I am willing", answered King Edward, in a loud, clear voice. The oath, similar to that administered to Queen Victoria at her Coronation, was then recited by the Primate.

"All this I promise to do", King Edward answered.

Then, kneeling on the steps of the altar, he laid his right hand upon the great Bible, and in strong, vibrant tones he declared: "These things which I have herebefore promised, I will perform and keep. So help me, God." As he kissed the Bible and signed the oath there was a deep silence in the Abbey.

The first part of the service was now over. Rising from the altar steps, King Edward VII moved to the chair made by Edward I to hold the famous Stone of Scone, the most ancient and the most romantic seat of coronation in the world, and sat on the Stone of Destiny to be anointed.

Before the anthem was ended, a glimmering pall of cloth-of-gold was carried out and held over King Edward by the four pall-bearers. The Lord Great Chamberlain disrobed the King of his crimson raiment, and a canon took the Ampulla and anointing spoon from the altar and poured out the holy oil into the spoon and presented it to the Archbishop who anointed the King on the forehead, breast and hands.

Oblation of the Sword

From this solemn moment King Edward technically became the sovereign. By a symbolic rite he had been made half churchman, half knight, and he was immediately invested with the priestlike vestments of his kingship. The Knights of the Garter gave back the pall to the Lord Chamberlain, and King Edward stood up, and an alb of white cambric was put on him, and over this was placed a short coat of cloth-of-gold called the Close Pall, and a sword-belt. Then the Archbishop of Canterbury took the kingly sword and placed it in the right hand of the King, with the customary exhortation. The sword was girded on the King by his Chamberlain, but the King ungirded it, and gave it to the Archbishop, who placed it again upon the altar of God. Lord Londonderry redeemed the sword from the Dean of Westminster at the price of a bag of silver, and bore it naked before His Majesty.

The King was then clothed with the Imperial Mantle and the Archbishop put on the fourth finger of his right hand the ancient wedding ring of England, which, by its legend, connects the weak little kingdom of Edward the Confessor with the vast empire of Edward the Peacemaker.

Afterwards seated in the chair made by Edward I, Edward VII received from the Archbishop the Imperial Robe and Orb. The Sceptre with the Cross was placed in his right hand, representing kingly power and justice ; and the Sceptre with the Dove, representing equity and mercy, was delivered into his left hand.

But at this supreme moment the apprehension which had ceased to be felt for the King, who had gone through his trying part with grave and manly dignity, began to be entertained for the aged Primate. Signs of extreme physical weakness became increasingly evident in his actions. Attended by a band of prelates, he went to the altar, and took in his hands the Crown and murmured, rather than recited, the Coronation prayer.

Assisted by his bishops, he almost stumbled down the altar steps, followed by a canon carrying the diadem on a cushion. As the Archbishop took up the crown, it was patent that the long ceremony had completely overtaxed his strength, that the aged and ailing Primate had almost succumbed. He raised the crown, and was

CORONATION NAVAL REVIEW

On August 16th, 1902, a week after his Coronation, King Edward VII reviewed the Fleet at Spithead. The ships, dressed with flags, were anchored in line between Southsea and Ryde, and King Edward and Queen Alexandra passed down the lines on board the Royal Yacht Victoria and Albert.

about to put it on the wrong way. With a gesture of infinite kindness, King Edward helped him to place it right. The tension lasted but a moment. Then the venerable Primate bent forward, and the crown descended gently and truly on the brow of the King. The Coronation was consummated. The vast multitude broke out in a triumphant shout of "God save the King". The bugles rang out, massed artillery at the Tower proclaimed to London the joyful tidings, and to the Empire in all the ends of the earth was flashed the glad news that the Emperor-King had at last been crowned.

And now the consecrated King rose up from the Stone of Destiny and, turning to the west, appeared before the multitude in Westminster Abbey, arrayed in all the attributes of majesty. Passing to his throne, he was lifted up into it by archbishops, bishops and peers. The great officers who had borne the Regalia assembled at his feet, and the Primate stood before him and cried :

"Stand firm, and hold from henceforth the seat and state of Royal and Imperial dignity which is this day delivered unto you, and the Lord God Almighty establish your Throne in righteousness, that it may stand fast for evermore, like as the sun before Him, and as the faithful witness in Heaven."

Homage of the Peers

The ending enthronization being thus completed, King Edward received the homage of the spiritual peers. The aged Primate was the first to kneel at the King's feet and make the declaration of fealty.

He then added, with deep emotion, "God bless you, sir ; God be with you, sir", and endeavoured to rise to kiss the King. But his strength failed him, and though King Edward rose from his throne and took him by the hands to help him to his feet, he must have fallen if three bishops kneeling by had not sprung up and supported him.

After the Archbishop had thus done homage for the spiritual lords, the Prince of Wales performed the same act on behalf of the Princes of the Blood Royal.

Then, arising, he touched the crown on his father's head and kissed him. As he was about to descend the steps, King Edward caught him by the end of his robe, and with his left hand drew him down by the shoulder. The Sovereign and the liegeman disappeared, and only a father and a son were face to face. With a gesture of infinite tenderness and fatherly love, the royal sire drew to his arms his only remaining son, and in the sight of his people kissed him twice and gripped both his hands and shook them in a strong emotion.

Then followed the homage of the temporal peers, a testimony to that continuity of tradition which gives to our institutions so wonderful a stability. When the homage was done, the drums were beaten, the trumpets were sounded, and all the people in the Abbey shouted, crying out : "God save King Edward ! Long live King Edward ! May the King live for ever !"

Queen Alexandra's Crowning

The Coronation of Queen Alexandra served as a graceful epilogue to the august drama of the sacring of the King. There were many points of difference between her crowning and the crowning of the King. She was crowned and anointed kneeling, while the King during the ceremonies sat in the Coronation Chair. The Queen, moreover, was anointed only on the head ; she did not take the orb, nor was she invested with special robes.

As she advanced from the altar, bearing nobly on her head the crown in which the Koh-i-noor flashed, and carrying in either hand her Sceptre and Ivory Rod, she made reverence in passing the King on her way back to her throne.

The Royal coach was waiting at the door of the minster. King Edward and Queen Alexandra entered it, and as they drove back to their palace, the children of London found themselves at last in that enchanted land where all beautiful dreams come true. They saw a real king with a real crown on his head, happy with his people's happiness, sitting by a crowned and radiant queen.

KING GEORGE AND QUEEN MARY AFTER THEIR CORONATION

The King and Queen are here seen at Buckingham Palace wearing the crowns and robes in which they had just driven back from the Coronation ceremony His Majesty is wearing the Imperial Crown and the Imperial State Robe with its ermine trimmings. Round his shoulders is the collar of the Order of the Garter

CHAPTER II

THE CORONATION OF KING GEORGE V AND QUEEN MARY

Magnificent in every way, the Coronation of King George V and his Queen was unique in that for the first time—indicative of their ever-growing importance— the Dominions and Colonies were fully represented at the age-old ceremony

NINETEEN hundred and eleven, the year of the Coronation of King George and Queen Mary, was a season of almost unequalled beauty, splendour and prosperity. The weather was unusually benign, as though Nature had combined with Man to lend the year a special charm. Summer started early, and by mid-May the land seemed one great garden. May merged into a still sunnier and warmer June, which lasted until a week before the date of the great ceremony and then turned into unusual cold with heavy clouds.

The period of national mourning ended in mid-May, and an amazingly brilliant social season at once opened. Public and private entertainment was planned on the most lavish scale. The gathering of the Imperial Conference, growing at each re-assembly in its importance and power, would alone have lent the year distinction. The Festival of Empire, produced at the Crystal Palace on a scale never before attempted in similar pageantry, was accompanied by other pageants and festivals in the provinces. The theatres showed their most alluring aspects. Sir Herbert Tree had prepared a Shakespeare Festival, done in his usual grandiose manner ; two plays by George Bernard Shaw were produced, one at the Criterion and one at the Little Theatre ; Laurence Irving had secured a new triumph in "Margaret Catch-

pole" ; Ellen Terry was at the Haymarket, and at Covent Garden Melba and Tetrazzini, Destinn, Sammarco and Sampiera were appearing.

For weeks beforehand the coming ceremonies dominated the national life. Here and there it must be admitted the enthusiasm of some people tended towards the ridiculous. Women wore Coronation dresses, red, white and blue. Men demonstrated their loyalty by wearing Coronation hats—that is, hats bound with Coronation ribbon. There were Coronation buttons and brooches galore. Coronation gardens became a craze in many suburbs, every borough had its plans for special celebrations, and one prominent feature in most of these was the emphasis laid on giving pleasure to the children and enjoyment, aid and comfort to the poor.

From the Ends of the Earth

One astonishing thing even to the experienced metropolitan in the days immediately preceding the Coronation was the variety of nations to be seen in the streets. Kensington Gardens and Hyde Park had become an armed camp, to accommodate the soldiers of the Empire arriving from all parts. Indian cavalrymen, dark-faced and turbaned, rode in brakes, seeing London. South African troops in khaki and with broad-brimmed soft grey hats, marched through the City, with the Guards Band at their head. The Canadians came in force and were welcomed everywhere. Men of colour abounded, men from Jamaica, from Bombay and Calcutta, native chiefs from East Africa, Burmese, Parsees, Bengal babus, and pure-blooded negroes. An Afridi in full war array walked down Fleet Street. Two types of Australians were numerous, the elder men, big-framed, heavily bearded and genial-mannered, and young Australia, the bronzed, lean, lithe men in their thirties, full of energy, purpose and ambition. From east and west, north and south, from tropics and Arctic zone, loyal subjects had come to join in the crowning of their King.

The crowds pouring into London were so great that the police became alarmed, and took elaborate precautions. Barriers were erected in a number of side streets, substantial gateways of solid wood, iron-bound, that could be closed to hold back the crowds.

Welcoming the Guests

The King and Queen returned to London from Windsor Castle on Saturday, June 17th, and were welcomed by enormous crowds that had gathered all along the line of route from Paddington to Buckingham Palace. They had barely arrived at the Palace before they set out again to meet the Empress Maria of Russia, Queen Alexandra's sister, who had come to visit her at Sandringham. The festivities started on Monday evening with a dinner by the King and Queen to all the available members of the Royal Family and all the foreign royal representatives, numbering eighty-seven, who had arrived for the Coronation. That same evening the Duke and Duchess of Sutherland gave a ball of extraordinary splendour at the then traditional home of the most sumptuous private entertainments in London, Stafford House. This is the mansion of which Queen Victoria had once said to a former Duchess of Sutherland, when coming from Buckingham Palace to visit her, "I have come from my house to your palace." There were over 1000 guests present, and among them more than 150 members of royal families. Wednesday was specially devoted to the Dominion

Premiers, who were received by the King and Queen at Buckingham Palace in the morning, and entertained by the Duke of Connaught at St. James's Palace later.

The main Coronation ceremonies were spread over two days. Thursday was to be Coronation Day, with a state procession from Buckingham Palace to Westminster Abbey, going by way of the Mall and returning along Piccadilly. On Friday the King and Queen were to make a royal progress to the City, visiting the Lord Mayor and returning by South London. Both days were being observed as Bank Holidays. On Saturday the King and Queen were to review the Fleet at Spithead.

The decorations in the streets were worthy of the greatest city in the world. Magnificent arches, marble pillars, gilded statuary and elaborate ornamental devices appeared as though by magic. The line of route of both processions had been transformed. Substantial wooden galleries, roofed and covered with cloth of red and gold, were erected in front of every shop and almost every private house. Places from where even a partial view of the processions could be obtained commanded a high figure, the income from the sale of seats in some comparatively small but well-placed houses running into thousands of pounds. In many of the main streets the houses were covered with a tracery of electric lamps.

New Zealand's Tribute

In the centre of Whitehall, New Zealand erected a triumphal arch designed by Frank Brangwyn, 35 feet high and 40 feet wide, draped in crimson and gold and capped by a large Imperial crown. Not far off the Government of Ontario had erected its arch. Piccadilly had adopted a uniform scheme of street decoration, Venetian masts connected by green festoons, with rows of yellow electric lights spread over the streets and amid the greenery. There were festoons and masts along most of the line of decoration. In Ludgate Circus these were joined by lines of red carnations, and in Cannon Street and Queen Victoria Street by pink and white carnations. The preparations to illuminate the heart of the City around the Bank of England were specially elaborate, great flares being placed at numerous strategic points. The lamps decking some buildings were numbered by the thousand.

Coronation Day opened with a sunrise salute of twenty-one guns, fired by the Royal Horse Artillery in Hyde Park, and by the Royal Garrison Artillery at the Tower. Other similar salutes were fired when the King left Buckingham Palace at 10.30 a.m., and when he was crowned there was a salute of forty-one guns in Hyde Park and at Windsor, and sixty-two guns at the Tower. Further salutes were fired later.

The whole of the processional route was lined with troops. One of the most moving sights was around Buckingham Palace, where two hundred Chelsea pensioners in their picturesque uniforms had places from which they could see the procession start and return. Near them were the Army Nursing Sisters in their uniforms, and children from military orphanages. Around the monument of Queen Victoria, facing Buckingham Palace, was a guard of honour of native officers from the Indian contingents. To the right was a guard of overseas troops, Canadians, Australians, New Zealanders and South Africans, and within

sight had been stationed a picked company of Boy Scouts.

The military arrangements were under the control of Lord Kitchener, and he himself was present early in the morning around Buckingham Palace to see that all was right. At 9.30 the first procession left the Palace, consisting of the representatives of foreign Imperial and royal houses. These included the German Crown Prince and Princess, the Grand Duke Boris of

TRIBUTE OF A GREAT DOMINION

The Dominions and Colonies not only sent troops to take part in the Coronation procession, but also made their contributions to the street decorations. One of the most impressive of these was the New Zealand Arch in Whitehall designed by Mr. Frank Brangwyn, R.A.

Russia, the Infanta of Spain, Prince and Princess Higashi Fushimi of Japan, the Archduke Charles of Austria, the Crown Prince and Princess of Sweden, and others in lessening importance down to the Hereditary Prince of Monaco. They were driven in state landaus, the more important having four matched horses with postilions and those of lesser rank a pair of bay horses without postilions. Then followed members of the British Royal House, each group in a state landau drawn by a pair of horses.

At 10.30 Their Majesties' procession began. An escort of Royal Horse Guards led the way, followed by the King's Royal Barge-master and twelve watermen. Then came members of the Household troops, and leading officers of the Army, three field-marshals, Lord Roberts, Lord Grenfell and Sir Evelyn Wood, two inspectors-general, Sir John French and Sir Ian Hamilton, and the Army Council. The King's marshalmen, Yeomen of the Guard, equerries and honorary aides-de-camp, an escort of Colonial and Indian cavalry, two divisions of the Royal Horse Guards and more of the King's Household made a varied array.

These immediately preceded the King

KING GEORGE AND QUEEN MARY APPROACHING THE ABBEY

The State coach, which is used only at the Coronation and the State Opening of Parliament, is here seen approaching Westminster Abbey. It was designed in the eighteenth century by the famous architect, Sir William Chambers, and its lavish details are clearly shown in the photograph. The panels were painted by Battista Cipriani, a Florentine artist, who also painted those of the Lord Mayor of London's coach.

CORONATION PROCESSION OF 1911 SEEN FROM BIG BEN

The route followed by the Coronation procession of King George V and Queen Mary on the way to Westminster Abbey was along the Mall, down Whitehall, and through Parliament Square. That for the return to Buckingham Palace was by way of Whitehall, Trafalgar Square, Pall Mall, St. James's Street, Piccadilly, and Constitution Hill. The photograph above shows the procession passing through Parliament Square.

and Queen in the gorgeous old state coach, drawn by eight cream horses. Behind them rode Lord Kitchener and a standard-bearer, followed by other high officials, more Life Guards coming at the end. The King wore his Cap of State, edged with minever, and a crimson cloak with a shoulder-lapel, also of minever. The Queen wore a dress of deep ivory satin, with gold embroidery, and no head-dress. People remarked that the King was pale and that his face showed clear traces of solemn mood, as though he had spent many hours in introspection and self-communion before undertaking the great responsibilities now awaiting him. The acclamations of the crowds all along the line of route were remarkably enthusiastic.

The interior of Westminster Abbey looked picturesque indeed, with the varied uniforms and elaborate dresses of the picked assembly. Here were officers of State of many degrees, champion, heralds and standard-bearers, prelates and Yeomen of the Guard, representatives of many historic regiments in uniforms of scarlet and blue, and foreign potentates like Desjamatch Kassa of Ethiopia, whose brow was encircled with a golden band surmounted by a strip of lion's mane. Bluejackets and Grenadiers lined the farthest end of the Abbey. The dim lights, the sombre walls, the deep shadows from the pillars, monuments and memorials, the flash of the rays from the candelabra against the shining metal on some of the uniforms made a scene never to be forgotten by those who witnessed it.

The Progress to the Altar

The King and Queen arrived at the west entrance of the Abbey, where they were received by the great officials of State, carrying their insignia and robes of office. The lords bore the Regalia and the bishops carried a Paten, a Chalice and a Bible. The procession towards the altar was a long one. The Abbey beadle led the way ; then came the clergy in increasing rank, starting with the humblest, officials of every kind and men of high degree, bearing the standards of the Empire, including the standards of the overseas Dominions and those of Wales, of Ireland and of Scotland. The standard of England was borne by the head of the family that for centuries has carried the proud title of the King's Champion, namely Mr. Frank S. Dymoke. Last among the standards came the Royal Standard itself, borne aloft by the Marquess of Lansdowne.

Four knights of the Order of the Garter, appointed to hold the canopy for the King's anointing, moved together ; following them came a number of statesmen, Lord Rosebery, Lord Morley and Mr. Asquith, the Prime Minister, in the uniform of a warden of the Cinque Ports. The Archbishop of York preceded the Archbishop of Canterbury, who has the right to crown the King. The Queen's Regalia came in front of the Queen, who was followed by her ladies and maids of honour. Then followed the King's Regalia, then the three swords—the Sword of Mercy, borne by the Duke of Beaufort ;

the Sword of Justice to the Temporality, borne by Lord Roberts ; and the Sword of Justice to the Spirituality, borne by Lord Kitchener. Kings of Arms followed, then the Lord Mayor of London and the Lord Great Chamberlain of England. The Sceptre, St. Edward's Crown and the Orb, all having their traditional part, were each carried by a duke.

The Paten, the Bible and the Chalice, borne by bishops, were carried ahead of the King, who was wearing his royal crimson robe of State, with the collar of the Garter and with the Cap of State on his head. The Bishop of Durham walked on one side of him and the Bishop of Bath and Wells on the other. Ten gentlemen-at-arms advanced on either side, while the King's train was carried by eight picked members of noble houses. More officials followed, and then twenty Yeomen of the Guard.

The members of the procession then took up their places, carefully marked out according to precedence. The Queen stood at the Chair of State on the south side of the altar, her ladies-in-waiting behind her. The King advanced to his Chair of State, also on the south side of the altar, and after making his humble adoration he and the Queen took their seats, the bishops, their supporters, remaining standing on each side, the lords bearing the four swords on the King's right hand and the lords bearing the Regalia standing about the King's chair. Near the pulpit were the bishops bearing the Bible, the Paten and the Chalice, while the train-bearers and others stood behind the King.

Ceremony of the Recognition

The anthem finished, the Archbishop of Canterbury, splendidly arrayed, advanced from his place to perform a ceremony that dates back hundreds of years to the earliest days of European monarchy. This is the presentation of a new king to the people for recognition. Supported by the Lord High Chancellor, the Lord Great Chamberlain, the Lord High Constable and the Earl Marshal, and preceded by Garter King of Arms, the Archbishop turned first to the

KING GEORGE V DRAWS NEAR TO THE ABBEY

King George V and Queen Mary entered Westminster Abbey through a specially-built annexe beneath the West Front, which the procession is here seen approaching. The annexe had a carriage-way through which the State coach drove, so that the King and Queen might alight at the entrance to the Robing-Room, whence they passed, escorted by the Great Officers of State, to their Chairs of State on the south side of the altar.

east side, then to the south, then to the west and then to the north, and each time announced in a ringing voice :

"Sirs, I here present unto you King George the undoubted King of this Realm ; Wherefore, all you who are come this day to do your homage and service, are you willing to do the same ?"

While the Archbishop was speaking, the King stood up by his chair and turned to the people in the direction to which the Archbishop spoke. The people replied with loud and repeated cries of "God save King George". At the conclusion the trumpets sounded.

Ritual of Church and State

The King resumed his seat and the bishops placed the Bible, the Paten and the Chalice on the altar, and then took their places. The Archbishop of Canterbury proceeded to the altar, where the Regalia, except the swords, were handed over to him by the Dean of Westminster and were laid on the altar. Then the officials representing the Church and the State took their stand on either side of the King. The Litany and part of the Communion Service were read, after which came a sermon by the Archbishop of York from St. Luke, chapter 22, verse 27 : "I am among you as He that serveth."

All these were the preliminaries. The King had put on his Cap of State "of crimson velvet turned up with ermine" during the sermon. He was now sitting in his Chair of State, in front of Anne of Cleves' tomb, the Bishop of Durham on his right, and the Bishop of Bath and Wells on his left, while behind him were the Master of the Rolls, the Earl Marshal and the bearers of the swords. The sermon finished, the Archbishop, standing before the King, administered the oath.

The King now rose from his chair, the Sword of State ahead. Attended by his supporters and by the Lord Great Chamberlain, he advanced to the altar, knelt upon the cushion placed on the steps, and, laying his right hand on the Gospels in the Bible which had been borne in the procession, he

took the Coronation Oath, kissed the book and set his royal sign manual on the transcript of the oath :

"The things which I have herebefore promised I will perform and keep. So help me, God."

The King signed his name to the parchment slowly and deliberately, as though weighing every stroke of his pledge to his people.

A still more solemn ceremony was yet ahead, the Anointing. The choir had sung the hymn "Veni, Creator Spiritus", while the King knelt in prayer. Then his crimson robe was taken from him by the Lord Great Chamberlain and he himself took off his Cap of State. He seated himself in St. Edward's Chair, placed in front of the altar, with a "rich canopy of cloth-of-gold" held over him by four Knights of the Garter, Lord Cadogan, Lord Rosebery, Lord Crewe and Lord Minto. The Dean of Westminster took the Ampulla containing the holy oil and poured some of it in the anointing spoon. With this the Archbishop of Canterbury anointed the King in the form of a cross on the crown of his head, saying, "Be thy head anointed with the holy oil, as kings, priests and prophets were anointed." Then the breast and the palms of the hands were anointed, with similar benedictions.

Knightly Investiture

Now came the decking of the King with the symbols of his high office. The Dean of Westminster invested him with the Close Pall of cloth-of-gold and Girdle. The Golden Spurs of Chivalry were no longer fastened to the King's heels as in olden days, but his heels were lightly touched with them.

A sword in a scabbard of purple velvet was handed to the Archbishop in place of the Sword of State. He took it to the altar, and prayed that the King might use it "as the Minister of God for the terror and punishment of evildoers and for the protection and encouragement of those who do well". Then, raising it, he carried it to the King and held the hilt of it towards him. As the King took it in both hands, the Archbishop bade him use it rightly. The sword was

[Sir Benjamin Stone

FIRST PHOTOGRAPH OF A CORONATION CEREMONY

The Coronation of King George V and Queen Mary was the first of which a photograph was taken. Their Majesties are seen seated in their Chairs of State on the south side of the altar. In the Royal Box above are, left to right, Princess Mary, Prince Albert, Prince Henry, Prince George, Princess Victoria, Princess Christian, Princess Louise, and Princess Beatrice girdled around him, ungirdled and replaced on the altar, where it was redeemed for one hundred shillings.

The Armil, a long strip of gleaming cloth-of-gold with which the King was invested by the Dean of Westminster, had a religious origin. The Royal Robe, a long and sleeveless garment, hanging in heavy folds to a train and buckling over the chest, was exceedingly gorgeous, consisting as it did of cloth-of-gold inwoven with brilliant flowers. Then came the Orb, symbol of the King's dominion, the King's Ring put on his right hand, the Sceptre and the Cross, and the Golden Rod surmounted by a white enamel dove with outstretched wings.

'God Save the King !'

The crowning followed. The Archbishop of Canterbury, supported by the Archbishop of York and the other bishops, came from the altar. The Dean of Westminster handed the Crown to the Archbishop, who, amid the breathless silence of that vast assembly, placed it upon the King's head saying :

"God crown you with a Crown of glory and righteousness, that by the ministry of this our Benediction having a right Faith and manifold fruit of good works, you may obtain the Crown of an Everlasting Kingdom by the gift of Him whose Kingdom endureth for ever."

As the last word was spoken, the drums began to beat, the trumpets were sounded, the peers put on their coronets, and the Kings of Arms their crowns, while the whole congregation shouted with a loud voice, "God save the King !" At the same moment the great guns of the Tower and the guns in the Park fired the first rounds of their Royal Coronation salute.

The King had paid his homage to the Church and the Parliament. Now came the Lords Spiritual and Temporal to pay their homage to him. The Archbishop knelt before the King, giving homage for himself and the other Lords Spiritual, who stood in their places, repeating the words after him. Then the Archbishop kissed the King's left cheek. The Prince of Wales came next, pledging himself and all other Princes of the Blood Royal. The Peers of the Realm, represented by their senior of each degree, followed.

The drums beat, the trumpets sounded, and again and again the congregation shouted : "God save King George ! Long live King George ! May the King live for ever !"

The anointing and crowning of the Queen followed. The ceremonial was the same as obtained at the coronation of Queen Alexandra, already described in an earlier page. When she returned to her place she reverently bowed to the King. During the offertory the King and Queen made their oblations, the King offering an altar cloth and an ingot of gold of a pound weight and the Queen an altar cloth and a mark weight of gold. The final portions of the Communion Service were then given. As the King and Queen passed out to the annexe they both bore traces of the fatigue after the long ceremony.

The return procession to the Palace had one specially dramatic moment. As the royal coach turned into St. James's Street from Piccadilly a lady in one of the stands began to sing the National Anthem. All around her, hundreds joined in. The Dominion soldiers near by forgot for one moment their discipline, and burst into cheers too, waving their rifles aloft, even their officers joining in.

After the Coronation

Thursday was the day of solemn ritual, Friday the day of widespread popular demonstrations. The royal progress to the City of London was made the occasion of a heartfelt demonstration by all classes of people.

There is no need to tell of the loyal addresses presented by the different authorities at various stages of the route, or of the way in which the City showed itself once more the fitting and graceful host of Their Majesties. To many the more touching aspect of the progress was the attitude of the people in South London. After the reception in the City was over, the royal procession swept over London Bridge and through the Borough, the home of poverty, past the "Elephant", and back again to Buckingham Palace across Westminster Bridge. The greeting of the King's poorer subjects was even more outspoken in its enthusiasm than that of those north of the Thames.

The illuminations that for two nights lit up cities and small villages, the bonfires that blazed from a thousand hills, the enter-

Garden, probably surpassing in splendour anything ever witnessed even there. The beautiful dresses, the flashing of superb tiaras and necklaces and the display of splendid orders all contributed to a spectacle of great magnificence.

On Tuesday there was a Royal Garden Party at Buckingham Palace, when 6000 guests assembled. One of the most notable figures here was an Indian prince

THEIR MAJESTIES ENTERTAINED BY THE CITY

On June 29th, 1911, the last of the royal progresses which marked the Coronation celebrations took place. The King and Queen, accompanied by Prince Edward and Princess Mary, drove in state to the City and attended a thanksgiving service in St. Paul's Cathedral. Their Majesties were afterwards entertained at luncheon by the Lord Mayor and Corporation at the Guildhall, where they are seen arriving.

tainments of children everywhere, the distribution of fine gifts to the poor, were merely outward expressions of the genuine national joy.

The return of the King and Queen from the impressive review of the Fleet at Spithead on June 24th was followed by a further series of festivities. On Monday, June 26th, there was a gala night at Covent

whose jewels were remarkable even in a gathering such as this. On Wednesday the King visited the Royal Agricultural Show at Norwich, and in the evening there was a second gala performance, this time at His Majesty's Theatre, when a variety of short scenes was given intended to present in dramatic form certain historic aspects of the British theatre.

The formal Coronation festivities came to a close on Thursday, when the King and Queen again made a progress to the City of London, attending a thanksgiving at St. Paul's Cathedral and taking luncheon with the Lord Mayor and City Corporation at the Guildhall.

That day the King issued a message which struck a responsive note throughout the Empire.

To My People

Buckingham Palace,
June 29th, 1911.

Now that the Coronation and its attendant ceremonies are over I desire to assure the people of the British Empire of my grateful sense that their hearts have been with me through it all. I felt this in the beautiful and impressive service in the Abbey—the most solemn experience of my life—and scarcely less in the stirring scenes of the succeeding days, when my people have signified their recognition and their heartfelt welcome of me as their Sovereign.

For this has been apparent, not only in the loyal enthusiasm shown in our passage to and from Westminster and in the progresses which we have made in different districts of London, but also in the thousands of messages of good will which have come to me across the seas from every part of the Empire. Such affectionate demonstrations have profoundly touched me, and have filled me afresh with faith and confidence.

Believing that this generous and outspoken sympathy with the Queen and myself is, under God, our surest source of strength, I am encouraged to go forward with renewed hope. Whatever perplexities or difficulties may lie before me and my people, we shall all unite in facing them resolutely, calmly, and with public spirit, confident that, under Divine guidance, the ultimate outcome will be to the common good.

GEORGE R.I.

DECORATING DOMINION TROOPS AFTER THE CORONATION

Each man of the military contingents from the Dominions and Colonies that took part in the Coronation procession received a medal specially struck for the occasion. At a final parade in the grounds of Buckingham Palace the King bade farewell to the Overseas troops and bestowed a number of decorations. The King and Queen with Prince Edward are here seen at the ceremony.

THEIR MAJESTIES

by

J. B. STERNDALE BENNETT

and

IRENE CLEPHANE

Biographical Sketches
of King George VI
and Queen Elizabeth

Photo] [Peter North

FIRST PORTRAITS AS "THEIR MAJESTIES"

This photograph was the first taken of King George VI and Queen Elizabeth after the accession. The King is wearing the uniform of an Admiral of the Fleet, a rank which he assumed immediately on succeeding to the throne, his previous rank having been that of Admiral. The King wears, among other orders and decorations, the sash and star of the Order of the Garter. On his birthday, which fell only two days after his accession, the King bestowed upon his Consort "the title and dignity of a Lady of the Most Noble Order of the Garter".

CHAPTER 12

THE LIFE STORY OF KING GEORGE VI

*In this chapter we follow the history of King George VI from cradle to Throne.
Of him the Prime Minister said immediately after his Accession that "more than
any of his Brothers he resembles in character and disposition of mind his Father."*

ON December 15th, 1895, the guns were booming in the Green Park and at the Tower of London to salute a royal prince born the day before at York Cottage, Sandringham. On that morning the child, who was later christened Albert Frederick Arthur George, was fourth in succession to the British throne, then occupied by his great-grandmother, Queen Victoria. Between him and the royal dignity which he was one day to assume were his grandfather (Edward VII), his father (George V) and his eighteen-months-old brother Prince Edward (Edward VIII). Between cradle and crown over forty years were to elapse.

His father, then Duke of York, had become heir presumptive three years earlier at the death of his elder brother, the Duke of Clarence. At this time, as during the short reign of his father, Edward VII, this prince was little in the limelight and was known to the public for the main part as an enthusiastic naval officer, devoted to his career, who, when he was one of a shooting party at Sandringham or Balmoral, had already proved himself to be one of the finest game shots in the country.

The infant Prince's mother, the Duchess of York, who before her marriage was known as "Princess May", was a daughter of the Duke and Duchess of Teck. The Duke, who held an ancient German title, married Mary Adelaide, daughter of the Duke of Cambridge and a cousin of Queen Victoria. Princess May was born in Kensington Palace, where she spent most of her childhood, her father and mother moving later to White Lodge, Richmond, a residence so closely associated with the early married life of the present King and Queen. Princess May had an entirely English up-bringing and one particularly fitted to the future consort and mother of kings. She had also the invaluable companionship of her brothers, one of whom, the King's uncle, the Earl of Athlone, was granted that title on the creation of the House of Windsor in 1917.

The childhood of the infant Prince Albert was spent in the normal sheltered obscurity of the British nursery. None of the fierce rays of publicity

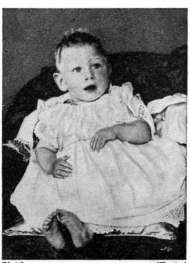

Photo]   [*Topical*

ALBERT, AGED ONE

Prince Albert, destined to become King as George VI, was born at York Cottage, Sandringham, on December 14th, 1895. He was the second child of the Duke of York (later King George V), a title bestowed upon the Prince himself in 1920.

which were to play round his own children shone on that sanctuary. Such harmless stories of childish pranks as were circulated were reserved for his volatile brother. Later photographs show him as a shy, retiring little boy, sometimes in a kilt, sometimes in naval uniform, but always, as it were, second in the picture.

When he was five years old his grandfather came to the throne as Edward VII and began a ten years' reign of exceptional social brilliance. Necessarily, his father, now Prince of Wales, succeeded to many more public duties, which brought him more in the public eye, but so overpowering was the personality of the new king that his son seemed always to live in an atmosphere of diffidence and self-effacement.

Photos]   *[Downey ; Elliott & Fry*

HAPPY HOURS OF PLAYTIME

Prince Edward, Prince Albert and Princess Mary, the three elder children of the Duke and Duchess of York, afterwards King George V and Queen Mary, are here seen in their early youth.   Princess Mary shared in all her brothers' games, even when they took a military turn, as the lower photograph shows.   Above is a photograph of the Princes and the Princess taken in 1901.

However, father and son had an excellent understanding and were in complete agreement on the important subject of the upbringing of the young Princes and their sister. Edward VII took a keen interest in the education of his grandchildren, who during his short reign were never far distant from him. In London they lived at Marlborough House; at Windsor, at Royal Lodge; and when the Court moved to Balmoral, the Prince of Wales moved to Abergeldie Castle. As a consequence, the royal children had the advantage of knowing their grandparents intimately. Very early they were left under their charge and supervision, for in March 1901 their parents left on a visit to Australia, where as Duke of Cornwall and York (he was not created Prince of Wales till his return) the late King George V opened the first Parliament of the Australian Commonwealth, and New Zealand. History was to repeat itself twenty-seven years afterwards, when as Duke of York the present King visited Australia and opened the new Parliament buildings at Canberra. He and his Duchess, too, had to leave behind an adored baby daughter to the loving care of her royal grandfather and grandmother.

In Nursery and Schoolroom

The education of royal princes must necessarily differ in many important particulars from that of all the King's subjects, however exalted. But Edward VII, who had suffered bitterly in his youth from the rigid curriculum imposed by his own parents, a curriculum which tended to isolate him from all but a few companions not of his own choice but of the royal advisers', had more enlightened views on the upbringing of children, however grave the responsibilities they might in future be called upon to shoulder. He had endeavoured to put these into practice, and his own two sons had far more liberty than had ever been allowed himself. Now with yet another generation demanding parental guidance he threw the weight of a grandfather's influence in the scale in favour of as much healthy freedom as possible, a

complete abandonment of forcing methods, and a concentration on essentials.

Nursery days for Prince Albert were happy and untroubled, spent always in healthy surroundings, the necessary discipline being administered by a much respected nurse, "Mrs. Bill", who, when her charges were off her hands, became in later years housekeeper at Buckingham Palace.

As the princes graduated from the nursery to the schoolroom, a small staff was engaged to direct their studies. Their tutor was Mr. P. J. Hansell, who had been educated at Malvern and Magdalen College, Oxford, had been a master at Ludgrove (Princess Mary's children recently attended this school) and Rossall, and was known to

Photo]   *[Topical*

EARLY INTEREST IN SPORT

The King has always been interested in all forms of sport and athletics. He is here seen, as Prince Albert of Wales, with his tutor, Mr. Hansell, and Lord Desborough, at the Amateur Athletic Associations meeting in London in 1908.

Photo]   [Central Press

TAKING GAMES SERIOUSLY

From his earliest days the King put his whole heart into everything he undertook, and in games he has striven hard and
successfully for efficiency. He began to play golf at an early
age and practised assiduously all that his coach taught him.

the Royal Family as a former tutor of Prince
Arthur of Connaught.   He had the assistance of Mlle Dussau and M. Hua for lessons
in foreign languages and also outside help
in the teaching of mathematics.

Prince Albert was an apt pupil, naturally
a studious youth with a keen desire to learn
and become proficient. His grandfather
said of him at this time, "Bertie has a
delightful nature, and is so clever, too."

Book-learning, however, was by no
means always in the forefront of the educa-
tional plan. Physical training did much to
establish the constitution of a delicate lad.
Drill was in charge of Sergeant-Major
Wright of the Coldstreams (who rose to be
Lieutenant-General Wright) and Pipe-Major
Forsyth of the Scots Guards. The soldierly

bearing of the Princes, later so noticeable
on ceremonial parades, owed much to this
early discipline.

But the physical side of their education
was not confined to the parade-ground.
They indulged in all the healthy sports of
boyhood. We hear of cricket matches with
the village lads of Sandringham or on the
lawn with the family circle. Prince Albert
was particularly deadly with his underhand
lobs and very early scored a hat trick,
clean bowling King Edward VII, his father
the Prince of Wales, and his brother
Prince Edward. Lawn-tennis, however,
soon became Prince Albert's favourite
game, and childish practice laid the foundation of that considerable skill he was to show
later in life, not only at tennis, but at that
even swifter racket game, "squash".

During these early years in the most
favourable surroundings of Windsor, Sandringham and Balmoral the young Princes
learned to ride, to shoot and to fish.
Prince Albert, with that diligence which
has characterized him all his life, slowly
but surely mastered these accomplishments.
With the example of his father before him
he could scarcely but be ambitious to be a
good shot, the gillies of Balmoral saw to it
that he knew what there was to know about
casting a fly, and his early performances in the
hunting field showed that his riding masters
had added skill to his own native pluck.

The Building of Character

But there was an element in the childhood
education of the future King immeasurably
of more value than the stereotyped instruc-
tions of his tutors. These were necessary
as a grounding in essential subjects, but
from infancy he had the incalculable advantage of the companionship of his wise
and kindly parents. From them he learnt
lessons that no tutor could convey. Their
example, a subtle influence from the beginning, taught him the manner of life led
by the selfless and devoted fathers and
mothers of this country. It taught him
how that life is led quietly and with dignity, and that a never-wavering devotion
to duty is the basis of all true happiness.

It taught him, too, that, while maintaining an exclusiveness necessary to an exalted position, it was possible to encourage and develop a sympathy with and understanding of the needs and outlook of all grades of society. That lesson once learnt never deserted him, any more than it did his brother the Duke of Windsor. From George V and Queen Mary all their sons learned to disregard class difference and to welcome even the collaboration of the extremist, if something could be gained to the solution of vital problems. The ever-increasing popularity of the House of Windsor is founded on this enlarged capacity to mix freely with every class of society, to enter into their troubles with sympathy, to understand the nature of their tasks with intelligence and to offer them not patronage but service.

§—The Training of a Prince in the Services

FOR the two elder sons of the heir to the throne a public-school career was not contemplated. Their first introduction to a world outside the family circle was when they entered the Naval Training College at Osborne. The young Prince Albert went there in the year 1909, when he was fourteen years of age. Possessed of an excellent grounding, he readily adapted himself to the normal training of a naval cadet. His natural bent was towards the scientific and mechanical branches of study which are the mainstay of the naval curriculum. There can be no question that the almost professional interest which he can take today in the most complicated machinery of the factory and the workshop has its origin in the mechanical training which he received at Osborne and at Dartmouth.

For the rest, leading the life of the ordinary cadet, he learnt the many splendid lessons which the naval training inculcates—habits of orderliness, instant obedience to command and, as a natural corollary, the power to take command. This period of his

SMILING CADET

The King was happy in his life as a cadet at Osborne and Dartmouth. He is here seen on board the Royal Yacht Victoria and Albert at Cowes in the summer of 1912.

life has no high-lights or fanciful stories. We must picture a conscientious and industrious lad, working hard and playing hard, fitting himself for a career which, had circumstances allowed it, he might well have made his own, and in which he would certainly have risen to distinction.

While at Osborne there occurred a major event in the history of his family. His grandfather, Edward VII, died, and his father ascended the throne as King George V. His new position as son of the reigning monarch and second in succession was not allowed to make a tittle of difference to his life as a naval cadet. When in 1913 he sailed in H.M.S. Cumberland (Captain Aubrey Smith) for an instructional cruise, he went with no more privileges than any of his fellows. This was his father's most strongly expressed personal wish and was a repetition of his own experience as a young naval officer.

Indeed, we can go further back to another sailor king, William IV, to find the same wise principle being observed.

That amiable monarch George III wrote to Admiral Hood:

I flatter myself that you will be pleased with the appearance of the boy who neither wants resolution nor cheerfulness which seem necessary ingredients for those who enter into that noble profession. . . . I desire that he may be received without the smallest mark of parade. I trust the admiral will receive him immediately on board. . . . The young man goes as a sailor and as such, I add again, no marks of distinction are to be shown unto him—they would destroy my whole plan.

The voyage in H.M.S. Cumberland provided the young Prince with his first introduction to the Empire overseas. The

OFF TO NIAGARA

In January 1913 the King, as Prince Albert, embarked on H.M.S. Cumberland for a cruise to the West Indies and Canada. He is here seen clad in oilskins preparatory to visiting Niagara Falls under the guidance of a stalwart official.

training ship cruised to the West Indies, Canada and Newfoundland, and the youngsters had plenty of opportunities of seeing life ashore. Here again Prince Albert, as the King's second son, was not treated with any special honour by the King's representatives. Naturally he attracted more than usual attention, and there is a story told of his reply to an autograph-hunter in Barbados, "I write awfully badly and I've got heaps of names. Do you want them all?"

Life as a Midshipman

The Prince saw something as well of Teneriffe, St. Lucia, Trinidad, Martinique, Dominica, Puerto Rico, Jamaica, Havana, Bermuda and several ports in Canada and Newfoundland. On his return from this voyage he was gazetted midshipman in H.M.S. Collingwood—the flagship of the First Battle Squadron (Vice-Admiral Sir Stanley Colville). The officer in command of the Collingwood was Captain (afterwards Admiral) James Ley, and in this ship the Prince, almost immediately after joining her, set sail for a two months' cruise of the Mediterranean, during which he visited Malta and Egypt.

The days of international crisis were drawing near, and after a period of training at Portsmouth and the Isle of Arran the Prince in the Collingwood proceeded to Devonport to take part in the great naval review which immediately preceded the War. When that calamity befell the world the Collingwood proceeded to her war station with the Prince on board. It was at this time, however, that the illness which was so sadly to hamper his naval career began to manifest itself. But, before touching on this unfortunate interlude, something may well be said of his character and abilities as a young naval officer.

He was always keen, always anxious to show his proficiency and always cheerful in the performance of the allotted task. He has been called the "engineer member of the family", his keenness manifesting itself in his particular delight in that aspect of his training. He is said also to have been particularly skilful in his handling of the picket boat. In his private relations with his fellow "snotties" he was extremely popular. He showed no trace of "side", was always ready to enter into a joke, however much youthful horseplay it involved, and was ready in all the give and take of life aboard ship. His nickname was "Mr. Johnston", and by this name he was known to all ratings.

Shortly after the outbreak of war the young Prince began to show signs of the most distressing gastric trouble. A rapid but incomplete diagnosis seemed to reveal the presence of appendicitis, and for this complaint an operation was performed. The surgeons, however, had by no means reached the seat of the trouble. Their patching up was purely temporary, although after a period of service ashore the Prince was able to rejoin his ship at Portsmouth in the following February. He was not really fit, and for months had a really miserable time battling against illness both aboard ship and ashore, where he was employed in the Operations Division at the Admiralty. In May 1916 he was once again able to rejoin H.M.S. Collingwood, this time on the eve of the greatest naval action of the War, the battle of Jutland.

Prince Albert played his part, and when on his accession to the throne he assumed the rank of Admiral of the Fleet he did so with the gratifying knowledge that he was the first British king to have fought in a first-class naval action since James II.

Photo]   [Topical

AFTER ACTIVE SERVICE

King George as Prince Albert was present at the battle of Jutland, serving on the battleship Collingwood as a midshipman. His post was in one of the forward turrets

His father had had a distinguished naval career; his ancestor William IV, who spent nine years in the Navy, was present at the relief of Gibraltar, but neither had experienced battle on the large and decisive scale. King George's two eldest sons both had the privilege, if privilege it is, of seeing war at first hand, and of Edward VIII it will be remembered that during the greatest war in history he took his place in the battle-line on the Western Front in France and in Italy.

The Collingwood in the 5th Division of the First Battle Squadron was not, in fact, very closely engaged, but her guns were in action and she was herself under fire. The future king's station was in one of the gun turrets, and for coolness and courage under fire he was mentioned in Admiral Jellicoe's dispatches. A humble task performed by him when shut up for hours in the ship's turret was brewing cocoa for the officer in charge and the gun crew.

Ill-health continued to dog him during the succeeding months, and he spent many weary weeks in hospital ships and in hospital ashore. He was gazetted to the Malaya battleship as Acting Lieutenant, but his period of active service in the Navy was drawing to a close, for in November 1917 duodenal ulcer was definitely diagnosed. An immediate operation was ordered and was successfully performed by Sir Hugh Rigby, but a long convalescence was necessary. It was felt that His Royal Highness should not again risk the rigours of service afloat in war-time. Parenthetically, it may be noted that this operation did clear away the trouble, and the immensely active life which the King has led during the past twenty years is sufficient proof that he was left with no permanent weakness.

Will power, patiently exercised to overcome all difficulties, is one of his outstanding characteristics, and while on this subject one must refer to another disability which has caused him great suffering and which he has conquered with immense courage. Since boyhood he was afflicted with a defect of speech which made public appearances an agony to him. He was obliged to stop completely in the middle of a speech, unable to articulate a particular word and undergoing the most painful mental struggles until he could accomplish the feat. What tortures he must have suffered only he could tell, but with great determination and perseverance he set about overcoming this difficulty. He pre-pared his speeches so as to avoid especially difficult words, one of which, ironically enough, was "king". Hence his constant references, with their added touch of intimacy, to "my father". He was persuaded that the trouble was purely physical and had no basis in a nervous affliction. Speech exercises were recommended and, under the care of a specialist, carried out day after day as a regular routine. No engagement or recreation was allowed to interfere with this disciplinary hour, and slowly but surely he reaped his reward. His broadcast speeches (of which there have been no fewer than thirty) and his later public utterances have shown him a clear and persuasive speaker seldom troubled with any form of hesitancy.

The closing year of the War found the young Prince Albert translated to another sphere of activity. Rejecting the shelter of invalidism, he was in February 1918 appointed to the R.N.A.S. station at Cranwell, where he performed duties as a ground officer. On the amalgamation of the R.N.A.S. and R.F.C. in April, he was gazetted Captain in the new Royal Air Force. As such he was on the staff of the R.A.F. cadet brigade at Hastings and later at Shorncliffe. Those who served with him bear testimony to the keenness with which he threw himself into this new phase of work. His duties implied setting an example of smartness and efficiency to the young cadets under him, and it is recorded that he never once missed that bugbear of all parades, P.T. before breakfast.

Photo] [Daily Mirror

SHARING A ROYAL TRIUMPH

King George V deputed Prince Albert to represent him at the triumphal re-entry of King Albert of Belgium to Brussels on November 22nd, 1918. He is here seen riding through the streets of the capital on the King's right hand. On King Albert's left hand is the Queen of the Belgians.

He was, however, to have one more glimpse of war at first hand. In October he was

THE KING—A MEMORY OF 1919

On November 11, 1919, King George VI was one of the royal mourners at the Armistice service. He is seen to the right, behind his father King George V, wearing the uniform of a Wing Commander in the Royal Air Force. On the left is his brother the Duke of Windsor, who was then Prince of Wales.

To face page 176

appointed to the staff of the Independent Force, R.A.F., whose headquarters were at Nancy under the command of Sir Hugh Trenchard. At this time the Independent Force had the most interesting and vital job, which was to carry the aerial war into the enemy's country and bomb their centres of munition production. The young Prince had the opportunity of meeting many dauntless airmen at this time and watching their nightly and most considerable contribution to final victory.

Then, on November 11, 1918, came the armistice. The future king was in no hurry to seek the safe if slightly tempestuous waters of demobilization. He stuck to his job and was appointed to the staff of Sir John Salmond, whose headquarters were at Spa. His first official task in that same month was to represent his father, the King, at the triumphal entry of King Albert to his capital of Brussels. There is a pleasing photograph (see opposite) of the British Prince riding with King Albert of the Belgians and his consort Queen Elizabeth, followed by their two children, the present King Leopold and Crown Princess of Italy, on that most momentous occasion. He had the opportunity of meeting and congratulating that day the second of the great national heroes of Belgium, the heroic Burgomaster Adolf Max of Brussels, who had just escaped from captivity in Germany.

But the War was now over, and other plans had to be formed for the future employment of Prince Albert. There was a moment when it was thought that he might return to his naval career, but clearly his

AS AIRMAN

After his health made it necessary that he should abandon a naval career, Prince Albert qualified as a pilot in the R.A.F. He is here seen at Croydon Aerodrome after a flight.

future responsibilities precluded any such course. As clearly also he was in need of a rest and change of environment. In that spirit of thoroughness, however, which must see a task that has been well begun, well finished and properly rounded off, he returned to the Air Force and qualified for his pilot's certificate, being promoted Squadron Leader in August 1919, and leaving the Force with the rank of Wing Commander.

At this time the ancient universities were offering a refuge to many young officers whose education had been interrupted by their services during the War. There was no intention in a number of cases that they should proceed to a degree, but that they should have the advantage of a university life and fill in some of the gaps in general scholarship which had necessarily been left open. It was decided that Prince Albert and his younger brother Prince Henry should be entered at the university of Cambridge. The Prince of Wales had already had some training at the university of Oxford, so that it was appropriate that the junior university should be chosen for the education of the younger sons. The two young Princes became members of Trinity College. They did not reside in college; a comfortable house was leased for the period, and Prince Albert's life-long friend, Wing Commander (now Sir Louis) Greig, who had been his M.O. at Osborne, and Mrs. Greig were installed as host and hostess. In the comparative freedom of a university, as useful in its way to the development of character as the rigid discipline of the services, Prince

Albert attended lectures in his chosen subjects. These were mainly in the schools
of history, economics and civics. It was
at this time that he founded a life-long
interest in industrial problems based on
scientific inquiry into their origins, which
has led him constantly to keep his knowledge in repair and to amass one of the
finest private libraries in this country on
the subject.

When the King was "Progged"

But during these happy, sheltered
months all was not dry as dust. One who
remembers him at this time tells the story
of how he vainly tried to elude a Proctor's
"bulldog", sent to apprehend an under-
graduate leaving the Union Society, who
was smoking a pipe whilst in academical
dress. He turned out to be Prince Albert.
The Proctor who interviewed the Prince
was Mr. T. R. Glover, of St. John's, the
present Public Orator.

The "bulldog", Mr. Lavis, who is now
on the retired list, recalls how the Prince
invited him in to have a drink when he
went to collect the fine of 6s. 8d. for the
offence. The Prince was highly amused
to hear that he had previously had a narrow
escape from being "progged" when leaving
the Corn Exchange after an inter-Varsity
boxing match without wearing a cap and
gown. He had been taken for one of the
boxers and not challenged.

The two royal brothers were regular
visitors at the Union Society weekly de-
bates, where they occupied chairs placed
in the centre gangway facing the President.
Lawn-tennis was the favourite outdoor
exercise of the King when he was *in statu
pupillari*, and he often played on the
C.U.L.T.C. courts at Fenner's.

He became a life member of many
University clubs, including the Hawks and
Union, and succeeded King George V as
Patron of the Amateur Dramatic Club.

This period of comparative leisure was
not uninterrupted by official duties. During this time the Prince of Wales was absent
for many months on his tours overseas, and
there were many occasions on which the

young Prince had to relieve his father and
act as official representative of the Throne.

Some reward was to come to him after
he had left the University and was about
to enter into the fullness of his public duties.
In the birthday honours of June 1920 he
was created Duke of York, Earl of Inverness and Baron Killarney, and "elevated
to the peerage". He had already on his
twenty-first birthday been made by his
father Knight of the Garter, but the dukedom of York gave him a title, not in any
sense hereditary, but reserved by tradition
for the reigning monarch's brother or second
son. As such he took his seat in the House
of Lords on June 23rd of that year, and as
such he was to be known to the British
public for the next seventeen years.

Back in his bachelor apartments in
Buckingham Palace, his daily programme
became regulated with the austerity observed by any other high public official.
He had his own secretarial staff, and he had
acting as his Comptroller his old friend
Wing Commander Greig. There were still
considerable periods of liberty and freedom,
but he had to hold himself constantly in
readiness for public duty, especially during
the Prince of Wales's absences abroad.
During the next few years he undertook
several important foreign missions as representative of his father, the King.

Official Duties Abroad

In February 1921 he again visited
Brussels, on this occasion to bestow, in the
King's name, a British decoration on the
gallant King Albert. This was the Distinguished Flying Cross, an apt tribute to
that monarch's intrepidity in the air and
his constant encouragement of aerial development. Burgomaster Adolf Max he invested with the insignia of Knight Grand
Cross of the Order of the British Empire.

In the following year he was present at
the marriage of King Alexander of Serbia
with Princess Marie of Rumania, and later
visited Bucharest to attend the coronation
of King Ferdinand. While at home he
attended innumerable public functions in
the interests of charity, industry or sport.

As he settled down to the normal routine of his duties the interests of the Duke of York began to flow along those channels with which his name became particularly identified. During the War much good work had been done for the welfare of the workers in munition factories. Their interests and well-being had been studied and ministered to far more thoroughly than had ever been the case under pre-War conditions. The results had been more than satisfactory, and it seemed a thousand pities that the good work should not be continued when industry returned once more to the direction of private enterprise. Men of high calibre, such as Mr. B. S. Rowntree and the Rev. R. R. Hyde, who had had the control in war-time, were at hand and ready to offer their services could encouragement be found to launch an effective scheme.

The King and the Workers

The Duke, who had always been interested in Mr. Hyde's efforts to ameliorate the conditions of boy workers, readily accepted the presidency of the newly formed Industrial Welfare Society. He accepted it not as a nominal gesture of patronage but as a definite task to be performed in the interests of the country as a whole. He saw in the office an opportunity of translating into terms of practical service an ideal very near to his heart, which was the betterment of the conditions under which the workers of this country performed their daily labours. It will be seen that throughout all his public life this ideal has been uppermost in his thoughts. It is the inspiration of his intense sympathy with the work of the Playing Fields Association and his encouragement of all good work in the interests of a healthier young Britain.

One of the chief aims of the Society is to promote a better understanding between all ranks in industry, and nobody has done more to foster this good spirit than the present King. He might have been speaking of himself when, as Duke of York, he said in one of his speeches :

"Nobody can lead, unless he has the gift of vision and the desire in his soul to leave things in the world a little better than he found them. He will strive for something which may appear unattainable but which he believes in his heart can one day be reached, if not by him, by his sucessors, if he can help to pave the way."

Again, on one occasion, speaking of sympathy as an essential quality in leadership, he said : "If you want to lead, you must be able to understand and share the joys and troubles of those whom you are trying to help. You must look at things from their point of view as well as your own."

Enthusiasm for Industrial Welfare

A man with so deep an understanding quickly realized that the foundation of his helpfulness would lie in an intimate knowledge of actual conditions. During the years that followed he never lost an opportunity of visiting factories and workshops, great or small, which offered any special points of interest. Often on his journeys at home or abroad he has risen early, or sacrificed his hours of leisure, to visit some centre of industry to which his attention has been attracted on the spot, but which was not included in the official itinerary.

Industrial welfare is not entirely a matter of canteens and clean overalls, of shower-baths and recreation grounds. It concerns the whole surroundings of the worker from the moment the blast of the siren calls him to his allotted task. It concerns the nature of the task itself. Of these facts the Duke was fully aware, and on his innumerable visits to industrial areas he has made it his business to examine with great thoroughness every process of manufacture in any particular industry. In this he has been greatly helped by his own natural enthusiasm and by his mechanical training. Whenever possible he has endeavoured to slip away from official ciceronage and see things for himself. He has always been pleased to listen to the humble workman explaining his job, and has a boyish pleasure in working the machine himself. In Glasgow they remember him driving a Corporation tram, during his Australian tour he more than once mounted the footplate and drove the engine, and when he visits a mining district he likes to descend the pit and wield a pick. In all this constant work for industrial welfare he realizes that the true goal is industrial peace.

"Our aim", he wrote, "is to create in our workshops such an atmosphere of mutual goodwill and fertile partnership that misunderstandings cannot thrive. This is just another instance of that old truth that the quality and happiness of our national life are the quality and happiness of each man and woman."

It was during the early days after the War that the Duke conceived a welfare scheme with which his name will always be associated. It had its origin in the visit to London of a party of industrial lads who wrote to the Welfare Society asking whether some football matches could be arranged for them. One of the fixtures was against a Westminster School eleven on the playground in Dean's Yard. The success of this meeting between two very different types of British youth gave the Duke his "big idea", and in the summer of 1921 the

first Duke of York's camp for public-school and industrial boys was held in a disused aerodrome on the Kent coast between Dymchurch and New Romney.

The Duke's scheme was to invite as personal guests of himself 100 boys from public schools and 100 from the industrial areas and mix them together for a week in a jolly open-air camping holiday. For messing and living they were split into sections, each with a section leader, an equal number from each category. Every year since this camp has been held, moving later to Southwold, and every year the founder has visited it, spending a whole day with the boys, entering into their sports, bathing with them, sharing their meals, joining in the camp-fire sing-song, and when able to do so sleeping under canvas.

The complete success of the idea was early established. It provided an opportunity for the exchange of points of view which could only have a broadening influence on both sides. Suspicions and differences were removed and in many instances enduring friendships made. There is no

Great Chief.

Photos]   [Keystone ; Topical

AMONG HIS YOUNGER SUBJECTS

The founding of the Duke of York's Holiday Camp at Southwold, where one hundred public-school boys and one hundred working boys spend a fortnight's holiday together, was one of His Majesty's most happy inspirations. In these photographs the King as Duke of York is seen during one of his visits to the camp where he is the Great Chief.

doubt that in his new sphere the King will continue to take an active interest in this personal experiment which has been so abundantly justified by its results.

Another national movement which has always enlisted his deepest sympathy and strongest support is the extension of available playing fields for the youth of the country. He became President of the National Playing Fields Association in 1925 and has always given it ready support.

There is a pleasant story of two London urchins who called at 145, Piccadilly, to complain that their cricket pitch on an L.C.C. site had been taken away from them. Could the Duke, please, see somebody about it? The Duke did see somebody, something was done about it, and the young enthusiasts were soon back on the site with bat and ball and a pile of coats for wicket.

The King's Marriage

The major event in the Duke's life at this time, however, was his betrothal to Lady Elizabeth Bowes-Lyon. The King's son and the daughter of a great Scottish noble house had been childhood friends and had met at intervals during the succeeding years. The story of their courtship and their marriage is told elsewhere in these pages. It was the perfect union of two kindred spirits, and as such it has remained unto this day.

The King's permission, which was readily granted, for his second son to marry into the Scottish nobility was greeted with the warmest approval by all classes of society. Modern opinion counted less and less the importance of finding consorts for Britain's princes amongst the daughters of reigning European sovereigns, and when the British people were presented with a Scottish lady, so engagingly lovely and so eminently fitted for her high position, their enthusiasm knew no bounds.

Those, however, who still felt that there was some sacred importance in the union of royal families could take comfort in the fact that the lovers were both descended from Robert II of Scotland. The Duke of York traced his ancestry from Robert II to James VI of Scotland (James I of England) and the Lady Elizabeth from Robert II through his daughter Princess Jean Stuart, who married in 1376 her ancestor, Sir John Lyon.

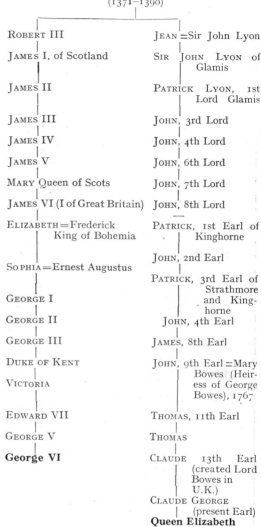

Robert II of Scotland
(1371–1390)

ROBERT III	JEAN = Sir John Lyon
JAMES I, of Scotland	SIR JOHN LYON of Glamis
JAMES II	PATRICK LYON, 1st Lord Glamis
JAMES III	JOHN, 3rd Lord
JAMES IV	JOHN, 4th Lord
JAMES V	JOHN, 6th Lord
MARY Queen of Scots	JOHN, 7th Lord
JAMES VI (I of Great Britain)	JOHN, 8th Lord
ELIZABETH = Frederick King of Bohemia	PATRICK, 1st Earl of Kinghorne
	JOHN, 2nd Earl
SOPHIA = Ernest Augustus	PATRICK, 3rd Earl of Strathmore and Kinghorne
GEORGE I	
GEORGE II	JOHN, 4th Earl
GEORGE III	JAMES, 8th Earl
DUKE OF KENT	JOHN, 9th Earl = Mary Bowes (Heiress of George Bowes), 1767
VICTORIA	
EDWARD VII	THOMAS, 11th Earl
GEORGE V	THOMAS
George VI	CLAUDE 13th Earl (created Lord Bowes in U.K.)
	CLAUDE GEORGE (present Earl)
	Queen Elizabeth

This double tree is compiled to show the line of descent from Robert II of Scotland on both sides. For King George's descent from the Anglo-Saxon sovereigns see page 296.

The engagement was announced in January and the marriage celebrated in April 1923. The honeymoon was spent at Polesden Lacey, at Glamis Castle and

Frogmore. And when the royal couple returned to town they took up their residence at White Lodge, Richmond, the childhood home of Queen Mary.

They soon entered into public life again as man and wife, one of their first duties being to attend as godparents the christening of the Crown Prince of Yugoslavia. Later in the summer of 1924 they paid an official visit to Northern Ireland. They spent a week in the northern province, receiving everywhere an enthusiastic welcome. One of the chief ceremonies of the tour was the unveiling by the Duke of a memorial to the members of Queen's University killed in the War, after which the honorary degree of LL.D. was conferred on both the Duke and Duchess.

At the end of 1924 they set out on the first of their tours of Empire, making a prolonged trip to East Africa and the Sudan. In some ways this was in the nature of a second honeymoon, enlivened by many exciting shooting expeditions. But it necessarily involved a number of official engagements of one kind and another, although the Duke himself referred to it as "quite an ordinary private visit".

They sailed from Marseilles with a small staff in the liner Mulbera on December 8th, the Duke receiving his initiation on crossing the equator, and landed at Mombasa, the port of Kenya, on December 21st. Here they were officially received and entertained both by the British colony and the native population, who treated them to exhibitions of their wildest dances. They moved on to Nairobi, the capital, and thence to their first hunting camp. Here the Duke bagged his first rhinoceros and his first lion. The whole of January was spent in a shifting camp life pursuing the varied game of Kenya, the Duke proving himself to be a fearless and resourceful shot. In early February the party was back in Nairobi, from which they set out on the second part of their journey through Uganda and down the Nile. They were met on their way to Entebbe by fleets of native canoes. Official receptions followed at

Photo]   [Keystone

WITH THE WOLF CUBS

To one with the welfare of the youth of the country so deeply at heart as the King, the Boy Scout movement has, naturally, made a great appeal. Above, he is seen during a Scout "jamboree" held at the Wembley Stadium, and a photo of the King in scoutmaster's uniform appears on page 186.

Entebbe, and at the native capital of Kampala, where they were greeted with native ceremonial and the presentation of many gifts. Then came a leisurely progress through Uganda until they reached the port of Nimule on the boundaries of Uganda and the Sudan. The most delightful part of their journey started when at Rejaf, on the Upper Nile, they embarked on the steamer Nasis and for five weeks travelled north.

Wherever possible, they landed and enjoyed good sport with the gun, or were invited to ceremonial displays by native chiefs, as, for instance, when in the neighbourhood of Tonga they were present at a parade of 12,000 Nubian warriors. They made more than one inspection of modern Sudanese development, and finished their tour at Khartoum, where they were given the most rousing reception. This was on April 7th, 1925, and after a few days' stay they embarked for home at Port Sudan.

The year 1926 was passed in the quiet but punctual performance of public duties at home, but it was a very happy year for the Duke and Duchess, for it saw the birth of their first daughter, who was named after her mother, Elizabeth. This arrival of the little Princess added the one needed touch to their domestic bliss, and it must have been a very great wrench indeed when in the following January the young parents were called upon to leave their nine-month-old baby and embark on an Imperial mission of the first importance. This was their tour of Empire, which was to culminate with the state opening of the new Parliament buildings in the new Australian capital of Canberra.

As has been said, their own parents, King George V and Queen Mary, had been called upon to make the same sacrifice years before, and they could offer the same recompense—their own loving care of the temporarily orphaned child.

In the interval between his two tours the Duke took over the presidency of the Wembley Empire Exhibition for its second year. It was typical of him that in undertaking a charge of this character he never contented himself by merely taking the chair at committee meetings or performing an opening ceremony. He took an assiduous interest in every relevant detail, kept himself constantly informed of progress, and added the great weight of his influence wherever it could be usefully applied. Naturally he made many useful contacts with men of influence overseas, and the experience proved of great value to him when he came to consider their problems on the spot.

§—The Great Imperial Mission

THE arrangements for the new tour were on a far more elaborate scale than for the "private" visit to East Africa. Months of preparation were necessary to prepare a programme which was to occupy five months and include many official ceremonies. The Duke and Duchess embarked in the battle-cruiser Renown at Portsmouth on January 6th, 1927. The chief of staff was that redoubtable War general the Earl of Cavan, while Lady Cavan was attached to the Duchess as Lady-in-Waiting. Mr. P. K. Hodgson was private, and Mr. (later Sir Harry) Fagg Batterbee political, secretary. Lieut.-Commander Colin Buist and Major T. E. G. Nugent, M.C., were the Duke's equerries. As soon as the ship had outdistanced her formal send-off the Duke settled down to the normal life aboard ship. He had a temporary squash-rackets court erected in which he played many energetic games with members of his staff and the ship's officers. He joined also in other games played aboard, but many strenuous hours had to be spent in his office with his chief of staff and his secretaries, planning the details of his tour, preparing his speeches and attending to a mass of correspondence.

One of the accredited correspondents

who accompanied the royal party, Mr. Taylor Darbishire, in his book "The Duke of York", describes a charming memory of the first afternoon at sea.   He writes :

"The four pressmen on board were bidden to afternoon tea in the Royal quarters, and as they entered the drawing-room they 'surprised' the Duke and Duchess making ready for their guests as would any young host and hostess.   The Duke held poised above his head a large chair, asking plaintively of a gaily laughing Duchess where it was to be put.   They had evidently done the arranging of the tea-table themselves, and took full charge of all the tea-pouring and cake-handing when the pressmen had

Photos]   [Central News
OUTWARD BOUND TO AUSTRALIA

On January 6th, 1927, the Duke and Duchess of York embarked on the battle-cruiser Renown on their way to open the first Parliament of the Commonwealth of Australia at Canberra.   Above, they are posing for a snapshot on deck, while top right is the ceremony of crossing the line into which both entered whole-heartedly.

settled down at their ease to enjoy their first meeting with those two whose almost every movement they were to chronicle during the next six months."

The first port of call was Las Palmas, where a landing was made in very choppy weather, but which proved useful as a rehearsal.   The British colony and the Spanish Governor both exerted themselves to make the Duke's first trip ashore a pleasant experience.

There followed the voyage across the Atlantic to Jamaica, which was reached on January 20th. Here the Duke revived many boyhood memories.   There were official receptions and informal visits ashore and an inspection of H.M. ships on the West Indian station. From Jamaica the Renown sailed to Colon and the Caribbean entrance to the Panama Canal.   The Duke paid official visits to the President

Photos] [Central News

ROYAL ACTIVITIES IN THE ANTIPODES

During their tour of Australia and New Zealand the King and Queen saw many aspects of life in the Antipodes. Our photographs show, top left, the Queen with a seven-pound salmon-trout at Tokaanu, New Zealand, and, top right, the King in the cab of the locomotive Passchendaele, which he drove from Arthur's Pass to Cass, near Christchurch. Below, the King and Queen are seen being welcomed at Sydney, Australia, by the school-children of the city.

Photo]   [Central News

HONOURING YOUNG AUSTRALIA

At Adelaide the King and Queen were guests of honour at a grand parade of three thousand Girl Guides and Boy Scouts drawn from every community in South Australia. Afterwards, the Queen inspected the Girl Guides and the King, accompanied by the Governor, Sir Thomas Bridges, presented cups to the Scouts.

The welcome to the Dominion began in Auckland harbour, where thousands of craft swarmed round the royal launch as it conveyed the Duke and Duchess ashore. This was followed by an enthusiastic "mobbing" in the streets. An interval for sport had been arranged before the official programme was entered upon, and in the Bay of Islands and its adjacent waters the Duke enjoyed some excellent game fishing. A visit was paid to Rotorua, the very centre of Maori life, where the Duke saw displays of native dancing and received many gifts. After a brief fishing and camping holiday the serious business of the tour began.

The royal progress lasted three weeks and included no fewer than fifty-three official receptions and the reading of fifty-three loyal addresses. Some of these visits were naturally little more than a brief halt at a railway station, but with his indefatigable energy the Duke took every opportunity of leaving the train and visiting points of interest. Particularly was he anxious to see any social effort in industry or agriculture which showed especial enterprise.

A great disappointment befell him in the middle of the tour when the Duchess fell ill with tonsilitis and was obliged to leave him to carry on alone. The disappointment was keenly felt by the New Zealanders themselves, but it did not detract from the hearty welcome which everywhere was accorded to the Duke himself. He visited Christchurch, Dunedin, and had a night with the "diggers". Mr. Darbishire records many amusing incidents of this time, not the least the occasion on which a local mayor, who had read his address of welcome, asked the Duke to accept "this unique gift". There were already half a hundred amongst his baggage.

Their month in New Zealand over, the Duke and Duchess set sail in the Renown for Australia. Here their duties were of a

of the Panama Republic and to the American Governor. A call at the Marquesas for the Renown to oil, and at the port of Suva in Fiji, were the only further interruptions on the voyage to New Zealand. In both places the royal party were afforded intimate glimpses of native life and were received very heartily by the native chiefs. In Fiji the chief, Ratu Popi, presented the Duke with a sperm-whale's tooth, a symbol of loyalty, and the Duke drank with him a loving-cup of kava, a potent ceremonial potion. The Renown reached New Zealand on February 22nd and remained there until March 22nd.

more strictly official character. Their first welcome was at Sydney, where again they were greeted with enthusiasm on their arrival in the harbour, where the streets were lined with cheering crowds, and where every reception was a mass demonstration of loyalty to the Throne and of personal affection for themselves. Indeed, in every city and township which they visited they had to face this spontaneous welcome, which often took the form of a lengthy procession, a march past the royal dais of all sections of the community, the big-wigs of the local clubs, the humble father wheeling a twin perambulator, and the eager "flappers" of Australia prepared to climb any lamp-post to get a snap of the royal pair.

After these exhausting ceremonies the Duke would slip away to study welfare conditions in Australian factories, to attend a reunion luncheon of ex-Service men, veterans of the Great War who had fought in Gallipoli and Flanders, of whom he could truly count himself one. Mr. Darbishire wrote that after one of these occasions "there was a huge children's display, miles away on the other side of the city, and then a university function to round off the afternoon. Mercifully that night's dinner was a private one, but there was a gala performance at the chief theatre in the evening. Yet despite all this rush the Duke fitted in a visit to a tobacco factory and a woollen mill, where he inspected not only the 'working parts', but more eagerly still the provision that had been made for the comfort and well-being of the workpeople."

The Australian tour was one long round of official visits most cheerfully paid by the Duke and Duchess, to Adelaide, to

Photo]   [Central News

THE FIRST CANBERRA PARLIAMENT OPENED

The culminating ceremony of the Duke and Duchess of York's tour in Australia was the opening of the first Parliament in the Parliament buildings of the new Federal Capital, Canberra. The photograph shows the scene in the Senate Chamber just after the Duke of York had delivered the message of King George V. Immediately behind the Duke is Lord Stonehaven, the Governor-General of the Commonwealth.

Brisbane and to Melbourne, where the Duke was present at a review of 25,000 ex-soldiers, headed by that brilliant Australian general Sir John Monash. At this parade there were present twenty-nine Australians who had been awarded the V.C. A flying trip was paid to the goldfields of Bendigo, and many other smaller towns were visited during the tour. Many opportunities were given to the royal party to see and to enjoy the sports of the country. A kangaroo hunt was arranged for the Duke, and such opportunities as were possible were given to him both to hunt and to fish.

But the main purpose of his visit was the opening of the new Federal Parliament buildings at Canberra. This ceremony was carried out with all due solemnity. Australia's great prima donna, Dame Nellie Melba, led the National Anthem. The Duke was asked by Mr. Bruce, the Australian premier, to unlock the doors. He

HIS EYE ON THE BALL

Like King Gustaf of Sweden, King George is fond of a good game of tennis. A left-handed player of more than ordinary ability, he entered for the Men's Doubles at Wimbledon in 1926 together with Wing Commander Sir Louis Greig. After a hard struggle, they succumbed before a crack pair in Gore and Roper Barrett.

Photos]   [Topical

A DAY'S HUNTING

One of the King's favourite relaxations is a day's hunting, and in the photograph above he is seen as the field moves off at the opening meet of the Quorn Hunt, the most famous pack in England, established in the eighteenth century.

declared the building open and delivered a message from the King. The chief object of the tour fulfilled, there remained only a brief visit to Perth and Western Australia before the royal party embarked once more in the Renown.

Back in the Old Country, the Duke settled down at once to the routine of his manifold duties. By his father's expressed wish, he of all his brothers identified himself most closely with the life of Scotland. Here the assistance of his Scottish bride was particularly helpful. In 1929 he represented the King as Lord High Commissioner to the General Assembly of the Church of Scotland. This was the year of the union of the Churches, and it was the first time for centuries that a son of a reigning

Photos]   [Topical: 'Times' ' Associated Press

THE CROWN MAKES CONTACT WITH THE PEOPLE

The Royal Family have always taken an active personal interest in the working life of the people, and have lost no opportunity to examine for themselves the conditions under which their humbler subjects live and work. Thus we see the King and Queen (top left) preparing to descend the Glamis Pit, Kibblesworth, Durham, in July 1936, while, next, the King is seen shaking hands with a workman at an ironworks in the Midlands. Below (left) the King is seen chatting to a disabled ex-serviceman at an annual reunion of the R.N.V.R., and (right) with General Sir Ian Hamilton on Armistice Day in Edinburgh.

monarch had filled the office. On more than one occasion the Duke visited Edinburgh to attend the Armistice Day celebrations, and it was he who led the Jubilee rejoicings in the summer of 1935. His last public appearance as Duke of York was made in Edinburgh, which he visited to be installed Royal Grand Master Mason of Scotland. Masonry had always claimed his enthusiastic interest, and at the time of his accession he held office as Provincial Grand Master of Middlesex.

Visits to industrial districts, such as the Tyneside, always occupied a considerable portion of the working year. He has thus always kept constantly refreshed his knowledge of working conditions and the steps taken to mitigate distress in the so-called depressed or special areas.

Two other causes may be mentioned with which he has closely identified himself. One was the Safety First movement, the other the British Empire Cancer Campaign. He has spoken eloquently in the interest of both these institutions, which are playing a vital part in safeguarding the happiness of the nation.

The King is not a man with any pronounced hobbies. He is fond of reading and fireside evenings, enjoys almost any form of sport, and is adept in several. He keeps himself fit with tennis and squash, enjoys a day with the rod or the gun, and when in Scotland likes to exercise his prowess as a deer-stalker. His handicap at golf has been as low as ten, and in 1930 he played himself in as captain of the Royal and Ancient with a drive of 180 yards. In 1926 he appeared in the All England tennis championships at Wimbledon partnered by Wing Commander Greig in a doubles match against A. W. Gore and H. Roper Barrett. This match was lost, but the Duke and Wing Commander Greig had earlier won the Air Force doubles in the Services championship. The King, like his brothers, is an excellent dancer, and enjoyed taking the floor at the many charity balls to which he gave his patronage.

Long may he reign! It may be prophesied with complete certainty that the longer he occupies the throne the more he will enter into the affections of his people, who in all confidence look to him to carry on the high traditions of his office.

Photo]   *[Bertram Park*

IN PRIVATE LIFE

Owing to the multitude of official engagements the King is called upon to fulfil, the majority of photographs depict him in either naval, military or air force uniforms. The above is the first studio portrait of the King to be taken after his accession showing him in his private capacity as the "First Gentleman in the land".

CHAPTER 13

THE ROMANCE OF OUR QUEEN ELIZABETH

The Queen is the first lady not of royal birth to be Queen since the days of Henry VIII. The romantic story of Her Majesty's life and many incidents showing how she has won the hearts of the people are related in this chapter

THE morning of April 26th, 1923, broke dull and chill. The thin line of spectators—mostly women and children—that had by nine o'clock already collected along both sides of the route of the wedding processions was hidden under a roof of umbrellas. Despite the unpromising weather, however, the line that had been one deep at nine was three and four deep at ten : when the rain stopped, the policemen folded away their waterproof capes, and the sun struggled to peep through the clouds. Long before eleven the crowd had grown into a dense swaying mass—a gay, good-tempered crowd desiring only one thing more to complete its happiness : that the sun also would play its part by the time the bride appeared.

Street vendors did a brisk trade in mementoes of the occasion—illustrated programmes, flags, pocket handkerchiefs adorned with portraits of the royal groom and his bride—and not the least flourishing trade was carried on by those who had brought stools to sell : at ten o'clock it was still possible to buy one for a shilling or so ; three minutes before the procession was due to pass, the price had risen to five shillings, so anxious were the people who had waited so long to make sure of seeing something of the procession. The many who were already prepared to rise to a higher level on their wooden stools made the others almost desperate in their desire to do likewise.

Eleven struck—and the crowd ceased to be a collection of individuals chaffing and joking good-humouredly with one another and became a cheering mass all alike intent on one thing : the procession that began with the passing of Queen Alexandra, than whom both for beauty and graciousness no royal lady has ever excited deeper warmth of affection among the British people. Her carriage was followed by another, in which rode the King and Queen, with Prince George (now Duke of Kent). As the royal parents passed, everyone agreed that they looked as happy as all parents should look who are about to see their son wedded to the woman of his choice with their entire approval. Another carriage came into view—and this time cheer upon cheer and a fluttering of flags and handkerchiefs marked its progress, for it contained the bridegroom with his brothers, the Prince of Wales—for so brief a time our King, and now the Duke of Windsor—and Prince Henry, now Duke of Gloucester.

The Coming of the Bride

And while the members of the Royal Family, preceded by military bands playing appropriately non-martial music, and escorted by companies of Life Guards, were proceeding from Buckingham Palace to the Abbey of Westminster, away in Mayfair outside the modest house in Bruton Street that was then the London home of the Earl of Strathmore another carriage stood, waiting for the bride. Exactly to the time arranged—at twelve minutes past eleven precisely—a small, slim figure stepped

Photo]   [Topical

LADY ELIZABETH LEAVES FOR HER WEDDING

Lady Elizabeth Bowes-Lyon, youngest daughter of Lord and Lady Strathmore, was married to the Duke of York on April 26th, 1923. Here we see the bride leaving her father's town house in Bruton Street, Mayfair, for the journey in procession to Westminster Abbey—the first appearance before the public eye of the future Queen.

last of her maidenhood and, even more onerous, the last she would take as a member herself of the people. It was the first time the people of England encountered the sweet, spontaneous smile that was to become famous, and instantly it won a place in the hearts of all who saw it for the young girl who was to become affectionately known throughout the Empire as "the Little Duchess".

The bride wore a floor-length gown of medieval style, made of chiffon moiré in an old ivory tint to match the marvellous old lace, lent by Queen Mary, that, arranged cap-wise on her head, flowed down at the sides to the hem of her gown and covered the train behind. Embroideries of pearls and silver thread enriched the gown's simplicity, and about the bride's shoulders was thrown a cape of ermine, the gift of the King.

Cheers greeted her on the threshold of her home, and cheers, growing louder and more affectionate, greeted her all along the route to the Abbey as, still smiling and self-possessed—a proof of her happy confidence—she rode beside her father to meet her royal groom. All the way she chatted happily with her father, turning from time to time from smiling at him to smile at the friendly, shouting crowd.

across the threshold. For the first time in her life the Lady Elizabeth Bowes-Lyon faced a London crowd—the heart and centre of their affectionate interest and curiosity. Despite her mere twenty-two years and her inexperience, she did not flinch. Her face was unveiled, and with a quiet self-possession that had no hauteur and no apparent nervousness, she paused a moment to smile at the spectators who had gathered about her home to wish her God-speed upon her momentous journey—the

Unlike the carriages that had passed before, with colour and jingling of martial gaiety, that in which the Lady Elizabeth rode had no brilliant escort : four policemen mounted on white horses preceded it, four more on light greys followed.

Inside the Abbey, the greyness of the morning made the dim light that always fills the great edifice dimmer than usual. But the guests began to assemble early, and soon the scarlet of uniforms, the glitter of gold lace, of ribbons and orders, and the infinitely varied hues of the wonderful dresses worn by beautiful women brought colour and brightness into the dim interior. Only the untenanted sacrarium, where stood the rows of white-and-gold chairs on which the families of the bride and bridegroom were to sit, was lighted.   There were no flowers, but the banners, the rich embroideries, the sacred vessels of gold that adorn the sanctuary glinted expectantly. And then at last the sun struggled through the clouds, and its cheerful light filtered through the lofty windows of the Abbey.

Queen Alexandra, dressed in purple velvet trimmed with gold lace, the King, and the Queen, wearing a gown of aquamarine blue embroidered with silver, arrived and were escorted to their places. Then came the bridegroom : he was wearing the grey-blue uniform of a Group Captain of the Royal Air Force, with the blue ribbon of the Garter across his breast. Just behind him walked his supporters— the Prince of Wales in the scarlet of the Grenadier Guards, also wearing the Garter ribbon, and Prince Henry, in naval uniform. They, too, reached their appointed places. As the Duke stood waiting a little apart from his brothers, Queen Alexandra rose impulsively from her place and kissed him.

SOLEMN CEREMONY OF ELIZABETH'S ROYAL WEDDING

The marriage of the Duke of York and Lady Elizabeth Bowes-Lyon was solemnized in Westminster Abbey, the ceremony being performed by the Archbishop of Canterbury, then Dr. Randall Davidson.   Members of the Royal Family seen in this photograph include the King and Queen, Queen Alexandra, and, to the right of the bridegroom, the Prince of Wales (best man) and Prince Henry.

The Queen smiled at him, and the King throughout the ceremony watched him with a look of loving friendliness.

Glancing at the cushions on which he and his bride were to kneel, the Duke made some remark to the Prince of Wales, who, with a laugh, stepped forward and re-arranged them. Then the organ began to play the Bridal March, and the Duke turned with shining eyes to meet his bride.

Escorted by her father, the Lady Elizabeth entered the Abbey. As she stepped through the door, a seemingly enormous figure clad in a vast scarlet gown approached her. From his great hand dangled a dainty white object—it seemed to be a handkerchief bag—which the bride had left in her carriage. She took it from him, with a smile of thanks, and walked forward. Then for a moment she moved to one side and stooped. When she stood up again, she no longer carried her bridal bouquet of white roses : she had laid it on the tomb of the Unknown Warrior.

The Earl of Strathmore's scarlet uniform threw the whiteness of the bride's gown into vivid relief ; and the train of eight bridesmaids who followed her, in dresses of cloudy white chiffon with floating side-panels of green, were a picture of virginal simplicity.

The bride and groom met before the altar, and throughout the familiar marriage service that is the same for prince and commoner, they seemed aware of none but

Photo]   *[Bassano*

ROYAL BRIDE AND BRIDEGROOM WITH THEIR PARENTS

This group, taken after the Royal Wedding on April 26th, 1923, shows the Duke of York and his Duchess, together with the Earl of Strathmore, the Countess of Strathmore, Queen Mary and King George V. The Earldom of Strathmore and Kinghorne is an ancient Scottish dignity dating back to the seventeenth century; the Earl is also Baron Bowes of the United Kingdom.

each other. The ceremony over, the joy-bells pealed out, and the bridal couple, now man and wife, headed the procession back to Buckingham Palace, where, at the wedding breakfast, the King announced that he had conferred on his daughter-in-law the title and dignity of Royal Highness. The Duke and his Duchess appeared on the balcony to acknowledge the acclamations of the people gathered about the Queen Victoria memorial. Both were full of joy and laughter, and

Photo]   *[Dorien Leigh*

HONEYMOON HOME OF THE DUKE AND DUCHESS

Polesden Lacey, a beautiful country-house near Dorking, Surrey, was lent to the Duke and Duchess of York by the Hon. Mrs. Ronald Greville for a few days of their honeymoon. The mansion, with its extensive grounds, once belonged to R. B. Sheridan, the playwright. It was often visited by King Edward VII.

on the face of the Duke as he looked down at his smiling bride was a truly winsome expression of delight in her happiness, and in the instantaneous success of her first public appearance.

Soon the time came for the bridal pair to set out on their honeymoon. For the journey to Polesden Lacey—a fine old house near Dorking lent by Mrs. Ronald Greville—the Duchess changed into a dress of *crêpe romain* in a soft shade of dove-grey with a slightly beige tinge in it. It had short sleeves and a coatee, and was embroidered all over in self-colour. With it went a travelling coat-wrap of *crêpe marocain* in the same shade, trimmed with wheels of drawn thread work of its own material. Her small hat, in tones of brown, had an upturned brim and a feather mount. Her sandal-shaped shoes were of beige antelope.

An open landau drawn by four grey horses emerged into the courtyard of Buckingham Palace on its way to Waterloo Station. In it sat the Duke and the Duchess, both looking supremely happy. They were met by a perfect fusillade of confetti aimed with a will by the royal princes, the bridegroom's brothers, and by the bridesmaids. From the balcony above leant Queen

Mary, to drop on the departing couple a shower of rose petals made by blind workers.

Thus was celebrated the wedding of our present King and Queen.

But what manner of woman was this young girl to whom the King's second son had plighted his troth? Some people have called the Lady Elizabeth Bowes-Lyon's romance a fairy-tale. But although it is true that, like Cinderella, the Lady Elizabeth had two elder sisters and was wooed and won by a prince, there the resemblance of her story to this favourite tale of the nursery ends. For no child ever had more loving parents or more loving elder sisters (and brothers) than the sedate girl who grew into the sedate and self-possessed woman who was to capture the heart of the Duke of York. "I find," said her father, the Earl of Strathmore, at the time of her engagement, "that Lady Elizabeth is most popular with all the tenants at St. Paul's Walden Bury and the villagers of Whitwell. They have known her since she first came there as a baby of less than a year. In her earliest days Lady Elizabeth was always sedate and restrained. She was always more interested in her dolls' houses and her dolls than in how to tease the workmen on the estate and her tutors. Not that she was above childish mischief, as many of the tenants will tell you, but she always preserved a sedate demeanour." And, looking at the pictures of her all through her childhood and girlhood that illustrate the Lady Cynthia Asquith's biography of her, one begins to understand the inner serenity of the nature that met with such natural self-possession so sudden a transformation from the seclusion of a sheltered home-life to the blaze of publicity that surrounds the wife of a king's son.

§—Childhood and Youth in Scotland and England

BORN on August 4th, 1900, the Lady Elizabeth Bowes-Lyon was the ninth child, and the third daughter, of the Earl and Countess of Strathmore. On her father's side she can trace her descent back to a certain Sir John Lyon of Forteviot, Chamberlain of Scotland, who in 1372 married the Lady Jean Stuart, daughter of King Robert II, and from the King received the Thanage of Glamis that has remained in the family ever since. On her mother's side she descends from Queen Elizabeth of York, daughter of Edward IV and consort of Henry VII, first of the Tudor monarchs, by whose marriage were at last united the long-warring and much-diminished houses of York and Lancaster.

The Lady Elizabeth was several years younger than the next youngest before her ; but a little less than two years later came David, last of the big family, her dearly loved brother and inseparable childhood companion. Together they played ; together they learned their first lessons with their mother as teacher, and until the time came for David to go to school they were scarcely ever apart.

Most of the year was spent at St. Paul's Walden Bury, the Queen Anne house near Welwyn in Hertfordshire where Her Majesty was born. With its rose-red brick, its green lawns and its flowers, no sweeter, friendlier home could be imagined. "It must have been lovely to be a child in the surroundings of St. Paul's Walden Bury", wrote Lady Cynthia Asquith. "On a summer's day the place has about it an especially delicious smell of country, and an insistent drowsy hum of bees and cooing of wood-pigeons. Lovely alleys of smooth green grass invite running feet, and in the garden are a dairy, a knobbly oak too stout for six children's outstretched arms to encompass, peacocks of clipped hawthorn, ilex and mulberry trees ; every variety of rose behind hedges of clipped yew, and an ambitious and wonderfully successful rock-garden."

Fragrant Memories of Youth

But best of all—and the feature of the garden which has remained most vivid in the Queen's memories of her childhood—is a small starfish-shaped wood of converging alleys so laid out that it gives a successful illusion of being part of a large forest. This, so Her Majesty told Lady Cynthia, is what she goes back to: "At the bottom of the garden, where the sun always seems to be shining, is THE WOOD—the haunt of fairies, with its anemones and ponds, and moss-grown statues, and THE BIG OAK under which she reads and where the two ring-doves, Caroline-Curly-Love and Rhoda-Wrigley-Worm, contentedly coo in their wicker-work 'Ideal Home'. There are carpets of primroses and anemones to sit on, and she generally has tea either in the shadow of the statue of Diana or near another very favourite one called the 'Running Footman' or the 'Bounding Butler' (to grown-up people known as the Disc-Thrower). These statues live in cut-out grassy places, and sometimes there are wild strawberries about them, sometimes bee-orchises . . ."

From their smiling Hertfordshire home the Bowes-Lyon family migrated each year for three months to Glamis Castle. Never were two dwellings in greater contrast. St. Paul's Walden Bury is an embodiment of the calm spirit of an age that knew not warfare. Glamis, with its turrets and its thick stone walls, dates from a darker era of social development when every man's hand was against his neighbours.' Not that a first glimpse at its exterior gives this impression, for Glamis is an admirable example of Scottish baronial architecture, from which style surely sprang the picture of every castle in fairyland. With its rounded towers capped by extinguisher-like turrets and its unordered piling of one turret above another, seen on a sunny day it has the typical aspect of the Fairy Prince's magnificent dwelling, the Sleeping Beauty's mysterious home.

The Queen's Ancestral Home

Most of the present structure belongs to the seventeenth century; but incorporated in it are remains far more ancient than that—some parts, indeed, are said to date from the eleventh century, when Macbeth was Thane of Glamis and slew King Duncan within its walls—though the accuracy of this location for that event is now disputed. Whether or not, however, Glamis was the scene of that particular tragedy, it has seen stirring times and doubtless witnessed many a treacherous deed in those dark days of Scotland's history when clan hated clan with a passion incomprehensible to the more sober-minded man of today. It contains dungeons, and massive walls fifteen feet thick, as well as gracious rooms in which a child of the twentieth century can feel at home; and the legends connected with it are many, the most famous being the mysterious secret never known to more than three people at one time—the reigning earl, his heir on reaching his majority, and the factor of the estate for the time being. What that secret is, no one knows save those to whom it is traditionally imparted, for none of these has ever betrayed it.

One legend has it that Patie, the wild Earl of Strathmore, who was "notoriously good at all the vices", having failed to persuade either friend or servant to join him in the wickedness of playing cards on the Lord's Day, swore that he would play with the "deil himsel" rather than give up his desire. His rash boast was heeded by the Evil One: a tall, dark stranger appeared

Photo]   [*Sport & General*

ENGLISH SEAT OF LORD STRATHMORE

The childhood of Queen Elizabeth was largely spent at St. Paul's Walden Bury (above), where she was born on August 4th, 1900, and became engaged in January 1923. This noble red brick house, which is near Welwyn in Hertfordshire, is therefore even richer in memories to the Queen than the Strathmores' historic seat in Scotland—Glamis Castle (see page 198)—with its very different character and environment on the threshold of the room to which the Earl had retired. For hours the two gambled, cursing horribly the while, and then suddenly the stranger vanished as mysteriously as he had appeared, having extracted from Earl Patie the bond usual to such meetings in payment of the debt the Earl had incurred in his reckless play. It was five years before the Earl died, but ever after strange sounds rang through the corridors, coming from the room where he had played his fatal game, until at last it was bricked up ; and now no one knows any longer where it is situated—unless, indeed, that is the secret handed down from generation to generation. Even in the nineteenth century quite matter-of-fact visitors asserted that they had heard strange and unaccountable noises and seen a huge figure in armour stalking about the castle ; and though, in these days of scientific miracles, one dismisses such "manifestations" as figments of the imagi-nation, there is no doubt that if any place has a claim to be haunted, that place is Glamis.

All about the great hall of the castle are hunting trophies and medieval armour. On the wall of the drawing-room hangs a portrait of Claverhouse by Peter Lely ; portraits of Charles II and James II, as well as paintings in the chapel, were done by Jacob de Wet for the first Earl of Strathmore, who found the castle bare after it had been occupied by Cromwell's troops. James II's son, the Old Pre-tender, spent a night there, with eighty of his followers, in 1715, his host going out to battle and death next day in support of his royal guest.

Sir Walter Scott stayed at Glamis in 1793. He was allotted a room in which, as he heard door after door shut, he began to feel that he was "too far from the living and somewhat too near the dead", so impressed was he by the eeriness of the

HISTORIC CASTLE OF GLAMIS IN THE COUNTY OF ANGUS

It was at romantic Glamis (pronounced "Glahms"), with its legends of Macbeth and Duncan and its historic memories of the Stuarts and Sir Walter Scott, that the future Queen spent as a child three months of every year on holiday. Glamis Castle is said to be the oldest inhabited house in the country, and is certainly a fine example of medieval baronial architecture.

antique structure : an impression that, one would have thought, ought to have been dispelled by the bumper he had drunk from the Lion Cup of Glamis, a silver beaker holding about a pint. Some thirty years earlier, Thomas Gray, who wrote the famous "Elegy", had visited Glamis and gone on a Highland tour with the then Lord Strathmore, whom he had known at Cambridge.

Such were the two homes in which the greater part of Her Majesty's youth was spent. There were, however, occasional visits to Streatlam Castle in Durham, another seat of the Earl of Strathmore, since sold, and to London, where the Earl then had a beautiful Adam house in St. James's Place. It was during one of these visits to London, indeed, that she first met the King. She was but five years old, and the occasion was a children's party given by Lady Leicester ; but the small girl made such an impression upon the schoolboy—then at the usually unimpressionable age of ten—that he recognized her at once when they met again thirteen years later.

She was, indeed, a child who never failed to make an impression, and a very charming one, on both adults and other children. Rarely is the child born that has this double gift, but Queen Elizabeth had it. Her sedateness, no doubt, earned her the interest of her elders ; her natural sweetness earned her the love of her contemporaries. "She was an extraordinarily graceful, dainty and engaging child", said an old friend of the family. Madame Matilde Verne, her music mistress, described her as a very intelligent pupil with a very good ear for music, and Madame Verne's sister, who gave the Queen her first lessons, - makes the illuminating remark, "She was a dear little girl. I used to lift her on and off the pianostool oftener than was necessary just

Photo]   [Lafayette

WITH HER BROTHER IN CHILDHOOD

The favourite companion of Lady Elizabeth during her early childhood days before the outbreak of the Great War was her youngest brother, the Hon. David Bowes-Lyon. Encouraged to lead a healthy and unspoiled life, the children are seen above dancing a minuet together.

because she was so nice to take hold of."

The adored David was her companion in music lessons as in dancing lessons and schoolroom tasks, and altogether delightful the two children were when, at the age of nine and seven, they gravely performed a minuet for the entertainment of the guests at Glamis. "She and her brother were like little fairies dancing about," said Mrs. Thompson, who served the family as housekeeper for nearly thirty years. "She had a very happy childhood, and always good health to enjoy it."

But then into this sunny life came the shadow of the Great War. On her fourteenth birthday, as she sat in a box at the theatre enjoying a birthday treat, the Queen heard that war had been declared. The people seemed to go mad with enthusiasm. But the harsh reality of war came home to the Strathmore family even earlier than to many, for within a few days of its outbreak her four elder brothers were under arms. The Queen went to Glamis—how different from all previous August arrivals, with their pleasant anticipations of romps in the castle, rides over the hills and the heather, cricket matches against teams from far and near! Glamis was being prepared as a war hospital. The Queen was too young to take any official hand in the nursing (her sister, Lady Rose, went through a course of training in a London hospital to fit her for the task); but her childish presence helped to cheer the wounded men who soon came to fill the silence left by the four absent brothers. Lessons were sadly neglected in favour of knitting comforters and making sleeping-bags for the soldiers, playing whist with the wounded, and carrying out obscure duties in scullery and pantry.

War-time Memories

The autumn of 1915 brought great sorrow : her brother Fergus was killed at Loos ; and early in 1917 Michael was reported killed. It proved afterwards that he had been taken prisoner ; but for a long while he was too ill to communicate with his family, and he was not repatriated until the end of the War.

The youthful Lady Elizabeth was an enthusiastic amateur photographer, and one of the many thoughtful things she did for the wounded men who found a brief haven at Glamis from the strain of war was the taking of snapshots for them to send to their friends and relations. This, unfortunately, on one occasion led to a sad misunderstanding. A certain Sergeant Pearne had been sent to Glamis with a shattered right shoulder, and his family had been warned (though the sufferer did not know this) that he might have to lose his arm. In due course the Lady Elizabeth took a portrait of him ; but it so happened that he was sitting in such a way that his right arm could not be seen.

When his parents received it, they thought that he had certainly had his arm amputated, and was trying to conceal the fact from them. A friend wrote to him begging him to tell them the worst, and at least relieve their doubts. Whereupon Lady Elizabeth took another snapshot, full face this time, showing clearly that the arm was still in place—and his mother's fears were set effectually at rest.

But even the stress of war-time and the presence in the grim old castle of acute physical pain could not, happily, altogether damp down the Lady Elizabeth's youthful good spirits. On one memorable occasion she entered the ward with her "cousin", a veiled "lady" dressed in cloak, skirt, furs and a becoming hat, who chatted brightly, in the manner of too many lady visitors of that day, with the men whom suffering had made more remote, if possible, from such inanities than they are in normal times. The soldiers listened to her amiably, voted her a pleasant lady, and were only aware of how they had been hoaxed when they were informed next day by brother David that he had been the "lady" visitor introduced to them by Lady Elizabeth as her cousin.

Fighting a Fire

It was during the War that the most exciting event in the Queen's otherwise happily uneventful early personal life happened. This was the great fire at Glamis. It occurred towards the end of 1916, and, beginning in the upper rooms of the central keep, which is nearly a hundred feet high, spread so rapidly, on account of the strong wind that was blowing at the time, that it seemed as though the whole castle would be involved in the conflagration. Luckily, the Lady Elizabeth noticed the smoke soon after the fire broke out. She immediately telephoned, not only to the fire brigades at Glamis and Forfar, but, fortunately, also to the fire brigade at Dundee. By the time 'the local brigade arrived, the roof was on fire in several places, and flames—perhaps when unconfined the most sinister sight in

Photos]   [Bedford Lemere ; Hoppé : Bertram Park

THE QUEEN AS LADY ELIZABETH AND DUCHESS OF YORK

Lady Elizabeth Bowes-Lyon, youngest but one of the ten children of the Earl and Countess of Strathmore, was born at St. Paul's Walden Bury on August 4th, 1900. This series of portraits shows (top left) a miniature by Mabel Hankey of Lady Elizabeth at the age of five : (top right) as a schoolgirl of fourteen ; (bottom left) at the time of her marriage in 1923 : and (bottom right) as Duchess of York the world—were leaping upwards. But the Glamis and Forfar firemen found they could do nothing : their hose-pipes were not long enough to enable them to use the waters of the Dean, flowing tantalizingly past a few hundred yards away. It began to look as though Glamis could not be saved. Still, there were things within it that could be rescued ; and, having first organized a party armed with brooms to guide safely down the stone stairs a torrent of water that flowed from a lead tank which had burst in the heat, the Queen then arranged a long queue of people who passed pictures, pieces of furniture and other valuables from hand to hand to the safety of the lawns outside.

At last the Dundee fire brigade arrived. Their equipment proved adequate for dealing with the situation, though the fire had got such a hold that at one moment the successful issue of their efforts was in doubt. But at last the flames were got under, and the inhabitants of the castle were able to go to rest in peace. The damage done, however, was considerable, and it was years before the necessary repairs were completed.

It was on this occasion that the Lady Elizabeth made the one sharp remark that has ever been recorded. One of the on-lookers who had gathered to watch the fire bothered her with many questions as to how the fire had started, and who was to blame, and so on and so on. "I've no time to make conversation," in an un-wontedly crisp voice, was the only response he got.

§—Her Life as Duchess of York

AT last the War years were over, though Glamis still sheltered damaged men until late in 1919, and the friends the Strathmores had made among the soldiers they had tended continued long after they had dispersed to their homes—some in far-away Australia and New Zealand—to correspond with their benevolent hosts. But during the period of hostilities the Lady Elizabeth reached and passed that important seventeenth birthday which is considered to change the society schoolgirl into the society woman. There were no Courts in those days, and, therefore, no presentations, no great balls and lavish musical parties in the great houses of Mayfair (now for the most part demolished) familiar to those who reached the age of "coming-out" in pre-War days. Very different was the entry into society of Lady Elizabeth from that of her sisters, who had made their début in fashionable society with all the pomp and circumstance customary in their circle. The Lady Eliza-beth, by virtue of the social status of the family to which she belonged, gradually under her mother's wing began to take her natural place in society without any formal coming-out.

Her gracious charm, her gentleness, her extraordinary power of putting others at ease, and, not least, her flower-like face, soon made her friends wherever she went ; and one of the warmest of her friendships was with the Princess Mary (now the Princess Royal)—a friendship that was publicly recognized by the Princess's choice of the Lady Elizabeth as one of her brides-maids when she married Lord Lascelles in 1922. After that event—spectacular, as befitted the first marriage in the family of the reigning sovereign—people began to notice that the Duke of York was often to be seen at gatherings that included Lady Elizabeth, and that they frequently danced together : neither circumstance perhaps so very remarkable, since they moved in the same circles, and Her Majesty was a good and indefatigable dancer who loved dan-cing. But many were the people who said, "I told you so", when on February 12th, 1923—not quite a year after Princess Mary's wedding—the King gave his formal consent "to the contracting of matrimony between His Royal Highness Albert Frederick Arthur George, Duke of York, and the Lady Elizabeth Angela Margaret Bowes-Lyon, youngest daughter of the Right Honourable Claude George, Earl of Strathmore and Kinghorne". Not till a good many years later did it become generally known that the Lady Elizabeth, feeling herself, like the sweet and modest person she is, unequal to the position that might one day be hers, had twice refused the Duke. Some say that after the second refusal Queen Mary pleaded her son's suit, some say the Prince of Wales pleaded his brother's. Possibly both urged her to change her mind—there is no doubt that they both rightly felt that this diffident young girl would be an ornament to the Royal Family. In any case, the Duke of York proved a determined lover, and, having been rejected in 1921 and in 1922, tried again in 1923, in that little wood at St. Paul's Walden Bury which holds so many memories of childish happiness for Her Majesty; and there at the third time he was successful.

"I am very happy, but quite dazed", wrote the Lady Elizabeth to a friend when matters were settled at last. "We hoped we were going to have a few days' peace first, but the cat is now completely out of the bag and there is no possibility of stuffing him back." So the King's second son won his bride, and two months later they were married in Westminster Abbey.

After spending a few days at Polesden Lacey—its beautiful views, splendid trees and spacious, secluded grounds must have made it a honeymoon paradise—the young couple went north to the Duchess's beloved Glamis. There they stayed until the end of May, when they came south again, to spend the last two weeks of their honeymoon at Frogmore. After that, they took up residence at White Lodge, the house in Richmond Park where Queen Mary spent her girlhood. This comfortable Georgian house (it was built by George II for Queen Caroline), with its dignified exterior, large rooms and pleasant gardens, must have proved a delightful home. It is not very far from London either; but even this short distance began to prove a serious handicap as the public and official engagements of the Duchess rapidly increased. She found herself inundated with requests to act as patroness, to lay foundation stones, to open buildings, to grace this, that and the other function with her sunny presence. To each such request she gave the most careful consideration. Many invitations had to be refused—even had the Duchess been convinced of the complete worthiness of every cause she was asked to countenance, no one human being could

Photo]   *[Central Press*

FIRST DAYS AS A ROYAL DUCHESS

This photograph of the Duke and Duchess of York was taken in the grounds of Polesden Lacey during the first few days of their honeymoon. At the time of her marriage the Duchess was only twenty-two years of age, being five years younger than her royal husband.

have fulfilled all the engagements this would have involved ; but, even so, her days and evenings became more and more taken up with appearances at Court and at public functions. The Duke and Duchess began to think of taking a house in London. During the 1924 season the Princess Mary lent them Chesterfield House (since pulled down to make room for a block of flats with the same name). Next year, on their return from a tour in East Africa—unlike the heroes of so many Victorian novels, the Duke did not go to shoot lions to recover from unrequited love; he took his young wife with him— the Duchess accompanied the Duke on a tour of the industrial North of England. In the autumn they spent a month at Glamis and another at Balmoral. When they went back to London, they occupied Curzon House for a time ; and then, in the spring of 1926, when Her Majesty was expecting the birth of her first child, they took up residence at her parents' house— the house from which she had been married—in Bruton Street.

There, on April 21st, 1926, the Princess Elizabeth was born, and still a new phase began in the life of the sedate little girl of Glamis and St. Paul's Walden Bury.

Even in those days it seemed highly probable that though the Duke and Duchess of York might never come to the throne, their child would inherit it, and there was a certain amount of disappointment when it became known that a princess and not a prince had been born. But then people began to tell one another that (save in the case of Mary Tudor, whose lamentable reign was conveniently forgotten) England had always enjoyed well-being under a female sovereign ; and when it was learned that the infant Princess was to be called Elizabeth, after her mother, this was taken as an omen of future prosperity—for under what sovereign had England risen to greater prestige than under the great Elizabeth Tudor ?—and it is safe to say that when the Duchess's second child was expected, not a few would have been disappointed if it had proved to be a boy. But that is anticipating.

The baby Princess was only eight months old when her mother was called upon to leave her for six months : the Duke had to go to Australia to open the new Parliament House at Canberra, and it was felt to be imperative that his wife should accompany him. The Duchess knew that she was leaving the infant in excellent hands—in the care not only of two devoted grandmothers, but also in the experienced charge of her own childhood's nurse. But it must have been a heartbreaking business to leave the small creature just at that moment when dawning intelli-

Photo]   [Fox Photos

RESIDENCE OF THE DUKE AND DUCHESS

The Duke and Duchess of York chose 145, Piccadilly, as their London town house after their return from their Empire tour in 1927, and lived there until a few weeks before their Coronation ten years later. No. 145 (left half of the central block) is on the north side of the street close to Hyde Park Corner.

gence was about to pass into speech and movement. Even the photographs that were faithfully dispatched to the royal parents by every mail must have added to the ache, though they unmistakably confirmed the fine progress the infant was making. But none of this private feeling was allowed to appear in the Duchess's public manner. She did not, as so many mothers less conscious of the obligations of such a difficult position might have done, spoil anyone else's enjoyment of that rare event, a royal visit to the Antipodes, by allowing her natural sadness at separation from her baby to show in her face.

Small wonder that, having perfectly fulfilled her public duties "down under", the Duchess on her arrival at Waterloo hurried from train to exit instead of making the very slow progress expected of royalties on such occasions. But she made amends to the crowd that had gathered to welcome her by driving to Buckingham Palace through drenching rain in an open carriage.

The Duke and Duchess, having lost so much of their daughter's babyhood, determined that, in order to combine the efficient fulfilment of their public duties with the home life they both like best, they must have a London house.

They decided eventually on a house in a row—a rather remarkable row, it is true, but a row nevertheless. They decided on 145, Piccadilly ; and there they lived for the most part until after their accession. For the first time in history, indeed, a King and Queen of Great Britain lived on a street, with only a couple of policemen at the gate to mark the fact that their particular house differed in any way from its neighbours.

Into this house they were able to introduce all those wedding presents that had

Photo]   [Thurstons Luton

PRINCESS ELIZABETH AT HER MOTHER'S HOME

Princess Elizabeth, elder daughter of the Duke and Duchess of York, was born in London on April 21st, 1926. This striking photograph was taken at St. Paul's Walden Bury, where she spent part of her first year in the care of Lord and Lady Strathmore during her parents' absence abroad.

not up till then found a permanent home— the beautiful pieces of furniture and plate given to them by public bodies and the City companies as well as by private friends. For they had both at the time of their wedding expressed a wish to receive gifts that would be useful in the setting-up of a home, and, except for the jewels given to the Duchess by her own and the bridegroom's immediate families, practically all their presents had been of the kind that pleased them best. The Princess Mary's, indeed, had taken the exceedingly practical form of a quantity of household linen.

Once across the threshold of 145, Piccadilly, one seemed to be in a different world. The stone-flagged courtyard, shallow as it is, helps to shut off the house from the noise of traffic. Pale colours and masses of flowers gave a sense of airy spaciousness, which was helped by the fact that a round glass dome roofs the well in which rises the staircase. The rooms are large and well-proportioned, and were furnished in quiet, good taste, without excess of pieces and with no touch of the ultra-modern. Sir Philip Sassoon's cousin, Mrs. Gubbay, whose knowledge of period furniture is well known, gave the Duchess much help in selecting the pieces that went to furnish her Piccadilly home. The public rooms are on the ground and first floors, while the nurseries occupy the top of the house, opening on to a circular corridor that runs round the glass dome. Behind the house lies a small garden protected from the public by a tall railing and a thick hedge, and beyond the garden lies Hyde Park, so that the back of the house has a feeling of openness very nearly as great as if it were really in the country.

In the early days of the Duke and Duchess's occupancy of 145, Piccadilly, crowds used to gather outside in the hope of catching sight of the little

Lower Photo,   [Marcus Adams

A DEVOTED FAMILY

Though there is more than four years difference in their ages, Princess Elizabeth and Princess Margaret Rose have been from the first devoted to one another. Above, they are at play at St. Paul's Walden Bury, the Queen's birthplace; and, below, Princess Elizabeth helps the Queen to nurse the new baby.

Princess—Lilibet, as she called herself—leaving the house with her nurse for a ride in her pram or a drive in a car, or racing about in the small garden on her tricycle with the fierce energy of a healthy, growing child. Occasionally her golden head was to be seen poked inquisitively between the long net curtains that shield the windows from the gaze of the passer-by and the glass, peering eagerly down into the street.

And then on August 21st, 1930, a baby sister came to join her. Their Majesties' second child was born at Glamis. She was the first member of

the Royal Family to see the light in Scotland since King James VI of Scotland became in 1603 King James I of England and moved his Court from the northern kingdom to the southern. Not since the birth of Charles I in 1600 had such an event happened north of the border. The Scots, who feel that Queen Elizabeth is peculiarly one of them, were delighted that she elected to bear her second child at her old home of Glamis.

Princess Elizabeth, by now four years old, had been wisely prepared for the newcomer's advent, and from the first the two have been friends and playmates as well as sisters.

"I'm four," declared Princess Elizabeth when she was telling a visitor about her new playmate, "and I've got a baby sister— Margaret Rose—and I'm going to call her Bud!"

"Why Bud?" inquired the visitor.

"Well, she's not a real rose yet, is she? She's only a bud."

Photos]   *[Topical : Fox Photos*

THE PRINCESSES LEARN TO KEEP HOUSE

Princess Elizabeth and Princess Margaret Rose are seen in the top photograph on a shopping expedition. Below, Princess Elizabeth is in the garden of her miniature cottage in the grounds of Royal Lodge, Windsor. The cottage and furniture were a gift to the Princess from the people of Wales on her sixth birthday. The rooms are only five feet high, but the cottage is complete in every detail with bells, a telephone, and a fully equipped kitchen. See also colour plate facing page 304.

There is something very attractive in the protective care which the youthful Elizabeth so clearly exercises over the still more youthful Margaret Rose in all the pictures taken of them together from the younger Princess's earliest days.

In their life, so full of Court functions and official engagements of all kinds, the peaceful family atmosphere of 145, Piccadilly, was an oasis to which the Duke and Duchess always returned with relief and delight. In the larger and yet more crowded sphere of activity to which they have been translated, one is sure that not even the multiplicity of their beautiful royal homes

Photo]   [Wide World

HELPING A GOOD CAUSE

Like all the members of the Royal Family, the Queen takes a deep interest in the work of the hospitals. Her Majesty is seen above accepting purses of money subscribed towards the cost of a new nurses' hostel at King's College Hospital, Denmark Hill, London.

Photo]   [Topical

CONCERN FOR CHILD WELFARE

The Queen, like Queen Mary, is a great child lover and everything connected with the welfare of children appeals strongly to her. She is here seen inspecting a "bouncing cradle" at the Heritage Craft Schools, Chailey, Sussex, an institution for crippled children.

will eliminate from their memories this happy domestic interior.

The two Princesses are still little girls, but they are growing up fast, and their education, particularly that of Elizabeth, has been a matter of anxious consideration. At first Their Majesties intended to send Princess Elizabeth to school, but after careful thought they were reluctantly forced to the conclusion that the disadvantages of such a course outweighed the advantages. The Queen herself taught her young daughter to read, and her subsequent education has been carried out by governesses and tutors. By the time she was ten Princess Elizabeth already had an excellent knowledge of French and German, as well as of the other subjects proper to a young lady of her age.

Neither of the Princesses takes after the Queen in appearance, though they both have much of her sunny temperament and of her ease and charm of manner. Queen Mary said on one occasion as she looked at the infant Elizabeth sleeping in her cot, "I wish you were more like your dear little mother." But the Princesses are fair, while the Queen is very dark. Her hair is dark brown, full of life. She wears it close to her head, parted in the middle and drawn down over her ears into a knot at the back, with just the suspicion of a fringe. Her complexion is clear and fresh, her brows dark and well marked; her eyes of deep blue are dark-lashed. She has a natural repose of manner, and she is never at a loss as to what to do with her slender, expressive hands. Always, whatever she is doing—opening a bazaar or an exhibition, listening to a speech (or even a series of speeches), receiving purses in aid of some charity, inspecting Girl Guides or a regiment of soldiers—she appears positively to glow with interest in the matter in hand; and the interest is genuine. Where she used in the early days of her marriage to speak those half-dozen words that are all that is expected of a woman in her position, she has in recent years trained herself to speak, and it has of late been her custom to make a speech lasting from ten to twelve minutes on all suitable occasions. Only those who have rarely tried, and perhaps ignominiously failed, to speak in public realize how thoroughly one must know one's subject to be able to talk interestingly on it for ten minutes ; and she does speak interestingly, on dozens of subjects, in a rather high-pitched, youthful voice that carries well.

The Queen is not tall—something under five feet six—and this has no doubt to some extent influenced her taste in clothes. She wears three-quarter or full-length clothes, in soft materials and soft pastel colours. She likes feminine but not over-ornamented gowns, and semi-slack coats, often with fur about the throat and wrists, that drape well. Except for strictly outdoor occasions in the summer, when she wears hats with unexaggerated brims, she prefers close-fitting hats, often with narrow upturned brims. Her high-heeled shoes (she takes a $3\frac{1}{2}$) are generally court-shaped.

She loves flowers and dogs. She plays a good game of tennis and used to dance a good deal—when she was first married, she was often to be seen at Ciro's and the Embassy. She does not care for shooting and hunting, though she used to ride to hounds.

Photo]   *[Topical*

OPENING A HOSPITAL

The King and Queen, as Duke and Duchess of York, opened the new buildings of the Middlesex Hospital, London, in May 1935. The Queen is here seen inspecting the nurses of the hospital, accompanied by the Matron.

of her marriage the secretary of the London headquarters of the Girl Guides paid the following tribute to her zeal and efficiency: "Although she was only twenty-one at the time of her appointment as District Commissioner, Lady Elizabeth has been responsible for the whole of the training, recruiting, and discipline of the Glamis branch for the past two years. She is an excellent officer, and has taken the very keenest interest in her work." She also interested herself in the Girl

Angling she delights in; but her favourite recreation has always been reading. She keeps in touch with all that is being written to-day, but her preference goes out to one or two older authors. Sir James Barrie she has always liked—partly no doubt on account of the proximity of Glamis to the Barrie country (the road to Kirriemuir, Barrie's "Thrums", runs close to the castle gates). She is an enthusiastic reader of Scott; and an even dearer friend is Jane Austen, Scott's own favourite novelist.

From her teens the Queen has taken a great interest in the Girl Guides. At the time

Photos]   *[Keystone : Fox Photos*

HOURS OF LEISURE

Above, the King and Princess Elizabeth are riding in Windsor Great Park on the Princess's tenth birthday. Below, the King and Queen, Princess Elizabeth and Princess Margaret Rose are seen at Glamis Castle on their way to witness a Military Display in the grounds, during one of their autumn visits to the Earl and Countess of Strathmore.

Guides of the village of Whitwell, near St. Paul's Walden Bury.

This interest she has never abandoned, and to it have been added a multiplicity of others. There is scarcely a charity or a movement for the betterment of the conditions of life of women and of children that has not at some time received the encouragement and recognition of her presence ; and when the Queen gives her countenance, in however small a degree, to any organization it has always meant that she knows a great deal not only about its objects, but also about the way in which it seeks to attain those objects.

By a happy combination of temperament and character, the woman who was once Lady Elizabeth Bowes-Lyon has shown herself to be perfectly fitted to fulfil the difficult role of Queen in a democratic country.

The face of the world has changed very much for women during the lifetime of Queen Elizabeth. She, indeed, was born into the century that has seen, at least in large measure, the realization of the aims for which the nineteenth-century pioneers of women's education and political freedom struggled. Women have not only acquired the privileges

Photo]   *[Dorothy Wilding*

FIRST LADY IN THE LAND

This photograph is one of the first taken of the Queen after the accession. Her Majesty is wearing a miniature of King George V set in diamonds and surmounted by a crown, a decoration bestowed by the late King on members of his own family.

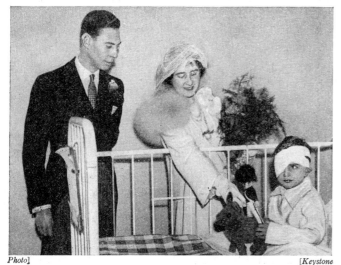

Photo]   *[Keystone*

MAKING FRIENDS WITH SHY PATIENTS

The King and Queen as Duke and Duchess of York are here seen at the bedside of a small and shy patient during a tour of the King George V Extension of the Royal Ophthalmic Hospital, City Road, London, just after the opening ceremony.

and duties of citizenship, but have penetrated into innumerable fields of usefulness and employment. It is, of course, impossible to doubt that women in this country owe much of the change that has come about in their condition to the Great War. It is not that they were not fully as capable before that terrible event as during and after it ; but that time of stress and strain gave them the opportunity to prove without possibility of doubt that they were capable of assuming all the burdens that go with the privileges of full citizenship, with personal and civic responsibility. The early years of the century were largely notable, in woman's sphere, for what appeared to the outsider as a far from dignified campaign for the vote. But that undignified campaign did more to spread the knowledge that a great many women wanted a vote than had the years of serious and dignified speech-making, pleading and pamphleteering that had preceded it. Then came the War, and the suffrage campaign ceased abruptly. The women who had been active in that campaign and the women who had opposed it were alike swept into the maelstrom of the times. Sheltered society girls like the Lady Elizabeth and her sisters found themselves tending men wounded in their country's service, from all ranks of life. They learned at first hand the realities of suffering and service in an abrupt way that their elders had been lucky enough to escape. Women of all grades of society penetrated into the hospitals as nurses, doctors, V.A.D.s ; into the Services in the various women's corps that were formed as the War went on ; into banks and offices and industry.

Hundreds of jobs that had been regarded as outside the range of women's capacity they proved that they could do, and do well. And though the ending of hostilities closed many of these newly opened doors, the knowledge that women were capable of good citizenship remained ; the concession of the vote, granted to them in 1918 with scarcely a dissentient voice, was an advance that no set-back could diminish.

Women now had a place in every politician's thoughts, for they had become as important in election campaigns as men, and as a result various pieces of legislation were passed improving women's status and opening doors to the legal profession and the Civil Service that had been obstinately closed. Women were given equal rights and duties with men in regard to property and to guardianship of children. Women have become successful doctors, lawyers, architects ; nor have they failed to emulate men by feats of endurance in the realms of sport and aviation that would have seemed monstrous fantasies to their great-grandmothers.

In the sphere of private life, too, improvements in lighting, heating and cooking devices, developments of design in flats and houses, simplification of taste in ornament and decoration have rendered women's lives more agreeable and less harassed. Fancifulness and furbelows have vanished from women's dress (and here the Queen sets an excellent example) ; and the invention of artificial silk has put daintiness within the reach of the poorest workgirl. Truly, Queen Elizabeth's lifetime has been coincident with a revolution in the lives and the outlook of women —a revolution whose force, we may be sure, is not yet spent.

Photo]   *[Topical*

THE QUEEN'S SMILE

The Queen is here seen leaving the Duke and Duchess of Kent's house in Belgrave Square to attend the christening of their infant daughter in the private chapel of Buckingham Palace.

CURIOSITIES OF CORONATION

by
E. W. F. TOMLIN
and
IAN COLVIN

Author of "The Safety of the Nations", etc.

Memorable Incidents
and Historic Events
Grave and Amusing

FIRST CROWNED ON A FIELD OF BATTLE

On August 22nd, 1485, Henry Tudor met Richard III in battle near Bosworth, in Leicestershire, and after two hours' fighting the King was defeated and killed. He had gone into battle wearing his crown and it was picked up by Lord Stanley and placed on Henry's head as an indication that he was now King. Henry VII's actual Coronation took place on October 30th, it having been delayed by his severe illness.

CHAPTER 14

HAROLD TO CHARLES I

CORONATIONS IN SCENES OF TUMULT AND PAGEANTRY

*In this chapter is shown the first stage of the evolution of the present-day
Coronation ceremony from the early scenes of disorder to the more
dignified proceedings at the Coronation of the second Stuart King*

OF the earliest coronations of English Kings we know little more than the fact that they took place, and sometimes we are driven to the conclusion that we know less. The only source of information at our disposal is the ancient chronicles, and, as every historian is aware, no chronicle can be judged wholly reliable. So few facts are we able to muster about these remote ceremonies that the most trivial detail becomes an object of curiosity. A chronicle, in fact, is merely a museum of such objects ; for the chronicler differs from the historian in that he records, without criticism, anything that strikes him as rare and unusual.

The chronicler may be unreliable, but his testimony is better than nothing ; and when we are concerned with a subject like the present, such testimony has a special appropriateness. For if the chronicler specializes in the rare and unusual, then he specializes in precisely the kind of facts we are interested in here. As recorder of the significant events of national life, he will inevitably attach particular importance to the leader of that life, the King ; and as recorder of the life of the national leader, he will naturally have much to say of the significant stages of his career, above all with his accession and coronation.

The earliest English King of whose coronation we possess reliable information is King Alfred, to whom historians have accorded the title of "Great" ; but apart from the story that he was "hallowed as

King" by the Pope in Rome at the age of five and crowned at Winchester in 871, few details of the actual ceremony have survived, though it is believed that a crown of "gold wyerworke, sett with slight stones and two little bells", was employed. Of the coronations of his successors, notably his grandson Athelstan and the wayward Ethelred the Unready, fairly elaborate descriptions have been preserved, but as these are mostly concerned with particulars of ritual—vitally important questions at the time, no doubt, when every detail had a symbolic value and every divergence from precedent was regarded as an omen—they need not detain us here.

Perhaps the first coronation at which a distinct divergence from precedent is recorded is that of Harold I (1037). After the death of Cnut the Dane in 1035, a struggle for the possession of the throne had taken place between his two English sons, Harold and Harthacnut, with the result that when, two years later, Harold obtained power, many people were disposed to regard him as a usurper. Among those who objected was the Archbishop of Canterbury, who, while consenting to officiate at the coronation service (for he jealously guarded his right as Primate), refused to give the new King his blessing. Placing the royal insignia on the altar, he said : "These are the crown and sceptre which Cnut entrusted to my charge. To you I neither give them nor refuse them, you may take them if you please ; but I strictly forbid any of my brother bishops to usurp an office which is the prerogative of my see.''

Needless to say, Harold did as he pleased; but the story has more than anecdotal significance, since it reveals the immense prestige of the Church at that time. We sometimes tend to regard the Divine Right of Kings as essentially an ecclesiastical doctrine. It was not; it was a doctrine formulated by the monarchy in order to resist the encroachments of ecclesiastical authority.

Such outbursts on the part of high dignitaries of the Church during the coronation service seem to us strange, but we must remember that public life in the eleventh century was much less stable than it is today. Today (at least, in this country) the force of law is paramount; at that time men were more accustomed to the law of force. Hence the coronation ceremony possessed a much more than symbolic significance; often it was a realistic demonstration that one faction (for there were no parties) had prevailed over another, or that authority had been entrusted to one man to rally the nation against a common enemy—perhaps a foreign claimant to the throne.

Rebuked by the Archbishop

The one institution in which authority was not subject to force was the Church; and thus it is not strange to find ecclesiastics continually inveighing against the lawlessness of the secular arm. At the coronation of Ethelred the Unready, for example, Archbishop Dunstan had taken the opportunity to accuse the new King of having murdered his brother (the late King Edward the Martyr), and to prophesy a series of disasters in the coming reign. It is highly probable, incidentally, that the accusation was unjust, since at the time of Edward's murder Ethelred was but ten years of age; but, unfortunately, many of the prophecies in which the Archbishop indulged were strikingly fulfilled—the new King's reign turned out to be a time of national calamity.

Edward the Confessor, Ethelred's son, who succeeded Harthacnut in 1042, was crowned with great acclamation; while the coronation of Harold II was one of those memorable occasions of which we have spoken, at which the task of rallying the country against a foreign claimant was entrusted to one man. The foreign claimant was, of course, William of Normandy, who—to pass over a tract of history familiar to all—was crowned at the new Abbey of Westminster in 1066. On this historic occasion the procession to the Abbey, which was accompanied with great pomp and magnificence, consisted of members of both nations; but William, knowing well that his task of conquest had not yet been completed, was careful to fill the Abbey precincts with a great body of soldiery.

Tumult and Disorder

The service started without disturbance, but owing to the presence within the Abbey of both Norman and English representatives, it was necessary, when the moment arrived for the form of popular election, to put the question twice, first in English and then in French; and this may have accounted for the fact that the resulting shouts of acclamation seemed, to those stationed outside, to be of more than usual strength. Hearing the shouts and suspecting that a riot had broken out, the foreign soldiers not only proceeded to set fire to the surrounding houses (which were of wood), but also started a wholesale slaughter of the English inhabitants of Westminster, thus causing the very disturbance against which it had been their duty to provide.

For some while the voices of the officiating clergy were drowned in uproar, and it is a great tribute to their presence of mind that the service continued at all. In a few minutes, however, most of the congregation had fought its way out of the Abbey on to the scene of massacre, there to loot, salvage or help restore order—the motives were impossible to disentangle in the confusion; and once the King and clergy were left to themselves, the ceremony was brought to a conclusion. But for William, and for the

Norman Conquest in general, it had been a narrow escape. Fortunately, he was the kind of man to profit by the warning.

Twenty-one years later the Conqueror was succeeded by his second son, William Rufus. The most interesting part of Rufus's ascent of the throne—and this applies also to his successor, Henry I—was the precautionary measures which he found necessary to adopt in order to secure it. His first act, on hearing that his father favoured his succession, was to lay hold of the royal treasure, which during this period was housed at Winchester, for without this rich accompaniment no King in those days could count himself secure. Having done this, he proceeded at once to London, where he received an enthusiastic welcome—natural perhaps in a people who had had little opportunity to learn anything of his true nature.

The accession of Henry I, Rufus's brother, was, if possible, even more abrupt and certainly less creditable. So eager was he to secure the royal treasure that, immediately upon his brother's decease, he journeyed post-haste to Winchester for this purpose. Meanwhile, the body of Rufus was trundled thither in a common cart and buried, without a vestige of ceremony, in the cathedral. It was said at the time of Henry's accession that "the present providing of good swords was accounted more essential to a king's coronation than the long preparing of gay clothes". Indeed, Henry did not stand upon ceremony ; he needed a more secure foundation.

Wishing to be succeeded by his daughter Matilda, Henry had extorted from Stephen, his nephew, a promise that he would support her claim. But directly Henry was

LAST SAXON KING OF ENGLAND

The photograph above of a part of the famous Bayeux Tapestry, illustrating scenes in the life of Harold II, shows, left, King Harold being offered the crown, and, right, the King enthroned after his coronation by Archbishop Stigand. It will be seen that he is holding the sceptre and orb, both very ancient emblems of royal authority. The latter, with its cross, is symbolic of monarchy subordinate to divine kingship. Harold was killed ten months later at the Battle of Hastings.

dead, Stephen repudiated his obligations to Matilda, and set about obtaining the throne for himself. Although he encountered some initial opposition from Canterbury and Dover, the fact that his brother was Bishop of Winchester made his appropriation of the royal treasure a matter of small difficulty; and thereafter nothing stood in his way to the throne.

His coronation, however, was not a success; very few dignitaries attended, and during the service certain omens occurred which were the cause of much public apprehension. Owing to mismanagement, for instance, the kiss of peace, to which so much symbolic importance attached, was left out; and it is also reported—though here we must allow for exaggeration—that before the Communion Service the Host unaccountably vanished and no trace could thereafter be found of it. Such facts may be challenged, but the fact that the succeeding nineteen years were years of anarchy is, unfortunately, not to be disputed.

Crowned before Accession

An even more interesting example of the lengths to which Kings in those days were prepared to go in order to consolidate their position is provided by the next King to ascend the throne, Henry II. So that there could be no dispute after his death as to who was the legal sovereign, Henry originated the happy idea of not waiting for that inconvenient moment. He arranged, in other words, to have his son crowned during his lifetime.

Various difficulties at first presented themselves. The right of crowning the Kings of England belonged, as we have seen, to the Archbishop of Canterbury, and the primate of that time—the famous Thomas Becket—refused to comply with the wishes of the King in this matter. Eventually, however, the Archbishop of York, openly defying the Pope and disregarding the scruples of his colleague, consented to perform the ceremony; and in 1170 the young Henry was crowned titular King.

Of all the coronation curiosities, this surely is the most curious. The traditional formalities were strictly observed, and the ceremony culminated in a magnificent banquet, not the least interesting feature of which was that the King insisted upon waiting on his son. When a courtier congratulated the young man on the honour of being attended by a monarch, King Henry wittily observed that "he thought it no such great condescension for the son of an earl to wait on the son of a king". Unfortunately, his precautions were of no avail; he outlived the son he had crowned by six years, and was succeeded by Richard the Lion Heart in 1189.

Massacred by Mistake

The coronation of Richard I, like that of William the Conqueror, was the occasion for a regrettable but quite unpremeditated massacre. On the previous day the King had ordained that neither Jews nor women (he probably referred to witches) were to attend the ceremony "for feare", says the chronicler Stowe, "of enchantments, which were wont to be practised". In spite of this edict, however, a number of Jews assembled at the Abbey; and as they belonged to the more prosperous class, it is natural to suppose that they wished to gain the sovereign's favour by an offer of rich gifts. No sooner was their presence detected, however, than the nobles set upon them and brutally drove them from the precincts.

The rumour immediately spread abroad that the King had ordered the slaughter of all Jews, and a terrible massacre (which later spread as far as Norwich, York and other distant places) followed. Hearing the tumult outside, the King is said to have inquired what was the matter; to which he received the reply: "Nothing, only the boys rejoice and are merry at heart." But when later the sounds betrayed the presence of less creditable passions than rejoicing and merriment, the King, having learnt the truth, at once ordered the ringleaders to be arrested. Next day they were put to death; but, as the chronicler sardonically observes, "they were not arraigned for the murder of Jews, but for some trifling offence against the Christians".

The chronicler also records how, at the close of the day, the citizens of Westminster were startled by a strange peal of bells from the towers of the Abbey. Of this occurrence the Abbey authorities were unable to provide an explanation, and the people, exhausted by the recent horrors, took it as an omen of singular misfortune. Nothing succeeded more effectively in subduing their inflamed passions.

Richard had spent a considerable portion of his reign in foreign lands, while his subjects had spent a considerable portion of the national revenue in rescuing him from foreign captors. He was succeeded by his brother John. A crude and undisciplined fellow at any time, John behaved at his coronation thoroughly disgracefully ; he seemed totally incapable either of concentrating on the ceremonial or of appreciating its significance for himself and for his subjects. Owing to the fact that he had assumed the title of Duke of Normandy as well as King of England, part of the service was specially devoted to his investiture in the former office ; but during this interlude (which he interpreted somewhat literally), he was repeatedly convulsed with laughter at a group of his companions who were amusing themselves in a corner.

When the time arrived for the formal presentation of the spear, he was in no more serious mood. So distracted was his attention, in fact, that he let the weapon fall, and it had to be restored by an indignant bishop. Finally, he became tired even of inattention, and, without waiting to receive the sacrament, hurriedly departed from the Abbey. Such facts were not easily forgotten by the people, who frequently called them to mind during John's subsequent misgovernment.

The coronation at Gloucester of John's successor, Henry III, a boy of nine, is remembered chiefly for the fact that, instead of a crown, the King was adorned with a simple gold fillet. The reason for this was that, during his predecessor's

BOY KING TWICE CROWNED

Henry III was nine when he succeeded King John and he was crowned at once. The ceremony was performed in Gloucester Cathedral by the Bishop of Winchester, in the absence of the Archbishop of Canterbury. The King was again crowned in Westminster Abbey four years later. The illustration is from a MS. in the British Museum.

reign, the crown and jewels had been lost on a disastrous journey across the Wash. A sidelight on the regard with which the coronation was then held is provided by the fact that after the ceremony an edict was issued ordaining that, for at least a month, every subject was to wear a chaplet. It was a way of symbolizing that the King had been crowned with public consent.

Before leaving this reign (Henry was actually crowned again four years later when London was no longer in the hands of the French), we cannot resist, in view of the crowds seen at the coronation of His Majesty King George VI, quoting a sentence from the famous annalist Stowe. "To this coronation", he writes in his account of Henry III, "resorted so great a number of all estates that the city of London was scarce able to receive them."

CROWNED DURING A SNOW STORM

Henry IV died on March 20th, 1413, and on April 9th Henry V was crowned in Westminster Abbey. The great snow-storm that raged during the ceremony was taken as an omen that the King had put behind him his previous wild life. The illustration is from one of two sculptures in Henry V's Chantry in Westminster Abbey showing the coronation ceremony.

ingenious, are very amusing (as we shall see later), not least because of the tone of pontifical solemnity in which the chroniclers are in the habit of recording them.

At the coronation of Edward I, however, the King entertained his subjects even more effectively than his subjects entertained him. Accompanied by King Alexander of Scotland (who was present to do homage for his realm) and a number of other nobles, the King rode to his banquet amid an unparalleled display of pageantry. "At the solemnitie of this coronation," writes Holinshed, "there were let go at libertie (catch them as catch might) five hundred great horses by the king of Scots and other noblemen." The horses, in other words, were let loose among the assembled spectators, who were given the chance of keeping as many as they might detain. It was a curious method of dispensing gifts, since the huge animals apparently made no docile surrender, and for a while all was confusion. But such hasty munificence was not out of harmony with the rough spirit of the time.

Of the coronations of Edward II, Edward III, Richard II (who fainted from exhaustion owing to the length of the ceremony), and the next three Henrys, the chroniclers have little to offer us in the way of curiosities. But the coronation of Edward IV, we are told, lasted two whole days, and concluded with a procession to St. Paul's, where, according to Stowe, "an angell came down and censed the king, at which time was so great a number of people in Paules as ever was seen in any days".

The splendour of Richard III's coronation, at which the embroidered trappings of the Duke of Buckingham's horse were so heavy that footmen were needed to support

As we approach nearer to modern times, we find the coronation becoming more and more of a public festival, an occasion for gaiety and rejoicing. Consequently, at these later coronations the chroniclers are wont to dwell upon the lavish entertainments which frequently took place at the conclusion of the ceremony at the Abbey. For many centuries (the practice is now discontinued) it was the custom on the day before the coronation for the new monarch, accompanied by the Regalia, to ride from Westminster Hall to the Abbey upon a specially-erected platform, decorated with flowers and cloth of "Tyrian dye"; and along the route the citizens would arrange side-shows and pageants at which the King was invited to pause and receive a loyal address,- this latter being often in verse and accompanied with allegorical masques. Some of the accounts of these pageants, many of which even today seem highly them on either side, was no doubt intended to dazzle the populace, and to distract their minds from the foul circumstances in which the King had acquired the throne. When, on the field of Bosworth two years later, Henry VII was presented with the fallen crown of Richard, public relief was perhaps even greater than public rejoicing, as well it might be at the close of a civil war. Although London gave Henry VII a great welcome, his coronation was not notable for magnificence; there was more display, and probably more satisfaction, when he married Elizabeth of York, thus healing the family feud.

His son, Henry VIII, whose reign saw so many vast changes in both Church and State, was crowned with all the magnificence and variety which we have come to associate with his character; but nothing remarkable seems to have been observed.

Edward VI was a delicate boy, but his coronation seems to have been a very vigorous affair. Never had pageantry been more elaborately and ingeniously devised. Not the least display of vigour, indeed, was given by an Aragonese, who, at one stage of the King's progress through the city, performed a series of acrobatic feats which, even allowing for exaggeration, must have been very remarkable and, for the performer, not without considerable risk.

To describe this scene in any other words than those of the chronicler would be to lose a great deal of its effectiveness, so let us listen to the rugged English of Holinshed. "As the king passed on the south part of Paul's churchyard," he writes, "an argosine came from the battlements of Paul's church upon a cable, being made fast to an anchor by the dean's gate, lying on his breast, aiding himself neither with hand nor foot, and after ascended to the middest of the cable, where he tumbled and played many pretty toys, whereat the king and the nobles had good pastime."

Had the country known the unhappiness which the reign of Mary Tudor was to bring to it, the pageantry of her coronation would no doubt have been less lighthearted than it was. Her ride through London was more than usually gay, for she

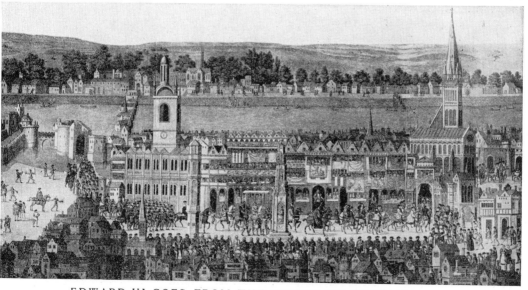

EDWARD VI GOES FROM THE TOWER TO WESTMINSTER

It was once usual for the King to pass to his coronation at Westminster Abbey from the Tower so that he might receive the acclamations of the citizens of London. This illustration, from a contemporary painting, shows the progress of the nine-years-old Edward VI along Cheapside to Whitehall on February 19th, 1547, the day before his Coronation. The houses were described as being hung with cloth of gold and cloth of silver and there were also tapestry hangings, streamers, and banners. On the right is Old St. Paul's.

loved finery ("the caule and circlet being so massy and ponderous," Stowe says, "she was faine to bear up her heade with her hand"); and of several of the entertainments with which she was greeted as she passed, we possess graphic and amusing descriptions. Here, for example, is one from Stowe:

"At the upper end of Grace Streete," he says, "the Florentines made a pageant. . . . There was an angell all in greene, with a trumpet in his hand, and when the trumpeter, who stood secretly in the pageant, did sound his trumpet, the angell did put his trump to his mouth as though it had been the same that had sounded, to the great marvelling of many ignorant persons."

In another case, Paul's steeple, which seems to have possessed a capacity for adapting itself to the public mood, once more featured. We are told how Peter, a Dutchman (it is interesting to observe how many of the entertainers on these occasions were foreigners), "strode the weathercock, holding a streamer in his hand of five yards long, and waving thereof, stood sometime on the one foote and shooke the other, and then kneeled on his knees to the great marvel of all people." In addition to these pageants, the common people were given free drinks from the conduits of Cornhill and Cheapside, which on this occasion ran wine.

Elizabeth's Complaint

Mary's reign ended in an atmosphere of intense gloom, with the result that when Elizabeth—who was known to be tolerant, perhaps even indifferent, in religious matters—ascended the throne, the enthusiasm knew no bounds. Historians do not relate any remarkable incidents concerning the ceremony, though we do know that the Queen, with characteristic frankness, complained of the anointing that "the oil was grease and smelt ill".

The coronation of James I, on the other hand, can hardly be described as a public ceremony at all. London had been visited by the plague, and every precaution was taken not to allow the assembly of a vast concourse of people; even the usual fair in Tothill Fields was prohibited. What is chiefly remarkable about this coronation, however, is the fact that, although it was a comparatively private affair, the expenses amounted to the sum of £37,000.

Omen of Evil

King Charles I, though not himself a spendthrift, was early beset with financial difficulties. Indeed, these difficulties were the ultimate cause of his downfall. But his coronation need not have been the poor thing that it was had he not required a large sum of money to finance a war with Spain. Being a Catholic, his Queen, Henrietta Maria, refused to be crowned with him in the Abbey, and would neither attend nor watch the service.

Possibly because he wore white satin instead of the more usual crimson velvet, and in spite of the fact that the chroniclers tell us that he looked "a proper person to all that beheld him", Charles was by some compared to a victim about to be sacrificed. Moreover, a singularly unfortunate episode took place when the King was formally presented to the people.

Leading him to the scaffold which, according to custom, had been erected in the centre of the church, the Archbishop said: "My masters and friends: I am here come to present unto you your king, King Charles, to whom the crown of his ancestors and predecessors is now devolved by lineal right, and he himself is come hither to be settled in that throne, which God and his birth have appointed for him: and therefore I desire you by your general acclamations to testify your content and willingness thereunto." For no apparent reason except that the people may have thought the Archbishop had something to add, there followed a most embarrassing silence. It was the kind of silence which, the longer it is maintained, the harder it is to break, and the people seemed virtually overcome by their own lack of demonstration. At length, after an almost intolerable pause, one of the nobles bravely tried to make amends for the lapse by telling the people to shout, "God save King Charles!"

CHAPTER 15

WHEN CROMWELL WAS OFFERED THE CROWN

The following arresting contribution by a famous journalist whose studies in historical subjects are well known for their erudition and independence of opinion has been amplified for the present work by its author from his original article in the "Morning Post"

TO those who would occupy the empty hours of convalescence with pleasure and with profit let me recommend a course in Clarendon. Reading that courtly and leisurely historian the other day, I was fascinated by the passage (in Book XV) where he describes how Oliver Cromwell was offered the crown.

It was proposed to him in the House of Commons in 1657. "The first motion for the making him King", says Clarendon, "was made by one of the most wealthy Aldermen of the City of London, and who served then for the City in Parliament", and it had very influential support. Yet there was such fierce opposition that—for the first time in his life—Cromwell hesitated, to the glee of the profane. Samuel Butler, greatest of our comic poets, wrote a ballad on the subject, which begins :

> As close as a goose
> Sat the Parliament-house
>   To hatch the royal gull ;
> After much fiddle-faddle,
> The egg proved addle
>   And Oliver came forth Nol.

We are given a wonderful picture of Cromwell's doubts and fears : "As his looks were extremely discomposed, and discovered a mind full of trouble and irresolution, so his words were broken and disjointed, without method and full of pauses." In the end he refused the glittering prize, and the historian thinks the decision was that first failure in courage which marked the declension of his power. "Many were then of opinion, that his genius at that time forsook him, and yielded to the King's spirit, and that his reign was near its expiration."

Truly, a marvellous passage—the usurper, at the supreme moment of his fate, mastered and defeated by the spirit of the King whom he had slain ! But who was the wealthy alderman who made this bold proposition—and why did he make it ? Clarendon does not give the citizen a name, but it is mentioned by some of his contemporaries; this member of Parliament who offered Cromwell the crown was Sir Christopher Pack, who had been Lord Mayor, 1654–5, and not only represented the City of London, but was Governor of the Merchants Adventurers of England.

The Fellowship of the Merchants Adventurers of England was a very old and at that time a very strong company. It was a Federation of the Merchants Adventurers of London, York, Norwich, Exeter, Ipswich, Newcastle and Hull, to mention its chief members, and it held a monopoly of the export of English cloth to Germany and the Netherlands.

If we were to trace it back to its origins we should find them in a certain fraternity of English mercers, calling themselves the Brotherhood of St. Thomas à Becket, who obtained a charter to trade in Flanders from the Duke of Brabant in the year 1296.

They were thus no doubt brought into conflict with the German Hansa, which then, and for two centuries after, held England (and Flanders) "under its thumb".

By the beginning of the seventeenth century, our Merchants Adventurers were victoriously seated in the Hanseatic city of Hamburg and the Dutch city of Middelburg, with a monopoly of the English cloth trade across the North Sea.

The company, says a memorial of the early part of the seventeenth century, "did transport for Germany and the 17 Provinces of the Netherlands 80 and 90,000 cloths yearly, besides a great number of coloured cloths and other woollen manufactures made and perfected in England".

Wheeler, the Secretary, who wrote his "Treatise of Commerce" at the beginning of the seventeenth century, says that even in 1550, in Antwerp alone, no fewer than 20,000 persons were fed and maintained for the most part by the trade of the Merchants Adventurers, besides another 30,000 in other parts of the Low Countries. The Freemen of the Company were said to number 3500 English merchants.

It was, then, the chairman of this powerful company, handling the greater part of the foreign trade of England, who tried to make Cromwell king. Why did he do it ?

English Only

The Fellowship, let us remember, was a national organization, composed of wholesale merchants — substantial men — who were not allowed to go into retail trade or cut the cloth they sold. They had to be English born, "of father and mother both English", and were not allowed even to marry a foreign wife or hold real property abroad. They held their charters from the Crown, which they were sworn to help with information and support.

It is undeniable, nevertheless, that they were one main support of Parliament against Charles. Possibly they gathered their flavour of Puritanism from the Netherlands in which they traded. Their rules, certainly, have a Presbyterian twang. They are governed by "24 of the most

sadd, discreet and honest persons of divers Fellowshipes of the same Merchants Adventurers". Their apprentices must not lodge "in anie Inns, Taverne, or Victuaillinge house" or "use anie excessive quaffinge or drinkinge", or "playe openly or secretely at cardes tables dyce or anie other game for above 4d. in a game", nor may they "comonly or inordinately use dauncinge, mumminge or walkinge abroad in the night seasone at undue hours". Brothers of the Fellowship are not permitted to keep "dogges used for sundry games and pastymes without licence of his Excellencie", nor are they allowed to carry parcels in the street (but this is a point of dignity) unless they can carry them in their sleeves or under their cloaks. They were certainly of the bourgeoisie !

Against the Stuarts

But they had besides a long-standing quarrel with the Stuarts. King James I had taken away all their privileges and put the trade in the too-confident hands of Alderman Cockayne, whereby the cloth trade of England was thrown into terrible disorder. Then Charles I, in 1640, to finance his expedition to Scotland, had seized the "treasure" of the Merchants Adventurers when it lay at the Mint, and although he had offered them security and interest, had again dislocated their trade. There were other matters—and, moreover, the Court leaned to the view that the Merchants, by their exercise of their monopoly, injured the cloth-workers and dyers of England. Thus it came about that the company supported Parliament against the King and helped to finance the armies of Essex and of Cromwell in the Civil Wars. It was, no doubt, in recognition of this support that Christopher Pack had been knighted by Cromwell, on September 20th, 1655.

Yet they could not have been altogether happy about it. Not only did their charters derive from the Crown, but there were forces let loose in England which threatened both trade and capital   In 1656 their privileges were so formidably attacked in Parliament that the Merchants Adventurers on (in Committee of the House) only by a narrow majority. The Levellers (the Communists of that time) were a power which even Cromwell found it hard to control.

"These hundred and forty honest men", he burst out, "could not govern; they attacked a settled Ministry; they flew out t liberty and property, insomuch that oth were like to have been destroyed; hey held that if one man had twelve cows, nother that had none ought to share with is neighbour. Who could have said anyhing was his own if they had gone on ?"

Here, then, are some excellent reasons why Sir Christopher Pack offered the crown of England to the Protector. But the Levellers and Democrats were too strong for him. "Those who still retained ome affection to the Commonwealth", ays a writer of the time, "fell so furiously pon Pack for his great presumption, that

they bore him down from the Speaker's chair to the Bar of the House."

In his "Last Years of the Protectorate, 1656–8", Mr. C. H. Firth gives a very full and interesting account of the controversy, from which it appears that it had long been agitated. As far back as December 1653, Lambert and his brother officers had offered Cromwell the title of King, and he had refused it; a year later, Augustine Garland, one of the regicides, had moved to have the Protector crowned, and he was seconded by no less a person than Sir Anthony Ashley Cooper; again, in 1655, a petition was circulated asking Cromwell to take the title of King or Emperor, and received many signatures before it was suppressed by the Council of State.

It was, therefore, a long-vexed question; but Cromwell long hesitated, long delayed, and finally refused. Probably he feared to

CROMWELL DOES NOT ACCEPT THE CROWN

March 1657 Cromwell's Second Parliament presented to the Protector a Humble Petition and Advice proposing a revision of the Constitution and offering the Protector the Crown. Cromwell's inclination was to accept, but he was doubtful of the feeling of some of his followers and is here seen making his final renunciation.

15

offend the fanatics not only of his party but also of the Army.

Lambert, for example, who led the Opposition, said that the re-establishment of kingship was contrary to the oaths and protestations they had all taken and to the principles for which the Army had fought and so much blood had been shed. And Thurloe, writing to Henry Cromwell on the subject, said that he (Lambert) will "put the Army in a ferment if he can".

Although Pack had a majority behind him—144 votes to 54—the Major-Generals were in the extremely violent minority, and Cromwell was afterwards approached on the subject by one hundred of the most powerful officers of the Army. The Protector lost his temper. He reminded them that Lambert himself had offered him the crown and that he had refused it, although the constitution and the liberties of the subject required some such "balance", to preserve their liberties. "This instrument of Government", he ended, "will not do your work. It is time to come to a settlement and to lay aside arbitrary proceedings so unacceptable to the nation." It is plain that Cromwell leaned to the proposal.

A Crown Refused

Nevertheless, in the end, to the bitter disappointment not only of Pack but of a large number of his most influential supporters, the Protector, as we have seen, refused the crown. It was after long debate and many hesitations. Pack had introduced his petition on February 23rd, 1657, and it was only on May 8th following that Cromwell gave his final decision. The constitution they offered was a good one in respect that it would give security to honest men "in that great natural and religious liberty, liberty of conscience"; but he remained unconvinced by their arguments as to the crown :

"I am persuaded, therefore, to return this answer to you, that I cannot undertake the government with the title of King."

Now, it will be admitted that the course of this great debate, even though it ended on a negative, amounts to a strong argument

for kingship. Cromwell saw plainly enough that the Crown was not only a popular institution, but a "balance" without which justice and freedom were on a very precarious footing. And it is notable that, although he did not accept the crown, he tried by ceremonial to convey the impression of kingship. This ceremony, indeed, is one of the strangest things in the strange story of Oliver Cromwell. Here is an abridged account of it from the pages of Clarendon (June 26th, 1657).

Enthroning the Protector

"On the day appointed, Westminster Hall was prepared, and adorned as sumptuously as it could be for a day of coronation. A throne was erected with a pavilion, and a chair of estate under it, to which Cromwell was conducted . . . with as much state (and the Sword carried before him) as can be imagined. When he was sate in his chair of state . . . the Speaker (Wythrington), with the Earl of Warwick and Whittock, vested him with a rich purple velvet robe lined with ermines, the Speaker enlarging upon the majesty and integrity of the robe. Then the Speaker presented him with a fair Bible of the largest edition richly bound ; then he, in the name of all the people, girded a sword about him ; and, lastly, presented him a sceptre of gold, which he put into his hand, and made him a large discourse of those emblems of Government and authority. Upon the close of which, there being nothing wanting to a perfect formal coronation but a crown and an archbishop, he took his oath . . ."

The rest of the story need not take long in telling. Cromwell died. The business men of London, fearing complete chaos, sent money and kind messages to the royal exile. Charles entered London amid such universal applause that he remarked it must have been his own fault to have stayed away so long. On January 1st, 1661, His Majesty granted the Merchants Adventurers a new royal charter, and Sir Christopher Pack, although he was disabled from holding any public office, continued to enjoy his wealth, and died at a ripe old age in the odour of sanctity.

CHAPTER 16

CHARLES II to WILLIAM IV

MAGNIFICENCE AND MUDDLE, 17th TO 19th CENTURIES

During the 18th century the splendour of the coronations increased and the pageant grew to such proportions as to become wearisome. That of William IV was the first to be shorn of some of the superfluous ceremonial

GAY, frank and extremely quick-witted —above all, determined not to meet with the same fate as his father—no man was better fitted than Charles II to pacify the discordant elements that remained as a result of the recent rebellion. His coronation, as might be expected, was an occasion for thanksgiving, jubilation and much broad merriment—for the Puritan spirit had become thoroughly distasteful to the common people ; and every effort was made to re-establish the traditions and precedents which, in spite of drastic innovations, the interregnum had failed to discredit.

As Charles was unmarried, no peeresses were present at the ceremony, which lacked that much splendour ; but so gorgeous, elaborate and extensive was the procession that, although Charles arrived at the Palace at seven o'clock, three hours elapsed before the column was ready to start. The liberality of the banquet, being such as had not been seen in England for many years, would certainly have scandalized men of the type of Zeal-of-the-land-Busy, had they been present.

Only two disturbances are recorded. The Barons of the Cinque Ports, who inherited the right of holding a canopy over the King during the procession, came into conflict with certain of the royal footmen, who, whether from ignorance or bravado, claimed this right for themselves. In spite of the convivial noise of the feast, sounds of the quarrel, which seems to have taken a pretty violent form,

reached the King's ear ; and immediately an equerry was dispatched to put the footmen under guard (they were later dismissed). The other disturbance was a thunderstorm which, accompanied by torrential rain, broke suddenly during the banquet.

The coronation of James II was distinctly more eventful. Being a Catholic, James experienced some doubts at first as to whether he should take the coronation oath, since by so doing he committed himself to upholding the Protestant faith. He solved the problem by omitting the Communion Service altogether.

Another innovation for which he was responsible was the abolition of the traditional procession through London on the day before the installation. These processions had always been exceedingly expensive ; and as James had already spent a large sum of money on jewels for the Queen, he decided to abolish the procession as a measure of economy. It is true that he endeavoured to curtail expenses in his own case by making do with the same crown as his father ; but since this was far too big for him, and assumed the most undignified angle on the royal forehead, the economy was false economy. Throughout the service Sir Henry Sydney, Keeper of the Robes, was obliged to support the crown with his hand ; and at one point he was heard to remark to the King : "This is not the first time, Your Majesty, that my family has supported the crown."

Superstitious persons, of whom not a few existed at the time, were quick to notice this circumstance, and upon no one did it prey more than the Queen. "There was one presage", she would say in after-life when history had so strangely altered her fate, "that struck us and that everyone observed. They could not make the crown keep firm upon the King's head. It appeared always on the point of falling, and it required some care to hold it steady." Within four years that crown had, indeed, fallen, and the royal signet was at the bottom of the Thames.

The instability of the crown was but one of many omens recorded of this coronation. It is also stated, for instance, that the moment the King had been crowned, the flag on the Tower was rent from top to bottom—a circumstance which, if it actually occurred, is difficult to regard as a coincidence ; but perhaps the fact that

the occurrence seems to have been noticed only by those to whom it appeared as a coincidence may not be a coincidence either.

Less open to exaggeration was an event which is recorded as having taken place during the twelve-hundred-and-forty-five-dish banquet that followed. In came the Champion (Sir Charles Dymoke) at the appointed time to issue his traditional challenge. Having done this, and having received the traditional reply of respectful, though always somewhat thrilling, silence, he walked solemnly towards the King with the intent of kissing his hand. Before reaching the royal presence, however, he unexpectedly tripped and, as the chronicler Pryme describes it, fell down "all his length in the Hall", though there appeared to be nothing in the way that could have occasioned so sudden a mishap. He remained thus for some moments, apparently unable to rise—a fact which he afterwards

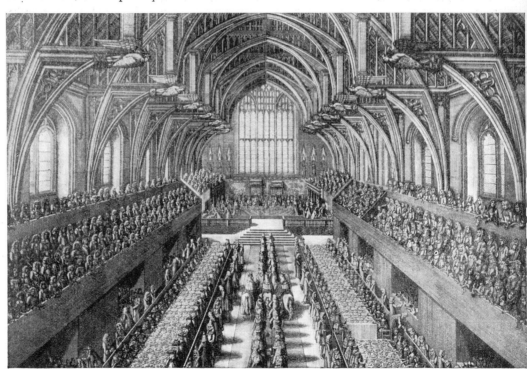

UNLUCKY CHAMPION OF THE LAST STUART KING

This illustration, after a contemporary drawing, shows the scene in Westminster Hall at the Coronation of King James II, when the King's Champion rode between the loaded tables to make his challenge to the King's enemies. When later he advanced on foot to kiss the King's hand, he fell headlong on the floor, an accident in which many saw an omen of ill for the King.

attributed (falsely, Pryme suggests) both to the excessive weight of his armour and to the fact that he had recently been unwell. "See you, love," the Queen remarked to her husband at the time, "what a weak Champion you have!" Dymoke proved to be not merely James's weakest Champion, but his last.

Robbed at his Coronation

The character of James II has fared none too well at the hands of historians, who tend to forget his magnificent services to the country, and, in particular, the Navy, as Duke of York ; and history books often give the impression that the transition to the reign of William and Mary was swiftly, easily and, above all, thankfully accomplished. It is not wholly true. Towards the end of his short reign James's popularity was certainly in the balance ; but there is every reason to suppose that, had he wished to do so (and Louis XIV offered him substantial help, which he refused), he could have weighed down the balance in his favour. We mention this because it throws some light upon the behaviour of William at the time of his coronation.

The date of the ceremony was fixed for April 11th, which, contrary to custom, was neither a feast-day nor a Sunday ; but just before the procession was due to start, William's composure was disturbed by the news that James had landed in Ireland, and—what was more serious— that nearly the whole of that country had declared in his favour. Almost simultaneously, so it is said, Mary (James's daughter) received the first letter from her father since his renunciation of the throne ; but, although it upbraided her for lack of loyalty, it did not affect her so deeply as the news of James's rally affected William. This information caught everybody unawares, and not a few opportunists and sycophants were busily engaged during the next few hours in thinking how best they could save their faces, perhaps also their lives, if James, with Catholic Ireland and even the fleet of Louis XIV behind him, should launch a successful counter-attack ; and William himself, possibly because he was only too conscious of the uncertainty of some of his followers, or possibly because he wished to take the opportunity to observe their reactions, postponed the procession by two hours.

In spite of the fact that the Archbishop of Canterbury refused to be present, and allowing for a somewhat tense atmosphere, the actual ceremony passed off without incident, except for a minor mishap towards the end. When the time arrived for taking the offertory, the King was surprised to discover that he had no money. After a hurried search it became obvious that he had been robbed—by whom, no one was ever able to ascertain. There was an exceedingly awkward pause, which was prolonged by the fact that the Queen, to whom the King had naturally turned, was also without money. At length, Lord Danby, who happened to be stationed near, hurried up to the distressed couple, and deposited the sum of twenty guineas in the plate. It was a satisfactory conclusion to what might otherwise have proved, by its very triviality, a ludicrous and undignified incident.

Carried to her Crowning

Crowned by her own wish upon St. George's Day, Queen Anne—a martyr to gout—was the first instance of a monarch who was too infirm to take part in the coronation service unaided. So crippled had she become by the time she ascended the throne that it was necessary to convey her to the Abbey in an arm-chair ; but in spite of this rather ignominious method of progress, she insisted upon wearing a beautiful and lengthy train which was upheld in the traditional manner by ladies of the Court. Much disapproval was caused at the time by the fact that the Queen's consort, Prince George of Denmark, was given no part in the service, though he was permitted to pay homage with the peers after the investiture, and to sit at the Queen's table during the banquet.

A coronation, as we have good reason to know, involves immense and lengthy preparation on the part of a great number of responsible persons ; but the preparations for the coronation of George I were complicated by the fact that the King, a complete stranger, knew no English, while the majority of high officials in this country knew no German. In order to communicate the more important directions for the conduct of the service, a medium less uncertain than that of vociferous gesticulation was required ; and the only language of which the King and his ministers possessed common knowledge was Latin. Latin, however, was by no means the ideal language in which to explain to a German monarch the traditional intricacies of the English coronation service, and the fact that the ceremony passed off as well as it did is a tribute as much to German intuition as to English organization.

A number of Jacobite nobles were present, but we learn from one of the ladies-in-waiting that they looked very disgruntled—probably because, in spite of a few minor riots in their favour, they realized they were the champions of a lost cause. Certainly George had the strongest elements of the country on his side ; though when the Archbishop of Canterbury presented the King to the people and demanded their consent, Lady Dorchester laconically remarked to her neighbour : "Does the old fool think that anybody will say 'no' to his question when there are so many drawn swords about ?"

Clearing the Tables

The coronation banquet has more often been the occasion for untoward happenings than the coronation ceremony ; and the banquet that followed the coronation of George I was certainly not without a memorable feature, even though this occurred when the meal was technically over. Thoroughly tired and hungry after serving so many guests, the numerous waiting-men decided to postpone the task of washing-up until after they had taken a meal. When they returned to the hall some while after, much refreshed and ready to tackle the enormous task of clearing

away, they found to their astonishment that their work was already accomplished. Not only were the tables completely bare, but everything—down to the tablecloths—had been removed. That thieves had been at work was only too apparent ; but how they had effected an entrance, how they had accomplished their work without noise, and, finally, who they were—these questions, but, above all, the last, never received a satisfactory solution.

Lighted by 4000 Tapers

Unlike George I, who had made little or no attempt to harmonize his own tastes with those of his subjects, George II had early found favour with the English people. This was due partly to the fact that, at the time of his father's coronation, he knew a great deal more about England, and certainly more of the English language, than the King, and partly to the fact that he had better and more ingratiating manners. In the arrangements for his coronation ceremony he displayed more than usual interest ; and the actual occasion—to which dignity was lent by the music of Handel—was one of great magnificence. A slight mishap occurred before the ceremony owing to the fact that the authorities of the Abbey remembered everything except the chalice and the paten (the plate for the bread in the Eucharist) ; and as these latter had to be presented along with the Bible and the Regalia, some delay and not a little embarrassment were caused.

Of the banquet following the rite, no feature was held to be more remarkable than the elaborate means employed for illumination—it is said that no fewer than 4000 wax tapers were used to fill the gilded candelabra which branched from the ceiling. Until the entry of the Queen, however, the entire hall was kept in darkness ; but within a minute after her presence was announced, the whole room, as if by a miracle, was a blaze of light—a notable technical accomplishment for those days. As for the populace, they signified their approval of the new King and his consort in the usual manner—they got hilariously drunk by the end of the evening.

No coronation of any English King was more full of untoward happenings than that of George III. It consisted of a series of incongruous mishaps—some serious, some awkward and some positively ludicrous.

Mishap after Mishap

In the first place, the procession was delayed at the eleventh hour owing to the discovery that certain parts of the Regalia were missing, including the Sword of State, and also the State chairs and the canopy used for the King and Queen at the banquet. As these could not be found, a canopy was roughly improvised and the ceremonial sword of the Lord Mayor borrowed. Evidently this last-minute scramble flustered the King, for he found the subsequent service so long and exhausting that, during the communion, he asked the Archbishop if he might remove his crown. The Archbishop replied that no precedent existed for such an action, but the King, asserting his sovereignty for the first time, removed the crown with the words, "Then there shall be one!" That the Queen wished to dispense with hers also is not surprising, seeing that it weighed about three and a half pounds; but, unfortunately, in her case, removal was not so easy, as the crown had been attached to her hair to prevent its falling.

After the ceremony, at the close of which the King had to be revived with smelling-salts, came the procession to the banquet; and it was during this procession that a large diamond fell out of the crown, though fortunately this was restored without difficulty. As the ceremony had ended late, the public saw very little of the procession, and what they did see looked, according to Walpole, more like a funeral.

The lateness of the hour, indeed, was responsible for one of the most disorderly events of the day. In harmony with the arrangements at the previous banquet, an elaborate system of lighting had again been installed in the hall, but since no illumination was permitted until the entry of the sovereigns, many of the guests experienced difficulty in finding their places. The fact that the seating arrangements were defective added complication to confusion, and those who did not stumble over chairs stumbled over one another, yells and curses being addressed indiscriminately to objects both animate and inanimate. But such disorder as prevailed previous to the lighting of the candles was nothing to that which followed. By an arrangement in which discretion was sacrificed to ingenuity, each chandelier had been connected with the next by a train of prepared wax; and within a minute of lighting the trains, all the tapers were burning brightly. But the engineers of this scheme had not calculated upon the fact that while the flame was travelling from one chandelier to another, the guests in the hall would be inundated with flakes of burning tow; and this is what, in fact, happened. For a few minutes something very like terror prevailed among the guests; and with so much inflammable material about, it is a wonder that no conflagration ensued. Fortunately, the rain of fire soon subsided.

Hungry Onlookers

The galleries were crowded with people who, owing to the long wait, were now very hungry; and numerous contrivances were employed to procure some of the food from the tables below. Not only were baskets let down by means of cords, but some of the more enterprising ladies sacrificed their handkerchiefs to construct a line for hoisting up bottles of wine, and meat.

The most ludicrous event of the evening occurred, however, with the entry of the Champion, who was accompanied by Lord Talbot. In order that he should face the King, both when he entered the hall and when he retired, the latter had been at great pains to train his horse to walk backwards. Unfortunately, the horse interpreted his master too literally, and insisted—much to the discomfiture of the rider and to the amusement of the spectators—upon entering the hall in the

LAST APPEARANCE OF THE KING'S CHAMPION

From the Coronation of Richard II in 1377 to that of George IV the King's Champion rode into Westminster Hall during the banquet and threw down his gauntlet in defiance of the King's enemies. This drawing by Charles Wild, now in the Victoria and Albert Museum, shows the scene at the Coronation of George IV. The Champion, in full armour, rides into Westminster Hall with the High Constable on his right and the Earl Marshal on his left.

way that he had been trained to leave it. Following upon this incident occurred a rather more mysterious event, of which there have been a number of conflicting accounts. It is said, for example, that when the Champion threw down his gauntlet, a reply came in the form of a white glove from one of the galleries— probably from a Jacobite. Certainly a silence fell upon the hall, for the rumour had gone round that the Pretender—who was almost certainly present at the ceremony—meant to accept the challenge.

Some say that after the Champion's glove had been cast, the attention of the public was distracted for some moments, and that when the Champion was about to leave the hall the glove was found to have disappeared. Still another version insists that while the audience was waiting for the Pretender to reply with his challenge, an old lady, whose knowledge of tradition must have been somewhat scanty, picked up the glove and, hastily returning it to the Champion, said : "Be careful with your fine gloves, young man."

King George had a sense of humour, but the mishaps of the day put a severe strain upon it, until at last he was prompted to complain to the Deputy Earl Marshal. The latter, tired with the work of organization, answered him as follows : "It is true," he said, "that there has been some neglect, but I have taken care that the next coronation shall be regulated in the best manner possible." The King was so taken aback that he had no alternative but to laugh ; but he gave the Deputy Earl a most effective punishment— he made him repeat the remark several times.

At the time of his accession King George IV was somewhat unpopular with his people owing to his treatment of his wife, Queen Caroline. In spite of the fact that she had been estranged from him for seven years, the Queen announced her right to be crowned with him at the Abbey. The prospect of a demonstration in her favour brought enormous crowds to London three or four days before the ceremony, and persons whose windows provided a view of the procession made huge profits. So thick were the crowds in the neighbourhood of the Abbey that ticket-holders, many of whom arrived as early as one o'clock in the morning, had to fight their way to their seats. In order to distract the public attention from the domestic scandal, the pageantry of this coronation was more than usually lavish, costing in all about £240,000 ; but although the Queen did not get her way—for when she arrived at the Abbey she was refused admission because she was without a ticket—the King's action was not calculated to make him popular.

The ceremonial, including the procession, lasted from 9.30 till 4 o'clock, and the day was more than usually oppressive. But George IV, who was a portly man, had evidently prepared for emergencies. In the Chapel of St. Edward, for example, he had arranged for the establishment of what can only be called a running buffet. The altar was used as a table upon which numerous bottles and plates of sandwiches were placed, and the King spent his time between this and the Abbey chancel.

While he was away the service was suspended, and according to all accounts it seems to have been suspended pretty frequently. When the time for the homage arrived, the King was almost prostrate, but, armed with smelling-salts and wiping his face with a supply of handkerchiefs which he handed on to the embarrassed Archbishop, he rallied sufficiently to express his changing sentiments as the leaders of the various parties in the State approached.

GEORGE IV'S CORONATION BANQUET

King William IV decided that his coronation should not be followed by a banquet in Westminster Hall. That decision was a result of the unfortunate incidents that had marred the Coronation banquet of George IV. After it was over the tables were stripped of all that they bore. The illustration, from a drawing by Charles Wild, shows the first course being served at George IV's banquet.

Yet more exhausting was the atmosphere of the banquet. Thousands of people were accommodated in the galleries and at the tables, which as usual were lit by candles; and so great was the heat of the burning wax that even the curls on the ladies' heads began rapidly to disappear. Not content with discomforting the guests from afar, the candles then proceeded to deliver a more direct assault by pelting the whole concourse with liquid wax. The resulting havoc, especially to the ladies' dresses, was tremendous; and hardly a person escaped unsullied. After the guests had left, the multitude from the galleries closed in upon the tables and, carrying off what they did not devour, stripped the hall of every vestige of finery.

A great contrast was the coronation of William IV. He hated display of all kinds, and would certainly have dispensed with a coronation if he had been allowed to. As it was, the ceremony was shorn of most of its picturesqueness, and the sentiments of the King, if not of the people, were perhaps best embodied in a statement that was issued before the day. "Those parts of the ceremony which had been fitted to a period when the outward senses were made panders to the all-absorbing superstition within, should be rejected, and only those retained in which an educated, inquiring people may see some relation between the nature of a kingly contract and its accompanying incidents." The procession, the Champion and the banquet were one and all cancelled, thus breaking a tradition of many hundreds of years.

In view of the fact that Princess Elizabeth attended the coronation of George VI, it is interesting to record that Queen Victoria, then a girl of eleven years of age, was not allowed to attend the coronation of William IV. Rumours spread that the exclusion was due to the King's disappointment that he could not be succeeded by a child of his own; others said that Earl Grey had deliberately excluded her owing to his annoyance over the King's abolition of the procession and banquet. Actually, the reason was that the Duchess of Kent feared for the young princess's health, and the King, all too reluctantly, had granted her leave of absence.

NINE PAGES TO BEAR GEORGE IV'S ROBE

Nine pages, all the sons of peers, bore the Coronation robe of George IV. They wore Elizabethan costumes with ruffs, doublets and puffed hose, and carried caps surmounted with ostrich plumes. The King, on entering the Abbey, wore the black Spanish hat of the Order of the Garter, surmounted with an immense mass of plumes. Lord Londonderry and Prince Leopold were the only other persons present at the Coronation with similar hats.

THE EMPIRE'S TRIBUTE

by

ERNEST SHORT

*Author of "King George the Well-Beloved", "The
Coronation, Its History and Meaning", etc., etc.*

How the British Empire
Overseas Celebrated the
Coronation of George VI.

IMPERIAL POMP AND CIRCUMSTANCE

The proclamation of King George VI in the cities of India was carried out with impressive ceremonial. In Calcutta the stately colonnaded façade of the Town Hall made a perfect setting for the proceedings. A carpet was laid on the imposing flight of steps, at the top of which all the notabilities of Calcutta were assembled, while native troops were lined up facing the building. Outside the railing a large crowd of spectators assembled. A closer view of the ceremony is given in page 263.

CHAPTER 17

ON THE CONTINENT OF AFRICA

In all five continents the Coronation was celebrated by subjects of the British Empire. In Africa the peoples of a great Dominion, of various Colonies, dependencies and Mandated Territories, each in their own way paid their tribute of loyalty to the King and Queen

THE Coronation of Britain's King on May 12th, 1937, was a vast historical symbol, and it had a twofold purpose. It served to dedicate George VI to his high task, but, in acclaiming their new King, his subjects at the selfsame time dedicated themselves to a loyalty even more eager and passionate than that they rendered to George the Well-Beloved and Mary the Queen Mother. As Mr. Alfred Noyes wrote of the last Coronation, the Empire crowns a British King in the "red dawn of its toil".

Accordingly, this tribute of the Empire, recalling as it does Coronation celebrations in many lands and among many peoples, will emphasize an act of Imperial dedication arising from the profound conviction :

This day, thy thousand years acclaim
The mightier morning of thy years to be !

The tribute will thus become a word-pageant of the Empire as it is, coupled with a record of the aspirations which its citizens reaffirmed on Coronation morning, in the belief that the trust which history has given into their charge will become still more potent for good, and, under George VI, add, if addition be possible, to the majesty of the British Crown.

Years ago, long before he had any expectation of coming to the throne, the King himself, then Duke of York, used these significant words. He was speaking at Canberra, and the occasion was the opening of the Commonwealth Parliament House. Not unnaturally, it prompted thoughts regarding a future of ever-increasing prosperity, which, in dreams at any rate, a loyal citizen at times indulges. Said the Duke :

"Today marks the end of an epoch and the beginning of another and one's thoughts turn instinctively to what the future has in store. One's own life would be hardly worth living without its dreams of better things, and the life of a nation without such dreams of a better and larger future would be poor indeed."

Pretoria's Acropolis

Among all the centres of Imperial celebration, none has a setting more impressive than the Acropolis, Pretoria. The genius of Sir Herbert Baker (who, with Sir Edwin Lutyens, also designed Imperial Delhi) has crowned the rough rock with a Parliament House which is at once the active instrument of South African rule under the British Crown, and an emblem telling that a thousand years of English history have united themselves with the destiny of British and Dutch from Table Bay to the Zambezi. A South African May is an English autumn, and the jacaranda was in bloom when the Union's Governor-General announced the crowning of its new King to South Africa. Not a few of the Coronation celebrants at Pretoria reached the Acropolis walking over a carpet of the jacaranda's purple-blue, while its shadowing branches echoed the colour overhead.

Photo]   *[South African Government*

CENTRE OF PRETORIA'S CORONATION CELEBRATIONS

When the Union of South Africa was formed in 1910, Cape Town became the legislative capital of the dominion and Pretoria the executive capital. To house the executive the Government erected a magnificent block of buildings on Meintje's Kop overlooking the city and forming a rallying point for all official celebrations. The building was designed by Sir Herbert Baker, the architect of many beautiful buildings in South Africa and England.

Mingled with this purple was the red of the aloes, both being set against the warm brown of the autumn leaves. The Acropolis, Pretoria, was the pulsing heart of South Africa on Coronation morning, and what the Governor-General, on behalf of his ministers and the people of South Africa, reaffirmed was the original message of dutiful homage sent to King George on his accession to the throne. The expression of loyalty was coupled with the hope and trust that his reign might be long and happy, and conducive to the peace, prosperity and development of all parts of his Dominions.

The Pretoria celebration was *primus inter pares* among South African Coronation rejoicings. The area of the Union, including the mandated territory of South-West Africa, is almost 800,000 square miles. It exceeds the combined area of Germany, France, Spain, Italy and Portugal, and nine Great Britains could be set within its wide spaces. In such a land there is necessarily decentralization. As Pretoria is the centre of administration, so Cape Town is the centre of legislature, and here, too, there were celebrations, eclipsed in

political significance by those at Pretoria, but in nothing else. The evening carnivals staged at the Mount Nelson or the Queen's Hotel were worthy of comparison with those in the West End of London—at the Dorchester, the Grosvenor or the Ritz. There were similar revels at the Carlton or the Lutjes-Langham, in Johannesburg, at the Marine Hotel, Durban, the Imperial, Pietermaritzburg, and other outstanding hotels in the capitals. In South Africa, at any rate, there was money to burn in the Coronation year. The gold mines had never been so prosperous, and how could unexpected gains be dissipated more pleasantly than in a "do" on a night which recurs only once in a generation ?

At not a few of South Africa's feastings men who had made money in diamonds toasted the fame of "The Cullinan", the stone that enabled South Africa to contribute not only the principal diamond to the Imperial State Crown of George VI' but the chief jewel in the Sceptre. The Cullinan weighed one and three-quarter pounds when it was unearthed at Pretoria, and measured four inches by two and a half by two, before it was cut into the jewels which are now included in the Regalia. The monster diamond resembled a block of rock salt in its primitive state, and it was plain that it could never be cut into a single brilliant. In the end nine big stones were made, the largest being the pear-shaped brilliant in the Sceptre, and the next largest the cushion-shaped brilliant in the band of King George's Crown, just below the Black Prince's ruby. This

Photos] [Wide World

FINE SETTING FOR CEREMONIAL OCCASIONS

Cape Town, in its romantic setting with a magnificent thoroughfare, Alderley Street, running through the heart of the city towards Table Mountain, affords an ideal background for public rejoicings. Above is the Union Parliament House as it appears when floodlit. On great occasions Johannesburg's celebrations centre round the Town Hall, a fine modern building seen illuminated below.

"Star of Africa" alone weighs 310 carats. The uncut diamond belonged to the Transvaal Government. When the South African Union became an accomplished fact, General Botha suggested presenting the stone to King Edward VII for inclusion in the Regalia, in token of the loyalty of the Afrikanders. And so it was.

Other South African Celebrations

The official celebrations in the Orange Free State were centred in Bloemfontein. Here Hoffmann Square, with its fountains, was as gay with flowers by day as it was lovely under the lights by night. Coronation Day was a public holiday, and South Africans, like most Dominioners, prefer to make holiday in the open. At Bloemfontein they forgathered among the roses of King's Park, or in the game reserve on Naval Hill, where the buck and the koodoo roam at will. Others sought the lovely riverside retreat, Mazelspoort, on the Modder River, with its superb bathing pool. If the folk of Bloemfontein sought an excursion which would take them farther from home, they picnicked in Basutoland, and watched the natives celebrating the Coronation of King George. From Durban, a motor run of three hours took Natalians to Eshowe, the capital of Zululand, where there were similar native rejoicings. An attractive town, Eshowe, with its white-walled and red-roofed houses, set in gardens gay with flowers! In Pietermaritzburg, Natal's capital, the City Hall was the centre of the celebrations.

Passing north, covering the miles of the karroo, in the Free State, with its thirsty red earth, or the monotonous green of the veld, which shows its full beauty only when the stars are looking down upon South Africa, the pageant of African celebrations draws us to the Rhodesias. The journey emphasizes the strange medley of racial types which have contributed to South African history. First the Bushmen, then the Hottentots and Bantus. After them, the early whites —Portuguese and Dutch, with an occasional French Huguenot or self-exiled German. And at last the British, in full flood.

At Salisbury, Sir Herbert Stanley, the Governor, was in charge of the proceedings outside the municipal offices, where he had proclaimed the accession of King George a few months before. The corner of Salisbury which displayed this sentiment most surely was the square with the Memorial to the Pioneers. It was only unveiled in 1935, but it enshrines all that Rhodesians desire to pass on to their sons and daughters. On Coronation Day, with the strange buzz of Britain's wireless still haunting their imaginations, the townsfolk of Salisbury came upon the Memorial to the Pioneers. And, coming, they stopped and read :

Fort Salisbury, 1890
The
Pioneer Corps
Specially recruited to become the first civil
population of
Mashonaland
under the Leadership of
Major Frank Johnson
and the
British South Africa Police.
Lt.-Col. Pennefather in command of the Column arrived here on the 12th September 1890.
On this spot the Union Jack was hoisted, signifying the Occupation of Mashonaland by the
British South Africa Company
Cecil John Rhodes
Being the Founder.

This was the type of self-dedication which a Rhodesian had in mind in mid-May, 1937, and it gave reality to his musings upon the rite enacted in the Church of St. Peter, Westminster. If he felt a bit hazy about the crowning of kings on the other side of the equator, the monument to his pioneers taught him something about British settlers in the "red dawn of their toil", and he felt the stronger for his share of the Empire's work.

In Northern Rhodesia, the celebrations centred upon Lusaka, the million-pound capital, cut from the jungle-like bush, which is now being built to the plans of Professor Adshead, of London University. The first brick was not laid until August, 1931, yet Lusaka could boast of sixteen miles of macadamized roads when King George was crowned. The Duke of Kent, then Prince George, laid the foundation stone of the Government buildings when he visited Northern Rhodesia in 1934. Fifty months before Coronation Day lions used to roam over the site of the Empire's new capital town.

The celebrations in Kenya, Uganda and the Sudan were carried through with special zest, as these colonies and dependencies chanced to be parts of the Empire which the King and Queen had visited. As Duke and Duchess of York, they landed at Mombasa just before Christmas in 1924, so early in their married life that the tour might almost be regarded as part of their honeymoon. They spent Christmas with the Governor at Nairobi and were welcomed by 2000 Kenya natives when they visited a new church. Somewhat to her surprise, Queen Elizabeth discovered that she had some skill with a big-game rifle, and a rhinoceros fell to her gun during the shooting expedition which commenced on Boxing Day. From Kenya the Duke and Duchess passed to Uganda. They were escorted across Lake Victoria Nyanza by 200 native war canoes, and the trip ended at Khartoum, in the Sudan. So came about that on Coronation night natives drinking their Chwala could boast that they had both seen and heard George King".

In Kenya, many of the

Photo]   *[Topical*

GOLD COAST CHIEF

Such an occasion as the Coronation affords the great Gold Coast chief, Sir Ofori Atta, a fresh opportunity to display that loyalty which has already won him the honour of a knighthood. He is the proud possessor of a number of crowns, the most ornate of which he wears on occasions of the highest importance

Coronation celebrations were markedly European, for here the uplands are a "white man's country". Nairobi has assembly rooms and hotels, where meals, music and dancing can be staged in something like the Piccadilly manner. Earlier in the day a Cross of Sacrifice in these East African colonies was a centre of pilgrimage for many, since no Imperial celebration can fail to bring back memories of the World War. There is such a Cross of Sacrifice in the South Cemetery, Nairobi, though one would have thought Kenya far enough away from "The Watch on the Rhine" to have spared the settlers their toll of death in the World War. The new Governor and Commander-in-Chief of the Colony, Air Chief Marshal Sir Henry Brooke-Popham, reached Kenya in March, in time to lead the Coronation celebrations. At Mombasa, the gun crews of the K.R.N.V.R. were much to the fore.

In December 1823, a naval detachment hoisted the British flag for the first time at Mombasa, and in 1887 the city became the capital of the protectorate of British East Africa.

Nigeria ("Lugard's Land"), unlike the Kenya Highlands, can by no stretch of imagination be regarded as white man's country. Nevertheless, it is the largest tropical dependency under the rule of George VI, with the exception of India. Its area of 332,000 square miles is equal to that of Germany and Italy combined, with Belgium

16

thrown in as a makeweight. It also has 15,000,000 people within its borders. On Coronation Day the market-place in Kano, the famous Kasua Kumari, where 6000 tribesmen in their blue and white raiment bargain at a time around the clay-built booths, was as characteristic a centre of celebration as any in West Africa. In Nigeria, a British Commissioner may be in charge of 100,000 natives, of many types and many tongues, so patriotic propaganda is not easy. But by speech and proclamation the district commissioners did their best to make it plain to Tuaregs, Kanuris, Arabs, and the rest, that a British King was being hallowed to the task of Empire-ruling in far-away London.

Among the African chiefs representing 50,000,000 loyal natives who acknowledge the suzerainty of King George VI is Sir Ofori Atta, who has already received a knighthood of the Bath for his services to the Crown in the Gold Coast, where he i Paramount Chief of Akyem Abuakwa Tshekedi Khama, David of Uganda and Yeta of Barotseland are other rulers of note

It is often forgotten how close is thei alliance with the Crown and how they valu the good that has arisen from the Imperia connexion. A few months ago, in Nigeria a tower of honour was erected in memor of Sir Robert Bower, the first Resident a Ibadan. Bower suppressed the slave traffi in his district and brought peace to th warring tribesmen, and the Nigerian chief wanted to show that they had not forgotten

At Khartoum, in the Sudan, there was a parade of troops and police, at which th Governor announced the Coronation i appropriate terms, standing on the step of Government House and speaking first i English and then i Arabic. On either sid were notables in robe of honour, representin the various tribes. I the provincial towns o the Sudan, in Wa Medani, El Obeid Fasher, and elsewhere were similar gathering so that every body o tribesmen in the pr tectorate might know o the majesty of Britain King, from the Baggara of the west to th "Fuzzy-Wuzzies" of th Red Sea hills. In th afternoon, at Khartoun a garden party was hel at the Palace, and in th evening a dance in th Grand Hotel. For th rest, wherever two o three Britons wer gathered in distant ou posts on the Sudan flyin routes the loyal toas were honoured.

Photo]   [Central Press

NATIVE CHIEFS IN FESTAL ARRAY

Among the subjects of the King are people of almost every race and creed, and none delight more to participate in public ceremonies than the native chiefs of the African colonies and protectorates. Nigerian chiefs are here seen in their bright-hued robes and strange head-dresses at the inauguration of the memorial to Sir Robert Bower, their great benefactor and protector at Ibadan.

CHAPTER 18

CELEBRATIONS IN TWO DOMINIONS

The people of Australia and New Zealand have many times given remarkable manifestations of their loyalty to the throne. Such occasions as Royal visits, the Silver Jubilee and the Coronation have called forth an enthusiasm unexcelled in any other part of the Empire

THE capital cities of Australia and New Zealand share with Kenya, Uganda and the Sudan the memory of a visit from King George and Queen Elizabeth. Their Majesties were there in 1927, a few months after the birth of Princess Elizabeth. On his return, speaking at the London Guildhall, the then Duke of York told of his landing in Sydney on a perfect summer morning and of the enthusiasm of the townsfolk as the Renown passed up Sydney Harbour. What would King George have said had he been able to witness the public excitement in the Australian capitals on May 12th, when his subjects "down South" acclaimed the Coronation of their King and Queen ?

King George would also have approved the undertone of re-dedication to the task of nation-building which accompanied the Hallowing of the Empire's King in Westminster. Sir Robert Borden, in Canada, once defined this task as "a partnership of the dead, the living and the as yet unborn", and some such thought would seem to have been the abiding impression which his visit to Australia and New Zealand left upon George VI. In his Guildhall address of 1927 (an address which was not unworthy to rank with the "Wake up, England" speech which George V delivered in the same place after the Australian tour made by himself and Queen Mary) the King paid a high tribute to the pioneer settlers of Australia and the sister Dominion, New Zealand.

"When one reflects on what the Dominions are today and what they were a hundred years ago, it is a tribute to British pluck and determination to have created such countries out of the wild."

In Australia and New Zealand it is not a matter of a thousand years of past history acclaiming the national destiny, but a bare century. Nevertheless, King George found no reason for doubting the future of the Dominions under the Southern Cross. He continued :

"Given a continuance of the spirit which animated the early pioneers, I see no limit to the development of these great countries, and I predict for them a wonderful destiny as population increases and industry and production grow and progress. Both countries are intensely British and determined that the future population must be of British stock. Both are desirous of welcoming kinsmen from home, to assist in the great task that lies before them. With wise development to increase their power of absorbing larger numbers, I am confident that they will be in the future one of the greatest homes of the British race. Not only will such an increase of population mean a great accession of strength to the Empire, but with the desire for reciprocal trade, which is part of the policy both of Australia and New Zealand, it will provide increasing markets for British industry, and will make for larger employment."

When King George and Queen Elizabeth came to the throne, Mr. Lyons, as Prime

Minister of Australia, recalled the King's visit, and "the charming presence of his wife, who is henceforth to be our Queen". Mr. Lyons added :

"The new King is a man whom we know and love. He takes with him to the throne a wife we also know and love. Less than ten years ago they were in Australia with us. We, in Canberra, particularly have cause to remember the visit, for it was the new King who opened the Parliament from the halls of which I now speak. We remember specially the new King's deep interest in the youth of this country and in the industrial conditions which prevailed here. From one end of Australia to the other their visit is fresh in our minds."

The proclamation of the accession was made in the presence of Lord Gowrie, the Governor-General, and took place at the foot of the statue of George the Well-Beloved in King's Hall, Parliament House, Canberra. This was also the place of the Federal celebration of the Coronation. Mr. Lyons, the Prime Minister, Sir Archdale Parkhill, Minister of Defence, and Mr. R. G. Casey, Treasurer, as well as a number of State Premiers, were in London, as members of the Coronation deputation which represented Australia at the Coronation and the Imperial Conference; but the Governor-General was supported by the ministers and senators who had remained in Australia to carry on the business of government. Parading in front of them were any Anzacs in the Federal territory and, on either side, Boy Scouts, Girl Guides and as many school children as Canberra can muster.

Man-, woman- and child-power are scarce at Canberra, so the real Coronation festivities were not in the planned capital which Australian pride has created at Canberra, but in the bigger centres of population. For characteristic Australian rejoicings one must turn to Sydney, Melbourne, Adelaide, Brisbane, Perth and Hobart, the State capitals. Here the Australian people mingled a public holiday with expressions of devotion to the King and the Empire which began, maybe, as a career of conquest, but has become a world-wide brotherhood.

In Sydney, the centre of Coronation rejoicings was Government House. With its battlements and towers, the Governor's house recalls a Tudor castle, though it was built only a hundred years ago. Set in spacious gardens behind Circular Quay, it has always been a central point in the urban landscape. To complete the picture, add the broad

Photo]   [*L.N.A.*

AT SYDNEY'S FLAG-DECKED PARLIAMENT HOUSE

In all the capitals of the States of the Commonwealth of Australia King George VI was proclaimed before a large assemblage of notable persons. The photograph shows Sir Philip Street, Lieutenant-Governor of New South Wales, reading the proclamation from the verandah of Parliament House, Sydney.

reaches of the harbour, the coves snuggling amid the hillocks, and see the whole of the vast riverscape dominated by the massy structure of Sydney's new bridge. Harbour and bridge alike are the best in the world, say Sydney folk, and few would care to dispute the dictum. It is very near to the truth. Ocean liners at Circular Quay (once Sydney Cove, where the Commonwealth of Australia had its birth in 1788) recall Australia's contacts with the world of commerce and trade. But more characteristic, at any rate on a public holiday, were the white-winged yachts and sailing boats in the harbour.

The wireless broadcasts from London were extended into the next day, owing to ten or eleven hours' difference in time between Eastern Australia and the Mother Country. Sydney folk were, therefore, free to treat Coronation Day as a holiday. Many attended race meetings or sports grounds. Randwick is the Flemington of Sydney, as Flemington is the Randwick of Melbourne. Many more made for one of the golden-sanded beaches between Sydney Harbour and Barrenjoey Head.

The water-slides, rotors, testers and other comic turns in the enclosed pools of Manly and other beaches were also prominent in Sydney's Coronation holiday. And, in the evening, dinner, with loyal toasts, dancing and listening-in to the broadcasts from London. The news of the actual Crowning came through in express time—only a few seconds, thanks to the wonder of 'wireless'. Then the bells rang out, as they were ringing in far-away Westminster. The Sydney Council organized a carnival for children in the civic playgrounds, and a civic ball, which alone cost £2000. The elaborate decorations of Sydney Town Hall were devised so that they might be used again for the 50th anniversary celebrations in 1938.

The Victorian Premier, Mr. Dunstan, was in London during May, but the State Governor, Lord Huntingfield, was in Melbourne as representative of the Crown. Apart from the State Parliament in Spring Street and Bourke Street, and Government

[*Wide World*

REMEMBRANCE AMID REJOICING

Within half a mile of Sydney Cove is the New South Wales War Memorial, an imposing stone structure. In front of it is the "Pool of Remembrance" and when the floodlit memorial is reflected in the still water, Sydney's great tribute to the dead is seen at its best.

House itself, the Shrine of Remembrance on the St. Kilda Road is a centre of communal celebration. Here was held the commemoration of Anzac Day on April 25th, and the Shrine was a place of pilgrimage three weeks later, on Coronation morning. Acts of homage had to be done to those who died in Gallipoli, on the Somme, during the storming of the Hindenburg Line. On Coronation Day Victorians recalled a tradition of public service which rivalled that of the early pioneers. If the pioneers established the Australian community, the heroes of the World War established Australia in the front rank of nationhood.

Similarly, the historic spot where John Batman, the founder of Melbourne, landed was not forgotten. It is marked by a

stone set into the footpath, at the corner of Flinders Street and William Street.

For the rest, picture Flinders Street railway station, with its great clock tower, gay with bunting, as it had been in October, 1934, when the Duke of Gloucester visited Melbourne for the city's centenary. Flinders Street has a heavier passenger traffic than any station in the world, and all the Melbourne lines converge upon it. The bridges over the Yarra—Prince's Bridge, Queen's Bridge, and the rest—were also beflagged. Apart from the Yarra, Melbourne cannot boast the natural attractions of Sydney. Its pride is in its ninety-nine-foot thoroughfares, its fine Gothic cathedral, its stately public buildings and business premises, the tree-lined roads radiating into such suburbs as St. Kilda, its cricket grounds, and the racecourses at Flemington or Caulfield.

As in Sydney, the broadcasts from London reached Melbourne towards midnight,

Photos]   *[Keystone Australian Trade Publicity*

IN A CITY OF THE COMMONWEALTH

The upper photograph shows Lord Huntingfield, Governor-General of Victoria, reading the proclamation outside the Parliament House in Melbourne in the presence of a great concourse of people. In front of him are the receivers of the loud-speakers that enabled him to be heard by all. Below is the Flinders Street station in the heart of Melbourne with the flood-lighting which the Dominion capitals, like London, have adopted to illuminate the streets at times of rejoicing.

Photo]   [Australian Trade Publicity

LEST WE FORGET

On every occasion of public rejoicing since 1918 the thoughts of millions have been turned to the dead soldiers of the Empire who by their sacrifice knit more closely that bond of loyalty to the Throne and Empire of which such impressive proof has been given this year. Melbourne's War Memorial is one of the finest in the Commonwealth. It is so built that at 11 o'clock on November 11 a ray of light coming through an aperture in the roof falls on the Rock of Remembrance within

owing to a ten hours' difference in time, so the waking hours of Coronation Day were free for holiday-making. A tramway run to Wattle Park for the frugal ; or a day on the foreshore at St. Kilda, on Brighton Beach, or at Karra Bend, where 520 acres of original "bush" have been enclosed as a national park. If a bigger expedition was desired, a picnic in the Dandenong ranges was a possibility, or at Healesville, amid the foothills of the Great Dividing Range. These ample facilities for open-air amusement characterize Australian urban life, and they distinguished their Coronation rejoicings from the gatherings in English, Welsh and Scottish cities.

The sentiment underlying all these Victorian celebrations echoed the promise of the State, which found official expression when Lord Huntingfield, with simple but stirring ceremonial, proclaimed George VI King from the steps of Parliament House, Melbourne, on December 14th, 1936. A feature of the proclamation was the firing of two royal salutes of twenty-one guns, the first at noon in honour of the King's birthday, and the second at 2.30 p.m., after the Governor had read the proclamation. It ended :

We now do hereby with one voice and consent of tongue and heart publish and proclaim that the high and mighty Prince Albert Frederick Arthur George is now become our only lawful and rightful liege Lord George the Sixth, by the Grace of God, of Great Britain, Ireland, and the British Dominions beyond the Seas, King, Defender of the Faith, Emperor of India, to whom we do acknowledge all faith and constant obedience, with all heart and humble affection, beseeching God, by whom Kings and Queens do reign, to bless the Royal Prince George the Sixth with long and happy years to reign over us.

Sir Harry Chauvel would have been in command of the Anzacs who paraded in Melbourne on Coronation Day, had he not been commanded to London to lead the defence contingent of 150 men, chosen to represent the Australian Commonwealth at the centre of Coronation rejoicings. He has been Australia's senior military officer since 1916, and may, perhaps, be regarded as the world's greatest cavalry leader. That, at any rate, is the opinion of Australians who served under him. The 150 men were divided equally among soldiers who served in the World War and the younger men serving in the Australian militia today, and there was a similar distinction in the ranks of those who honoured King George's Hallowing by parading on Coronation Day.

In Adelaide, Government House, the acknowledged link between South Australia and the Crown, lies in a belt of parkland, near the centre of the town, with the two spires of St. Peter's Cathedral rising near by. The Torrens River has been artificially dammed to form a lake at this point, and its banks are fringed by gardens, with Government House, Parliament House, the State Library, the War Memorial, the Museum, the University and the School of Mines amid the lawns and trees. Lord Bryce, who had known many cities in many lands, said of Adelaide that it was the nearest approach to a garden city he had seen. North Terrace, on the banks of the Torrens, was the centre of Adelaide's Coronation celebrations, with Major-General Sir Winston Dugan as the representative of George VI. As at the time of the King's proclamation from the steps of Parliament House on December 14th, 1936, there were a few full-blooded aborigines present to remind men of British blood that they were not the first inhabitants of the island continent.

Nor was the historic gum-tree at Glenelg forgotten. Here Captain John Hindmarsh, of the brig Buffalo, and Colonel Light pegged out the first South Australian settlement under the shadow of Mount Lofty. The bending gum is almost dead today, but it recalls the spot where the establishment of the colony was proclaimed on December 28th, 1836, and it was fitting that it should be kept in mind when the State's new King was crowned. The sentiment animating South Australia was summed up by Mr. Butler, the Premier, when he said of George VI:

"What struck me most about

Photo]   [Australian Trade Publicity
BRISBANE'S CITY HALL

Brisbane, the capital of the State of Queensland, though one of the smaller cities of the Commonwealth, has a high sense of civic pride. Its magnificent City Hall, in Queen Street, seen above, is a centre to which the people rally at a time of public rejoicing.

the Duke of York when I met him in South Australia was his quiet sincerity, clean and high ideals and determination to grasp and understand the problems of the people. The Duchess will bring added lustre to the Throne, which Queen Mary did so much to brighten and glorify. On behalf of South Australia I say with all sincerity, 'God bless them both!'"

For the rest of Coronation Day Adelaide men and women were free to enjoy the Morialto Cascade and other picnic haunts in the hill-country surrounding the capital. The Boy Scouts and Girl Guides "corroboreed", as they had been taught to do by Sir Percy Everett, whose visit from Scout Headquarters did so much for the movement in South Australia.

In Brisbane, the capital of Queensland, Anzac Square was the centre of Coronation rejoicings. Here, in the heart of the city, is a memorial colonnade, with its bronze altar from which lifts the eternal flame that burns in honour of Queenslanders who died in the World War. The City Hall, Brisbane's pride, also had its part in the celebrations. As in Pretoria, the jacaranda scatters its powdery blue blossoms in Brisbane in a Queensland "fall", and its petals coloured many a path taken by Coronation celebrants. It was in Queensland that George VI first took tea brewed in a "billy" can—Australia's famous "billy tea". At Beaudesert, outside Brisbane, he also watched the bullock-drafting competitions, with their amazing displays of horsemanship, which characterized more than one holiday gathering in Queensland on Coronation Day.

Australian Memories

Western Australia was founded as long ago as 1829, following upon the voyage of Sir James Stirling, aboard the Success, with a view to forestalling a possible occupation by the French in the Swan River area. Later came the exploration era, associated with the revered name of Forrest. In one case, John Forrest (later Lord Forrest) and his brother Alexander travelled overland to Adelaide, a journey of five months, which entailed tremendous hardships. The discovery of gold still further contributed to the Western Australia which celebrated the crowning of Britain's King with such generous loyalty. West Australians remembered how the Duke and Duchess of York had "received" the greater part of the State in Perth's park ten years earlier.

In Tasmania

Lastly, in Hobart (the second oldest city in Australia, though the capital of the smallest State), the City Hall, Parliament House and Government House all had their part in the Coronation festivities. With Mount Wellington at its back and the River Derwent winding through the estuary to Sullivan Cove, Hobart is another of the dream cities which characterize Australia. Sydney, Brisbane, Adelaide and Hobart: it would be hard to name four capital towns better favoured by Nature. The turrets of Tasmania's Government House rise on an isolated hillock overlooking the mouth of the Derwent. Parliament House is close to the wharves surrounding Sullivan Cove, Hobart's deep-water harbour. When the civic celebrations ended, Tasmanians were free to finish the holiday picnicking on the slopes of Mount Wellington, or listening to the "water-music" made by the cascade of Cora Lynn, as lovely in its way as that which Handel made for an earlier George on the broad banks of Thames.

Nevertheless, it may be doubted whether the pulsing heart of Australia is in any of these favoured capitals. May it not be that the Coronation of George VI was celebrated by the typical Australian, when some old bush "humpy" boiled his billy and drank to the King and Queen in tea? Today, Australia is a country of primary production and the great cities of the Commonwealth are secondary growths. In the karri forests, where the foresters watch the giant trees towering above the undergrowth; on Tambourine Mountain, in sun-drenched Queensland, where butts only less mighty lift their bodies and heads out of the ferns and palms; or in the river-flats where grow the gnarled red gums

—here we find an Australia which the poets and painters of the land regard as truly characteristic. Again, there is the mountain country of New South Wales, cut by the railroad which ends at Alice Springs, whence trails run out, north, west and south, though in the last two directions there is desert for the most part. Eastward and northward of Alice Springs, however, is cattle country, thanks to the artesian wells which British capital and Australian energy have provided.

In the out-stations pioneer work is still being done. Here Australians are still rejoicing in the red dawn of their toil—on sheep runs, or on cattle plains, where a boundary-rider may ride for a week and not come upon a fellow Briton. These men did not forget King George and Queen Elizabeth on Coronation morning. Nor did the fruit farmers in the Murray valley, with its groves of orange-trees or bowers of raisins and currants.

The drovers, some in a job, some on the tramp, with the gaunt Bushwomen who bear them company, also had their good wishes for the happiness of Britain's King and Queen, even if they were prefaced by nothing more than a muttered, "Blimey! Why, it's Coronation Day!"

§—In the Dominion of New Zealand

WHEN King George and Queen Elizabeth reached Auckland, "Queen City of the North", during the voyage on the Renown in 1927, the then Duke of York said, "The Duchess and I want to see as much of the New Zealand children as possible." In a later speech at Wellington the Duke coined and applied the phrase, "Take care of the children and the country will take care of itself." He could not have found a sentiment more certain to endear himself and his wife to New Zealanders. The Dominion is justly proud of its record in connexion with the saving of infant life and the training of New Zealand women in mother-craft. The reforms, which broke all world records, were primarily due to Sir Truby King, Lord Plunket, a former Governor-General, and Lady Plunket, and the Royal New Zealand Society for the Health of Women and Children, with its badge "To help the mothers and save the babies."

In a community with such a record, children naturally had a foremost place in the Coronation celebrations. Gatherings in the schools and patriotic demonstrations by young people were to be seen in practically every town.

No part of the Empire is more definitely Imperial in its outlook, and very many New Zealanders made a special trip to England for the Coronation. Indeed, all berths on the passenger liners were booked after January, so that tourist traffic to the Dominion virtually ceased, as it was impossible for visitors to secure passages. Mr. Savage, the Prime Minister, joined Mr. Nash, the Finance Minister, in London, for the Coronation and the Imperial Conference, leaving Lord Galway, the Governor-General, and Mr. Peter Fraser, the Minister for Education, Health and Marine, in charge of the home celebrations. Mr. Savage's words at the time of King George's accession summed up New Zealand's attitude to the Coronation :

"The loyalty of this Dominion to the Crown is as strong and enduring as ever it was, and the people of New Zealand will honour and serve the new King with all the traditional affection and sincerity."

The doings on Coronation Day showed that Mr. Savage had not misjudged his fellow Dominioners. The centre of the celebrations was the capital, Wellington. An English May was New Zealand's autumn. Though the native evergreens persisted, the English planes and other imported trees had shed most of their leaves, but Wellington is always delightful, lying as it does between the water of Port

Photos] [*L.N.A.*

CEREMONIAL DANCE OF MAORI MEN AND MAIDENS

There are about 75,000 Maoris in New Zealand, who have proved themselves loyal citizens of the Empire and good craftsmen and farmers. They have abandoned their warlike ways, but on occasions of national rejoicing they bedeck themselves in native finery and join in action dances. those of the men being founded on what were originally war dances

Nicholson and the abiding hills, which characterize so much of New Zealand's scenery, both in North and South Island. Parliament Buildings are only half finished, but, inside and outside, there is enough to suggest the noble pile which, when it is completed, will fitly represent New Zealand's seat of government.

On Mount Cook, near by, the carillon in the War Memorial Tower rang out its message of a peace that had arisen from strife. Londoners will remember the carillon in Hyde Park in 1930.

At New Zealand's Birth-place

Another centre of Coronation rejoicing was Waitangi, with its old-time Residency, which recently passed into the possession of the people of New Zealand, owing to the generosity of Lord and Lady Bledisloe. In front of the Residency the treaty of 1840 was signed, which brought New Zealand into the Empire. To British-born and Maori alike, the Residency and its surrounding park are holy ground, "the shrine where the Government and the Church of New Zealand were born", as a Maori leader once said.

At Christchurch, too, in the South Island, the fine Gothic cathedral had its service of personal and national dedication. It would have stirred any Englishman, perhaps because Christchurch is the most English of the New Zealand cities, and actually has its own River Avon winding through the town. If Christchurch strikes one as English, Dunedin, capital of Otago, is pronouncedly Scottish and Presbyterian. It was founded by pioneers from north of the Tweed, and there is a statue of Robbie Burns in Dunedin's Octagon. Still farther south is Invercargill. In all these towns the streets were decorated by day and illuminated by night. Under the general direction of the mayor in charge, Anzacs or members of the Defence Force, paraded, along with school children, Boy Scouts and Girl Guides. Their endeavour was to strike the community note as strongly as the sturdy individualism of the typical New Zealander permitted.

The Europeanized towns occupy only the foreground of the pageant which constitutes "Ao-Tea-Roa", or the "Long White Cloud", as the Maoris described New Zealand when their war canoes first broke into its silent seas. In New Zealand, as in Australia, there was also the farmer in his homestead, who gathered his family about him on Coronation Day and "listened-in" to the broadcasting. In some cases London was picked up direct. More often there were relays from such a station as "YA Auckland".

And the Maoris? King George saw them in their native surroundings at Rotorua and was privileged to witness a performance of a *haka*, or warrior dance, of immense proportions and efficiency, while the Maori girls obliged with a *poi* dance, in which they play with balls made of flax and hanging upon a long string.

These Maoris inhabited North and South Islands twenty-five generations before the men of Britain reached New Zealand. Tall, muscular, black of hair and olive-brown in complexion, they are among the pick of the Empire's native population, and in 1840 their assent to the governance of Queen Victoria did much to ensure the prosperity of the newly-founded colony.

In the South Seas

Lastly, there were the celebrations in the ocean outposts of New Zealand—in Cook Islands, in Bounty Islands (a discovery of Captain Bligh), in Chatham Island with its Moriori inhabitants, and elsewhere. The celebrations at Avarua, on the island of Rarotonga, were led by the Ariki or native king, who "rules" with the aid of a Resident Agent. Each inhabited island in the Cook group has its Island Council and its Ariki, and none forgot its duty to the Empire on May 12th. Even in Samoa, the National extremists ceased their passive resistance. Mr. Langstone, the Minister of Lands, recently spent a month in Samoa, upon a mission of pacification in this mandated territory. As a result Western Samoa accepted the fact of King George's rule well before his Coronation Day.

CHAPTER 19

CANADA'S TRIBUTE OF LOYALTY

In every great city, small towns and remote settlements, from the Atlantic to the Pacific, loyal Canadians made Coronation Day one of enthusiastic rejoicing, the celebrations among French Canadians being no less whole-hearted than those of British Canadians

UNLIKE Australia and New Zealand, it was spring in Canada when King George was receiving his Hallowing in the Abbey. The frost was out of the ground in the prairie fields, and the farmers were getting to work with their seeding. In the Rockies and the Appalachian mountains, the snows were melting, while the Great Lakes were once more free of ice. In a word, Canada was awake to a sunshine as full of tonic force as that of an English June. Picture the maple leaves displaying their tenderest green, and only at dawn and eventide showing those hints of fiery red which at times suggest a forest ablaze to the wondering Canadian.

There are 3,684,000 square miles in Canada—a territory larger than the United States. Putting out of the reckoning the mountain areas—the Rocky Mountains, with forests and minerals on the west, and the Appalachians to the east—where shall we fix our first gaze on Coronation morning? The central plain alone is as big as France and Germany combined, and of this at least half is rich prairie. One of these prairies was once the bed of a vast glacial lake. When its waters drained into the Hudson the rich alluvial was revealed in which to-day the wheatfields of Manitoba come to flower, fruit and seed.

It is true that almost one Canadian in three is a farmer. Nevertheless, on Coronation Day, Canada's loyal sentiments became vocal, not in the open prairie, but in the Dominion capital, Ottawa. Here, only a

few months before, on the occasion of the Proclamation, Mr. Mackenzie King, Prime Minister of the Dominion, had sent this message to George VI, on Canada's behalf:

"On this day of your Majesty's accession to the throne, I desire respectfully to convey the expression of the heartfelt loyalty and respect of the Government and people of Canada, and also on their behalf feelings of homage and attachment to the Queen. Our thoughts, too, are of their Royal Highnesses Princess Elizabeth and Princess Margaret Rose, each of whom already holds a place in our hearts. We pray for the happiness of all the members of the Royal Family, and that your Majesty may be greatly blessed in your home and your reign."

A Link Strong as Steel

In Rideau Hall, Ottawa (Government House), and the new House of Parliament, with the Peace Tower as its crowning glory, the feelings of Canadians found official expression. When the lovely carillon of fifty-three bells rang out from the tower on Parliament Hill, proclaiming the crowning of the King in London, not only the people of Ottawa but every Canadian knew he had membership in one far-flung Empire and that the binding force was the British Crown. Sir Herbert Marler, the Canadian Minister to the United States, addressing the Pilgrims of the United States earlier in Coronation Year, put into words what British and French Canadians alike desired to say to the world :

"While we are a free and sovereign nation, no Canadian, no matter before what altar he may worship or what language he may have learned at his mother's knee, is forgetful that our political institutions are founded on those of that little island in the northern sea. We are not forgetful of the splendid traditions of Great Britain. We are not forgetful that our political development has progressed step by step with hers, and, while now our political ties rest only on the fact that the King of Canada is the same as the King of Great Britain, that slender link is reinforced and made as strong as bars of steel by reason of those common traditions and developments which we in Canada and Great Britain equally venerate."

A slender link, but strong as bars of steel !

Ottawa and the great pile of Government buildings on Parliament Hill alike were worthy to be the scene of Canada's chief rejoicings on Coronation Day. In 1916 Parliament House was burnt to the ground, with the exception of the charming octagon behind the Library. When it was rebuilt, the central feature in the great Gothic pile was the Peace Tower. Here is the Memorial Chamber, with its Altar of Remembrance. Within are preserved the names of Canadians who died in the World War. Rideau Hall, now the Ottawa Government House, has arisen from the home of a pioneer. Successive Governors-General have added to it, and today it has the charm of a building which speaks of several decades and the progress of many interesting owners. The Marquess of Lorne and Princess Louise, a daughter of Queen Victoria, Lord Dufferin, Lord Lansdowne, Lord Minto, Lord Aberdeen, and the Duke of Connaught are some of the Governors-General who have left memories in Rideau Hall. Lord Tweedsmuir, better known as John Buchan, the novelist, is representing the Crown in Canada today and was the leading spirit in the Coronation celebrations, which centred round Government House.

Photo]   *[Wide World*

CENTRE OF CANADA'S CELEBRATIONS

Since the disastrous fire that destroyed Canada's Parliament buildings in 1916 a magnificent new block has been erected at Ottawa to house the Dominion Legislature. The wide open space in front of it makes it the natural rallying point of the people at all public rejoicings.

As Washington has become a shrine of national aspirations in the United States, so Ottawa enshrines all that is best in the national sentiment of Canada.

The Dominion's Royal Society, its Historical Association, the headquarters of the Canadian Boy Scouts, and other movements with a national or Imperial appeal have their homes here. Though Ottawa is often regarded as a city created by the whim of Queen Victoria as a Government centre for Canadians, who could not decide between Montreal or Kingston, Toronto or Quebec at the time of federation, it really has something like 300 years of history behind it. Champlain visited the site in 1613, when his creation, Quebec, itself was no more than a tiny encampment. However Queen Victoria's decision may have appeared in 1858, Ottawa has long justified the distinction conferred upon it.

Its delightful situation amid and around the waters of the Ottawa River, and the tree-clad heights upon which the Federal Parliament buildings and Government offices were to arise, alone justified the wise old Queen's decision. If not the present City, then the River Ottawa links up Dominion history with the progress of Canada from the earliest days. The Ottawa was the highway whereby the fur-traders of primitive Canada brought their skins to Montreal from the trading posts in the Far West. Later, the Ottawa was the river of the lumberers. Its broad reaches displayed the vast rafts of squared timber from which the French lumberjacks sang their delightful folk songs:

> Derrier chez nous, y-a-t-un étang,
>   En roulant ma boule.
> Trois beaux canards s'en vont baignant,
>   En roulant ma boule.
>   Rouli, roulant, ma boule roulant,
>   En roulant ma boule roulant,
>   En roulant ma boule.

On Coronation evening there were gala celebrations at such places as the Château Laurier Hotel. The illuminations, too, gave the capital a new beauty. The "White Coal", generated by the waterfalls in the upper reaches of the Ottawa River, make such civic illumination easy. Reflected in the mirror of the stately river, the Rideau Canal and other waterways, with

the silhouette of the Peace Tower standing out against the deep blue of the sky, Ottawa in its garb of light took on the mysterious loveliness of a dream city.

The French Canadians

If Ottawa is the marriage home of federated Canada, Quebec was the cradle of the infant community. Even today the many-towered city is full of historic memories. These begin with the city's foundation by Samuel de Champlain, in 1608. More than a century earlier, John Cabot, out of Bristol, had "discovered" Canada, and in 1534 Jacques Cartier, the mariner of St. Malo, sailed into the Gulf of the St. Lawrence and up the river for 1000 miles. He took possession of Lower Quebec on behalf of the French Crown. Cartier reached the site of Montreal, where he was stopped by the rapids. The first permanent colony was established by Champlain at Port Royal in 1605. The foundation of Quebec followed speedily, thus establishing the rights of France in the St. Lawrence basin.

Quebec itself, with the headland of Cape Diamond towering three hundred feet above the river, is a dominating point on the St. Lawrence waterway, but on Coronation Day the centre of historic interest moved westward to the neighbouring Plains of Abraham, where Wolfe won Canada for Britain. After many decades of Franco-Canadian fellowship there were few to grudge Britain the memories of their century-old victory. If there had been, Quebec could offer them the memorial in the Governor's Garden, overlooking the St. Lawrence, which Montcalm, the French commander, shares with Wolfe.

Compared with Quebec, Montreal is a vast metropolis. Its population is well over 1,000,000 people, and it is not only the second seaport in North America, but the greatest grain port in the world. Cartier reached the tiny Indian village of Hochelaga and gave the name Mont Royal to the height which towered behind it. Today, Mont Royal is Montreal—French, with an English accent. The same may be said of the city as a whole, for the broad lawns and the greenery of the elms which grow so freely in the suburbs of Montreal recall England, even if the maples seem less homely to the average Englishman. The numerous convents and monasteries in Montreal, and the fact that so many streets are named after saints are other unfamiliar notes. The haggling and bargaining in the vegetable markets, too, are un-English. But the sentiment is Canadian through and through, and the demonstrations of loyalty to Canada's King in Montreal during the Coronation festival heartened every lover of Empire. They suggested that Wolfe's conquest has proved to be one of the few successful wars in world history. As in South Africa, the cruel wastage of the past has given Mankind an example of two races, two languages and two historic cultures blending into a fresh unity which is as vital as either of the stocks from which it sprang.

The broadcasts from Westminster Abbey and the London streets were available to Canadians in their entirety. Their time was four or five hours behind that of London, so Canadians did not have to stay up late as did Australians or New Zealanders, in order to listen-in to the doings at Westminster. There were loudspeakers in the streets of Toronto, Montreal and Ottawa, so that no one who wished should miss King George's Coronation.

Canada's War Veterans

Of all the Canadian "listeners-in" none felt the tug of patriotic Imperialism more strongly than the men who had served with the Dominion contingents in France and Flanders and, maybe, made the solemn pilgrimage to Vimy Ridge in the summer of 1936. The memories of these Canadians were mingled with sorrowful memories, not only of comrades who fell on the battlefield, but of a well-loved leader to whom the Fates had also been less than kind—the man who, when Prince of Wales in 1919, said in Toronto:

"The War has shown that our free British nations can combine without loss of freedom as a single unit in vigorous defence of their common interests and ideals. The unity of the Empire in the War was the feature least expected by our enemies, and the most effective in saving the liberties of the world."

A contingent of 300 Canadian soldiers, many of whom were War veterans, represented the Dominion in London during Coronation Week.

Beside Lake Ontario

As Montreal is the metropolis of eastern Canada, so Toronto is the metropolis of the West. The name arises from an Indian word, meaning "the place of meeting". It still has its old-time significance, for here is gathered the trade which flows from the Prairie Provinces, by way of the Great Lakes. On Coronation Day Toronto was at its loveliest, when the illuminated city was mirrored in the broad reaches of Lake Ontario. Earlier, the Cenotaph by the Old City Hall was a gathering point. There were also official celebrations in Parliament Buildings, Queen's Park, while the twenty-three-bell carillon rang out its greetings to the newly-crowned King and Queen from the Soldiers' Tower in Toronto University.

When the holiday spirit manifested itself fully later on Coronation Day, the open spaces of the Exhibition Park were thronged with loyalists, bent upon recording their affection for Canada's Royal Family. A granite boulder in the Exhibition grounds marks the original "place of meeting" on the shores of the lake, which after centuries of effort was to be transformed into the chief manufacturing and distributing centre of Canada. If not all roads, then all railroads, lead to Toronto. In the vast Union Railway Station, which Edward VIII, as Prince of Wales, opened in 1927, the Canadian Pacific and Canadian National Railways meet. Three hundred and fifty trains arrive and leave the Union Station daily. The C.P.R.'s Royal York Hotel, which was a centre of celebration on Coronation night, is the tallest building in the British Empire.

Nevertheless, the illuminations, fed by generous supplies of electricity generated by the Niagara Falls, were Toronto's outstanding contribution to Coronation pageantry.   The double image of the Canadian Bank of Commerce, first against the azure of the sky and then in the deep blue of the still lake, was the focal point in the glorious mingling of stygian gloom and radiant light. Toronto is proud of her "sky-scrapers", and they had a twofold loveliness.

If the sentiments animating Canadians on May 12th had to be put into words, none more fitting could be quoted than those which the members of the House of Commons of Canada used in their loyal address to the King and Queen, when the accession was formally recognized.

"We believe that, under the blessing of Divine Providence, Your Majesty will be vouchsafed guidance and strength to meet the responsibilities of your noble heritage, and to fulfil your purpose to strengthen the foundations of mutual trust and affection between the sovereign and his people. We pray that, amid the confusion of the world and the uncertainties of the times, Your Majesty's throne may be established in righteousness, that Your Majesty's counsellors may be endowed with wisdom, and that all the endeavours of Your Majesty's reign may be directed to the well-governing of your peoples, the preservation of freedom and the advancement of unity and peace."

The Province of Ontario, like its capital, Toronto, is also a "place of meeting".   It stands between the Maritime Provinces,

Photo]   *[Canadian Pacific Railway*

FIREWORKS BEFORE CHÂTEAU FRONTENAC

Quebec by night, with the lights of the upper town built on the cliff glimmering above the lower town, is always a beautiful spectacle and the conformation of the city lends itself remarkably well to special illumination.   The photograph shows a firework display in front of the Château Frontenac, which could be seen from all parts of the city.   The Château Frontenac is a magnificent hotel built in 1892 in medieval French style on a bluff alongside the St. Lawrence.

17

over which the Atlantic sheds its salty savour, and the wide spaces of the Prairie Provinces. After leaving the bustle of the manufacturing and distributing city, Ontario yields a wonderful diversity of lake, field and forest scenery. Of the first, Wilfred Campbell once wrote :

> How I long for Huron's shore :
> How I long for Huron's beaches,
> Where the wind-swept shining reaches
> Wind in mists and are no more.

But the rivers, fields and forests of Ontario and Quebec reveal a Canada which is also deep-rooted both in the Dominion's past and present. Unlike the prairie West, with its wheatfields, this is a mixed-farming country, while its waterfalls provide power for the Canadian factories. As historical time moves, this part of North America was the only Canada until relatively recently. In the eighteenth century the Prairie Provinces were exploited only by a few fur-traders, using the canoe routes, from Montreal westward to the trading posts on the Red River. To the north there was an alternative route westward, used by the fur-traders of the Hudson's Bay Company, but, owing to ice, this was open for a few weeks only in summer-time.

In the Prairie Provinces

To gain a full picture of Canada's tribute to King George and Queen Elizabeth, one must recall many a Quebec and Ontario farmhouse, with the portrait of the new King and Queen framed by a Union Jack and wreathed with spring flowers. Each had its wireless set, and the inmates easily picked up the booming of the royal salute from Hyde Park and the Tower, as they picked up the Abbey bells which rang out the news that the Hallowing in the church was over and the King and Queen were being acclaimed by their people in the London streets.

It was the same in the Prairie Provinces —in Winnipeg, where Portage Avenue was thronged by excited crowds ; in Regina, with its ever-growing industrial population ; in Calgary, where ranchers

vied with oil and gas producers in expressions of loyalty ; and little Coronation, on the Canadian Pacific Railway, which laid itself out to show how an Alberta prairie town could justify its quaintly appropriate name. In the Prairie Provinces there are numerous thriving towns, but there are very many more solitary ranches, where the owners were careful not to leave the Coronation of George VI unobserved. During a royal progress some years ago, a train with the then Prince of Wales passed such a ranch. On the roof was to be seen the ranch-owner, at attention and "presenting arms", as the royal train went by. There were scores of similar actions on Coronation Day, 1937.

Across the Rockies

Whereas the three Prairie Provinces are mostly wheat areas, British Columbia is a land of fruit-trees, vegetables and poultry farms. Crossing the peaked ranges of the Rockies, perhaps by way of Kicking Horse Pass, we may see in imagination a man with a coiled lariat, halting for a moment to rest his horse and recall the fact of Coronation Day. Again, the solitary rider, looking up at the line of the Rockies, may be a member of the Royal Canadian Mounted Police, of which the Duke of Windsor, when Prince of Wales, was Honorary Commandant. This was the man whom Canadians once called "Ed", and in those days he had a farm "down Alberta way". In his broad-brimmed Stetson hat, "Ed" looked a very Canadian, and he was not forgotten by the solitary riders in the Prairie Provinces and the Rockies area on Coronation Day.

In British Columbia, to the west of the Rockies, the Coronation celebrations were somewhat apart from those in Eastern Canada. Victoria, British Columbia, is pronouncedly English in outlook, and the official doings in Parliament Building and the less official celebrations in such a social centre as the Empress Hotel were equally English. The last British naval base in Canada was in these waters, and a number of naval men retired to British Columbia when their term of service ended. These formed an enthusiastic nucleus for Coronation doings. The fur-trading companies worked their posts across the Rockies early in the nineteenth century, and in 1843 Fort Victoria, on Vancouver Island, was established by the Hudson's Bay Company. Later, after the colony of British Columbia was formed, the island and mainland settlements were united, with Victoria as the capital. British Columbia entered the confederation in 1871 and was linked up with Eastern Canada by the Canadian Pacific Railway, but its real progress came in the twentieth century. Today the trade of Vancouver and Victoria, British Columbia, is in rivalry with that of the ports of Eastern Canada.

Lastly, there were the men of the far north —the miners of Whitehouse and Dawson, out to paint the townships red on Coronation Day, their pockets metaphorically "stuffed with gold dust". And still farther north, the Canadian Eskimo, within the Arctic Circle, who dreamt vaguely of some "Great White Father" in far-away Britain, representing all that the Eskimo knew of earthly rule. Yet the Yukon valley and the ice-ridden lands of the Eskimo are a thought too remote for a typical picture of Canada paying its tribute of loyalty and affection to its new King. Let the concluding gaze rest upon the national parks, in which the Canada of pre-settlement times so happily mingles with the Canada of post-War prosperity. In the

national parks, the original flora and fauna of North America are conserved for holiday-making Canadians. Among them are the mountain reservations in the Rockies and the Selkirks, including Banff Park, with its superb Alpine scenery, and Lake Louise, amid its circle of snow-capped hills. Prince Albert Park in Saskatchewan is a canoeing and fishing centre, while Riding Mountain in Manitoba is forest land, and includes one of the largest wild elk herds in Canada. All the national parks had their visitors on Coronation Day, and the loyal celebrations of the holiday-makers were as heartfelt as any in the Dominion.

Photo] [*Canadian Pacific Rly.*

SOLITARY CELEBRATION

In the great cities of the Empire Coronation Day was a public holiday in which the people could rejoice together. In the distant outposts of Empire such men as this solitary horseman in the Rockies could celebrate Coronation Day only in their thoughts.

CHAPTER 20

INDIA'S TRIBUTE TO THE KING-EMPEROR

*Though in due course India will have in the Coronation Durbar an
equivalent of the ceremony at Westminster, yet the Crowning of King
George and Queen Elizabeth was made the occasion for a great display
of loyalty throughout the Indian Empire*

INDIA is a part of his Empire that George VI has not yet visited. The people of India are looking forward eagerly to the Coronation Durbar, which will make the King-Emperor their very own. The accession of King George was proclaimed at Delhi with fitting ceremonies, those in the forecourt of the Viceroy's House being impressive in a high degree. The Viceroy, Lord Linlithgow, and the Commander-in-Chief were accompanied by their staffs, all in full uniform, and they were supported by the Viceroy's Council in levee dress. A great assembly of civilians echoed the message of loyal congratulations which the Governor-General in Council cabled to King George, amplifying the personal telegram which the Viceroy had sent on behalf of the princes and peoples of India, expressing the hope that His Majesty and the Queen-Empress would long be spared to reign in happiness and prosperity.

India, with its 350,000,000 inhabitants and its 220 vernaculars, is so vast and varied that no summary of its homage to the King-Emperor can even dimly suggest the fantasy, charm and interest of the whole. With a Coronation of its own in prospect, it could not be supposed that the ceremony at Westminster would arouse the lively excitement which that at Delhi will do next year. But religion plays so large a part in the lives of a Hindu, Moslem, Buddhist, Sikh or Jain that the significance of the Hallowing of Britain's

King was not lost upon India. Following the governmental divisions, there were official celebrations in the Bengal, the Bombay and the Madras Presidencies in the United Provinces of Agra and Oudh in the Central Provinces and the Punjab and in Bihar, Orissa, Assam and Burma In each case the Governor, as the represen tative of the British Parliament and the Secretary of State for India, was the foca point. But there were also the celebra tions in the native States—Baroda Gwalior, Kashmir, Hyderabad, and the rest—where the chiefs of the ruling familie controlled the celebrations and ordained what was fitting to exemplify his or he loyalty to the Crown.

Imperial Delh

In Delhi, India's capital, the spirit, thoug not the details, of the pageant was base upon that memorable gathering on Ne\ Year's Day, 1877, when on the Daheer pore Plain, Lord Lytton, then Viceroy read Queen Victoria's proclamation, "Give at Our Court, at Windsor, the 28th day c April, 1876, in the thirty-ninth year of ou reign." In this historic document th Queen made an addition to the roya style and titles appertaining to the Imperia Crown of the United Kingdom and so be came Empress of India. Sixty-three rulin princes were present, testifying to th importance of the occasion. After th proclamation was read in English, it wa translated into Hindustani and the new was acclaimed by a salvo of artillery, fired by half-batteries, that is, by three guns fired as one. When thirty-four salvos had been fired to eastward, the infantry, 13,680 in number, drawn up in two lines and extending for a mile and a half, fired a *feu de joie*, which ran from east to west and back again with astonishing quickness and precision. Then the batteries to westward took up the firing, and there came yet another *feu de joie*. Only when 303 guns had contributed their quota of gunpowder and noise did the salvo end. Whereupon the Royal Standard was hoisted and the massed bands broke into the National Anthem. The ceremony reached a dramatic close when the Scindia rose to his feet and exclaimed :

"Padshah, Shah-au-Shah, be happy !"

These words sum up the wish that came from the heart of India on May 12th, 1937, when the peoples from Cape Comorin to the Himalayas learnt that their new

Emperor and Empress had been acclaimed, anointed and crowned. "Be happy !"

On New Year's Day, 1877, Delhi was a city of tents, extending over seven square miles. Since then, the Delhi of Sir Edwin Lutyens and Sir Herbert Baker has arisen, a much more fitting background for the acclamation of a King-Emperor. The Delhi of Lutyens and Baker is the eighth known to history, and is worthy to rank with any of its seven predecessors. The transfer of the capital of India to Delhi was announced by George V, but the city was not officially opened until 1931, so the crowning of George VI was the first to be proclaimed in New Delhi. Very happily, the task fell to Lord Linlithgow, who is already known as "The People's Viceroy", owing to the interest he has displayed in rural betterment and public health in India. To Lord Linlithgow will also fall the task of inaugurating the new Constitution, in which the strongest link

Photo] *[Times*

PROCLAIMING THE KING-EMPEROR

An impressive ceremony was enacted at New Delhi, capital of the Indian Empire, when the proclamation was read from the steps of the Viceroy's House by the Secretary to the Home Department in the presence of the Viceroy, the Commander-in-Chief and a large gathering of officers and officials. The steps were lined by the Viceroy's Bodyguard in their brilliant uniforms and other troops were posted in front of them. The proclamation was also read in Old Delhi.

binding India to the rest of the Empire will be the Throne. In India, even more than in the Dominions and Colonies, reverence for a personal King is dominant over the reverence which associates itself with the authority of the King's Government. The typical Indian prefers a measure of kindly understanding such as arises from government by an individual human being, far above the efficiency of the best machine-made rule.

As for the background of the Viceregal celebrations at Delhi, picture the domed house of the Viceroy as the central point in a vast architectural scheme, designed to express the power of Britain and the House of Windsor. The classical columns and the stone lanterns in front, which give character to Sir Edwin Lutyens' exterior, happily support the twofold purpose of the architect. He was building for Britons as well as Indians. From the great portico of the Viceroy's House, with Sir Herbert Baker's Council House at its side, extends the King's Way. Its vista ends in the All-India Memorial Arch, which commemorates the Indians who fell in France, Flanders, Mesopotamia, Persia, and on the North-West Frontier between 1914 and 1918. The names of 14,000, with their ranks and regiments, are inscribed upon the Arch. As November 11th, Armistice Day, comes round each year, the Smoke of Commemoration ascends from the summit of the Arch, telling that, for the first time in Indian history, all races and religions united against a common foe.

Imperial Delhi, with its war memorial, is a visible token of the fact which was in the minds of many on Coronation morning. Earlier Delhis have been sacked and burnt by invading hosts—Bactrians, Kushans, Scythians, Turks and Pathans. One of the last was led by Nadir Shah, who brought about the massacre of 1739 and, incidentally, took loot from the seventh Delhi to the value of £70,000,000, including the Koh-i-noor. The presence of the historic diamond in the diadem with which Queen Elizabeth was crowned at Westminster was yet another augury for the faith that Delhi's troubles have ended,

Photo]   [Keystone

INDIA'S FIRST CAPITAL FLOODLIT

Calcutta, which was the capital of India from 1774, when Warren Hastings took up his residence there, until 1912 when New Delhi took its place, is a city rich in historic memories. Government House, seen above, floodlit for Empire rejoicings, was the home of the Governor-General until the new capital at Delhi was built.

thanks to the power and justice of the Raj, and its visible head, George VI.

In Calcutta, still the metropolis of British India, though the governmental activities have passed to Delhi, the Coronation celebrations centred around the Governor of the Bengal Presidency. Belvedere House, formerly the residence of the Viceroy, Fort William, the University and other centres of Calcutta life all had their place in the rejoicings. So had the All-India Queen Victoria Memorial Hall, opened by the Prince of Wales in 1921

Photo]   *[Keystone*
CIVIC CEREMONY IN CALCUTTA
The King was proclaimed in all the chief cities of India as well as at Delhi. In Calcutta the ceremony took place on the steps of the Town Hall. The photograph shows the Sheriff of the City, Mr. C. G. Arthur, reading the proclamation. On his right are the judges of the High Court in their robes. Another aspect of this ceremony is shown in page 236.

as a tribute to the first "Empress of India." The art of the interior mirrors Indian history under the British Raj. Bombay, the Gateway of India, was the foremost centre of celebration on the opposite side of the peninsula. An island, eleven miles long and four miles broad, it was ceded to England in 1661, as part of the dowry of Catherine of Braganza, when she wedded Charles II.

The offices of the big companies, and such European centres as the Taj Mahal Hotel and the Hotel Majestic, vied with the native bazaars in rendering their happy homage. Madras, the first outstanding British settlement in India and for many a year India's chief port, was the focal point in Southern India. Here the Hindus are lightly built men, who afford a sharp contrast to the rugged races of the North. On Coronation Day, when the historical sense was alert, many an Anglo-Indian in Madras looked upon Fort St. George and gave thanks for Clive, the pioneer of British rule in India. In Calcutta, Bombay and Madras, the red dawn of the Empire's toil has a somewhat different connotation from that in ꙭ the self-governing Dominions, though Coronation Day still left the conviction of "the mightier morning" which

awaits the Indian Empire in years to be.

Other centres of Anglo-Indian life which celebrated Coronation Day, each in its characteristic way, were : Lahore, capital of the Punjab, where, as in Peshawar, the burly men of the North-West Frontier jostle against the smaller and lighter plainsmen in the busy bazaars ; Muttra, with its temples ; Amritsar, the city of the Sikhs ; Agra, in the pride of its Taj and its crenellated Fort ; and the rose-pink town of Jaipur, capital of Rajputana.

Darjeeling, too, the hill station of Bengal. On Coronation Day the weather was warm enough to encourage a trip by rickshaw or pony to Tiger Hill, whence the Himalaya heights could at least be seen—Jabanu in the foreground and beyond Kanru, Jannu, Kinchinjunga, and, in the farthest distance, Everest. Tibetans, Nepalese, Lepchas and Limbus supported the Anglo-Indians of the hill station in celebrating May 12th, 1937.

The immediate future of the Indian Empire cannot be foreseen. Difficult problems of statecraft will have to be faced and solved, but the Coronation rejoicings seemed to assure the British Throne of whole-hearted support from the Indian princes and the peoples of the Native

ILLUMINATIONS IN BOMBAY

The statue in Bombay of Queen Victoria, first Empress of India, stands at the conjunction of Esplanade Road and Mayo Road, two of the chief streets of the city. The ornate Gothic structure in which the statue is placed lends itself to effective illumination.

States in the task. The names of some of these rulers must suffice to recall their partnership in the task of Empire-building. May is a hot month in India, and Indian rulers who were not at Westminster were at hill stations. But minor durbars were organized in connexion with the Native States and were attended by the local grandees, in full ceremonial raiment. A minority of the intelligentsia of India may want *purna swaraj*, that is, complete independence, but not the millions of people in the Native States.

A gay happy folk with dark eyes and dark hair are the Kashmiris, living in a land of pleasant pastures, flower gardens and lakes, set between the sun-baked plains of the Punjab and the ice-capped heights of the Himalayas. But what of the beyond-land, where Nada Nevi lifts its head 25,000 feet above the Indian plains and reduces Man to littleness? Here sheep, laden with Tibetan borax or Indian tea, may be seen winding through the passes, showing that here, too, are subjects of King George who did not forget their King on the day of his crowning; perhaps a trader, more often a political agent. Between the Oxus and the Indus rivers, amid these Himalayan heights, is the Gilgit Agency. A labyrinth of valleys issues from the ivory peaks of the Hindu Kush, the Pamirs and the Karakoram. And here a British agent raised his glass to his King on Coronation night and wished himself in a busier haunt and one more suited for good fellowship.

And this recalls a score of jolly mess dinners in cantonments at Quetta, at Fort Sandeman, at Chaman, at Peshawar and elsewhere. Peshawar holds the key to the North-West Frontier, and here there is no permanent peace. A soldier honours the Crown, with his sword-arm free.

Nevertheless, the typical Indian is not to be found in these busy trading towns or military cantonments. The real Indian is a peasant, owning a pair of oxen, and farming, maybe, five or ten acres. Six out of seven Indians are village-dwellers, and of the villagers, eighty per cent are agriculturists. The moving picture, displayed in a dust-ridden tent which has been carried round the countryside on a lorry, and broadcasting have taught them something of King George and his Empire. These things will help to drive home the significance of the Coronation at Westminster well before India's own Durbar is due. Among these Indian villagers family life is a religious cult. In many a home the younger members of a family daily take the dust from the feet of the father, as a token of his benediction. Such simple folk look upon a King of Britain as the father of a family, embracing the world, and what they treasure in his legend is such a family life as radiated from the home of George the Well-Beloved and Queen Mary for a quarter of a century. They, and still more their leaders, are looking for a similar example from the father and mother of Princesses Elizabeth and Margaret Rose.

Still Farther East

In lands where the mercury is continually striving to thrust its way out of the thermometer, patriotic celebrations cannot be expected to follow the London pattern. In the Far East, in the majority of cases, all that is possible is a convivial feast on the evening of the great day, with dancing to gramophone music. If atmospherics are absent, listening-in to an Empire station also brings the Englishman a bit nearer home. May is a warm and wet month in Ceylon, and the weather dictated the celebrations. Colombo, one of the busiest ports east of Suez, offered the planters and traders Coronation junketings at the Galle Face and the Grand Oriental hotels. Earlier, and in more sober mood, Englishwomen refreshed the flowers in the Kanatte cemetery, where stands that unfailing emblem of Empire, the Cross of Sacrifice, with its hushed memories of the World War. Other Englishmen forgathered inland at Kandy, with its lake, its spice gardens, and such points of interest as the Elephants' Bathing-place at Kantugastota. The Government House celebrations in Ceylon were under the guidance of Sir Reginald Stubbs.

In colourful Burma, from Rangoon to Mandalay, wherever there were Britons there were patriotic assemblies; in Singapore, too, and Penang and Hong Kong,

yes, and in British North Borneo, that curious appendage of the British Empire. It is an island five times as big as England and Wales, and yet so far off the sea track between Singapore and China that it escaped discovery by Europeans until Magellan's ships found the place when searching for Spice Islands. In 1838 Sir James Brooke, on a yacht of 140 tons burden, came to Borneo and aided the then Sultan against Dyak rebels in the province of Sarawak. As a reward Brooke was made Rajah of Sarawak, and there the Brooke family maintain their benevolent rule to this day, under the protectorate of George VI, as was officially recognized on the King's Coronation Day. Hong Kong has been British since 1842, when the "Island of Fragrant Streams" was ceded to the Empire as a stopping-place for foreign traders forced to leave Canton. A million people were there on Coronation Day to acclaim their King.

Aden, Cyprus, the Seychelles, Ascension and Mauritius also come to mind. The

IN AN OUTPOST OF EMPIRE

In Singapore, Britain's great port and naval base in the East Indies, the proclamation ceremony was the occasion of an imposing military parade in the presence of the chief Government officials. It took place in the open space in front of the fine new Municipal Buildings fortified island of Ascension is under the Lords Commissioners of the Admiralty, and the Coronation festivities were those of a British battleship. Tristan da Cunha, in the southern Atlantic, with its strange history and social system had its celebrations. A company of British artillerymen took possession of the island in 1817, as an extra precaution against the escape of Napoleon from St. Helena. From three of these soldiers and a few whalers arose the tiny community of today. Property is held in common and the oldest inhabitant acts as governor of the settlement. To him fell the happy task of acclaiming the Coronation of King George on May 12th. Truly, a strange assembly of very varied parts constitutes this Empire of ours.

The West Indies

Lastly, there were the celebrations in the Colonial Empire which preceded Dominion rule and, indeed, Dominion aspirations. From the beginning, the West Indies have associated peace and prosperity with the Union Jack, and a common allegiance to the Crown is the only association of the islands and mainland possessions with world politics. But how happy an element in the diadem of Empire which George VI assumed when he ascended the Throne of Britain! The Crown of St. Edward, to the people of the West Indies, is the historic symbol of that other diadem, in which each island is a jewel of worth and loveliness. Trinidad, which the earliest Indian inhabitants called "Tëre", the "Land of the Humming Bird"; Jamaica, the home of the banana and Blue Mountain coffee, with its sandy beaches, fringed by palms and framed by hills which have the fantastic beauty of stageland, rather than of reality.

St. Lucia and Grenada, in the Windward Islands, are still French in type, and the native speaks a French patois, but the sentiment is as English as it is in French Canada. The headquarters of the Governor of the Windward Islands is in the land-locked harbour of St. George, with its grey fort, its red-roofed houses and its bathing beach of Grand Ance.

At Nassau, the capital, the Union Jack was flying over Government House on Mount Fitz-william, and, together with the parade of the island garrison, recalled the decades of hard fighting which had held the West Indies for the British Crown. For the rest, there were very many jolly feastings and loyal toastings under the beach umbrellas in the gardens of the Nassau hotels.

Photo]   [Sport and General

PROCLAIMED ON THE QUARTER-DECK

George VI was proclaimed King at the port of Haifa, Palestine, by Mr. Edward Keith-Roche, the District Commissioner for Northern Palestine. The ceremony took place on the quarter-deck of H.M.S. Delhi, a light cruiser of 4,500 tons. The Commissioner is seen reading the proclamation and on his right is the captain of the Delhi.

POMP AND CIRCUMSTANCE

by

E. ROYSTON PIKE

and

J. B. STERNDALE BENNETT

Claims to Serve the King
at his Crowning : the Story
of the Ancient Royal Regalia

BY THE KING

A PROCLAMATION

Declaring His Majesty's Pleasure touching His Royal Coronation and the Solemnity thereof

GEORGE R.I.

WHEREAS We have resolved, by the Favour and Blessing of Almighty God, to celebrate the Solemnity of Our Royal Coronation, and of the Coronation of Our dearly beloved Consort the Queen, at Westminster upon Wednesday the Twelfth Day of May next ; and forasmuch as by ancient Customs and Usages of this Realm, as also in regard of divers Tenures of sundry Manors, Lands, and other Hereditaments many of Our loving Subjects do claim and are bound to do and perform divers Services on the said Day, and at the Time of the Coronation, as in Times precedent their Ancestors and those from whom they claim have done and performed at the Coronations of Our famous Progenitors and Predecessors, Kings and Queens of this Realm ; We, therefore, out of Our Princely Care for the Preservation of the lawful Rights and Inheritances of Our loving Subjects whom it may concern, have thought fit to give Notice of and publish Our Resolution therein ; and do hereby give Notice of and publish the same accordingly : And We do hereby further signify, That, by Our Commission under Our Great Seal of the Realm, We have appointed and authorized

OUR Most Dear Brother and Counsellor His Royal Highness Henry William Frederick Albert, Duke of Gloucester ; Our right trusty and right entirely beloved Counsellor the Most Reverend Father in God Cosmo Gordon, Archbishop of Canterbury, Primate of All England and Metropolitan ; Our right trusty and well beloved Cousin and Counsellor Douglas McGarel, Viscount Hailsham, Our Chancellor of Great Britain ; Our right trusty and right entirely beloved Counsellor the Most Reverend Father in God William, Archbishop of York, Primate of England and Metropolitan ; Our right trusty and well beloved Counsellors Stanley Baldwin, Prime Minister and First Commissioner of Our Treasury ; and James Ramsay MacDonald, President of Our Council ; Our right trusty and well beloved Cousin and Counsellor Edward Frederick Lindley, Viscount Halifax, Keeper of Our Privy Seal ; Our right trusty and right entirely beloved Cousins and Counsellors Bernard Marmaduke, Duke of Norfolk, Earl Marshal and Our Hereditary Marshal of England ; George Granville, Duke of Sutherland, Lord Steward of Our Household ; Henry Hugh Arthur Fitzroy, Duke of Beaufort, Master of Our Horse ; and William John Arthur Charles James, Duke of Portland ; Our right trusty and entirely beloved Cousins and Counsellors James Edward Hubert, Marquess of Salisbury ; Lawrence John Lumley, Marquess of Zetland, one of Our Principal Secretaries of State ; and Robert Offley Ashburton, Marquess of Crewe ; Our right trusty and right well beloved Cousins and Counsellors Rowland Thomas, Earl of Cromer, Lord Chamberlain of Our Household ; Edward George Villiers, Earl of Derby ; David Alexander Edward, Earl of Crawford and Balcarres ; James Richard, Earl Stanhope, First Commissioner of Our Works and Public Buildings ; Richard William Alan, Earl of Onslow ; and Alexander Augustus Frederick William Alfred George, Earl of Athlone ; Our right trusty and well beloved Cousin and Counsellor Philip, Viscount Swinton, one of Our Principal Secretaries of State ; Our right trusty and well beloved Counsellor the Right Reverend Father in God Arthur Foley, Bishop of London ; Our right trusty and well beloved Counsellors Gordon, Lord Hewart, Lord Chief Justice of England ; William, Lord Thankerton, Lord of Appeal in Ordinary ; Robert Alderson, Lord Wright, Master of the Rolls ; Clive, Lord Wigram ; Sir John Allsebrook Simon, Robert Anthony Eden, William George Arthur Ormsby-Gore, Alfred Duff Cooper, Malcolm MacDonald, and Walter Elliot Elliot, six of Our Principal Secretaries of State ; Alexander Henry Louis Hardinge ; Sir Joseph Austen Chamberlain ; David Lloyd George ; Winston Leonard Spencer Churchill ; John Robert Clynes ; Sir Samuel John Gurney Hoare, First Commissioner of Our Admiralty ; Arthur Neville Chamberlain, Chancellor and Under Treasurer of Our Exchequer ; Hastings Bertrand Lees-Smith ; Sir Archibald Henry Macdonald Sinclair, Baronet ; Wilfrid Guild Normand, Lord Justice General and President of the Court of Session in Scotland ; and Clement Richard Attlee ;

Or any five or more of them to receive, hear, and determine the Petitions and Claims which shall be to them exhibited by any of Our loving Subjects in this Behalf ;

AND We do hereby appoint such of Our said Commissioners as may be summoned for that Purpose to sit in the Council Chamber at Whitehall upon the first convenient Day to be hereafter notified by Publication in the *London, Edinburgh,* and *Belfast Gazette,* respectively, and from Time to Time to adjourn as to them shall seem meet, for the Execution of Our said Commission, which We do thus publish, to the Intent that all such Persons whom it may anyways concern may know when and where to give their Attendance for the exhibiting of their Petitions and Claims concerning their Services before mentioned to be done and performed at Our said Coronation :

AND We do hereby signify and declare that it is Our Royal Will and Pleasure that such Part only of the Solemnity and Ceremony of the Royal Coronation of Ourself and Our dearly beloved Consort the Queen as is usually upon the Coronation of the Kings and Queens of this Realm solemnized in Westminster Abbey, shall take place.

AND We do further by this Our Royal Proclamation signify and declare that We do for Ourself and for Our dearly beloved Consort the Queen dispense, upon the Occasion of this Our Coronation, with the Services and Attendance of all Persons who do claim and are bound to do and perform any Services which, according to ancient Custom or Usage, are to be performed in Westminster Hall or in the Procession.

AND We do hereby further graciously declare that such Dispensation shall not interfere with the Rights and Privileges of any of Our loving Subjects to claim the Performances of such several Services or any of them at any future Coronation. And We do hereby, by and with the Advice of Our Privy Council, declare and make known to all such of Our loving Subjects as it may concern, that it seems good to Us that the Committee of Claims shall, upon the Occasion of this Our Coronation, exclude from their Consideration as well such Claims as may be submitted to them in respect of Rights or Services connected with the Parts of the Ceremonial in Times past performed in Westminster Hall and with the Procession as also such Petitions and Claims as have been received, heard and determined by the Committee of Claims appointed and authorized by the Commission under the Great Seal of the Realm bearing date the twenty-eighth Day of May last, save in so far as to the Committee of Claims, authorized and appointed by Us as in this Our Proclamation hereinbefore recited, it may appear that any such Petition or Claim should rightly be by them received, heard and determined by reason of any Change of Tenure of any Petitioner or of any Change in the Nature of the Service to be performed.

AND We do hereby declare that any Determination made by the said former Committee of Claims shall have effect and hold good as if the Petition or Claim concerned had been heard and determined by the Committee of Claims appointed and authorized by Our aforesaid Commission under Our Great Seal of the Realm.

AND We do, by this Our Royal Proclamation, strictly charge and command all Our loving Subjects whom it may concern that all Persons, of what Rank or Quality soever they be, who either upon Our Letters to them directed, or by reason of their Offices and Tenures, or otherwise, are to do any Service at the time of Our Coronation, other than Service anciently done and performed in Westminster Hall or in the Procession, do duly give their Attendance at the said Solemnity on Wednesday the Twelfth Day of May next, in all respects furnished and appointed as to so great a Solemnity appertaineth and answerable to the Dignities and Places which every one of them respectively holdeth and enjoyeth, and of this they or any of them are not to fail, as they will answer the contrary at their Perils, unless upon special Reasons by Ourself under Our Hand to be allowed, We shall dispense with any of their Services or Attendances.

Given at Our Court at *Buckingham Palace,* this Eighteeenth Day of *December,* in the Year of our Lord One thousand nine hundred and thirty-six, and in the First Year of Our Reign.

GOD SAVE THE KING

CHAPTER 21

PETITIONERS TO THE COURT OF CLAIMS

*One of the most important antecedents of the Coronation is the Court which adjudi-
cates upon the Petitions advanced by persons who, through hereditary right or by
virtue of their Office, make claim to places in the Coronation Procession or Ceremony*

AMONGST the most curious of the courts of one kind and another in His Majesty's dominions is the ancient tribunal of the Court of Claims.

Ancient indeed it is, for it came into being soon after the accession of Richard II in 1377. He was a minor—a boy of ten—and the arrangements for his Coronation were undertaken by his uncle, John of Gaunt — "time-honoured Lancaster" as Shakespeare styles him—as "steward of England". To him in the Palace at Westminster came persons claiming to perform certain services at the great ceremony, amongst them being one petitioning to act as constable, two who both claimed the right to act as King's Champion, and the Barons of the Cinque Ports who then, as only the other day, petitioned to carry a canopy over the King during the service.

The precedent set in 1377 has been followed at every subsequent Coronation, though since the days of Henry VIII the claims have been submitted to a body of Commissioners instead of to the Lord High Steward. On every occasion, some months before the date fixed for the ceremony, a proclamation has been issued by the sovereign "declaring His Majesty's Pleasure touching the Royal Coronation and the Solemnity thereof", and in this it is stated that—to quote from the Proclamation of King George VI (reprinted opposite by permission of the Stationery Office): "We do hereby appoint such of Our said Commissioners as may be summoned for that Purpose to sit in the Council Chamber at Whitehall upon the first convenient Day to be hereafter notified by Publication in the *London, Edinburgh*, and *Belfast Gazette*, respectively, and from Time to Time to adjourn as to them shall seem meet, for the Execution of Our said Commission, which We do thus publish, to the Intent that all such Persons whom it may anyways concern may know when and where to give their Attendance for the exhibiting of their Petitions and Claims concerning their Services before mentioned to be done and performed at Our said Coronation."

Seven months before, on May 28th, 1936, a similar proclamation had been issued by King Edward VIII, and the Commissioners appointed by the King for the purpose of hearing the claims had met at the Privy Council Office in Downing Street on November 25th and had reached a decision on all the claims submitted. Then followed the extraordinary event of the King's abdication, and it became necessary to constitute a fresh Court. As so short a time had elapsed, however, the proclamation of December 18th contained a clause providing that "the Committee of Claims shall, upon the Occasion of this Our Coronation, exclude from their Consideration as well such Claims as may be submitted to them in respect of Rights or Services connected with the Parts of the Ceremonial in Times past performed in

Photo]   [Keystone

THE COURT OF CLAIMS MEETS IN FULL SESSION

As is stated in the accompanying text the Court of Claims is one of the most ancient of British tribunals, for it has been called into being on the occasions of the Coronations of the last 550 years. This photograph is of the Court that met on November 25th. 1936, at the Privy Council Office, Whitehall, London, to hear the claims advanced in respect of the Coronation of King Edward VIII. Its decisions, save in the case of the claim of the Lord Great Chamberlain, were held valid in respect of the Coronation of King George VI. Seated from left to right are : the Earl of Cromer, the Duke of Norfolk, Lord Thankerton, Lord Chief Justice Hewart, Lord Wright, the Earl of Onslow, and Lord Normand.

Westminster Hall and with the Procession as also such Petitions and Claims as have been received, heard and determined by the Committee of Claims appointed and authorized by the Commission under the Great Seal of the Realm bearing date the twenty-eighth Day of May last, save in so far as to the Committee of Claims, authorized and appointed by Us as in this Our Proclamation hereinbefore recited, it may appear that any such Petition or Claim should rightly be by them received, heard and determined by reason of any Change of Tenure of any Petitioner or of any Change in the Nature of the Service to be performed".

The Court of Claims that assembled on November 25th was presided over by Lord Hewart (Lord Chief Justice), in the absence of the Lord Chancellor, Lord Hailsham; and the other Commissioners were the Duke of Norfolk (Earl Marshal), the Earl of Cromer

(Lord Chamberlain), the Earl of Onslow (Chairman of Committees, House of Lords), Lord Thankerton (Lord of Appeal in Ordinary), Lord Wright (Master of the Rolls), and Lord Normand (Lord Justice General and President of the Court of Session in Scotland).

Clergy of the Abbey

The first claim submitted was that of the Dean and Chapter of Westminster Abbey, who petitioned to "instruct the King in the Rites and Ceremonies, and to assist the Archbishop of Canterbury, and to retain the Robes and Ornaments of the Coronation in the Vestry of the Collegiate Church of St. Peter in Westminster, and to have certain allowances and fees". The claim was allowed on the same terms as were granted in respect of the Coronation of King George V in 1911, i.e. :

It is considered and adjudged by the Court that the claim of the said Dean and Chapter be allowed except as to the retaining and keeping the Robes and Ornaments in the Vestry of the Collegiate Church of St. Peter in Westminster, which the said Commissioners do adjudge to be kept there unless His Majesty shall at any time be pleased to order the same to be kept elsewhere, and also that the fees claimed by the said Petition be referred to the pleasure of His Majesty.

Next came the claims of the Bishops of Durham and of Bath and Wells "to support His Majesty at the Coronation, and to have certain privileges"; these were formally admitted as having been granted aforetime.

Then Mr. H. J. Scrymgeour-Wedderburn claimed the right "to carry the Royal Standard of Scotland as Hereditary Royal Standard Bearer for Scotland". After satisfying the Commissioners that he was the grandson of the Henry Scrymgeour-Wedderburn whose claim was allowed in 1902 and 1911, his right was allowed with "the same order as on the former occasion".

The claim of the Barons of the Cinque Ports to "bear the canopies if used in the Procession in Westminster Abbey, or, if canopies are not used, to be assigned a station within the Abbey in attendance upon the King, and that their ancient privileges may remain undisturbed", was the next to be allowed. The canopies borne by the Barons in ancient Coronations were made of cloth-of-gold or purple silk, with a silver-gilt bell at each corner, supported by four silver-covered staves, each borne by four Barons; after the service the Barons received the canopies, bells and staves as their perquisites and sat down to dine on the King's right hand at the Coronation banquet.

The succeeding claims that were advanced may be recorded in the brevity of the formal phrasing. Each was read out by Sir Claud Schuster, Clerk of the Crown, and in most cases the Lord Chief Justice declared that "There will be the same order as on the previous occasion", referring to the Coronation of King George V in 1911.

The Walker Trustees, "to be present by deputy within Westminster Abbey at the Coronation, by virtue of the office of Hereditary Usher of the White Rod, or Principal Usher for Scotland".

The Clerk of the Crown, "to record the proceedings in Westminster Abbey, and to be assigned a suitable place therein to discharge his duties, and that the Registrar of the Privy Council may be associated with, and assistant to, the Clerk for this purpose; also to have five yards of scarlet cloth".

Lyon King-of-Arms, Heralds and Pursuivants of Scotland, Ulster King-of-Arms and Dublin Herald-of-Arms, "to be assigned usual places at the Coronation".

The Earl of Erroll, "to walk as Lord High Constable of Scotland, and to have a silver baton or staff, of twelve ounces weight, tipped with gold at each end, with His Majesty's Royal Arms on one end and the Petitioner's on the other end".

A Glove for His Majesty

The executors of the late Duke of Newcastle, Henry Pelham Archibald Douglas, Duke of Newcastle-under-Lyme, "to provide a glove for the King's right hand and to support His Majesty's right arm while he is holding the Sceptre by virtue of the tenure of the Manor of Worksop; ask to perform the services by deputy (the Earl of Lincoln)". These rights have been attached to the Manor of Worksop since the reign of Henry VIII, before which time they were appurtenances of the Manor of Farnham Royal in Bucks. They were recognized by the first Court of Claims in 1377, and were apparently first granted by the Conqueror.

The Earl of Shrewsbury, "to carry a white wand as a symbol of his office of Lord High Steward of Ireland, if invited by His Majesty to be present in that capacity".

The Marquess of Cholmondeley, "to perform the duties and services of the office of Lord Great Chamberlain of England, and to have such profits as thereto of right belong, together with all privileges as His Majesty may be pleased to determine".

The Mayor and Commonalty and Citizens of the City of London, "for the Mayor to attend the King within Westminster Abbey during the Coronation, and bear the Crystal Mace".

The Lord Great Chamberlain who claimed above was, it will be seen, the Marquess of Cholmondeley. The office is vacated at the beginning of every new reign, and is held in turn by the representatives of three great noble families—Cholmondeley (in alternate reigns), Willoughby and Carrington (the two latter holding office alternately in the intervening reigns). On King Edward's abdication in December 1936, therefore, Lord Cholmondeley's brief tenure came to an end, and it became the Earl of Ancaster's turn to enjoy the privileges and responsibilities of the office. He made claim thereto at a meeting of the newly-appointed Court of Claims, which met on February 11th, 1937, and was composed as before save that it was presided over by the Lord Chancellor. In his petition Lord Ancaster claimed that by virtue of his office he should be granted a box, specially erected for his use in Westminster Abbey, and also forty yards of crimson velvet for his robes. Other privileges granted to his predecessors were stated to include lodging in the King's Court at all times ; that on the day of the Coronation he should have the right to dress the King with all his apparel ; and that he or his deputies should carry the

royal robe and Crown, the Sword of State and scabbard, and the gold to be offered by the King at the High Altar. One further claim was mentioned, but not formally presented : "to serve His Majesty with water on the day of the Coronation and to have the basins and towels and the cup of assay for his fee".

After some deliberation it was announced by the Lord Chancellor that :

The Court considers and adjudges that the erection of a box in Westminster Abbey is not one of the rights appertaining to the office of Lord Great Chamberlain.

The Court adjudges that the petitioner may exercise such duties as have heretofore appertained to the office of Lord Great Chamberlain, and have such privileges and profits as his Majesty may be pleased to determine.

It may be of interest to quote the claim advanced by Lord Ancaster's father to be Lord Great Chamberlain to Edward VII :

That he may have livery and lodging in the King's Court at all times, and bring to His Majesty on the day of His Majesty's Royal Coronation His Majesty's shirt, stockings and drawers : that your Petitioner together with the Lord Chamberlain of the Household for the time being may dress His Majesty to all his apparel on that day : and that your Petitioner may have all profits and fees thereunto belonging, viz., forty yards of crimson velvet for his robes against the day of His Majesty's Coronation, together with the bed wherein the King lays the night previous to the Coronation, with all the vallances and curtains thereof, and all the cushions and clothes within the chamber, together with the furniture of the same : and also the night robe of the King wherein His Majesty rested the night previous to the Coronation, and likewise to serve His Majesty with water on the said day of his Royal Coronation and to have the basins and towels and the cup of assay for his fee.

So much for the unopposed claims in respect of which orders were made by the Court. Now we have two in which the precedent of 1911 could not be invoked, as they were not made on that occasion, and in respect of which the Court decided to make no order.

The first was advanced by Mr. Frank Scaman Dymoke. He claimed "to bear the Standard of England as King's Champion by virtue of the tenure of the Manor of Scrivelsby". It was stated on his behalf that he had carried the Standard of England

THE CROWN JEWELS AND ROYAL REGALIA OF ENGLAND

1) the King's Royal Sceptre with the Cross ; (2) the Imperial State Crown ; (3) the Queen's Sceptre with he Dove ; (4) the Jewelled Sword of State ; (5) the King's Orb ; (6) the Crown of England (St. Edward's Crown) ; (7) the Queen's Orb, unused since the dual monarchy of William and Mary.

To face page 272

in 1902 and 1911 after the matter had been referred to the King in Council : in 1937 the Court decided that the matter did not come within their terms of reference and, as just stated, no order was made.

Flinging Down the Gauntlet

But the claim is an intensely interesting one, for the challenge of the King's Champion was the most dramatic and picturesque element of bygone Coronations. Immediately after the ceremony on May 12th, 1937, King George VI and his Consort returned in state to Buckingham Palace ; but their predecessors used to walk from the Abbey to Westminster Hall, there to participate in a splendid banquet. Preceded by heralds, the newly-crowned king was installed on a throne before the table, and then the viands, contained in gold dishes, were brought in by Gentlemen-Pensioners and three of the great Officers of State riding their horses.

But before the dishes were placed by the Clerks of the Kitchen on the board the Lord High Constable and the Earl Marshal entered the hall on horseback, escorting the King's Champion, armed *cap-à-pie*, accompanied by trumpeters, serjeants-at-arms, herald and equerries. The trumpeters sounded a fanfare, and then the herald proclaimed in a loud voice that "if any person, of what degree soever, high or low, shall deny or gainsay our sovereign lord . . . to be the right heir to the imperial crown of this realm, or that he ought not to enjoy the same ; here is his Champion, who saith that he lieth, and is a false traitor, being ready in person to combat with him ; and in this quarrel will adventure his life against him on that day soever he shall appoint". Whereupon Dymoke— the office of King's Champion has been hereditary in the Dymoke family for hundreds of years—threw down his gauntlet, which lay on the ground for a short space until it was returned to the Champion by the herald. Thrice this little ceremony was performed—at the door, in the middle of the hall, and just before the throne. This done, the king drank the challenger's

health in a gilt cup which he then had delivered to him. Dymoke drank in turn the king's long life and then retired, taking the cup as his fee. The last occasion on which this ancient rite was performed was at the Coronation of George IV in 1821 ; there is no record of the gauntlet's ever having been picked up.

The second of the undecided petitions was that of the Rev. H. Cotton Smith, who "claimed to be present at the Coronation by virtue of his ownership of the lands of Nettleham, Lincoln, where he alleges Edward I invested his son first Prince of Wales". Two further claims—by the Marquess of Exeter "to exercise the Office of Almoner as possessor of the Barony of Bedford" and by the Duke of Roxburgh "to carry the staff of St. Edward"—were not pursued.

Only one contested claim came before the Court : who should carry the Great Spurs in the Coronation procession. Three claims to do so were advanced. The Countess of Loudoun, Viscountess St. Davids, Lady Flora Anne Rawdon-Hastings, Mr. J. W. L. Butler-Bowdon and the Hon. Dame Lelgarde Harry Florence Bellingham petitioned on behalf of their deputy ; the same claim was made by Lord Hastings ; and Lord Churston asked that he should carry the spurs in person.

Who Shall Carry the Spurs ?

All of these claimants traced their right through their common ancestor, Sir John de Hastings, first Baron Hastings (1262–1313), whose ancestor, John Marshal, bore the spurs at the Coronation of Richard I in 1189. Then the Grey de Ruthyn family acquired the barony of Hastings, and at the Coronation of Edward VII in 1902 claims were advanced on behalf of the Grey de Ruthyn family and also by Lord Hastings. The matter was left undecided, and the matter was now further complicated by the claim of Lord Churston, who was descended from one Lady Barbara, Baroness Grey de Ruthyn, who married a Marquess of Hastings and thereby became the ancestress of the five claimants in the first category.

18

Photo]   *[Fox*

CLERK OF THE COURT

At the Court of Claims the claims were read out by the Clerk of the Crown in Chancery, Sir Claud Schuster, K.C.B., seen in this photograph arriving at the Privy Council offices in Downing Street for the meeting on February 11th, 1937.

After deliberating in private, the Court announced that it "considers and adjudges that each of the claimants has established a claim to perform the service of carrying the Great Spurs, and that it be referred to the pleasure of His Majesty to determine how such service shall be performed".

Just as the proceedings were terminating, claims were advanced by Mr. G. F. Tracy Beal and Vice-Admiral A. F. Beal, who claimed to be Chief Butler of England and his assistant respectively. No order was made in regard to these, as they were connected with the banquet which, as already mentioned, has not been part of the ₋Coronation proceedings since 1821. At some future Coronation the banquet may possibly be revived, and in contemplation of this eventuality the Proclamation of December 12th, 1936 (printed in page 268), says that though "We . . . dispense, upon the Occasion of this Our Coronation, with the Services and Attendance of all Persons who do claim and are bound to do

and perform any Services which, according to ancient Custom or Usage, are to be performed in Westminster Hall or in the Procession", "We do . . . . graciously declare that such Dispensation shall not interfere with the Rights and Privileges of any of Our loving Subjects to claim the Performances of such several Services or any of them at any future Coronation".

In olden days the Chief Butler received as his fee the gold cup and cover in which he proffered wine to His Majesty as well as certain other wine-vessels, the wine left over, and all the pewter and earthenware pots and cups in the wine-cellar. The Lord Mayor of London and twelve of his burgesses acted as assistants to the Chief Butler and were allowed to retain a gold cup as their fee. The Mayor and eight citizens of Oxford, acting in a similar capacity, were granted three maple cups.

Many other ancient services were attached to the banquet. The Grand

EARL MARSHAL OF ENGLAND

Earl Marshal and Hereditary Marshal and Chief Butler of England, Premier Duke and Earl, His Grace of Norfolk is a busy and prominent figure in the Coronation Year. On him in particular devolves responsibility for arranging the procession.

Panneter provided, as the name implies, the bread, and was in charge of the salt and carving-knives ; he was permitted to take away the salt-cellars, knives and spoons from the table. The Chief Lardiner had all the meats left in the larder after the guests had been fed. The Lord of the Manor of Lyston presented the King with a charger of wafers, and the Duke of Atholl, Lord of the Isle of Man, followed next with a brace of falcons. Another claim rested with the Lord of the Manor of Addington, in Surrey, who presented a mess of "dillegrout"—gruel flavoured with dill according to one authority ; a mixture of almonds, milk, brawn, sugar, spices and chicken, according to another. The origin of this service may be detected in the fact that the Manor of Addington was granted by William the Conqueror to his cook.

The King's almoner collected and distributed alms in and from a silver dish ;

LORD GREAT CHAMBERLAIN

The office of Lord Great Chamberlain rests in the families of Lords Cholmondeley, Willoughby and Carrington, whose representatives hold office in accordance with an established sepuence. Under George VI the Earl of Ancaster (Gilbert Heathcote-Drummond-Willoughby) seen above, is the holder.

this service appertains to the barony of Bedford, and, as stated above, a claim was preferred in 1936 by the Marquess of Exeter as the holder of the barony. The almoner received as his fee a tun of wine, the dish in which he had collected the alms, and the carpet on the pathway from the Abbey to Westminster Hall over which the King had walked.

The first cup was proffered by the Lord of the Manor of Great Wymondley, who claimed the silver-gilt cup as fee. The napier had the custody of the table-linen.

Then finally there was a herb-strewer, who with her attendant maidens scattered flowers on the dais. At George IV's banquet the herb-strewer was Miss Fellows.

Not only antiquarians may regret the passing or the abeyance of these ancient offices, but the Court of Claims still retains sufficient business to constitute it a most interesting link in our nation's story.

Photo]   *[Fox*

LORD HIGH CHANCELLOR

As chief of the temporal hierarchy of the realm, the Lord Chancellor holds numerous posts and dignities, and amongst them is the important but seldom occurring presidency of the Court of Claims. Here we see Lord Hailsham leaving Downing Street after the hearing that decided the claim of the Lord Great Chamberlain preferred by Lord Ancaster.

CHAPTER 22

GLORIES OF THE CROWN JEWELS

The priceless treasures of Gold and Gems which form the British Regalia and which, with a few exceptions, are used only at the Coronation, have an historic interest as fascinating as their intrinsic beauty. The vicissitudes that have befallen many of the objects make a remarkable page in History

THE British Regalia, every item of which has its symbolic significance, are of immense intrinsic value, but for the main part of no great antiquity, for the ancient Crown Jewels of England were broken up and sold at the time of the Commonwealth (1649).

Amongst the collection brought from the Tower of London for use at the Coronation there are very few pieces which have played a part in the crowning of earlier English kings : the ampulla, or golden eagle from which the sacramental oil is poured ; the gold spoon, also used in the anointing ; and four historic gems in the Imperial State Crown—Edward the Black Prince's ruby, a sapphire which is said to have been set in Edward the Confessor's ring, the Stuart sapphire from the Crown of Charles II, and Queen Elizabeth's pearl ear-drops.

Everything else was lost, and although one cannot but deplore the ruthless marketing of objects of such great historical value, it is only fair to acquit Cromwell of being the only vandal to disperse a contemporary collection. For centuries the jewels were regarded as the personal property of the monarch and his to pawn or sell at times of financial stringency. Both Edward III and Henry V pawned their jewels, and though their action met with some disapproval, no one questioned their right.

The Regalia, for long housed in Westminster Abbey, were not always as securely guarded as they are today, and there is no doubt that valuable pieces were lost through the connivance of thieving priests. Following an attempt made to rob the Abbey treasury in the reign of Henry III, the greater part of the king's treasure was removed to the Tower and a jewel-house built for it in the south wall of the White Tower. After the Restoration the new jewels were housed in the Martin Tower, where they remained until the reign of Queen Victoria, when they were transferred to their present home in a chamber in the Wakefield Tower.

The most elaborate devices were later installed to prevent any possible chance of theft. In his book, *The Jewel House*, the present keeper, Major-General Sir George Younghusband, without committing himself to any definite statement, darkly hints that the intrepid burglar must suffer the risk of electrocution or decapitation.

The most historic attempt to steal the jewels—one which came near to being a complete success—occurred shortly after they had been restored in the reign of Charles II. This was effected by an Irish adventurer, Colonel Blood, who gained the confidence of the assistant keeper—an aged man named Edwards. With two accomplices, Blood overpowered Edwards and but for interruption would certainly have got away with the State Crown and the Orb. For some unexplained reason, Charles II rewarded the thief with a post on his bodyguard and a pension of £500. One theory is that Blood was acting for him and that the King was anxious to replenish his empty pockets by stealing and selling his own crown !

The British Regalia today include seven crowns. Of these the most important is known as the Crown of England or St. Edward's Crown, made to resemble as far as possible Edward the Confessor's Crown, which, as stated above, was destroyed at the Commonwealth. This crown is used only at the actual ceremony of Coronation and is of such a weight (between six and seven pounds) that the sovereign is required to wear it for only a few minutes. Queen Victoria, indeed, could not support it at all, but respected its traditional importance by ordering it to be carried during the ceremony of her Coronation.

St. Edward's Crown is of gold, and heavily bejewelled with diamonds, rubies, emeralds, sapphires and pearls. The two arches edged with pearls which surmount it, and which are themselves surmounted by the orb and cross, are symbolic of hereditary and independent monarchy. Inside the crown is a crimson velvet cap of maintenance or estate—not to be confused, by the by, with the Cap of Maintenance which is worn by the King on his way to the Abbey and during part of the service.

The Crown the People See

A far more interesting and valuable crown is that known as the Imperial State Crown. This was re-made for Queen Victoria in 1838 and with it she was, contrary to the usual practice, actually crowned. It has been re-set and other jewels have been added for successive monarchs. It is the crown used by the monarch on all State occasions and is worn at the Coronation after St. Edward's Crown has been discarded.

This crown is a mass of diamonds, containing no fewer than 2783 of these stones as well as 277 pearls, 17 sapphires, 11 emeralds and 5 rubies. Amongst the most famous of these stones is the Second Star of Africa, cut from the Cullinan diamond, the largest in the world, which

was given to Edward VII by the South African Government after the Boer War. By his direction this great stone was cut into sections, all of which found a place in the British Regalia.

Historic Gems

Historically more interesting is the Black Prince's ruby, another very large stone about two inches long and one and a half broad. In 1367 this was owned by a king of Granada in Spain, who was murdered by a neighbouring prince, Don Pedro of Castile, who coveted the stone. He gave it to the Black Prince, who wore it in battle, as did Henry V at the battle of Agincourt, and Richard III at Bosworth field. After that monarch was killed the King's crown was found hidden in a hawthorn bush and was used to crown Henry VII, the first Tudor king. The ruby, which was inventoried by the Commonwealth valuers as worth but £4, was mysteriously recovered at the Restoration and resumed its place in the State Crown. It is related that during Captain Blood's escapade it fell from its setting and was found in the pocket of one of his accomplices.

A diamond cross surmounts the crown, and set in this is another historic gem, a sapphire which is said to have been the chief ornament of Edward the Confessor's Coronation Ring in 1042. It was buried with Edward in his Abbey of Westminster and was lost again when his shrine was desecrated and his jewels stolen. How it came to be returned to the British Regalia is a complete mystery.

Another sapphire, the famous Stuart sapphire, adorns the State Crown. This gem was carried to France by James II, and after many wanderings George III recovered it in the year 1821. Its position now is at the back of the crown. Edward VII provided a further addition of historic interest in the shape of Queen Elizabeth's pearl ear-drops, which came to light during his reign. They hang from the point where the two arches cross. The intrinsic value of this crown must be very great. For one Coronation, that of George IV, £60,000 was

CROWN OF INDIA'S EMPEROR

The crown which the King will wear at the Durbar is one of the newest pieces of the Regalia. It was made for the Durbar of King George V in 1912, when it was found that neither of the other crowns could legally be taken out of England.

spent on it, and much of value has been added since.

A similar sum was spent in 1912 on the construction of the Imperial Crown of India, which was specially designed for George V's durbar at Delhi. By tradition the St. Edward's and State Crowns were not allowed to leave the country, which necessitated the making of this new crown. It contains some very fine gems amongst its 6,170 diamonds, 4 sapphires and 6 emeralds.

Another interesting crown in the Regalia is that which belonged to James II's queen, Mary of Modena, which was also used at the Coronation of Mary II. Accompanying this crown is Mary of Modena's diadem, which she wore on her way to the Abbey. This alone is said to have cost £110,000.

The present Queen Mary's crown is an example of beautiful workmanship, the making of which she superintended herself. It is set entirely with diamonds and contains amongst them three magnificent and historic gems. First is the celebrated Koh-i-Noor, which

weighs 108 carats. It is set in the centre cross and is detachable so that it can be worn as a pendant on high State occasions. This famous stone has changed hands many times, and has been responsible for much bloodshed since it is first heard of as belonging to Ala-ed-din (1288–1321), a sultan of Central India. It came into British possession when the Punjab was annexed by the East India Company in 1849. It was presented to Queen Victoria and became a very popular feature of the great Exhibition of 1851. Queen Victoria used it as a brooch, but at King Edward VII's coronation it was incorporated in Queen Alexandra's crown. There is a superstition that it brings misfortune to its male wearer but not to women, which may account for the fact that it was not set in one of the King's crowns.

The other gems are the Second and Third Stars of Africa, cut from the Cullinan diamond. These, with the Koh-i-Noor, are regarded as the property of the Crown, but apart from them Queen Mary's crown is her personal property. A new crown is made for every queen consort, and the Koh-i-Noor from Queen Mary's crown was detached to form part of the crown of Queen Elizabeth, mounted throughout in platinum.

A crown which is unlikely to be used again for many years is the Prince of Wales's crown, of simple design, without any valuable gems. This is used by the Prince at Coronations and at State Openings of Parliament. It is distinct from the coronet, used by the last Prince at his investiture. This is kept at Carnarvon Castle, and was made of Welsh gold in 1911 by Messrs. Garrard.

Insignia of Authority

Next in importance in the Regalia to the royal crowns come the sceptres and the orbs, which, when used at the Coronation, have a symbolic significance of the first importance. There are five sceptres, each of which has its own history and symbolic value. First among them is the King's Royal Sceptre with the Cross, called in the Coronation ceremony the Baculum.

The use of the sceptre as a sympol of royal power is of extremely ancient origin, probably of earlier date than the crown itself. It is seen amongst Egyptian hieroglyphics, tipped by the lotus, the papyrus flower or other emblem. An oath sworn on the sceptre is of special solemnity in the *Iliad*. Each of the sceptres in our Regalia has its own special symbolism.

The King's Royal Sceptre is "the ensign of kingly power and justice". The present rod was originally made for Charles II by Sir Robert Vyner, but it has been much added to and beautified. It is about three feet in length, richly jewelled, with a centre portion of plain gold. Its head is most elaborate and now contains the Great Star of Africa, part of the Cullinan diamond, which weighs 516½ carats and is the largest cut diamond in the world. (*See* colour plate facing page 272.) This has been attached by clasps and can be detached for the adornment of the Queen on high State occasions.

Above it is an orb of amethyst of great beauty, surmounted by a jewelled cross, made entirely of diamonds with a central emerald. The hilt is also heavily encrusted with jewels. Beyond the Coronation, the only occasion on which this sceptre is used is the lying-in-state and funeral of the monarch when, with the orb and crown, it is placed on the coffin. As Sir George Younghusband has said, "When the King holds this sceptre he may veritably be said to have in his hand a king's ransom."

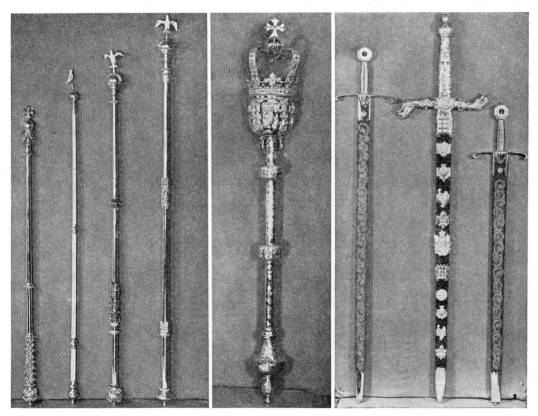

SYMBOLS OF MOST KINGLY POWER

The four Sceptres, left to right, are the Queen's Sceptre with Cross ; the Ivory Rod, placed in the Queen's right hand after the Coronation ; the Queen's Sceptre with the Dove made for Mary the wife of William III but never since used, and the King's Sceptre with the Dove. Centre is one of the eight Maces, and, right, three of the swords : from left to right, the Sword of Justice to the Spirituality, the Sword of State, and Curtana, or Sword of Mercy.

The Royal Sceptre is placed in the King's right hand, while in his left he receives the Sceptre with the Dove. This, too, was made for Charles II, and is a gold rod three feet seven inches in length. It is thus officially described :

"At the top is a monde or orb of gold with a fillet round the centre studded with diamonds. From the top of the monde rises a golden cross on which is sitting a white enamelled dove with extended wings, its eyes, beak, and feet of gold. Below the monde is a band studded with diamonds, and beneath this another band with drooping designs, ornamented with coloured gems and diamonds.

"In the centre of the sceptre is an ornamental band of enamels and gems and gold open work with coloured gems, enamels and diamonds. Nearer to the bottom of the sceptre is another band with large jewels. The boss at the foot of the sceptre is encircled by two bands, one jewelled, the other enamelled."

The dove is symbolical of the Holy Ghost, who controls the action of kings. As the Royal Sceptre is the emblem of power and justice, its companion is the "Rod of Equity and Mercy". In the words of the liturgy pronounced by the Archbishop to the King when he places this sceptre in his left hand : "Be so merciful that you be not too remiss ; so execute justice that you forget not mercy."

Emblems of Queenly Dignity

The other three sceptres in the Regalia have been used by queen consorts and one queen regnant. The Queen's Sceptre with the Cross was made for Mary of Modena, James II's queen. This is only two feet two inches in length, and is made of gold and richly ornamented with diamonds. The cross has a large diamond in the centre and one on each arm, and the boss is also richly jewelled.

This sceptre is placed in the Queen's right hand after her Coronation. In her left is placed the Ivory Rod, emblem of "the powerful and mild influence of her piety and virtue". The rod, which is

surmounted with a gold orb and white dove, is made of three pieces of ivory linked together with gold bands. The dove of white enamel has closed wings, the beak, eyes, and feet being of gold. This sceptre was also made for Mary of Modena, and is used only by queens consort at their Coronation.

The remaining sceptre in the Regalia, the Queen's Sceptre with the Dove, has been used only once, at the crowning of Mary II, for whom it was specially made. It is of the same design as that of the King but is smaller, and ornamented with coloured gems and diamonds and enamel. This sceptre was at one time altogether mislaid, but was recovered in the early nineteenth century, dust-covered, at the back of a cupboard in the Tower jewel-house.

Orbs in the Royal Hand

There are two orbs amongst the Crown Jewels, but only one is used at the Coronation. It is placed in the King's right hand after he has assumed the royal robe. It is presented only to a reigning monarch, and the presence of a second orb in the Regalia is accounted for by the fact that one was specially made for Queen Mary II when, with William III, she was crowned queen regnant.

The orb, surmounted by the cross, symbolizes the Christian domination of the world. The King's Orb, known as the Orb of England, is a golden globe, heavily ornamented with rubies, sapphires and emeralds surrounded by diamonds. The fillet which surrounds the orb and the arch are lined with small pearls. A large amethyst of exceptional quality surmounts the arch, and on the top of this is the cross, decorated with diamonds and pearls. The orb was executed by Sir Robert Vyner for Charles II.

When the Archbishop places the Orb in the King's right hand he thus adjures him : "When you see this Orb . . . remember that the whole world is subject to the power and Empire of Christ our Redeemer."

Queen Mary IIs' Orb is smaller, but very similar to the King's Orb.

An important part in the Coronation ceremony is played by the swords included in the Regalia, particularly by the jewelled Sword of State. So heavily are the hilt and scabbard encrusted with jewels of great value that as an ornament, if not a weapon, it must be one of the most valuable swords in existence. One square emerald set in the hilt is said to be worth nearly £3000, and the value of the sword as a whole cannot be less than £20,000.

Sword of Justice

At the head of the hilt is a large diamond surrounded by four rubies. The cross-piece between the hilt and blade is heavily set in diamonds. The whole of the gold scabbard is jewelled ; amongst the designs picked out in precious stones are the rose of England, the thistle of Scotland, and the shamrock of Ireland.

This sword is the only one the King wears during the Coronation service. It is placed on the altar by the Archbishop, then handed to the King, and girt about him by the Lord Great Chamberlain. After being abjured "With this Sword to do justice" and "stop the growth of iniquity", the King unbuckles it and places it on the altar as a symbol that the power it represents belongs to God and devolves upon the King not by right but by Divine permission.

Technically the sword then becomes the property of the Church—but it is redeemed from the Archbishop after each Coronation by the keeper of the jewel-house on payment of 100 shillings. It is typical of the carelessness all too often accorded to priceless objects—in the past—that this sword was mislaid for many years during the reign of Queen Victoria. It came to light in what looked no more than a dusty gun-case found in a dusty cupboard.

Another Sword of State is amongst swords used at the Coronation. This is the sword carried before the King at the opening of Parliament. It has a gold hilt and quillion (cross-piece) and a crimson velvet scabbard, on which are various designs in gold such as the rose, thistle, harp, fleur-de-lis, portcullis,

etc. The length of the blade is 32 inches and it is 2 inches in width. This sword was used by King George V when he knighted his son, Edward, Prince of Wales, Knight of the Garter.

The three other swords are known as the Curtana or Sword of Mercy, the Sword of Justice to the Spirituality, and the Sword of Justice to the Temporality. These are copies of a set sent by the Pope Clement to Henry VIII as Defender of the Faith. The swords are long and straight, and their blades are of the same pattern, but there is a variation in their points.

The Curtana, for example, is broken off, leaving a blunt point which signifies the element of mercy. The Sword of Justice to the Spirituality has an obtuse end which is said to symbolize the limited power of the ecclesiastical courts ; that of the Sword of Justice to the Temporality a sharp point. They are carried in the Coronation by distinguished noblemen.

Minor Pieces of the Regalia

Another item in the Regalia which now plays only a minor part in the Coronation ceremony is the gilt spurs known as St. George's Spurs. These were made for Charles II and are symbolic of knighthood and chivalry. They have gold-embroidered straps—but are no longer strapped on. The King's heels are merely touched with them, after which they are placed on the altar. The right to carry the spurs has been much contested, and at the Coronation of George V, in 1911, the coveted honour was divided between two noble peers who carried a spur apiece.

The Coronation ring plays a part in the ceremony and symbolizes the union of the King to his people. It is placed on the King's finger after he has taken the orb. Traditionally a new ring is made for each monarch, whose personal property it is. Those exhibited in the Tower were worn by Queen Victoria, King George V, and Queen Mary. A completely disused part of the Regalia are the bracelets, once regarded as an emblem of sovereignty. The

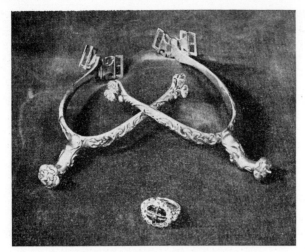

KINGSHIP AND KNIGHTHOOD
SYMBOLIZED

The Coronation Ring—the only part of the Regalia which is the King's private property—is the "ensign of Kingly Dignity". St. George's Spurs of solid gold, made for the Coronation of Charles II, are the symbol of knightly chivalry.

trumpet has a silk banneret embroidered in red and gold with the Royal Arms and Cipher.

The Holy Oil and its Vessel

There remains only to describe the most ancient and sacred of all the precious things used at the ceremony. These are the ampulla and the spoon used in the anointing of the King and Queen, which are laid ready upon the altar before the ceremony. The ampulla is a gold vessel in the shape of an eagle with outstretched wings, standing about nine inches in height and weighing some ten ounces. The ampulla and spoon are undoubtedly of great antiquity, though the ampulla may have been restored by Sir Robert Vyner. There is nothing directly to connect them with earlier Coronations, though it is highly probable that they have been used many times and escaped the vandalism of the Commonwealth by the fact that they were secreted in the

pair still in existence were made for James II, but there is no record in existence which shows that he ever wore them.

Amongst other minor items still used may be mentioned St. Edward's Staff, a gold rod about four feet seven inches in height tipped with a steel shaft and surmounted by an orb and cross. It was once presented to the King on his entrance to the Abbey, symbolically a staff to guide his footsteps, but in recent Coronations it has been merely carried in procession by a nobleman.

There are eight royal maces lodged in the Tower jewel-house, and these make an appearance at royal proclamations and are carried at the Coronation by the Sergeants-at-Arms. Here, too, are stored the State trumpets, of which there are fifteen. They are used only on great State occasions, of which the Coronation is one, when the trumpeters blow fanfares to acclaim the King. Each

STATE TRUMPETS OF SILVER

The State Trumpets of solid silver, with silk bannerets embroidered with the Royal Arms and Cipher, are used for sounding fanfares at certain points in the Coronation ceremony and on a few other State occasions, including the Proclamation of the Sovereign.

ecclesiastical treasury of the Abbey. The handle of the finely-chased gold Coronation spoon is set with four pearls. The sacred oil is poured from the beak of the golden eagle into the anointing spoon, into which the Archbishop dips his finger.

There is an ancient legend attached to this holy oil. When Thomas à Becket, Archbishop of Canterbury, was at Sens in France during his exile from England as a result of his quarrel with King Henry II, the Virgin Mary is said to have appeared to him, carrying in her hands a golden eagle and a small phial of stone or glass containing oil of an altogether priceless description and of the extremest rarity—oil that was possessed of a peculiar virtue for the consecration of monarchs.

MOST ANCIENT AND MOST SACRED

The anointing of the King with holy oil is one of the most important parts of the Coronation ceremony. The Ampulla (of great antiquity) seen at the top of the photograph is filled with oil by the Dean of Westminster, and the Archbishop of Canterbury anoints the King with oil poured into the spoon, said to date from the twelfth century.

Eagle, phial and oil were given to the kneeling Archbishop, with the injunction that they should be confided for safe custody to a certain monk at Poictiers, who, on receiving them, hid them under a stone in St. Gregory's church.

There—so the story goes on—they remained for nearly two hundred years, when they came into the possession of the Black Prince, who had the phial and the eagle or ampulla conveyed to the Tower of London. On discovering its existence, Richard II wished to be reconsecrated with the oil, but it was first used at the Coronation of his successful rival, Henry IV.

While in the realm of legend, we may recall that of Edward the Confessor's ring, the stone of which is in the Imperial State Crown. Edward, the "royal saint", one day, it is said, was asked by a beggar for alms. He had given away all he had to give—all save a valuable ring, which he immediately withdrew from his finger and handed to the old man. Not long afterwards two English pilgrims in the Holy Land met an ancient traveller who, learning that they were from England, extended to them bounteous hospitality, and then, just as he was about to leave them to pursue their journey, announced that he was the Apostle John and asked them to hand to their king on their return to England a ring which he had received from him. The astonished pilgrims took the ring and returned it to the Confessor, who recognized it as the one he had handed to the old beggar.

Apart from the Regalia the solemn religious ceremony of the Coronation owes much of its symbolism to the vestments worn by the sovereign. The King arrives at the Abbey in what is known as the Royal Crimson Robe of State, but after the anointing he is invested in the priest-like vestments of his kingship.

The first of these is known as the Colobium sindonis, an alb or rochet, which is a sleeveless surplice made of fine white cambric, trimmed with lace. The next garment is the Supertunica, called the Close Pall, a coat or tunic reaching below the knees, of cloth of gold lined with crimson silk. In earlier Coronations the buskins, hose and sandals followed, and then the "kingly sword" was girded on.

Next in order of the vestments is the Armil, which represents an ordinary ecclesiastical stole. It was at one time attached to the sovereign's shoulders by ribbons, but now the ends hang down; they have crosses of St. George embroidered on them. But the most important of the vestments is the Imperial Mantle, known as the Pallium or the Open Pall. This is of cloth of gold and resembles a cope in shape.

There is a theory that this may formerly have been a square put over the head like a lozenge with the points hanging down before and behind, but that so inconvenient did this become that it was divided in front and buckled on. The four corners of the mantle signify the four quarters of the world "which are subject to the power of God". National emblems have been traditionally embroidered on the Pallium for many centuries.

After the investiture and anointing of the Queen, and when the King with his Queen Consort have taken the Sacrament, during which celebration both their crowns are removed, they pass, again wearing their crowns, into the traverses prepared for them in St. Edward's Chapel behind the high altar. There the regal robes are put off and the Parliament mantles and State crowns are put on, while the clergy divest themselves of their copes. Finally the royal procession is formed again, and in the same order as that in which it entered it leaves the Abbey by the west door, the King with the sceptre in his right hand and the orb in his left. He is at this time wearing the Imperial State Crown.

The Queen's Coronation

The coronation of the Queen is a less elaborate ceremony. During her anointing four peeresses hold over her a "rich pall of gold". Her ring is placed on the fourth finger of her right hand. She is crowned with her own crown, at which moment all the peeresses present put on their coronets. Then she receives from the Archbishop the Queen's sceptre in her right hand and the Ivory Rod with the Dove in her left.

The Queen wears a gown of ivory satin with symbolic embroidery made of gold thread. Precedent is being followed in the Queen's dress, made by the Royal School of Needlework. The Queen's velvet robe is embroidered with gold and is attached with golden tassels to the shoulders. The cape and the lining are of ermine. The Mistress of the Robes and six daughters of peers clad in simple white dresses carry the Queen's train.

By courtesy of]   *[Garrard & Co.*

QUEEN ELIZABETH'S CROWN

The Queen's Crown, specially made for the 1937 Coronation, consists entirely of diamonds set in platinum. In the front just above the circlet is the famous Koh-i-Noor, and in the cross is the Indian drop brilliant from the Treasury of Lahore.

FROM ACCESSION TO CORONATION

by

OSBERT LUMLEY

and

GILSON MACCORMACK

Chronicle of the Eventful Months from Edward VIII's Abdication to the Crowning of George VI.

King Edward VIII's Message to Parliament

Fort Belvedere,
Sunningdale,
Berkshire.

MEMBERS OF THE HOUSE OF COMMONS,

AFTER long and anxious consideration, I have determined to renounce the Throne to which I succeeded on the death of my father, and I am now communicating this, my final and irrevocable decision.

Realizing as I do the gravity of this step, I can only hope that I shall have the understanding of my peoples in the decision I have taken and the reasons which have led me to take it.

I will not enter now into my private feelings, but I would beg that it should be remembered that the burden which constantly rests on the shoulders of a Sovereign is so heavy that it can only be borne in circumstances different from those in which I now find myself.

I conceive that I am not overlooking the duty that rests on me to place in the forefront the public interest when I declare that I am conscious that I can no longer discharge this heavy task with efficiency or with satisfaction to myself.

I have accordingly this morning executed an Instrument of Abdication.

[This Instrument is reproduced
in facsimile in page 291.]

MY execution of this Instrument has been witnessed by my three brothers, Their Royal Highnesses the Duke of York, the Duke of Gloucester, and the Duke of Kent.

I deeply appreciate the spirit which has actuated the appeals which have been made to me to take a different decision, and I have, before reaching my final determination, most fully pondered over them. But my mind is made up. Moreover, further delay cannot but be most injurious to the peoples, whom I have tried to serve as Prince of Wales and as King and whose future happiness and prosperity are the constant wish of my heart.

I take leave of them in the confident hope that the course which I have thought it right to follow is that which is best for the stability of the Throne and Empire, and the happiness of my peoples.

I am deeply sensible of the consideration which they have always extended to me both before and after my Accession to the Throne, and which I know they will extend in full measure to my successor.

I am most anxious that there should be no delay of any kind in giving effect to the Instrument which I have executed, and that all necessary steps should be taken immediately to secure that my lawful successor, my brother, His Royal Highness the Duke of York, should ascend the Throne.

EDWARD R.I.

CHAPTER 23

HOW GEORGE VI CAME TO THE THRONE

The element of drama is by no means rare in British History, but seldom in their
"rough island story" have the British People lived through such dramatic incidents as
those that accompanied in December, 1936, the Abdication of King Edward VIII

ON Thursday, December 10th, 1936, the British Parliament met for one of the most momentous and dramatic sittings in its long history.

For a week the public had known that a constitutional crisis had arisen owing to differences between King Edward VIII and his advisers, but the Prime Minister, when questioned in the House, had pleaded for patience and had promised to make a statement as soon as he was in a position to do so. On Wednesday, December 9th, it was known that Mr. Baldwin would make his full and final pronouncement on the following day.

Never had the House of Commons been more crowded than on December 10th; never had it been more anxiously expectant. The buzz of excited talk that usually pervades the House on important occasions was subdued. The gravity of the decision members were about to hear obviously weighed upon them. They knew that King Edward's decision had been communicated to the Cabinet in the morning, and there was little doubt as to what it was.

The scene when the House assembled was impressive. It is seldom that all the Commons are present together, and a full assembly means that the chamber is filled to overflowing.

On December 10th, every bench was crowded. Those members who could not find seats sat on the steps of the gangways, clustered behind the Bar or found refuge in the side galleries or on the steps of the Speaker's chair. Yet amidst all the excitement and agitation the House of Commons followed its time-honoured procedure—prayers by the Chaplain ; then "Prayers are over," and the roll of questions.

Soon after 3.30 Mr. Baldwin entered the House and was received with subdued cheers by all parties. He took his accustomed seat on the Treasury Bench. Questions went on to the end ; and, as though to show that the nerves of the House were steady at this moment of crisis, supplementary questions were more numerous than usual. At last the Speaker called upon the Prime Minister. Mr. Baldwin bowed and walked to the Bar of the House and, addressing the Speaker, said : "A message from His Majesty the King, sir, signed by His Majesty's own hand."

Abdication !

With another bow, he advanced and handed the message to the Speaker. Mr. Baldwin retired and the Speaker, in a voice tinged with emotion, read the message that appears in the facing page.

It was received in complete silence. The House had anticipated King Edward's decision, but the irrevocable words stirred such emotions as cannot find voice.

When the reading of the message was over, Mr. Baldwin rose in his place to move "that His Majesty's most gracious message be now considered". His reception showed that members of all parties realized how well he had played his part, how truly he

Photo]   [*Keystone*

OUTSIDE NO. 10

The Prime Minister's official residence in Downing Street was watched with anxious interest as the crisis concerning King Edward's proposed marriage drew to its inevitable conclusion. This photograph shows No. 10 when the street had been cleared by the police of all save Press-men and photographers.

had reflected the opinion of the Empire and how faithfully he had served his Sovereign. Mr. Baldwin said :

"No more grave message has ever been received by Parliament and no more difficult, I may almost say repugnant, task has ever been imposed upon a Prime Minister. I would ask the House, which I know will not be without sympathy for me in my position today, to remember that in this last week I have had but little time in which to compose a speech for delivery today, so I must tell what I have to tell truthfully, sincerely and plainly, with no attempt to dress up or to adorn."

After recalling his first conversation with

King Edward on the proposed marriage, Mr. Baldwin continued :

"I saw the King on Monday, November 16th, and I began by giving him my view of a possible marriage. I told him that I did not think that a particular marriage was one that would receive the approbation of the country. That marriage would have involved the lady becoming Queen. I did tell His Majesty once that I might be a remnant of the old Victorians, but that my worst enemy would not say of me that I did not know what the reaction of the English people would be to any particular course of action, and I told him that so far as they went I was certain that that would be impracticable. . . .

"Then His Majesty said to me—I have his permission to state this—that he wanted to tell me something that he had long wanted to tell me. He said, 'I am going to marry Mrs. Simpson, and I am prepared to go.' I said, 'Sir, that is most grievous news and it is impossible for me to make any comment on it today.' . . .

"He sent for me again on Wednesday, November 25th. In the meantime a suggestion had been made to me that a possible compromise might be arranged to avoid those two possibilities that had been seen, first in the distance and then approaching nearer and nearer. The compromise was that the King should marry, that Parliament should pass an Act enabling the lady to be the King's wife without the position of Queen ; and when I saw His Majesty on November 25th he asked me whether that proposition had been put to me, and I said 'Yes.'

"He asked me what I thought of it. I told him that I had not considered it. I said : 'I can give you no considered opinion.' If he asked me my first reaction informally, my first reaction was that Parliament would never pass such a Bill. But I said that if he desired it I would examine it formally. He said he did so desire. Then I said : 'It will mean my putting that formally before the whole Cabinet and communicating with the Prime Ministers of all the Dominions,' and I asked was that his wish. He told me that it was. I said that I would do it.

"On December 2nd the King asked me to go and see him again. I had intended asking for an audience later that week, because such inquiries as I thought proper to make I had not completed. The inquiries had gone far enough to show that neither in the Dominions nor here would there be any prospect of such legislation being accepted. His Majesty asked me if I could answer his question. I gave him the reply that I was afraid it was impracticable for those reasons. . . .

"That decision was, of course, a formal decision, and that was the only formal decision of any kind taken by the Cabinet until I come to the history of yesterday. When we had finished that conversation, I pointed out that the possible alternatives had been narrowed, and that it really had brought him into the position that he would be placed in a grievous situation between two conflicting loyalties in his own heart—either complete abandonment of the project on which his heart was set, and remaining as King, or doing as he intimated to me that he was prepared to do, in the talk which I have reported, going, and later on contracting that marriage, if it were possible. During the last days, from that day until now, that has been the struggle in which His Majesty has been engaged. We had many talks, and always on the various aspects of this limited problem.

"The House must remember—it is difficult to realize—that His Majesty is not a boy, although he looks so young. We have all thought of him as our Prince, but he is a mature man, with wide and great experience of life and the world, and he always had before him three, nay, four, things, which in these conversations, at all hours, he repeated again and again—that if he went he

would go with dignity. He would not allow a situation to arise in which he could not do that. He wanted to go with as little disturbance of his Ministers and his people as possible. He wished to go in circumstances that would make the succession of his brother as little difficult for his brother as possible ; and I may say that any idea to him of what might be called a King's party, was abhorrent. . . .

"I have something here which, I think, will touch the House. It is a pencilled note, sent to me by His Majesty this morning, and I have his authority for reading it. It is just scribbled in pencil :

"Duke of York. He and the King have always been on the best of terms as brothers, and the King is confident that the Duke deserves and will receive the support of the whole Empire.

"I have only two other things to say. The House will forgive me for saying now something which I should have said a few minutes ago. I have told them of the circumstances under which

Photo]   [Fox

LONDON WAITS WHILE EVENTS MOVE FAST

Though little information was given to the public, it was sensed that great events were afoot, and on the afternoon of December 10th, 1936, the pavements of Whitehall and Parliament Square were thronged with anxious folk. There was little visible excitement and no "demonstrations", but on every hand signs of deep sympathy with the prime movers in the drama that was being played in Palace and Parliament. Above we see the crowd watching outside the House of Commons for Mr. Baldwin's car.

I am speaking, and they have been very generous and sympathetic. Yesterday morning when the Cabinet received the King's final and definite answer officially they passed a Minute, and in accordance with it I sent a message to His Majesty, which he has been good enough to permit me to read to the House, with his reply.

" 'Mr. Baldwin, with his humble duty to the King.

" 'This morning Mr. Baldwin reported to the Cabinet his interview with Your Majesty yesterday and informed his colleagues that Your Majesty then communicated to him informally Your firm and definite intention to renounce the Throne.

" 'The Cabinet received this statement of Your Majesty's intention with profound regret, and wished Mr. Baldwin to convey to Your Majesty immediately the unanimous feeling of Your Majesty's servants.

" 'Ministers are reluctant to believe that Your Majesty's resolve is irrevocable, and still venture to hope that before Your Majesty pronounces any formal decision Your Majesty may be pleased to reconsider an intention which must so deeply distress and so vitally affect all Your Majesty's subjects.

" 'Mr. Baldwin is at once communicating with the Dominion Prime Ministers for the purpose of letting them know that Your Majesty has now made to him the informal intimation of Your Majesty's intention.'

"His Majesty's reply was received last night.

" 'The King has received the Prime Minister's letter of the 9th December, 1936, informing him of the views of the Cabinet.

" 'His Majesty has given the matter his further consideration, but regrets that he is unable to alter his decision.'

"My last words on that subject are that I am convinced that where I have failed no one could have succeeded. His mind was made up, and those who know His Majesty best will know what that means.". . .

"Where I failed . . ."

It would not be true to say that the Prime Minister received an ovation when he sat down—this was not the moment for such a demonstration—but members of all parties in the House showed obviously their agreement with Mr. Baldwin's own words when he said: "Where I failed, nobody could have succeeded."

Later in the day Mr. Baldwin brought in a Bill to give effect to the King's wishes, and this was passed through the next day.

In moving the second reading the Prime Minister explained that it concerned the Dominions as well as the Parliament at Westminster, and that four of the Dominions had asked to be associated as assenting to its text. The Bill gave effect to the King's abdication and provided for the succession by excluding King Edward and his issue. It also exempted King Edward from the Royal Marriage Act of 1772, which established a measure of control over the marriage of persons who might succeed to the throne.

Opposition in Line

Mr. Attlee, for the Opposition, said that the Labour Party supported the Bill because they insisted that the will of the people must prevail, and that the thoughts of the people should be turned quickly once more to the pursuit of peace and the elimination of poverty. Sir Arthur Sinclair, as leader of the Liberal Party, expressed his agreement with the speakers who had preceded him.

After a few other speeches the Committee stage was begun, and the Attorney-General explained that all King Edward's titles, with the revenues attached to them and the Civil List, would pass automatically to the new King exactly as if there had been a demise of the Crown.

As there were no amendments there was no Report stage, but on the third reading the Prime Minister spoke a few words of appreciation of past services of King Edward VIII to the Empire. Mr. Baldwin said :

"This is the last Bill that will be presented for the Royal Assent during the present reign. The Royal Assent given to this Bill will be the last act of his present Majesty.

"I should not like the Bill to go to the House of Lords without putting on record what I feel sure will be the feeling of this House, and of the country, that, though we have this duty to perform and though we are performing it with unanimity, we can never be unconscious of, and we shall always remember with regard and affection, the whole-hearted and loyal service that His Majesty has given to this country as Prince of Wales and during the short time he has been on the Throne.

"Like many of his generation, he was flung into the war. He has served us well in trying to qualify himself for that office which he knew must be his if he lived. For all that work I should like to put it on record that we are grateful and we shall not forget."

The proceedings in the House of Lords were short and the Bill was passed in less than ten minutes. Lord Halifax explained its purpose in a few sentences, and Lord Mottistone and Lord Snell voiced the assent of the Liberal and Labour Parties.

Then came the final scene of the drama. The Lords Commissioners—Lord Onslow, Lord Stanhope and Lord Denman—authorized by the King to declare his assent to the Bill, entered the House. Lord Onslow instructed Black Rod to inform the Commons that the Lords Commissioners desired their attendance.

In a few minutes the Speaker, followed by Ministers and members, entered the House and advanced to the Bar. Lord Onslow then called upon the Reading Clerk to read the authorization of the Commission. The parchment document, sealed with the Great Seal and signed by the King himself, was read. Lord Onslow then told the Clerk to declare the title of the Act to which assent was to be given. "His Majesty's Declaration of Abdication Act," was the reply.

As soon as these words were spoken the Clerk of Parliaments, standing on the other side of the table, pronounced the final words, "*Le Roy le veult.*"

A moment or two later the Speaker with the Commons returned to the Lower House and heard the Speaker report the Royal Assent. After the Prime Minister had spoken a few words stating that the Accession Council would be held on the following day and that the Commons would meet in the afternoon to take the Oath of Allegiance, the motion for adjournment was carried in silence.

INSTRUMENT OF ABDICATION

I, Edward the Eighth, of Great Britain, Ireland, and the British Dominions beyond the Seas, King, Emperor of India, do hereby declare My irrevocable determination to renounce the Throne for Myself and for My descendants, and My desire that effect should be given to this Instrument of Abdication immediately.

In token whereof I have hereunto set My hand this tenth day of December, nineteen hundred and thirty six, in the presence of the witnesses whose signatures are subscribed.

SIGNED AT
FORT BELVEDERE
IN THE PRESENCE
OF

Edward RI

Albert

Henry

George

Proclamation of His Majesty King George VI

WHITEHALL, Dec. 12, 1936.

This day the Lords of the Privy Council assembled at St. James's Palace and gave orders for proclaiming His Majesty, who made a most gracious Declaration to them.

WHEREAS by an Instrument of Abdication dated the Tenth day of December instant, His former Majesty King Edward the Eighth did declare His irrevocable Determination to renounce the Throne for Himself and His Descendants, and the said Instrument of Abdication has now taken effect, whereby the Imperial Crown of Great Britain, Ireland and all other His former Majesty's dominions, is now solely and rightfully come to the High and Mighty Prince Albert Frederick Arthur George :

We, therefore, the Lords Spiritual and Temporal of this Realm, being here assisted with these of His former Majesty's Privy Council, with Numbers of other Principal Gentlemen of Quality, with the Lord Mayor, Aldermen and Citizens of London, do now hereby with one Voice and Consent of Tongue and Heart, publish and proclaim, that

The High and Mighty Prince Albert Frederick Arthur George

is now become our only lawful and rightful Liege Lord

George the Sixth

by the Grace of God, of Great Britain, Ireland and the British Dominions beyond the Seas,

King, Defender of the Faith, Emperor of India:

To whom we do acknowledge all Faith and constant Obedience, with all hearty and humble Affection : beseeching God, by whom Kings and Queens do reign, to bless the Royal Prince George the Sixth with long and happy Years to reign over us.

Given at St. James's Palace, this Twelfth day of December in the year of our Lord One thousand nine hundred and thirty-six.

Henry, Arthur, Cosmo Cantuar, William Ebor, Athlone, Stanley Baldwin, J. Ramsay MacDonald, E. A. FitzRoy (Speaker), Halifax, John Simon, Norfolk (Earl Marshal), Devonshire, Cromer, N.Chamberlain, Zetland, Huntly, Walter Runciman, Duff Cooper, W. Ormsby-Gore, Malcolm MacDonald, John C. C. Davidson, Vincent Massey, Wigram, Beaufort, S. M. Bruce, Austen Chamberlain, W. Nash, Anthony Eden, C. T. te Water. Swinton, Walter E. Elliot, Firozkhan Noon, Oliver Stanley, Kingsley Wood, Salisbury, S. M.

L. O'Keefe, William Shepherd Morrison, Ernest Brown, Crewe, Craigie M. Aitchison, Hewart, C. R. Attlee, Lancelot Sanderson, J. R. Clynes, L. S. Amery, Arthur Greenwood, Mottistone, Rhayader, FitzAlan of Derwent, David Margesson, Rockley, Lloyd, A. V. Alexander, Henry Slesser, Fred. O. Roberts, T. M. Cooper. George Lambert, Wright, Euan Wallace, W. G. Normand, Philip Sassoon, Stanley, Dennis Herbert, H. J. Mackinder, Moyne, Bayford, Lytton, Alness, Goschen, Charles A. McCurdy, Douglas H. Hacking.

Onslow, George Stanley, Archibald Sinclair, Charles Trevelyan, Southborough, T. W. H. Inskip, F. Boyd Merriman, Crawford and Balcarres, John Gilmour, Inverforth, Gerald W. Wollaston (Garter), Henry Norman. Liverpool, Thomas Wiles, Leslie Scott, Robert Horne, Ronald Graham, Wilfrid Greene, Stanmore, Guy Fleetwood Wilson, Daryngton, Geo. T. Broadbridge, G. Wyat Truscott, T. Vansittart Bowater.

[One hundred other Lords of the Council were also present.]

God Save the King

CHAPTER 24

TAKING UP THE BURDENS OF KINGSHIP

As soon as King Edward had decided upon his unparalleled Act of Renunciation, the machinery for the Proclamation of his Successor was set in motion. First in London and then in all the principal cities and towns of the Empire, George VI was proclaimed King-Emperor with all the time-honoured forms

THE Accession Council was held at St. James's Palace at 11 o'clock on Saturday, December 12th. To most meetings of the Privy Council only a few members are summoned, and they are as a rule Cabinet Ministers or officers of the King's Household. To an Accession Council, however, all the members are summoned, the official description of those present being "the Lords Spiritual and Temporal of this Realm, being here assisted with those of His Former Majesty's Privy Council, with numbers of other Principal Gentlemen of Quality, with the Lord Mayor, Aldermen and Citizens of London".

In addition to those named in the order for proclaiming the new King, representatives of the Overseas Dominions and of the Indian Empire attended at St. James's Palace.

The King left his residence in Piccadilly shortly before half past eleven. His Majesty, who was wearing the uniform of an Admiral, was attended by Rear-Admiral Sir Basil Brooke, his Comptroller and Equerry, who rode with him in the first car. It was followed by another in which were Sir Eric Miéville, Private Secretary, and Commander Harold Campbell and Mr. Thomas Coke, Equerries.

A large crowd had assembled outside 145 Piccadilly, and the King was loudly cheered as he drove away, first to Buckingham Palace and then to the garden entrance of St. James's Palace, which was reached at 11.25. Outside St. James's Palace the

crowd was larger, and when the royal car appeared there was a spontaneous outburst of cheers. At the Palace His Majesty was received by the Lord Chamberlain and the other principal officers of the Household, and conducted to the Throne Room, where Privy Councillors wearing

Photo]   [*Wide World*

FIRST STEPS AS KING

The King made his first public appearance as Sovereign when on the day after his accession he proceeded to the Accession Council at St. James's Palace. His Majesty is here seen leaving 145, Piccadilly, for the Palace, attended by Rear-Admiral Sir Basil Brooke.

His Majesty's Declaration to His Privy Council

AT THE COURT OF ST. JAMES'S, THE 12TH DAY OF DECEMBER, 1936.

His Majesty, being this day present in Council, was pleased to make the following Declaration:

YOUR ROYAL HIGHNESSES, MY LORDS AND GENTLEMEN:

I MEET you today in circumstances which are without parallel in the history of our country. Now that the duties of Sovereign have fallen to me, I declare to you my adherence to the strict principles of constitutional government and my resolve to work before all else for the welfare of the British Commonwealth of Nations.

WITH my wife as helpmeet by my side I take up the heavy task which lies before me. In it I look for the support of all my peoples.

FURTHERMORE, my first act on succeeding my brother will be to confer on him a Dukedom, and he will henceforth be known as his Royal Highness the Duke of Windsor.

Whereupon the Lords of the Council made it their humble request to his Majesty that his Majesty's most gracious declaration to their lordships might be made public, which his Majesty was pleased to order accordingly.

M. P. A. HANKEY.

Present

The King's Most Excellent Majesty, His Royal Highness the Duke of Gloucester, His Royal Highness Prince Arthur of Connaught, *Archbishop of Canterbury, Archbishop of York, Prime Minister, Lord President, Mr. Speaker of the House of Commons, Lord Privy Seal, Earl Marshal, Master of the Horse, Duke of Devonshire, Duke of Atholl, Marquess of Huntly, Marquess of Salisbury, Marquess of Londonderry, Marquess of Zetland, Marquess of Crewe, Marquess of Willingdon.*

Lord Chamberlain, Earl of Crawford and Balcarres, Earl Stanhope, Earl De La Warr, Earl of Bessborough, Earl Winterton, Earl of Donoughmore, Earl of Onslow, Earl Granville, Earl of Lytton, Earl of Liverpool, Earl of Athlone, Earl of Midleton, *Lord Richard Cavendish, Lord Eustace Percy, Viscount Goschen, Viscount Wimborne, Viscount St. Davids, Viscount Fitz-Alan of Derwent, Viscount Cecil of Chelwood, Viscount Dunedin, Viscount Sankey, Viscount Swinton, Viscount Dawson of Penn, Lord Stanley, Viscount Wolmer.*

*Lord Hugh Cecil, Bishop of London. Lord Denman, Lord Stanmore, Lord Southborough, Lord Weir, Lord Ernle, Lord Inverforth, Lord Illingworth, Lord Hewart, Lord Mildmay of Flete, Lord Daryngton, Lord Blanesborough, Lord Merrivale, Lord Stonehaven, Lord Lloyd, Lord Atkin, Lord Lugard, Lord Thankerton, Lord Craigmyle, Lord Bayford, Lord Amulree, Lord Greenwood, Lord Russell of Killowen, Lord Dickin-*son, *Lord Macmillan, Lord Noe*l *Buxton, Lord Howard of Penrit*h, *Lord Moyne, Lord Rhayader, Lor*d *Wright, Lord Rankeillour, Lor*d *Rennell, Lord Mottistone, Lor*d *Bingley, Lord Rockley, Lord A*ness, *Lord Wigram, Lord Maughan*, *Lord Roche, Lord Strathcarron.*

*Secretary Sir John Simon, M*r *Secretary Eden, Mr. Secreta*ry *Ormsby-Gore, Mr. Secretary Du*ff *Cooper, Mr. Secretary Malcol*m *MacDonald, Mr. Secretary Ellio*t *Sir George Stanley, Mr. Oliv*er *Stanley, Sir William Forbes E*r*skine, Major Alexander Harding*, *Sir Austen Chamberlain, Mr. Re*g*inald McKenna, Mr. Winst*on *Churchill, Mr. Walter Runcima*n *Sir Herbert Samuel, Sir Charl*es *Hobhouse, Mr. George Lambe*rt *Sir Guy Fleetwood-Wilson.*

[Sixty-six other Lords of the Council were also Present.]

HIS Majesty, at his first coming into the Council, was this day pleased to declare that, understanding that the law required he should at his accession to the Crown take and subscribe the oath relating to the security of the Church of Scotland, he was now ready to do it this first opportunity, which His Majesty was graciously pleased to do, according to the forms used by the Law of Scotland, and subscribed two instruments thereof in the presence of the Lords of the Council, who witnessed the same.

And His Majesty was pleased to order that one of the said instruments be transmitted to the Court of Session to recorded in the Books of Sed runt, and afterwards to forthwith lodged in the Publ Register of Scotland, and th the other of them remain amor the records of the Coun and be entered in the Coun book.

their robes were assembled to hear his Declaration, printed in the opposite page.

When the King had read it the Council requested that it might be made public, and the King made an order that this should be done as stated. His Majesty also took the Accession Oath and the Oath relating to the security of the Church of Scotland. In the meantime, the representatives of the overseas Dominions and India had assembled near the door of the picture-gallery. Those present were Mr. Vincent Massey for Canada, Mr. S. M. Bruce for Australia, Mr. Nash for New Zealand, Mr. C. T. te Water for South Africa, and Sir Firozkhan Noon for India.

Before the King's arrival a Privy Council had been held, presided over by Mr. Ramsay MacDonald, Lord President of the Council, at which the Proclamation had been approved and signed by all those present in the Throne Room, the first four to sign being the Duke of Gloucester, Prince Arthur of Connaught, the Archbishop of Canterbury and the Prime Minister.

After the Council the King's first act was to speak to the overseas representatives. They were presented in turn by the Lord Chamberlain and conveyed to His Majesty the loyal greetings and good wishes for his reign from the Dominions which they represented. The King gave individual replies to all, thanking them for their greetings and expressing his hope for the welfare and prosperity of his peoples in the overseas Dominions.

After the Council came the ceremony of proclaiming the King at four points in London—St. James's Palace, Charing Cross, Temple Bar and the Royal Exchange. The proclamation at St. James's Palace was watched by the King, Queen Mary, Princess Elizabeth and Princess Margaret Rose from a window of Marlborough House and by the Princess Royal and her two sons from the gardens of Marlborough House. The Queen was unable to be present owing to an attack of influenza.

Some of the splendour which usually marks such a ceremony was lost, for it took place in the failing light of a dull December day.

Photo]   *[Keystone*

TO THE ACCESSION COUNCIL

The King who, like King George V, received his early training in the Navy, wore the uniform of an Admiral when he attended the Accession Council, as he had not then assumed the rank of Admiral of the Fleet. This photograph shows His Majesty on his way to the Council.

At St. James's Palace, however, the gloom was artificially relieved, for a powerful searchlight was directed across the courtyard on to the balcony from which the Proclamation was to be read, while the windows behind were brightly illuminated. The unfavourable weather proved no deterrent to the crowds.

Just before three o'clock the trumpeters appeared on the balcony, followed by the Earl Marshal and Garter Principal King of Arms, Sir Gerald Wollaston, carrying the parchment roll on which the Proclamation was inscribed.

Garter King of Arms advanced to the front of the balcony. Behind him were Clarenceux King of Arms, Norroy King of Arms; the Heralds, Lancaster, Somerset,

THE ROYAL LINE OF DESCENT FROM THE ANCIENT SAXON KINGS

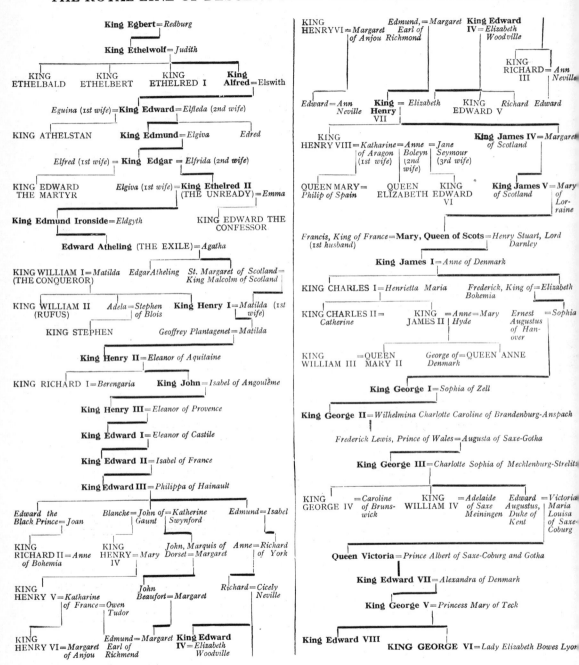

NOTE.—Names of kings and queens set in black type are English or Scottish monarchs in the direct line of descent who have occupied the throne. Black rules indicate the complete line of descent from Egbert to George VI.

Chester, Richmond, Windsor and York ; and the Pursuivants, Rouge Dragon, Rouge Croix and Bluemantle. It is only on the demise of the Crown, at the State opening of Parliament and at the Coronation, or on the occasion of a declaration of war or peace that they appear in their gorgeous tabards, relics of a past age of pageantry.

On the occasion of the proclamation of King George VI, lit up by the searchlights, they were seen in their full splendour. As soon as they had taken their places, the troops came to attention, and the State trumpeters sounded a double fanfare.

Then in measured tones Garter Principal King at Arms read the Proclamation already printed in page 292. When the reading was finished he paused. Then in ringing tones he said : "God Save the King !" Once more there was a fanfare from the trumpeters, the Guard of Honour presented arms, and the band played the National Anthem. First those near at hand took up the words, then those on the outskirts of the crowd, until the whole vast assembly joined in the song of prayer for the new King. Then three cheers for His Majesty, and the Kings of Arms, Heralds and Pursuivants disappeared into the Palace.

A few minutes later there emerged through Marlborough Gate the State carriages which were to convey the Officers of Arms to the three other points at which

[Photo]   [Evening Standard

KING GEORGE VI PROCLAIMED TO HIS PEOPLE

The King was proclaimed at four points in London. The first ceremony took place at St. James's Palace, and above we see the scene just after Sir Gerald Wollaston, Garter King of Arms, had read the Proclamation. Between the mace-bearers, left to right, are Clarenceux King of Arms, the Earl Marshal, Garter King of Arms, and Norroy King of Arms. Drawn up in the courtyard is the Guard of Honour, saluting with the King's Colour dipped. As the day was gloomy a searchlight was trained on the balcony.

the Proclamation was to be read. Along the troop-lined streets, escorted by Household Cavalry, the procession passed to the first point, Trafalgar Square. The light of a winter afternoon was fading fast when a halt was made before the statue of King Charles I on the south side of the Square. There from his carriage Lancaster Herald read the Proclamation, his voice being relayed by loudspeakers to the huge crowd. When he had spoken the last words—"God Save the King"—there were hearty cheers from the many thousands assembled.

As the procession moved along the Strand towards Temple Bar it was brilliantly lit up by the blaze of street lamps and the lights of shops, cinemas and theatres. At Temple Bar a huge crowd had assembled, and though it was a half-holiday

for most of the workers in the neighbourhood, many of them had lingered on to watch the ceremony, every window and vantage point being occupied.

At this point the interest of the proceedings was increased owing to the fact that the Heralds had to obtain the permission of the Lord Mayor before they could cross the City boundary, marked by a red silk cord stretched across the street.

Shortly before three o'clock the Lord Mayor, Sir George Broadbridge, with the Sheriffs, Aldermen and the chief officers of the City, drove up and, alighting from their carriages, took up a position east of the Griffin. Almost exactly as the clock on

Photos]   [Keystone
WITHIN THE CITY BOUNDS

After the procession of Kings of Arms, Heralds and Pursuivants had obtained the Lord Mayor's permission to enter the City, a halt was made at Chancery Lane. Here, in the presence of the Lord Mayor, the Sheriffs, and other City dignitaries, the Proclamation was read by Norroy King of Arms, seen in the top photograph.

the Law Courts struck half past three, the sound of the bells of St. Clement Danes Church told of the approach of the procession. West of the City boundary it halted. The trumpeters came to the front and sounded a fanfare answered by another from the City trumpeters.

Immediately the City Marshal, mounted on a white charger, advanced to the boundary and in ringing tones asked "Who comes there?" From the opposite side of the barrier Bluemantle Pursuivant advanced and replied, "His Majesty's Officers of Arms, who demand entrance to the City of London in order to proclaim His Royal Majesty King George VI."

Bluemantle was then allowed to cross the boundary without escort and was conducted to the Lord Mayor, to whom he delivered the Order in Council requiring the Proclamation to be read. The Lord Mayor, having examined the credentials of Bluemantle, assented to the admission of the Heralds. The City trumpeters sounded again and the Common Crier and Sergeant-at-Arms read aloud the Order in Council. Bluemantle returned to the cavalcade, which then advanced across the boundary.

The Lord Mayor and those with him took up a position opposite Chancery Lane, where Norroy King of Arms rose in his carriage and read the Proclamation, at the conclusion of which the crowd cheered enthusiastically. The Lord Mayor then returned to his carriage and the civic procession preceded the Heralds eastward to the Royal Exchange. As soon as the

Heralds, the Lord Mayor, and the representatives of the City had taken up their position on the steps of the Royal Exchange, the guard of honour of the Honourable Artillery Company presented arms, and the State trumpeters sounded a fanfare, answered by the City trumpeters from the balcony of the Mansion House. The Proclamation was then read for the last time by Clarenceux King of Arms. Another fanfare was sounded, the band played "God Save the King", which was taken up by the crowd, the Lord Mayor called for three cheers for the King, and the ceremony was over.

On the day of his proclamation the King sent messages to the Royal Navy, the Army, the Royal Air Force and the Civil Service.

Photo]   [L.N.A.

ON THE STEPS OF THE ROYAL EXCHANGE

For the fourth and last time the King was proclaimed from the steps of the Royal Exchange in the presence of the Lord Mayor and representatives of the City who had driven in the procession from Chancery Lane. The photograph shows the scene in the late afternoon when, after Clarenceux King of Arms had read the Proclamation, the Lord Mayor called for three cheers for the new King.

The King's Message to His Navy

ON my accession to the Throne I recall with pride that, as my dear father did before me, I received my early training in the Royal Navy.

IT has been my privilege to serve as a Naval officer both in peace and in war ; at Jutland, the greatest sea battle of modern times, I saw for myself in action the maintenance of those great traditions which are the inheritance of British seamen.

IT is my intention always to keep the closest touch with all ranks and ratings of the Naval forces throughout the Empire and with all matters affecting them.

I SHALL do so in the sure knowledge that they will be worthy of the implicit trust placed in them by their fellow-countrymen and that in their hands the honour of the British Navies will be upheld.

GEORGE R.I.

The King's Message to His Army

ON my accession to the Throne, I wish to assure all ranks of the Army that their welfare will be one of my chief concerns.

IT was a notable event in my life, four years ago, when my father appointed me a Major-General in the Army, and that association has only served to enhance my admiration for the courageous and efficient manner in which their duties, however onerous they may prove, are invariably undertaken.

THE task that lies before me is fraught with difficulties, but I know well that the heavy burden of my responsibilities will be lightened by the faithful allegiance of all ranks of the military forces of the Crown throughout the Empire.

GEORGE R.I.

On the same day the King was proclaimed in the Dominions. The ceremony in Canada was synchronized to coincide with that in London. The Canadian Cabinet met at 9.30 in the morning and passed an Order in Council proclaiming the new Sovereign.

Immediately after the Cabinet meeting Lord Tweedsmuir, the Governor-General, signed the Order at Rideau Hall. At 10 o'clock the Cabinet listened to the broadcast of the Proclamation from London. When it was over the King was proclaimed over the Canadian national broadcast, Mr. Mackenzie King making the Proclamation in English and Mr. Lapointe, the Minister of Justice, in French.

In Australia the King's accession was proclaimed at Canberra in the presence of the Governor-General, Lord Gowrie, the Prime Minister and other members of the Government at the foot of the statue of King George V in King's Hall, Parliament House and at Sydney (*see* illustrations p. 244), Melbourne (p. 246), Adelaide and Perth.

At a special meeting of the Executive Council at Wellington, New Zealand, the Governor-General, Lord Galway, and the members of the Cabinet took the oath of allegiance to the new King and Lord Galway sent a message to His Majesty on behalf of the Government and people of New Zealand.

In the Union of South Africa the Proclamation of King George VI was

The King's Message to His Air Forces

*O*N *my accession to the Throne, I hasten to assure the Air Forces at home and overseas that I look forward to the maintenance of my close connexion with them, which has been such a happy feature of my life ever since I became a junior officer in the Service in 1918 and served with the Independent Air Force in France.*

*A*S *Air Chief Marshal, I have watched with keen appreciation the way in which the Service has proved more than equal to the many tasks which a rapid expansion has imposed upon it.*

I KNOW *full well that the Air Forces of the Empire will maintain to the full the great traditions that they have already established, combining with the highest efficiency and zeal a fine chivalry of service and a deep and steadfast loyalty.*

GEORGE R.I.

The King's Message to the Civil Service

I DESIRE, *on my accession to the Throne, to express to all grades of the Civil Service my appreciation of the ability and devotion with which they have always discharged their varied duties, whether at home or overseas.*

*T*HE *record of the British Civil Service is indeed unique, and I recognize with satisfaction the great position which its members have won for themselves in the life of the community. Its great traditions and those of the Dominions Services, of the Indian and the Colonial Services, are well known to me, and I am sure that I can depend on that spirit of steadfast devotion to duty which has at all times animated them.*

*W*HATEVER *difficulties may lie ahead, I know that I can rely on their lasting loyalty.*

GEORGE R.I.

---

nnounced by the firing of a salute of twenty-ne guns and the Governor-General sent a ᴍessage to the King assuring him of the ᴏyalty of the Union.

In Newfoundland, the Governor, Vice-dmiral Sir Humphrey Walwyn, pro-laimed King George VI from the steps of ᴛe Colonial Building.

In Gibraltar and Malta, Jamaica, Kenya, ᴌong Kong and all the other British ᴏssessions the Proclamation was also made ᴎ Saturday, December 12th, and loyal ᴍessages were dispatched to the King.

On Monday, December 14th, the King as proclaimed in Scotland, in the Indian ᴍpire and in the principal English cities ᴎd boroughs. The proclamation in Delhi ᴏok place in the forecourt of the Viceroy's

House, in the presence of the Viceroy and the Commander-in-Chief with their staffs and the Executive Council, and many high officials. (*See* illustration p. 261.)

The ceremony in Edinburgh with its medieval pageantry was quite as impressive as that in London. The first part took place at the historic Mercat Cross in the High Street, the heart of old Edinburgh.

As soon as midday had sounded from the bells of St. Giles's, Lord Provost Gumley read the Proclamation "to the people of Edinburgh" from the gallery of the Cross. Lyon King of Arms then read it twice, first "to the people of Scotland" and then, at the request of the Sheriff of Peebles and the Lothians, "to the people of the Sheriffdom". Each reading was

George II	1714-1714
George III	1727-1727
George IV	1760-1760
William IV	1820-1820
Victoria	1830-1837
Edward VII	1837-1901
George V	1901-1910
Edward VIII	1910-1936
	1936
George VI	1936

Photo]   *[Keystone*

THREE KINGS IN ONE YEAR

Many elderly people of the nineteenth century knew no other sovereign than Queen Victoria, but the present century has seen four Kings in less than twenty-seven years. Above, the beginning of the new reign is being recorded on a board outside the famous city inn that has seen more than a dozen reigns.

the Central Hall of the Parliament House in the presence of a large and distinguished official gathering.

On Monday, December 14th, the King celebrated his forty-first birthday. At His Majesty's wish the official celebrations were postponed until a later date, but flags were flown on public buildings and salutes were fired in Hyde Park and at the Tower of London, while the Court Circular contained the following announcement :

> The King has been pleased on the occasion of His Majesty's birthday to confer upon the Queen the title and dignity of a Lady of the Most Noble Order of the Garter.

On Monday, December 14th, when Parliament met, a message from the King to Lords and Commons was read. This is given at the top of the next page.

Special meetings of both Houses of Parliament took place on Saturday, December 12th, in order that the members might take the oath of allegiance.

followed by a fanfare, and, when the last one had been sounded, Lyon King of Arms called for three cheers for the King. From Mercat Cross the procession drove to the Castle, where the Proclamation was read by Falkland Pursuivant. Next it was read in the forecourt of the Palace of Holyrood House by Albany Herald, and lastly at Leith by Unicorn Pursuivant.

The Proclamation of the King in Belfast did not take place until Thursday, December 17th. After a meeting of the Privy Council at which the Proclamation was signed, it was read by the Governor, the Duke of Abercorn, at noon in

Photo]   *[Topical*

PROCLAMATION IN SCOTLAND'S CAPITAL

King George VI was proclaimed in Edinburgh from the Mercat Cross in the oldest part of the city. The photograph shows the Lord Provost reading the proclamation from the gallery of the Cross, with City halberdiers on either side of him. Below are he Heralds and Pursuivants in front of the Guard of Honour, the City Councillors and the Senators of the College of Justice in their robes.

I HAVE succeeded to the Throne in circumstances which are without precedent and at a moment of great personal distress, but I am resolved to do My duty and I am sustained by the knowledge that I am supported by the widespread good will and sympathy of all My subjects, here and throughout the world.

It will be My constant endeavour, with God's help, supported as I shall be by My dear Wife, to uphold the honour of the Realm and to promote the happiness of My peoples.

GEORGE R.I.

Mr. Baldwin then moved :

"That a humble address be presented to His Majesty to offer to His Majesty our loyal thanks for his gracious message and to express to His Majesty our devotion to his Royal person and to Her Majesty the Queen, and to assure His Majesty of our conviction that his reign, under the blessing of Divine Providence, will safeguard the liberties of the country and promote the prosperity and contentment of his people.

"His Majesty speaks of a moment of great personal distress and I can assure the House that that is no exaggeration and no mere formal phrase.

"When the one who succeeds is a brother with the tie of affection that always has bound those brothers, the occasion cannot but be one of poignant distress.

"But, Sir, I have the honour of knowing the new King well and I would tell the House—if they do not already know—that what will endear him to his people, if it has not already endeared him, is that, more than any of his brothers, he resembles in character and disposition of mind his father, whose loss we were lamenting eleven short months ago."

For the Opposition, Mr. Attlee and Sir Archibald Sinclair spoke briefly in support of Mr. Baldwin. On the following day the King received at Buckingham Palace twenty Privy Councillors, headed by the Prime Minister, who presented to His Majesty the loyal address of the Commons in reply to His Majesty's message. After his formal reply, the King added the message which appears at the foot of this page.

On January 26th another message from the King was read by the Prime Minister. In this the King asked Parliament to make provision for the purpose of facilitating the uninterrupted exercise of the royal authority not only during the minority of the Sovereign at his accession, but also during any incapacity of the Sovereign and his absence from the realm.

To meet the King's wishes the Regency Bill was presented to Parliament on January 29th and passed through all its stages without opposition. It provided for all the contingencies mentioned in the King's message. In the event of the Sovereign being under eighteen years of age at the time of his accession, the next heir to the throne if he be twenty-one shall be appointed Regent. In the event of the illness of the Sovereign or Regent or his absence from the country, he may delegate certain of his functions to the Counsellors of State, they being the wife or husband of the Sovereign, if the Sovereign is married, and the four persons next in the line of succession to the Throne.

GENTLEMEN, may I add that I am sure that I can count on your sympathy in the sad circumstances in which I have acceded to the Throne.

I have suffered a very real loss by the decision of my brother, for by his going I am deprived of a close friendship which I valued highly.

However, the fact that I have received this address at the hands of many old friends fills me with encouragement for the future.

CHAPTER 25

FIRST FUNCTIONS OF THE NEW REIGN

The exceptional circumstances in which King George VI ascended the Throne made it necessary that he should at once take up the full burdens of Kingship not only in the great affairs of State, but also in regard to public and official functions

AFTER his accession to the throne, following the abdication of Edward VIII, the first official act of King George VI was to hold a Privy Council at St. James's Palace on the morning of December 12th, 1936, as described in the preceding chapter of this Section.

The first official engagement King George VI was called upon to fulfil after his accession to the throne took place on February 9th, 1937, when His Majesty drove to St. James's Palace to hold the first levee of his reign.

Accompanied by the Duke of Beaufort, Master of the Horse, the King, wearing the full-dress scarlet and gold uniform of Colonel-in-Chief of the Grenadier Guards, left Buckingham Palace soon after eleven o'clock. His Majesty rode in a semi-State coach, accompanied by a captain's escort of the Life Guards, their uniforms hidden by scarlet cloaks. Large crowds gathered in the Mall and cheered as the procession drove by to St. James's Palace, where, at the garden entrance, the King was received by a guard of honour of the Welsh Guards.

The levee was attended by about a thousand people, and the scene in the State salons, where the Gentlemen-at-Arms and the Yeomen of the Guard were on duty, was most striking as the various uniforms mingled in a mass of brilliant colour. At the beginning of the ceremony, in accordance with tradition, the "states" of the Royal Artillery and of the Royal Engineers were presented to the King by Field-Marshal Lord Milne and Lieut.-General Sir Ronald Charles respectively. These are documents presented to the King on the occasion of his first levee by the Colonel-Commandant of these regiments, showing their strength or "states".

The Ambassadors and Ministers of forty-nine countries were then introduced by the Marshal of the Diplomatic Corps, Lieut.-General Sir Sidney Clive, and presented to the King by the Lord Chamberlain, the Earl of Cromer. These having been introduced in order of precedence, presentations of the staffs of the Embassies and Legations were made.

After the ceremony, which lasted about an hour, and at which the Duke of Gloucester and the Duke of Kent were present, the King drove back in state to Buckingham Palace.

Princess Alexandra Christened

In the afternoon he was present with the Queen at the christening of the infant daughter of the Duke and Duchess of Kent, which took place in the private chapel at Buckingham Palace. The Archbishop of Canterbury officiated, assisted by the Domestic Chaplain to the King, Prebendary L. J. Percival. The gold font made for the christening of Queen Victoria's eldest child was brought from Windsor Castle, and the baby was sprinkled with water from the River Jordan.

The child, who is sixth in the line of succession to the throne, was given the

_oto]   [Studio Lisa

HAPPY GLIMPSE OF ROYAL HOME LIFE

Guided by their strong sense of duty, the King and Queen have always put their public obligations before all
else, but once those obligations have been discharged they enjoy to the full a happy domestic life.   This scene
outside Princess Elizabeth's Welsh cottage in the grounds of Royal Lodge (see also page 207), showing Their
Majesties enjoying a "romp" with the Princesses and their pets, gives a charming glimpse of their home life.
This delightful picture appears in "Our Princesses and Their Dogs", by Michael Chance (John Murray).

To face page 304.

names of Alexandra Helen Elizabeth Olga Christabel.

On February 13th, 1937, the King and Queen fulfilled their first public engagement together since His Majesty's accession, when they visited the new People's Palace in the Mile End Road. The new building, opened in December 1936, was erected on a site adjoining the old building, part of which—the Queen's Hall—was destroyed by fire in 1931.

There was a typical warm-hearted East End welcome for Their Majesties as they drove through Commercial Road, Burdett Road and into Mile End Road. Everyone waved flags or streamers, and the humble decorations of many a small home in the dingy side-streets evoked those homely scenes of loyalty which had so touched the heart of King George V at the time of his Silver Jubilee.

Among the crowds of people gathered along the pavements there must have been many who remembered how, when they were children, they had seen Queen Victoria and the Prince of Wales drive to the Mile End Road to open the first People's Palace in May 1887.

The King, who was met by Mr. W. C.

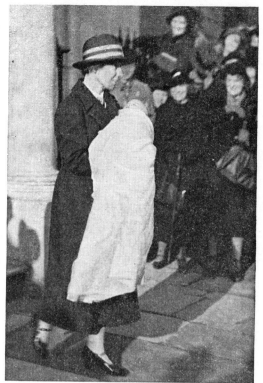

Photo]   *[Fox*

YOUNGEST PRINCESS

The infant daughter of the Duke and Duchess of Kent, born on Christmas Day, 1936, was christened in the private chapel of Buckingham Palace on February 9th. The photograph shows the Princess in the arms of her nurse leaving for the ceremony.

Johnson, Chairman of the Governors, inspected the guard of honour provided by detachments of the Queen Victoria Rifles (9th London Regt.), Tower Hamlets Rifles (17th London Regt.), the British Legion and the Jewish ex-Service Men's Legion. Their Majesties then entered the Main Hall, where a number of presentations were made, after which a little girl handed a bouquet to the Queen, timidly asking Her Majesty to give her love to Princess Elizabeth. This little girl was a descendant of the child who presented a bouquet to Queen Victoria at the opening of the previous People's Palace, fifty years before.

After an inspection of the building the King and Queen witnessed, in the Small Hall, a gathering of 500 representatives of various youth organizations—Boy Scouts,

Photo]   *[G.P.U.*

PRINCE CHARMING

The elder brother of the little Princess Alexandra was born on October 9th, 1935. This happy photograph shows Prince Edward out for an airing in the gardens in front of the Duke and Duchess's residence in Belgrave Square.

20

Photo] [Fox

QUEEN MARY GOES TO THE
CHRISTENING

The photograph shows Queen Mary with the Duchess of
Gloucester leaving the Duke and Duchess of Kent's residence
in Belgrave Square to attend the christening of their infant
daughter, Her Majesty's sixth grandchild.

Sea Scouts, Girl Guides and so on—and
then, returning to the Queen's Hall, where
they took their places in the Royal Box,
they listened to a poem written by Mr.
John Drinkwater for the occasion, and
spoken by Miss Margaretta Scott.

There followed a performance of selec-
tions from Edward German's opera "Merrie
England" by the People's Palace Choral
and Orchestral Society, and a recital on the
new organ by Dr. Reginald Goss-Custard.
As the King and Queen left the building
after the National Anthem had been
played, they were given an enthusiastic
send-off by the crowds assembled in the
Mile End Road—so enthusiastic, in fact,
that the police were unable to keep the
cheering crowds in bounds.

On February 15th the King and Queen
took up their residence at Buckingham
Palace. The move was marked by no
ceremony. The Queen had that day visited
the British Industries Fair at the White
City, and after returning to 145 Piccadilly
for tea she drove to the Palace. The small
crowd which cheered her departure was
quite unaware that she had left her former
home for the last time.

Earlier in the day the King had driven
straight to the Palace from Royal Lodge,
Windsor Great Park, where he had been
spending the week-end with the Queen
and their two daughters. Their Majesties'
suite of apartments is on the first floor,
and is the same as that which was formerly
occupied by King George V and Queen
Mary. The rooms set apart for the
princesses are on the second floor, and
from Constitution Hill the windows can
quickly be identified by the white-painted
bars placed across the lower part as a
safeguard against accidents.

After his return to the Palace the King
sat for Sir William Goscombe John, R.A.,
the well-known sculptor, who had been
commissioned to execute the new Great Seal
of England. It was Sir William who designed
the regalia and medal for the investiture
of the Prince of Wales in 1911, and also
the King's Silver Jubilee medal in 1935.

In view of the short interval between the
King's accession and his Coronation, both
he and the Queen were frequently called
upon to grant sittings to artists and photographers, in order that official portraits of
Their Majesties might be available and to
enable suitable Coronation medals to be
struck. For the official medal, struck at
the Mint, bearing on the obverse the head
of the King and on the reverse that of
Queen Elizabeth, Their Majesties sat to
Mr. Percy Metcalfe.

The fact that the British Industries Fair
has grown, since its inauguration in 1915,
into one of the greatest national trade fairs in
the world has received of late years generous
recognition from the Royal Family, and
since its inception Queen Mary has visited
the fair no less than thirty-four times.

[*hotos]   [*Sport & General ; Fox*

STATE OCCASION AND FAMILY PARTY

The first State function of the new reign was a Levee held by the King at St. James's Palace on February 9th.   The King and Queen were not then in residence at Buckingham Palace, but the Royal procession started from and returned to the Palace.   It is seen above on the return journey.   After the Levee the King and Queen were present at the family luncheon-party given by the Duke and Duchess of Kent before the christening of their daughter.   They are seen in the lower photograph leaving to attend the ceremony in the private chapel of Buckingham Palace.

In 1937 the fair was visited twice by the King and three times by both the Queen and Queen Mary. On February 16th, when they all visited the fair together, they brought with them the Princess Royal and the Duke and Duchess of Kent. The presence of six members of the Royal Family at a public exhibition at one time is an event probably without precedent. The King and Queen entered Olympia by the Addison Road entrance at 10.30 a.m. and found the remainder of the royal party near the British Empire exhibits.

Royal Interest in Industry

They were welcomed by Mr. Walter Runciman, President of the Board of Trade, and officials of the British Industries Fair, and afterwards made a close inspection of the many stands. During their tour they bought a number of articles, and at one point the King left the party to visit a display of sports goods on the first floor. There he was observed trying several tennis rackets, and he later remarked that he intended to take up the game again soon. It will be remembered that the King, as Duke of York, was a player of more than usual ability, and has played at Wimbledon. As a souvenir of his visit, the King was presented by a Sheffield cutlery firm with a canteen of scissors, made in 1827 for presentation to King George IV.

The visit was not without its amusing moments. An exhibitor offered to show the King a camera capable of taking 3000 pictures a minute, and His Majesty, who is a miniature-camera enthusiast, made to follow the demonstrator, but so dense was the crowd, he could not get through. So, shrugging his shoulders, the King remarked with a smile that he would have to leave it until some other time.

The following day the King visited the White City section of the fair, where he was received by Lord Derby and Captain Euan Wallace, Secretary to the Department of Overseas Trade. The White City housed the textile section of this great industrial exhibition, and the King was greatly interested in the vast array of stalls decked with fabrics, silks, lace, carpets and clothes.

During this visit the King was shown specimen sections of the carpets used in Westminster Abbey for the Coronation, and he expressed his admiration of the colours. Again, his visit was marked by a complete absence of formality, and the element of comedy was not lacking when Lord Derby, who could not resist testing a settee by sitting on it, found considerable difficulty in rising unaided. For an hour and three-quarters the King walked round the halls, showing keen interest in the numerous exhibits.

The first investitures of the new reign were held at Buckingham Palace on February 24th and 25th, when the King conferred honours awarded in the New Year list upon 147 persons.

The first day's investiture being an official function, uniform or levee dress was worn and the Grand Entrance of the Palace was used for the reception. The ceremony took place in the Throne Room, where His Majesty's Bodyguard of the Honourable Corps of Gentlemen-at-Arms was on duty. The King's Guard of the 1st Battalion Coldstream Guards, with the King's Colour and band of the regiment, was mounted in the Quadrangle. Those to be honoured were severally introduced into the King's presence by the Lord Chamberlain, and His Majesty invested them with the insignia of the honour bestowed upon them. Among those decorated was the Right Hon. H. A. L. Fisher, who was awarded the rare Order of Merit.

Second Investiture

The second day's investiture was more of a private function, and morning dress was worn, as most of the recipients of honours were civilians. Those present were introduced into His Majesty's presence by the Home Secretary, Sir John Simon. During the investiture a selection of music was played by the String Band of the Welsh Guards.

Prior to their Coronation Their Majesties had little leisure for theatre-going, but on

FIRST PUBLIC CEREMONY OF THE NEW REIGN

On February 13th the King and Queen performed the first public ceremony of the new reign when they drove to the East End and opened the new People's Palace in the place of that destroyed by fire in 1931. Above, the King is inspecting the Guard of Honour while the Queen awaits him at the entrance. Their Majesties were acclaimed by huge crowds, who testified their loyalty to King George VI with enthusiasm equal to that which they had shown at the Silver Jubilee of King George V.

Photo]　　　　　　　　　　　　　　　　　　　　　　　　　　　　　　　　　　　　　　　[Fox

QUEENS AT THE BRITISH INDUSTRIES FAIR

The Queen and Queen Mary are deeply interested in the welfare of British manufactures, and both spent many hours inspecting the display at the White City and Olympia during the British Industries Fair of 1937.　The Queen, with the King and Queen Mary, is seen at the Fair accepting a silver gilt and enamelled toilet set presented to the Queen by the Birmingham Jewellers' and Silversmiths' Association, to mark the Golden Jubilee of the Association.

March 4th they attended the Haymarket Theatre to see "The Amazing Dr. Clitterhouse", which Queen Mary and the Princess Royal had enjoyed the previous Saturday.

The Queen, who is a lover of the ballet, and who, as Duchess of York, often attended performances of the Russian Ballet at Covent Garden, graciously consented to be present at a ballet performance in aid of the National Council of Girls' Clubs at the Piccadilly Theatre on March 8th. Among the stars who delighted the Queen were the great English ballerina Lydia Sokolova, the brilliant Irish dancer Anton Dolin, Argentinita, Harold Turner and Alicia Markova.

The King and Queen gave the first party of their reign at Buckingham Palace on March 11th, when nearly a hundred ambassadors, ministers and heads of foreign missions, together with their wives, partook of a buffet tea in the Blue Drawing-room. In the evening Their Majesties gave a dinner-party to some thirty of their personal friends, after which a talking film was shown for the first time at the Palace. Five days later the King and Queen held an afternoon party at the Palace, to which 450 guests were invited.

On March 16th Their Majesties held an afternoon party at Buckingham Palace. This function had originally been planned for March 24th, but when it was pointed out that, Easter falling so early in the year, the royal party would actually come into Holy Week, the Queen at once altered the date.

On March 17th the King visited the Manor of Kennington, the London estate of the Duchy of Cornwall, and this tour, undertaken on the 600th anniversary of the promulgation of the Duchy Charter, marked His Majesty's first visit to any Duchy property. After visiting King's George's House, Stockwell, the Christ Church Boys' Club and the headquarters of the Church of England Waifs and Strays Society, the King planted a crab-apple tree in the newly made gardens of Dennis Crescent.

His Majesty then drove to the Old Tenants' Hostel in Newburn Street, where a number of presentations were made, and concluded his visit by inspecting the homes of some of his tenants on the estate.

The official announcement made on December 15th, 1936, that the King intended to maintain the royal stable and breeding stud was warmly welcomed by every lover of the "Sport of Kings". Their pleasure was made all the greater

Photo]   *[Keystone*

READY FOR THE GREAT RACE

Like his father before him, the King takes a keen interest in the "Sport of Kings". Here we see him with the Queen just after their arrival in the Royal Box at Aintree for the Grand National of 1937. In the background stands Lord Derby.

Photo]   *[Keystone*

KENNINGTON ACCLAIMS ITS NEW ROYAL LANDLORD

As befits a good landlord, the King took an early opportunity of visiting some of the estates in South London that are amongst the properties of his Duchy of Cornwall. Loyalty knows no class-distinctions, and His Majesty received a tremendous reception as he passed from place to place on his tour of inspection of a thickly populated working-class neighbourhood. Here the King is acknowledging the greetings of 500 children outside the headquarters of the Waifs and Strays Society in Kennington.

when His Majesty intimated his desire to be present at the Grand National, and the storm of cheering which greeted his appearance in the Royal Box at Aintree on March 19th was not only a token of personal esteem, but also a manifestation of delight that the King should continue that interest in the Turf which had been shown both by his father and grandfather.

Their Majesties, who during their visit stayed as the guests of the Earl of Derby at Knowsley, Lancashire, arrived at Huyton station on March 18th, and watched the races from Lord Derby's private stand on the following day, when, after a thrilling race, the Grand National was won by Royal Mail. On the same day a new race was inaugurated, named after the King— the George VI stakes— when Queen's Shilling carried Lord Harewood's colours first past the post.

The royal racing establishment and breeding stud includes the royal stables at Egerton House, Newmarket, the Hampton Court stud and the Sandringham stud. Brigadier Tomkinson is manager of the royal establishment, and the King's trainer is Mr. W. R. Jarvis. The royal stud is managed by Captain Charles Moore, a leading authority on bloodstock and a former Steward of the Irish Turf Club.

Apart from Polonaise, entered for the 1000 Guineas and the Oaks, no royal horses were entered for the classic races of 1937, but in 1938 there will be royal nominations for all the great events.

At Easter Their Majesties took up their residence at Windsor Castle for a stay of nearly five weeks. This was the first time

Photo] [Keystone
RADIANT SMILE

The heart, not only of Great Britain, but of every part of the Empire which the Queen has visited has been captivated by Her Majesty's smile. It is indicative of her desire to put all those with whom she comes in contact at their ease.

the Court had been in residence at the Castle since Ascot Week of 1935.

On April 20th the King unveiled the memorial to King George V in the Guards' Chapel, Wellington Barracks, and on April 23rd he performed a similar ceremony for the Windsor Memorial. On April 27th, accompanied by the Queen, the King opened the National Maritime Museum at Greenwich, to which he went by water. On May 2nd Their Majesties attended service at the new Royal Military College Chapel, Sandhurst.

Shortly after his return to London, the King was presented, on May 4th, at Buckingham Palace, with the baton of a Field-Marshal. The presentation was made by the Duke of Connaught as senior Field-Marshal of the British Army. About thirty inches long, this baton was made of 18-carat gold by Messrs. Garrard and Co., goldsmiths to the Crown. It is covered in red velvet, studded with gold lions, and surmounted by a finely worked gold model of Saint George and the Dragon.

One of the last engagements fulfilled by the King before his Coronation was on May 7th, when he acted as host to the Empire Premiers and members of the legislatures of the Empire at a luncheon given by the Empire Parliamentary Association in Westminster Hall. On May 11th Their Majesties received addresses from the Prime Ministers of the Dominions and representatives of India and the Colonial Empire, and entertained to luncheon at Buckingham Palace representatives of the British Commonwealth.

BEHIND THE SCENES OF A CORONATION

by

GILSON MacCORMACK

and

ERNEST SHORT

An Account of the Decorations and Rejoicings arranged for the Celebration of the Great Day

CHAPTER 26

Pageantry in Preparation

CHAPTER 27

Britain's Coronation Dress

FROM AUSTRALIA TO THE CORONATION

In brilliant sunshine the Australian Contingent which took part in the Coronation procession marched through the streets of Adelaide (as seen above) on their way to Government House, in the grounds of which they were inspected by Major-General Sir Winston Dugan, the Governor of South Australia. The contingent included men of the Australian Navy, Army and Air Force. After the inspection the officers and men were entertained at luncheon by the Lord Mayor at the Town Hall.

PREPARING FOR THE CROWDS

On Coronation Day some hundreds of horses that had never before faced a cheering London crowd were employed to draw the carriages of distinguished visitors from Overseas to Westminster Abbey. The photograph above shows a stage in the training the horses underwent to ensure that they would face the ordeal quietly. Barriers much stronger than those formed by the friendly arms of the London police were necessary to keep the Coronation crowds within bounds. Steel barriers such as those seen, left, in course of erection in Pall Mall were put up at many points on the route.

CHAPTER 26

PAGEANTRY IN PREPARATION

Five or six months of intensive work were required to prepare for the Coronation, for not only was every detail of the actual ceremony worked out and rehearsed, but there was in addition an immense amount of constructional work to be done

A CORONATION, with all its attendant pageantry, takes but a few hours: its preparation involves months of careful planning. In this chapter are described some of the manifold activities which spring into life as soon as a Coronation is imminent. Before the actors can make their appearance, the stage must be set, and that which goes on behind the scenes of a Coronation is by no means the least interesting part.

One of the busiest and most prominent persons in the country during the preparations for a Coronation is the Duke of Norfolk, Hereditary Earl Marshal and Marshal of England.

The Earl Marshal ranks as the eighth of the great officers of State, and as head of the College of Arms is responsible for the appointment of Kings-of-Arms, Heralds and Pursuivants. In addition to attending the Sovereign at the opening of Parliamentary sessions, he arranges all State processions and ceremonials, notably Coronations, royal marriages and funerals

On the occasion of the Coronation of King George VI the onerous duties of this high office were performed by the twenty-nine-year-old Bernard Marmaduke Fitz-Alan-Howard, sixteenth Duke of Norfolk. On his shoulders fell the task of arranging the whole of the complicated ceremonials, the processions to and from the Abbey, the order of precedence, the issuing of invitations to those entitled to be present in the Abbey. and "the determining and ordering

of all matters touching Arms, Ensigns of Nobility, Honour and Chivalry". Furthermore, he had to superintend and enforce the correct dressing of the peers and peeresses, direct the manufacture of the robes worn by the King and Queen, and appoint the gold-staff officers and other temporary officials whose services are required at the ceremony.

In these duties he was assisted by a special staff, by the College of Arms, of which he is the head, and by a specially appointed Coronation Executive Committee.

This Coronation Executive Committee, constituted on December 21st, 1936, consisted of twenty-eight members, among whom were, in addition to the Earl Marshal, the Archbishop of Canterbury, Lord Wigram and Sir Philip Game. Further, an Empire Coronation Commission was appointed on January 14th, 1937, consisting of the members of the Coronation Committee of the Privy Council and representative bodies for Canada, Australia, New Zealand and South Africa, "to meet in London for the purpose of considering those aspects of the arrangements for the Coronation which are of common concern". The chairman of this Commission was the Duke of Gloucester.

Some three hundred gold-staff officers were appointed by the Earl Marshal for duty within the Abbey, and recruited for the most part from retired officers or the relatives of peers. The office was no sinecure,

NEW ORGAN AT WESTMINSTER

For the Coronation of King George VI a new organ was constructed in West-minster Abbey by the famous Durham firm of Harrison and Harrison at a cost of £20,000. This cost was entirely defrayed by a public subscription sponsored by the *Daily Telegraph*, and the organ, some of the pipes of which are seen above was erected during the spring of 1937.

It is an immense task which devolves upon the Office of Works in preparing a worthy setting for the greatest cere-monial pageant that ever takes place within our realm. To ensure sufficient time for the necessary preparations, West-minster Abbey was closed to the public on January 4th, 1937. On the following day the building was formally handed over to the Office of Works, the task of pre-paring it for the Coronation ceremony having been placed by the Earl Marshal of England in the hands of His Majesty's First Commissioner of Works.

Before work could start, authority had to be obtained from the Dean of Westminster to import into the church the timber, scaffolding and other materials needed. The business of transforming the Abbey then rapidly got under way.

In point of fact, a beginning had already been made previous to the closing of the Abbey, for the old organ had been removed, and the new one, used for the first time at the Coronation, was in process of completion, the swell organ being already in place.

To clear the ground for the work in hand all the existing seats were taken away, save the choir stalls, after which a final survey was made of the total space available. Normally, the seating capacity of West-minster Abbey is about 2500 ; to provide accommodation for the great congregation due to assemble there on May 12th, this seating capacity had to be increased to 7700, and this entailed the construction of stands and galleries all round the interior.

For the erection of this additional seat-ing accommodation, a plan was adopted analogous to that used in theatre practice. The scaffolding was erected against the walls of the Abbey, and "floors" were

for they were required to be on duty at 5.30 a.m., and did not leave the Abbey until more than eight hours later. Their dress was either full uniform, in the case of officers, or Court dress, with a badge of office on the left arm. The "gold staff" they carried was of wood, painted red and gold, bearing the royal monogram and a crown. These they were allowed to retain as mementos, otherwise the office was a purely honorary one. In addition to their work in the Abbey during the service, these gold-staff officers had also to attend several rehearsals during March and April.

established. From each of these floors rows of seats were carried to the rear in rising tiers, and thus the utmost use was made of the available space.

At the Coronation of King Edward VII much apprehension had existed with regard to injuries to which the old church might be subjected during its transformation. On former occasions monuments had been broken, shields and statuettes removed and never replaced, canopies and finials destroyed. Today scientific progress has manifested itself even in so commonplace a business as the erection of scaffolding, and the employment of relatively light steel tubing, with metallic bracing, eliminated the risk of damaging the fabric of the church or of endangering the security of the stands themselves.

But to avoid any risk where irreplaceable treasures were concerned, the Abbey authorities removed most of these, notably the priceless picture of Richard II (probably the earliest painting of an English sovereign made during his lifetime), the fifteenth-century altar-piece from Henry VII's Chapel, and the tapestry from the sanctuary.

The first matter to be taken in hand was the covering of the entire floor of the Abbey, in order to protect the stonework, with its many hallowed inscriptions, from damage during the erection of the stands. Upon it was laid a covering of felt, and on top of this was placed a "false floor" of thick planks, some two and a half inches above the ordinary level. This took about a fortnight, after which work was begun on the seating.

Before the workmen started on the tiers of seats, nine-inch-square balk timbers were laid on the boarding to take the loads. Then, as, in order to prevent unnecessary congestion within the Abbey itself, it had been arranged that guests having seats in stands

against the wall of the north-nave aisle should reach their places by means of staircases built outside the church, the stained glass had to be removed from certain of the windows, and temporary doors fitted into the apertures.

It took several hundred workmen, employed in shifts for fourteen hours a day, many weeks before the huge tiers of seats rested solidly on heavy steel girders. In addition to the triple tiers erected in the transepts for the peers and peeresses, and the double tiers erected in the nave for other honoured guests, immediately to the south of the sanctuary a special box was erected for members of the Royal Family, though special seats, apart, were provided for Queen Mary and Princess Elizabeth. Further seating was arranged in the triforium, and a balcony was erected over the west door.

At the point of intersection of the choir and transepts, facing the high altar, was built a large raised platform, officially termed the "theatre", for upon this the actual ceremonies of investiture and enthroning were to take place. A dais

Photo]   *[Planet News*

MAKING ACCESS EASY

The fact that over 7000 people were present in Westminster Abbey rendered the ordinary doors quite inadequate for ingress and egress. Temporary entrances—one of which is shown here in course of construction—were therefore made at the east end of the building by removing the glass from some of the windows so that spectators could pass direct to their seats.

ascended by five steps was constructed, upon which the King's Throne was later to be placed, and a similar dais, though with three steps only, was placed upon the left to receive the Queen's Throne.

By the end of January the interior of the Abbey presented an extraordinary appearance. Along the whole length of the nave and out of the west door ran trolley-lines to facilitate the carrying of the enormous quantity of timber needed for the stands. Derricks swung outwards from the triforium, huge joists ran from pillar to pillar of the nave, ladders and trestles were everywhere in profusion, and the noise of hammer and saw was never still. In Henry VII's Chapel draughtsmen pored intently over tables on which were spread out the blueprints of every constructional detail.

In addition to all the work carried out inside the Abbey, the Office of Works had also to erect temporary buildings outside, of which the most important was the great annexe adjoining the west door.

On the site of the old almonry where, four centuries ago, William Caxton set up his press, was built a one-storeyed edifice, designed under the direction of Sir James West, chief architect at the Office of Works, which, while more modern in treatment than the poor pseudo-Gothic structure erected for the Coronation of King George V, did not conflict with the architecture of the Abbey itself. Though only a temporary structure, it was built with much care, of steel framing with a wood filling, finished externally in plaster toned to match the stonework of the Abbey. Inside, the walls were generally covered with stone-coloured Glamis fabric over fibre boarding.

Of unusual interest is the fact that the entrance doors of the annexe and some of the interior doorways were covered with a veneer of elm taken from timber rings placed round some of the piers of Waterloo Bridge over fifty years ago to prevent ballast from being washed away from the bases. No normal wood could be found of the silver-grey tint desired, but the half a century of immersion this particular timber

Photo]   [News Chronicle
DRAWING OFFICE IN HENRY VII'S CHAPEL

The plans for the constructional work rendered necessary in Westminster Abbey in preparation for the Coronation ceremony were worked out in Henry VII's Chapel, which was transformed for a few months into a drawing office. The photograph shows the scene during working hours. To the right of the central drawing-table is the High Altar, the Silver Jubilee gift to the Abbey of the Order of the Bath. whose Chapel this is. Behind the altar a portion of the tomb of Henry VII can be seen.

had undergone had resulted in a particularly beautiful shade of the needed colour.

Within this annexe, which effectually screened and disguised the west front, and which harmonized well enough with the "chamber called Jerusalem" and the old College Hall upon which it abutted, were arranged a vestibule for the reception of royalty, an entrance for the peers and peeresses, the royal retiring-rooms and a hall for marshalling the procession.

This temporary portico enabled the

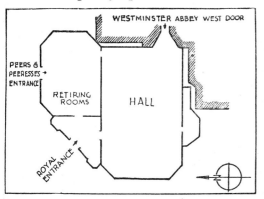

assembled clergy, on May 12th, faithfully to fulfil the first rubric in the day's service, which exhorted them "to assemble outside the west door of the church and await the approach of Their Majesties".

Within the hall of the annexe was placed a table covered with a crimson cloth. This was for the Regalia to rest upon after they had been brought from the Jerusalem Chamber until such time as the various items should be handed to those whose office it was to carry them in the procession. The Great Hall, the royal entrance hall, the

peers' and peeresses' entrance hall and the royal retiring-rooms were richly decorated and hung with tapestries, among them some fine pieces of sixteenth-century Flemish work lent by the Duke of Buccleuch, and some belonging to the collection of Lord Duveen.

While all these arrangements were going on, electricians were no less busy planning an elaborate arrangement of lights, for owing to the height to which the seating had to be taken, most of the windows in the side aisles of the nave and the lower windows in both transepts had been obscured. New switchboards and wiring were installed, so that the normal lighting of the Abbey could be reinforced by a system of auxiliary lighting near the roof, and at the same time electric lighting was installed throughout the annexe. An increase of current capable of providing at least 200,000 candle power was made available. Cables and microphones were also installed for the broadcasting of the ceremony.

In addition to the wiring of the Abbey for supplementary lighting, an elaborate

(Office of Works

ANNEXE TO THE ABBEY

It was formerly customary for the sovereign to go first to Westminster Hall, where the procession of the clergy and the great Officers of State bearing the Regalia assembled before passing to Westminster Abbey. For the last five Coronations an annexe in which the procession was marshalled was built beneath the Abbey towers. Top left is the ground plan of the 1937 annexe, and, below, the architect's drawing for the complete building.

system of telephones was installed to facilitate control of the procession and of the service, and a special telephone exchange was fitted up in St. James's Palace, for general control. In this way was avoided the contretemps which occurred at the Coronation of King Edward VII, when the signal denoting His Majesty's arrival was given too early and the whole of the anthem had to be rendered over again.

The instruments and switchboard were completely hidden. The latter was erected near the organ, in the nave, and the operator was in direct communication with the switchboard at St. James's Palace.

Not until the seating accommodation was ready could the decoration of the Abbey be taken in hand, but for a long time previously loom-hands and needle-women, weavers and dyers had been hard at work fashioning the fabrics, the patterns for which had been chosen long before carpenters plied their saws in the Abbey, to allow time for the actual process of manufacture.

The leading motif of that symphony of colour provided by the interior decoration of the Abbey was blue and gold : chairs and stools covered in blue velours and gold braid, stand frontals of blue with fringes and braiding of gold, blue carpet and cloth of gold for theatre and sanctuary.

From the west door of the Abbey, through the centre of the nave, and past the choir stalls, up to the rostrum of the Coronation theatre, ran a long processional way, seventeen feet wide, covered with a plain blue chenille Axminster carpet, the side fillings being in a darker shade than the central portion. This magnificent carpet, one hundred and seventy-three feet long, was woven in Glasgow on one of the largest looms in Scotland. The Great Hall of the annexe was covered with a carpet of the same colour as the sides of this processional carpet.

On either side of the processional way the stand frontals were

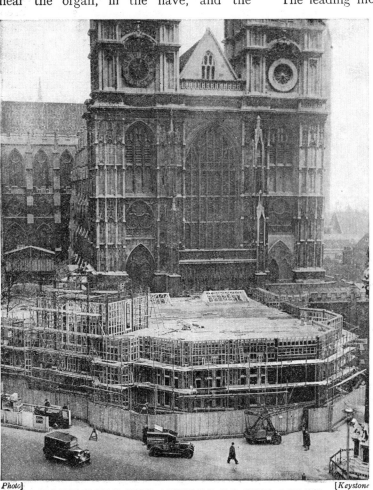

Photo]   [*Keystone*

BUILDING THE ANNEXE TO THE ABBEY

The photograph shows the annexe to the Abbey in course of construction. The plan and a drawing of it are given in the preceding page. The framework, of steel, with wood filling, was covered with plaster carefully tinted to harmonize with the stones of the Abbey. The façade was decorated with the arms of Great Britain and the Dominions, and heraldic devices appeared on the canopy over the entrance.

covered with a specially designed brocatelle, the main features of which were the Imperial Crown, Tudor roses, oakleaves and fleurs-de-lis, arranged in a repeating diaper pattern, the background being woven of gold thread and the design in blue. These ornamental frontals were finished off with a simple bullion fringe.

The chairs of the peers and peeresses continued the blue-and-gold motif and were enlivened with embroidered royal ciphers on the back. The royal box carried the additional decoration of a richly embroidered royal coat of arms.

Not until shortly before the ceremony was the Coronation Chair removed from the Chapel of Edward the Confessor and placed in front of the high altar, together with the Queen's Chair, each having before it a desk and faldstool. A special chair, richly upholstered in purple velvet, was placed in readiness for the

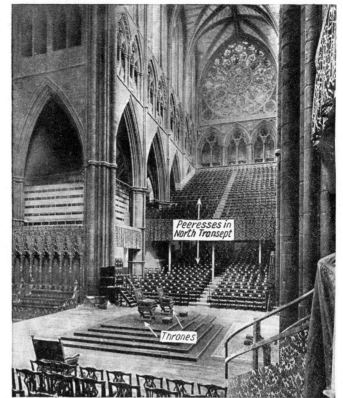

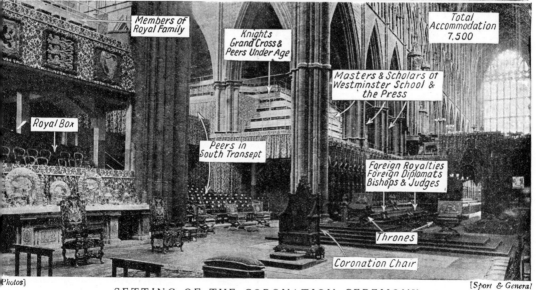

SETTING OF THE CORONATION CEREMONY

[*Sport & General*]

The two photographs in this page show that part of Westminster Abbey in which the Coronation ceremony actually took place. The top photograph was taken from the south transept, in which the peers had their seats, looking across the choir to the north transept, which was reserved for peeresses. Below is the choir taken from in front of the high altar, looking towards the nave, with the royal faldstools, St. Edward's Chair and the thrones. The throne on the right is that of the Queen.

Archbishop of Canterbury. This, according to tradition, becomes the Primate's perquisite.

Two Chairs of State, known as the Recognition Chairs, on which the Sovereign and his Consort sit until the actual ceremony of crowning, were placed on the south side of the altar, and the thrones, used for the ceremonies of enthronization and homage, were stood upon the raised theatre. The Recognition Chairs had high backs and were covered with crimson satin : the thrones, designed after the historic early-Stuart chair known as the Knole Chair, now in the possession of Lord Sackville, were covered in crimson velvet, with gold braid and fringes, and bore the initials of the King and Queen worked in gold. For the first time tenders were invited for making the thrones, whereas at previous Coronations one firm had the exclusive privilege of making them. This departure from tradition was due to the present high standard of craftsmanship.

Once the decoration of the Abbey had been completed, and a short while before the actual ceremony, the necessary rehearsals of the complicated ritual began. Just as in the case of an elaborate theatrical production, a series of sectional rehearsals were held to begin with, and groups of people engaged on various specific duties, such as ushers, pages and the general clergy, were shown exactly what to do.

The musical part of the service called for long and careful rehearsal after the Privy Council Committee had approved the form of service prepared by "the Director of the Music at the Solemnity of Their Majesties' Coronation".

The Director, Dr. Ernest Bullock, organist and master of the choristers at Westminster Abbey, arranged the programme of music in conjunction with Sir Walford Davies, "Master of the King's Musick". Special compositions were contributed by several well-known composers, including Sir Walford Davies himself.

Early in the year invitations were sent to many of the leading singers and instrumentalists to take part in the chorus or orchestra at the Coronation. The chorus itself numbered over four hundred singers, and there was an orchestra of seventy musicians, mostly members of the leading London orchestras.

At the final rehearsals two people were chosen by the Earl Marshal to represent the King and Queen, and the entire ceremony was gone through, including the procession of the Regalia from the west door and the crowning. For this, dummy Regalia were used—wooden swords and cardboard crowns. A few days before the Coronation the King and Queen themselves visited the Abbey to witness the rehearsal.

Photo]   *[Keystone*
FINAL TOUCHES TO THE CORONATION CARPET
The above photograph shows part of the great carpet laid in Westminster Abbey for the Coronation, being carefully smoothed, so that no obstruction should impede or catch in the frail material of the trains of the royalty and peeresses who walked on it. This carpet was woven at Glasgow on one of the largest looms in Scotland.

CHAPTER 27

BRITAIN'S CORONATION DRESS

In the manufacture of flags, banners, souvenirs of all kinds and the numerous other forms of decorations for the Coronation, thousands of men and women found employment, and many more were engaged on the erection of stands. Flood-lighting and illuminations were general throughout the Country

THE "official" preparations for King George's Coronation have been set out. But the efforts of the Earl Marshal, the Lord Great Chamberlain and other high officers of State, important as they are, constitute only a small part of the work behind the scenes which goes to the hallowing of a British King. What of the "unofficial" efforts?—the builders of the miles of grand-stands on the processional route; the makers of the millions of yards of bunting which fluttered overhead during Coronation Week; and the artists, whose imagination and ingenuity made the display worthy of the national pride and joy which brought it into being?

Officially, the simplest of British Coronations was that of William IV, which cost only £40,000. It was the time of the Reform Bill agitation. Moreover, William followed George IV, a monarch who never studied economy at all, and, in fact, enjoyed the most luxurious of all British Coronations. The bill for crowning George IV totalled £238,000, that is, more than three times as much as the £70,000 which sufficed for Queen Victoria's hallowing. If we allow for the higher post-War costs, the official bill for George VI's Coronation may well have been seven times as much as sufficed for Victoria. But, if this is the case, it will be little in comparison with the real public expenditure, and still less in comparison with the material benefits which accrued to British trade. Borough councils and other local authorities up and down the country

alone spent upwards of £2,000,000 upon Coronation decorations, presentations to school-children and similar celebrations. The hire of seats on the processional route accounted for at least another million, while the tourist traffic arising from the Coronation totalled forty or fifty millions sterling. The extra food, clothing, housing and entertainment called for intensive organization and constituted no small part of the work behind the scenes incidental to a Coronation. So did the refurbishing of the great hotels and restaurants.

Directly the death of George the Well-Beloved made a Coronation certain, an international struggle began as to who should secure the bulk of the £10,000,000 worth of bunting, street decorations and souvenirs which could be looked for. Japan, with characteristic promptitude, at once sent a trade deputation to London to organize a manufacturing campaign. Happily, in November 1936, the Government imposed a special duty of 100 per cent *ad valorem* upon imports of Coronation novelties, flags and other articles from December 15, 1936, until July 31, 1937, for a heavy influx of cheap goods from Japan, Czechoslovakia, Germany and other countries was feared.

British manufacturers responded nobly to the demand for British wares. For many months a single Birmingham firm was making a million flags every month, its customers ranging from British Columbia to Malaya, and from the Orkneys to New

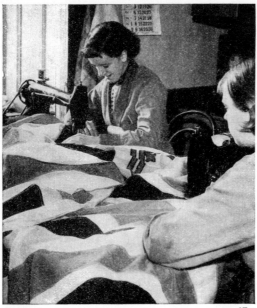

Photo]   *[Fox*

MAKING CORONATION FLAGS

Much skilled labour was employed in making the flags for the Coronation, for the thirty pieces which go to make a Union Jack must be sewn together with absolute accuracy. This photograph shows girls at work in a Glasgow flag factory.

Zealand. Flag-making may appear a simple operation, but in fashioning a single Union Jack thirty separate pieces may have to be sewn up. High skill is also required in printing bunting, work which was done in bulk at Bridgnorth, Shropshire. Cutting Crown emblems and adding ropes and toggles to flags were other operations which called for skill.

Building the Grand Stands

The construction of the stands along the processional route to and from the Abbey was of particular interest. In the old days stands were laboriously built up in wood, and this meant hundreds of carpenters sawing and hammering heavy timbers and then hoisting them slowly into place. The modern method entails the employment of a few mechanics armed with spanners and wrenches. With their aid hundreds of miles of steel tubing were put into place in a few weeks and built up into stands which were both lighter and more rigid than the old-time wooden

erections. The Silver Jubilee of George V represented, indeed, a triumph for steel tubing as applied to stand erection, but even that record was eclipsed when George VI and Queen Elizabeth went to their crowning.

The stands ranged from modest five- or six-tier constructions to the monster in the Marble Arch area, where twenty tiers were set up. Marvels of ingenuity, these stands—especially to Londoners who were lucky enough to see them in the making and could recall the maze of steel bars which underlay the finished product.

Strains and Stresses

In the old days the method of testing a wooden stand was to secure the presence of burly London policemen, and make them dance in broken time on the erections. In 1937 a mathematician acquainted with steel stresses could assure the maker of a stand that his erection was disaster-proof. All that was needed was to follow the specifications of the engineer in charge.

The sites taken by the Office of Works along the processional route included the Mall, Constitution Hill, the Victoria Memorial Gardens, East Carriage Way in Hyde Park, Parliament Square, Whitehall Gardens, New Palace Yard and Whitehall. They accounted for 85,000 seats. In addition, standing-room for 60,000 specially invited guests of the Government, including delegates from the leading Trade Unions, was provided. There were also numerous stands built by private enterprise. On Crown property, in particular, only British steel, Empire wood and British textiles were used.

As for the cost of seats, who can gauge the worth of a spectacle which normally recurs only once in a generation ? Seats in the stands built by the Office of Works were offered at less than cost price, and, therefore, the price was not open to criticism. Elsewhere, considerable profits were made. A first-rate seat to view King George's Coronation cost twenty-five guineas including luncheon, but there were rich men and women who willingly paid

much more for a place in such favoured sites as opposite the Annexe. Here the King and Queen could be seen leaving the State coach, or re-entering it, robed and crowned, for the return journey to the Palace. Fifty guineas were paid for front seats outside Westminster Hospital. As the money went to the rebuilding fund of a worthy philanthropic institution, those who could afford the amount may well not have grudged it. Naturally, there was an occasional outcry against alleged "profiteering", but on examination this was shown to be scarcely justified by hard figures. Thus, the

[Photos]   [Keystone

WEAVING WEBS OF STEEL

Tubular scaffolding is an innovation since the last Coronation. The photograph above of stands being erected in the Queen's Gardens, around Buckingham Palace, shows clearly how the steel tubes are locked together ; the framework, with its countless interlacing lines, has a certain aesthetic appeal which was unfortunately lacking in the finished stand. The top photograph shows the statue of Abraham Lincoln in Parliament Square nearly hidden by a stand in course of construction.

authorities of St. Margaret's Church, Westminster, sold 6000 seats to ticket agencies and transport companies at an average of £16 a seat. Insurance against a postponement of the Coronation—an absolutely necessary precaution—however, cost from 12½ to 20 per cent, and when necessary expenses were considered, 25 guineas was found to yield no extravagant profit. High prices have been paid for Coronation seats in the past. Horace Walpole, writing of George III's crowning, informs us that "a platform from St. Margaret's roundhouse to the church door, which formerly let for £40, went this time for £2,000". At the Coronation of George IV, too, single seats were sold for five guineas; nevertheless, the range of prices in 1937 broke all records.

If the cost of a front seat for the Coronation procession seemed high to those with slender purses, no one could grumble at the background to the spectacle. Never have the local authorities been more generous in the expenditure of municipal funds. The City of Westminster alone spent £25,000, £14,000 being expended upon street decorations. The Westminster colours—white, blue and gold—were dominant in Whitehall, Parliament Square and other thoroughfares in the Council's area. The floodlighting of the charming Gothic façade of the Middlesex Guildhall vied with that of Westminster Abbey and the Houses of Parliament near by. The Office of Works was, of course, responsible for the Government Offices in Whitehall, and here the Bailiff of the Royal Parks was generous in supplying the window-boxes with fresh plants and flowers. The use of growing plants and fresh flowers, indeed, was a feature of the street decorations in 1937. The London Passenger Transport Board in Broadway made a feature of window-boxes, displaying red, white and blue blossoms, and Regent Street was another centre which displayed a unified scheme of window-boxes filled with real flowers.

In Bond Street the scheme of decoration, devised by Mrs. Acland, was particularly happy. A series of huge banners was hung along the sides of the street in such a way that sightseers could view the whole effect. In contrast with the vivid white of the big banners were coloured Plantagenet crowns, while trays of flowers were borne upon the upstanding staves. At night, the banners were floodlit. The Bond Street design was one of many shown, early in 1937, at the Royal Institute of British Architects. The exhibition was full of

[Office of Works

THE MALL BEDECKED WITH BANNERS

The decorations in the Mall, along which the Coronation Procession passed on its way to the Abbey, had both dignity and simplicity. From masts erected at intervals of about fifty feet, two white-and-gold banners embroidered with the Royal Arms were hung ; each mast was surmounted by the Imperial Crown and Lion in gilt.

suggestion for flag and floral designs, as well as for floodlighting suitable buildings and for street illumination. A rubber-treated fabric was available in all the Coronation colours, and was guaranteed to withstand the worst of thunderstorms. In general, it was found that vertical treatment was best for the decoration of streets mainly consisting of small shops, while roomy thoroughfares, with big stores, could usefully display horizontal designs. With gaily coloured banners hung between the windows, these horizontal designs were very effective in such an open road as Oxford Street. Apart from colours dictated by heraldic considerations, the outstanding Coronation hues were a rich crimson and a delightful blue, developed from Royal blue, Union-Jack blue and gentian-blue.

The Coronation colours were specially devised and selected by the British Colour Council, and this body issued a most useful brochure upon bunting colours, which circulated widely in the Dominions as well as in Britain. Later, a Coronation Souvenir Book of Traditional Colours was issued by the Council. Forty-two varying colour schemes were suggested, based upon a range of twelve Coronation colours, these being white, gold, spectrum green, larkspur (heraldic azure), spectrum orange, Garter blue, silver-grey, peacock-blue, satinwood, jade, signal-red, and Stewart blue.

Mr. Robert Wilson, art director of the Colour Council, was careful to emphasize the need for co-operation between house-owners and shopkeepers in a given area. Largely owing to his advice, the occupiers of shops, club-houses and other premises on the route co-operated generously with the Office of Works, the Westminster City Council and the Marylebone Borough Council. In the Mall and Constitution Hill the Office of Works was in sole control and a unified decorative scheme was easy. Masts were put up at intervals of fifty feet, and from each were hung two banners, emblazoned with the Royal Arms. The Admiralty Arch and the buildings on either side were decorated with white ensigns, hung vertically, while a large

Photo]   *[M. O. Henchoz*

THE EMPIRE'S TIME-PIECE

When it is floodlit at times of national rejoicing the Clock Tower of the Houses of Parliament, with the face of Big Ben lighted from without, reveals an unexpected beauty of form and detail.

floral crown was placed above the central arch, amid blue and gold flowers. Baskets of flowers were also hung within the lesser arches, while at the base of each column were trophies of flags.

Another area for which the Office of Works accepted sole responsibility was Hyde Park. The Marble Arch, at the entrance to the East Carriage Drive, was decorated with trophies of flags, with still larger trophies on either side, over the central archway. Between the Marble Arch and Hyde Park Corner were six groups of trophies, each based upon eight masts, carrying emblems. Red and white banners, emblazoned with the Royal Arms and surmounted with the Imperial Crown and the Lion, hung from the masts. Lastly, the marble screen of Hyde Park Corner was decorated with flowers at the parapet level—rhododendrons, hydrangeas, blue cinerarias and white marigolds.

The Metropole building, in Northumberland Avenue, was draped at the first-floor level with trophies of flags, while Dominion and Colonial flags hung from the fifth-floor level. The headquarters of the Royal Empire Society, once the Royal Colonial Institute, another recent addition to Northumberland Avenue, also displayed Dominion emblems in profusion in honour of the great occasion.

Floodlighting and Illuminations

Naturally enough, off the actual route of the procession there was a tendency to rely upon floodlighting and illumination which would be effective by night, rather than upon bunting or floral emblems. In the City of London the civic colours—red and white—were dominant. The Corporation made itself responsible for the decoration of the principal thoroughfares

within the city boundaries; and Sir Giles Scott provided the basic designs.

All the London buildings which were floodlit for King George V's Silver Jubilee were illuminated also in May 1937, among them the Clock Tower with Big Ben, the London County Council Hall, the Mansion House and the Royal Exchange. This floodlighting in 1937 proved a vast improvement on anything possible at the last Coronation, when gas flambeaux and other devices were the main source of London illuminations. In 1911 the main lines of the Bank of England were outlined with gilded wreaths, displaying the rose, shamrock and thistle. Since then Sir John Soane's exterior has been replaced by that of Sir Herbert Baker, which allowed of a much more impressive illumination. The Mansion House, the Royal Exchange and the headquarters of the big banks

Photo]   *[Fox*

CENTRAL LONDON'S CELEBRATIONS

Trafalgar Square is to most people the heart of London, for, except for the great parks, it affords the only open space where large crowds can assemble. The National Gallery on the north side, Canada House to the west, South Africa House to the east and Whitehall stretching away to Westminster on the south side give it a dignified setting. It is here seen floodlit with the National Gallery on the left, the church of St. Martin's-in-the-Fields, famous for its broadcasts, in the centre, and South Africa House and one of the lions at the foot of the Nelson Column on the right.

made the heart of the City a place of magic loveliness during Coronation Week.

Another addition to the illuminations of London was Broadcasting House. The upper storeys of the building were lighted by powerful floodlamps, the aerial and masts being very conspicuous against the deep blue of the sky. Red, white and blue floral designs mingled with the silvery floodlighting. Shell-Mex House, Unilever House in Blackfriars, and Imperial Chemical Industries, Millbank, were other newcomers that contributed nobly to London's Coronation floodlighting, which was not confined to May 12th but continued until Whit Monday, May 17th. The London Associated Electricity Undertakings made no charge for electricity thus consumed, and the Electric Lamp Manufacturers' Association, representing the manufacturers of floodlighting equipment, met the authorities with corresponding generosity.

§—Festivities Souvenirs and Regalia

THE Abbey Church at Westminster and the route of the procession were necessarily the focal points in the celebrations on May 12th. But from them spread many and varied ramifications, devised to express the glad assent of every part of the British Isles in the national homage to King George and his Queen. If street decorations and illuminations of charm were prepared for mid-London, the outer Metropolitan boroughs and civic authorities all over England, Scotland, Wales and Ulster also laid generous plans for the local celebrations of the Coronation.

In Stepney, Poplar and Bow, typical East End districts in London, public subscription lists were opened to supplement the efforts of borough councils. Twopence or threepence a week was contributed for months before Coronation Day, in order that certain East End streets might be worthily decorated. The Poplar Council showed its appreciation of this public-spirited support by contributing free electricity on Coronation Night. Elsewhere, the local efforts benefited by the generosity of the London Associated Electricity Undertakings, which (as stated above) gave free current for the illumination of public buildings and street-decoration lighting. Neon lighting, too, added many happy colour effects.

In the poorer London areas the celebrations were by no means confined to street decorations. The collections of weekly pence covered the cost of teas, which were served on Coronation afternoon. In Battersea a huge tea was organized for twelve thousand pensioners and a week's holiday at the seaside was given to a thousand poor children of the borough. Twenty thousand Battersea school-children also received a booklet describing the Coronation in its historic and symbolic aspects, as a souvenir of the crowning of their King and Queen. At Barking the festivities included special facilities for the entertainment of the blind, while East Ham organized a splendid firework display for the Saturday night preceding the Coronation. The school-children of the Borough were treated to a free cinema display.

In Walthamstow local efforts were concentrated upon celebrations likely to satisfy the school-children and the aged. In Wood Green great play was made with floodlighting in the public parks, the shimmer of multi-coloured lights amid trees and shrubs being fully up to the standard set by the Office of Works in St. James's Park. A novel scheme at Wood Green was the staging of a cricket match in the Albert Road Recreation Ground, played in the old-time manner, with cricketers appearing in top hats, knee-breeches and buckled shoes.

Barnet organized a fair in Wrotham Park, and concluded the day with a brilliant firework display, while Southgate had its fête in Broomfield Park. A complete record of the local celebrations in Outer London alone would fill a book. These typical efforts must suffice to suggest scores of similar efforts.

To pass to the English provinces, Norwich naturally made a big effort to ensure that the capital of King George's own county should celebrate the crowning in worthy fashion. The King was born at York Cottage, Sandringham, on December 14th, 1895, so he is a Norfolk man. Under the general guidance of the Lord Mayor a Norwich pageant, with tableaux illustrating the history of the city, was organized for Coronation Day, following a service for all denominations in the Cathedral. Every Norwich child received a Coronation souvenir, which took the form of a book setting out the significance of the rejoicings, and the Norwich Chamber of Commerce subscribed £1200 for the

decorations of the streets. Another happy idea was to extend the village signs, which were a feature of Norfolk celebrations in 1911, when George V was crowned. Wolferton, Flixton, and various other Norfolk villages can offer inspiration to artist designers for such abiding souvenirs.

In Bournemouth Coronation Day opened with a general ringing of church bells, and ended with the illumination of the sea front, a torchlight procession and fireworks. In between were fêtes for children in the public parks, and feastings for the poor and the unemployed. Eastbourne, Brighton, Worthing, Weymouth, Torquay, and numerous other south-coast resorts devised similar schemes. At Bath the Mayor and Corporation opened Coronation Day with a State visit to the Abbey, while an elaborate floodlighting of the historic buildings in the city was organized for Coronation Night. At Warwick the Castle,

HISTORIC HOME LIKE A FAIRY PALACE

Many historic castles and houses were floodlit for the Coronation rejoicings, and so revealed an ethereal beauty that was strikingly impressive. The photograph shows the residential part of Warwick Castle and Caesar's Tower floodlit and mirrored in the still waters of the River Avon, which flows through the grounds.

Lord Leycester's Hospital, Westgate, Eastgate and the Beauchamp Chapel were among the old-time buildings which revealed new and unsuspected beauties. Warwick Castle, reflected in the cool shallows of the Avon, gained a haunting loveliness which even its most devoted admirers scarcely looked for. Earlier in the day there was a Fun Fair at Warwick and in the evening open-air dancing and fireworks.

Among the great manufacturing areas of the North, Birkenhead offered a capital example to the country. Parties of unemployed men and women collected material and erected miles of bunting and other devices. One novel effort was an eight-foot portrait of the King in naval uniform, in which nothing but household paint was used. In Liverpool, near by, attention was drawn to the new Mersey Tunnel by adorning the entrance in pleasantly modern style, due to the fact that the local art school had taken up the task of providing appropriate decoration for the public buildings. The art students also devised a delightful scheme for the decoration of Castle Street, Liverpool, just as the Sheffield School of Architecture was happily inspired in its schemes for floodlighting and decorating the local University buildings. The two Newcastles, Grimsby, the wool centres of Yorkshire, the cathedral towns of the North Country, including lordly Durham, queenly Ripon and regal York, were other centres which made it plain that civic pride, apart from devotion to the Crown, demanded a worthy display on Coronation Day.

In Glasgow, an effort was made to avoid the errors of the Silver Jubilee celebrations. In 1935 the City was

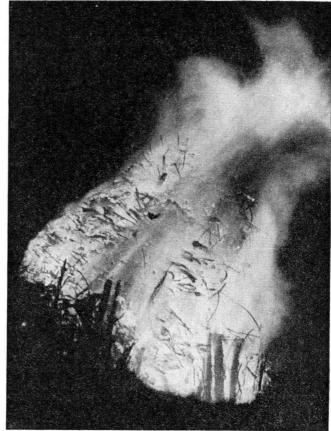

Photo]   *[Keystone*

FESTIVE FIERY BEACONS

Among the most spectacular of the Coronation celebrations was the great chain of bonfires which flamed from practically every high point in the United Kingdom. One of these monster beacons, whose light could be seen for many miles around, is seen in the photograph above.

meagrely decorated because the Corporation preferred to confine its efforts to entertainments for the aged, the sick and the young. The motive was understandable, but in 1937 the big Glasgow business houses got to work and plans were laid in good time for the decoration and lighting of such a centre as Buchanan Street.

In Edinburgh there were better natural opportunities for decorative and lighting effects. Prince's Street calls for generous and ingenious scheming, and it received it. The electric standards in the centre of the famous roadway each received a "barber's pole" colour treatment, while the gardens at the side were floodlit with delightful ingenuity. At intervals pylons, which alternated with the monuments in Prince's Street, and light latticed standards on the south side of the street carried gay stretches of bunting. St. Andrew's crosses and Scottish lions afforded a particularly happy colour scheme, alternating between silver and blue and gold and red. Charlotte Square and St. Andrew's Square offered more difficult problems to the designers, but again effective use was made of the blue and white colour scheme arising from St. Andrew's cross. The foot of Leith Walk, Toll Cross, Haymarket, Portobello Town Hall and Hamilton Place were other centres of festive decoration in the Scottish capital.

Fully three thousand monster bonfires blazed from the hilltops of Britain on the night of King George V's crowning. In 1937 the bonfires lit in honour of George VI were equally numerous and no less impressive. London was hemmed in by a vast circle of burning beacons, which carried their fiery messages north, south, east and west.

Blackheath, Streatham, and Wimbledon Commons, Greenwich Park and Richmond were some of the beacon points in the London area, and they joined hands with the fires that arose on such heights as Box Hill, near Dorking, or the Hog's Back, Guildford. Close upon a hundred beacons were fired in the West Riding of Yorkshire, while the summits of Snowdon, Cader Idris, and Ben Nevis thrust out fiery limbs, as they doubtless did after the defeat of the Spanish Armada in the far

Photo]   ROYAL OAKS   *[Topical*

In many parts of the country trees were planted to commemorate the Coronation, and so, too, were thousands of acorns collected in Windsor Great Park. The photograph shows Windsor acorns being dispatched to all parts of the Empire.

distant times of an earlier Queen Elizabeth.

The Boy Scout movement deserves full marks for its efforts on behalf of the Coronation bonfires.

It is good to remember that the Coronation of George VI brought about tree-planting on a large scale. Lady Leconfield was a pioneer in national tree-planting, but the movement, throughout the Empire, owed most of its driving force to that admirable institution, "The Men of the Trees". Practically every county was enrolled in a scheme to plant groups of nine trees, from Land's End to John o' Groats. The scheme was to plant the trees in the shape of a King Arthur's shield, having an oak in the centre. Planting began in the Duchy of Cornwall before the abdication of Edward VIII, and it was continued with equal vigour when his brother came to the throne. As the point of the "shield" of trees faced the prevailing south-west winds, the method of planting ensured the strongest wind resistance. A commemorative plaque was placed upon all trees planted under the auspices of the Coronation Planting Committee. The plaque included a crown, the date 1937, and the inscription :

CORONATION PLANTING COMMITTEE

PLANTED TO COMMEMORATE
THE CORONATION OF
KING GEORGE VI

The communal or semi-communal efforts which went to the organization of the

The King's cypher and the heraldic crown were particularly well suited to decorative purposes and shields showing them on a plain background looked very effective.

Photos] [*Fox ; Sport & General ; Keystone*

CORONATION EMBLEMS, SOUVENIRS AND DECORATIONS

The Coronation produced an unexampled demand for objects designed for commemoration and decoration.   Above is the interior of a British Legion factory in London where the Coronation emblems, the designs for which were approved by the King, were made.   The proceeds from the sale were divided between the British Legion Pension Fund and King George's Jubilee Trust. Top right are Coronation cushions, tea-cosies and other commemorative objects.

Coronation by no means exhaust the record of those behind the scenes. The souvenir mugs, for example, recall an interesting episode, which may well be treasured in the memory of their possessors years hence. For King George's crowning—or rather for that of Edward VIII—a group of British pottery manufacturers determined that a special effort to produce a worthy object should be made. Accordingly, they asked Dame Laura Knight to prepare a design. Half the surface was devoted to the Royal Arms and the rest to a profile portrait of the King, set between a St. George and the Elephant of India. The handle was in the form of an heraldic lion and each mug was signed "Laura Knight". The immense production enabled a twelve-coloured mug to be offered at one shilling and threepence, and lively demand ensued from the oversea Dominions, India and the Colonies.

When King Edward's abdication necessitated two royal heads in place of one, Dame Laura Knight made the essential

CORONATION MEDAL

The official Coronation medal bears on the obverse (left), the effigy of the King, and on the reverse (right), the effigy of the Queen. It was struck in two sizes in silver and gold and, in a smaller size, in bronze.

changes. The result was a sale which amazed all but the courageous traders who planned the scheme. The potters who originated the idea permitted any British firm to manufacture the mug, and even provided the necessary moulds and colour transfers. All they asked was that a proper standard of craft should be maintained. The personal popularity of the Duke of Windsor ensured a big public demand for many souvenirs designed for his Coronation and thus prevented heavy losses by manufacturers and dealers.

The London Mint commissioned Mr. Langford Jones to design a double-head portrait of King George and Queen Elizabeth for incorporation in the medals which municipal and other bodies required for distribution to school-children. The design was made at the suggestion of the Federation of British Industries, which felt a standardized portrait of Their Majesties was desirable, even if the reverses of the medal differed. The official commemorative Coronation medal was designed by Mr. Percy Metcalfe. This, in accordance with precedent, displayed the head of King George on the obverse and that of Queen Elizabeth on the reverse. The preliminary studies were made at Sandringham, from special sittings given by Their Majesties.

Official Coronation medals go back at least as far as the time of James I, who caused a small silver coin to be made and thrown among the spectators

Photo]   [Sport & General

COMMEMORATION MEDAL

Besides the Coronation medal this double portraiture of the King and Queen was designed at the Royal Mint to be used with special reverses by municipal and other public bodies for distribution in commemoration of the Coronation.

Photos] [Topical

THE CORONATION MUG

For months before the great day 70,000 workers in the Potteries were busy producing some 5,000,000 Coronation mugs, beakers and other souvenirs. On the right a batch of Coronation pottery is being taken out of the oven in which it has been baked for several days, and above is the officially-approved mug.

Photos] [Topical; Fox

DECORATING THE DECORATIONS

In many of the decorative schemes applied to streets and buildings in honour of the Coronation, crowns and medallions of the King, surrounded by laurel wreaths, found a prominent place. They were made of papier-maché and coloured by hand, and above we see two girls applying the colours. On the left Britain's most famous woman artist, Dame Laura Knight, R.A., is painting a de luxe edition of the mug.

335

Charles I had two medals for his Coronation, one struck for England and the other for Scotland. Thenceforward Coronation medals became a regular custom, as was their distribution during the ceremony of crowning.

Coronation busts of the King and Queen; Coronation spoons; heraldic shields; replicas of the crowns, the anointing spoon and other items in the Regalia; and a representation of the State coach, complete with eight horses and postilions, were other souvenirs produced which will pass down to coming generations. The

Photo]   *[Fox*

ROYAL STATE COACH

The State Coach of England, seen above, was built for King George III in 1761. Designed by Sir William Chambers and decorated with panels painted by Cipriani, it measures 24 feet in length, is 12 feet high and weighs four tons. The whole structure is richly ornamented.

printing trade, too, did a lively business in souvenir books, among which should be mentioned the Official Souvenir Programme, published by the King George's Jubilee Trust.

Photo]   *[Keystone*

FOR DECORATION AND COMMEMORATION

Busts of the King and Queen painted in life-like colours formed a part of many schemes of decoration, and were also in great request both at home and in the Dominions as souvenirs of the Coronation. The photograph shows a girl at work in a London factory colouring a bust of the Queen.

Among the contents of its 32 pages were "A Prayer for the King's Reign" by the Poet Laureate; "The King's Majesty", an article by the late John Drinkwater; "The Coronation Ceremony" described by Garter Principal King of Arms; a life of King George VI and the Order of Service. Copies of this book were on sale throughout the Dominions as well as in the United Kingdom, and it was the first programme to be officially published for any Coronation.

And writing of these souvenirs recalls that the State coach itself was duly sent to the Chelsea workshops of Messrs.

Photo] [*Photopress*

SILK FOR THE QUEEN'S ROBE

The robe of royal purple velvet worn by the Queen at the Coronation was made from silk produced at Lullingstone Park, Kent, where Lady Hart Dyke is making an attempt to revive the English silkworm industry. Above, girls are at work spinning the silk.

Hooper & Co. for renovation and regilding. The coach was 176 years old in Coronation year and in good running order, but it had not been regilded since its manufacture and fresh gold leaf was essential.

Robes, Uniforms and Regalia

Nor must the embroiderers and others responsible for the robes of peers and peeresses, the copes of clergy and the uniforms of officers of State be forgotten. For the first time the silk for the robe of a British Queen was spun in England, the source being Lady Hart Dyke's silkworm farm at Lullingstone Castle, Kent. The royal velvet was woven on a hand-loom at the Braintree Mill, in Essex, which also prepared the velvet for the robes of the Duchess of Gloucester and the Duchess of Kent. Only at Coronation times is velvet of such quality in demand, and the supply of skilled machinists is necessarily small.

The robes of peers and peeresses were largely the work of London firms such as Ede & Ravenscroft, of Chancery Lane, which was making Coronation robes when Queen Anne reigned and has had a long experience of making robes for the legal profession.

The robe of a duchess cost 320 guineas, assuming Her Grace unwilling to substitute the inferior white rabbit for the costly ermine. The fee for the robe of a marchioness was only 290 guineas ; for a countess, 275 guineas ; for a viscountess, 255 guineas ; and for a baroness, 235 guineas. The reason for the difference was the varying length of train. Whereas the train of a duchess required seventeen yards of velvet and a corresponding amount of white fur, that of a baroness could be made with fifteen yards of material. The gold girdle and tassels on a peeress's robe accounted for £5, while the value of a coronet varied from £15 to £25.

Photo] [*Fox*

PREPARING THE CANOPY

The golden canopy of cloth-of-gold embroidered with silver eagles which, supported by four silver poles, was held over the King and Queen during the Coronation ceremony, was embroidered at the Royal School of Art Needlework, South Kensington. Here embroiderers are shown at work on the canopy.

22

Apart from the Coronation robes were the gowns of the peeresses. A single London Court dressmaker employed four hundred embroidery hands in his workrooms during the Coronation season. Not a few peeresses desired such special silver or gold embroidery upon their Coronation gowns, as were allowed by the regulations. They might embody, perhaps, the white rose of a Yorkshire family or the red rose of a Lancastrian or some other device.

Lastly, there were the tailors whose speciality is military uniforms, among them a famous Tooley Street firm, which can guarantee an outfit for a Yeoman of the Guard at the shortest notice.

Backstage inquiry into the men, women and things that contribute to a British Coronation carries one into unfamiliar fields, and not a few of them have a curious charm, owing to their old-world associations. How pleasant, for example, it would be to watch the craftsmen of the Crown Jewellers, Messrs. Garrods, at work upon the crown for Queen Elizabeth, perchance actually putting the Koh-i-Noor diamond into its place in the newest item in the Regalia ! Or, again, the craftsman might be making the changes which fit the Imperial State Crown for its new wearer —changes small in themselves, but calling for the nicest judgment. The second Star of Africa, cut from the Cullinan diamond, is one of the things of price which was in the man's care. The ruby of the Black Prince, which Henry V wore in his helmet at Agincourt, was another. Jewels and jeweller alike could a strange tale unfold. And so it is with many of those who work behind the scenes of a Coronation.

Photo]　　　　　　　　　　　　　　　　　　　　　　　　　　　　　　[Fox

STATELY SIMPLICITY OF PEERESSES' ROBES

The photograph shows the Queen at the British Industries Fair watching a parade of fashions which included Coronation robes
The robes worn by peeresses are cut on simple but stately lines, the only ornamentation being lace at the sleeves and some embroidery
Both robe and train are of velvet trimmed with ermine, the material being of British manufacture. Peeresses place their coronets
on their heads for a few moments when the Queen is crowned.

THE SCENE & THE CEREMONY

by

J. B. Sterndale Bennett
K. Janet Maitland
E. Royston Pike
Osbert Lumley
and
Gilson MacCormack

ARTIST'S IMPRESSION OF THE SCENE IN THE ABBEY

The culminating ceremonies of the Coronation took place before the High Altar, the King sitting in the chair of St. Edward, beneath which is the Stone of Scone. Upon this the Kings of Scotland were crowned for many centuries. Edward I removed the Stone to Westminster for his own coronation, and since then it has been used by every English king.

CHAPTER 28

WESTMINSTER ABBEY
HALLOWED BY THE CROWNINGS OF NINE CENTURIES

Scene of the Coronations of our sovereigns since the Norman Conquest, the Collegiate Church of St. Peter at Westminster, to give it its official style, provides a setting of incomparable majesty for the sublime Pageant

IT is to be regretted that the many thousands of visitors to the Coronation will never see Westminster Abbey in its everyday dress. Some of them may see it in all its draped splendour, but weeks must elapse before the scaffolding and the stands are removed and the Abbey is once again the great, grey, noble edifice which is the first shrine of pilgrimage to the British peoples. There is not a man of feeling who must not be moved as he sees here the monuments to those whose names have been familiar to him since childhood. Here lie Edward the Confessor and the very latest of our own famous dead. (Rudyard Kipling entered last into this noble company.) It is true that it is a jumbled Pantheon, for every generation has chosen its own heroes; but we must remember that even of Sir Cloudesley Shovell, whose sprawling monument has for long been the butt of wits, Sir Roger de Coverley said, "A great man, sir—a very great man."

The purpose of this short chapter is to show how Westminster Abbey became the scene of all Coronations since that of William the Conqueror, how it became the burial-place of kings and those who, as the French say, "deserved well" of their nation. A cry arises after a great war; here are thousands of missing soldiers, "known unto God". Let us at least disinter one of these unidentified bodies and bury it as an Unknown Warrior with great honour. Just as through the centuries the pilgrims filed past the shrine of St. Edward, so today do the great crowds which visit London for football matches and arrive in the morning, detach large numbers to pay their first homage to the Unknown Warrior. And of what we know of Edward the Confessor and of the great army of missing soldiers, theirs undoubtedly is the worthier shrine; for the Unknown Warrior died nobly at his post, whereas Edward lived in exile while Danish kings reigned in England and, as history tells us, was a perfectly incompetent monarch when he did come to the throne.

He may be pictured, however, as a genial soul, sufficiently popular as a king, a good huntsman and devoutly religious— two qualities to this day not incompatible. He liked Westminster as a place of residence (not in those days very far from his hunting-grounds), and there he built himself a palace and a church. His church, built in the Norman style—for he had lived long in Normandy—was little smaller than the present Abbey, and far exceeding in magnificence any other ecclesiastical building of its time. When he died he was buried there, and his tomb became one of the costliest monuments in the world.

It is doubtful whether his successor Harold was crowned in the Abbey, but William the Conqueror had little doubt where he should present himself for the ceremony. We owe it to Edward, therefore,

341

THE UNKNOWN WARRIOR'S TOMB

At this sacred spot within the Empire's ancient Temple of Fame, thousands pay their homage year by year to the nameless heroes who so nobly gave their lives during the Great War in the cause of King and Empire. Past this honoured tomb came the procession of the Coronation in all its splendour.

scene of the present Coronation when, in the middle of the next century (1245), Henry III, another devout spendthrift, set about rebuilding Edward's Norman Abbey. He demolished the Norman chancel, tower and transepts. In nine years, with from six to eight hundred men at work, he had built up in the Gothic style the first section of the new Abbey. It seems not a far cry from the twentieth to the thirteenth century to learn from one authority (Mr. A. L. N. Russell, F.R.I.B.A.) that "the second section, hampered by civil war, strikes of workmen and financial difficulties, proceeded much more slowly". But in 1269 the unfinished building was consecrated. Hereafter remained a century and a half of diligent work, without much help from improvident kings, before

that Westminster—rather than York or Canterbury, St. Albans or Winchester—should by tradition have become the church of kings. Edward, who himself was crowned at Winchester, may truly be said to have made London the capital of England.

Edward's church was begun in 1045 and consecrated in 1065, shortly before his death. He left to it his whole private fortune. His posthumous sanctity grew in the minds of men until, nearly a hundred years later (1161), Edward was canonized and became St. Edward.

The influence of the Abbey was thereby increased and the Abbot was granted a mitre. This honour was rudely torn off him by an offended Papal legate, but he had at least the satisfaction of knowing that at that very same synod (of 1176) the Archbishops of Canterbury and York came to fisticuffs in his Abbey over the matter of precedence.

We come a little nearer to the actual

IN THE ABBOT'S YARD

At the end of this beautiful little courtyard in the shadow of the Abbey towers stands the fourteenth-century Abbot's house, the most famous part of which is the Jerusalem Chamber. The name of the latter is held to have been derived from tapestries of the Holy City which once hung on its walls.

the Abbey in its present form took on a wellnigh complete shape.

The devotion of medieval architects and builders which raised this "high memorial fane" to its present splendour, the close association of the Abbey with the monarchy, the natural corollary that it should become the burial-place of Britain's illustrious men—these things should not be allowed to obscure its long religious history. We must picture it throughout the course of the Middle Ages as a monastery occupied by the order of Benedictines, with Abbot and all the other officials and servants of a religious order leading the regulated life of a dedicated community. To some of these abbots and their humble workers we owe many present beauties of the Abbey.

Photo]   [Fox

SANCTUARY AND HIGH ALTAR

The fine reredos is composed of red and white alabaster, and in the niches are figures of Moses. St. Peter, St. Paul and David. The representation of the Last Supper is executed in Venetian glass mosaic. Before the Altar is a curious old mosaic pavement brought from Rome in 1268 by Abbot Ware.

There was one, John Islip, under whose reign the Abbey reached the completed state we recognize today, for it was during his abbacy in the early years of the sixteenth century that the last three bays of the nave were vaulted in and the windows glazed. He was fortunate, too, to serve under a pious monarch who added to the Abbey one of its chief glories— Henry VII's chapel.

The monastic side of the Abbey's life disappeared at the time of the Reformation, but perhaps it was its intimate association with the Crown that prevented its becoming a particular object of vandalism. On the other hand, it is said that much of the damage to the fabric which occurred during succeeding centuries was directly traceable to injuries inflicted through the erection of temporary scaffolding for Coronation ceremonies. As Cockney children swarm lamp-posts to watch a Lord Mayor's procession, so did their more illustrious ancestors think nothing of profaning the monuments of the Abbey to obtain a better view of their new monarch.

But if the fabric remained substantially the same, and Westminster still held its unique place in English life, nothing could arrest the depredations on its store of treasures. These were always at the mercy of marauders of high and low estate, and it is interesting to speculate to what extent the magnificence of the present Coronation might have been added to had the present Dean and Chapter inherited their rightful legacy.

But jewels and vestments are of little account compared to the building itself, and it is remarkable that this should have escaped the marauding instincts of ambitious architects as successfully as it has. However much the restorer may have constructed crumbling details to his own design, the majestic fabric remains the same. When architectural detail is covered with the rich furnishings of a Coronation,

THE CORONATION CHAIR

This has been used at the Coronation of every English monarch
since Edward II. It contains beneath its seat the Scone stone
whereon it is said the Celtic kings of Scotland were crowned
many centuries ago.

the scene cannot have differed greatly
throughout the ages.

Those furnishings, however, do so alter
the whole appearance of the Abbey as
to leave it unrecognizable to the ordinary
visitor or worshipper. A description of
its magnificence when prepared for the
Coronation ceremony will be found elsewhere, but something must be said of the
normal aspect of the Coronation scene.

The visitor at ordinary times enters by
the north door, passing along the north
transept with its huddled masses of political
statuary, and finds himself immediately
between the choir and the sanctuary.
The sanctuary with the altar behind it
provides the background to the theatre
for the Coronation. Here stand the chairs
of the king and queen, and here are grouped
during the ceremony the chief actors.

Behind the altar is the chapel of St.
Edward. Here are placed the Confessor's
shrine, the tombs of Henry III (the
Abbey's benefactor), of Eleanor of Castile,
of Edward I, of Edward III, of Richard
II, and of Anne of Bohemia. This chapel
is made use of by the King as a retiring-
room during certain parts of the ceremony.

But the two ornaments of the chapel
most intimately connected with the Coronation are kept against the screen at the
west end. These are the Sword and
Shield of State, carried before every
sovereign at his Coronation since Edward
III, and the Coronation Chair.

This, the most famous chair in the world,
was built to the order of King Edward I
to house the famous Stone of Scone which
he had captured during his victorious
Scottish campaigns. The chair itself—
now a very simple, ancient oak affair—
was at one time far more elaborate, gaudily
painted, and studded with jewels. Shorn
of these adornments, it has also suffered
defacement at the hands of initial-carvers.
One set of these is attributed to a P.
Abbot who was unfortunate enough to find
himself locked in the Abbey one night and
thus amused his hours of incarceration.
The story that he slept in the chair seems
a little far-fetched, as there would have
been benches accessible on which to lay
his weary length. The other initials may
be attributed to the vandalism of schoolboys of the adjoining foundation.

Made in 1300 at a cost of 100 shillings, it
has been used at the Coronation of every
sovereign since Edward II, and the design
is familiar to every schoolboy, one of its
distinctive, although more modern, features
being its feet of four carved lions. One of
its more serious adventures was in June
1914, when an enthusiastic advocate of
votes for women placed a bomb under it,
the explosion of which did some damage.

The famous Stone of Scone has an
almost entirely legendary history. It was
for years thought to be Jacob's pillow
brought to Ireland by Scota and captured
by the invading Scots. But the material-
istic geologist has proved without a doubt

that the stone is West-of-Scotland sandstone, so that the legend must go the way of many others.

The actual origin is obscure, but it is known that in the ninth century it was set up at Scone in Perthshire and that all Scottish kings were henceforth crowned seated upon it. Edward I himself was crowned king of the Scots upon the stone. Once in England, no efforts of the Scots availed to secure its return, and for 600 years it has remained a precious relic in the Abbey, and upon it every sovereign has been crowned. Such was the potency of its tradition that Cromwell removed it to Westminster Hall for his installation as Lord Protector, when it was placed "under a princely canopy of State". It may be noted here that the Anglo-Saxon kings from Edward the Elder to Ethelred are believed to have been crowned on a stone at Kingston-on-Thames. Legend identifies as the veritable crowning-block a stone now standing close to the old town's Guildhall.

The King and Queen, preceded by a magnificent procession of clergy in their rich copes, and high officials of State in their even more resplendent uniforms, enter by the west door and proceed up the nave. Under the circumstances of the Coronation they can see little of the monuments which adorn the north and south aisles of the nave, for stands are erected along their length; but they miss but little, for this is by no means the most interesting part of the Abbey. After passing the organ-screen and reaching the crossing in front of the sanctuary, there is far more of beauty to be seen. At the bottom of the south transept is a wonderful stained-glass window through which radiating lights shine on the Coronation scene.

Photo]   [Fox
POETS' CORNER

Many British poets and men of letters have been given honoured burial or memorial in this corner of the Abbey's South Transept. The ashes of Rudyard Kipling were interred here in 1936.

Photo]   [Underwood
OLD CROWNING BLOCK

At Kingston-on-Thames is preserved this Stone, traditionally supposed to have been used as the King's seat during the crowning of several of our early Anglo-Saxon sovereigns.

Underneath this window are perhaps the most famous sculptures in the Abbey— the censing angels, which are better seen from the dizzy heights of the triforium, but still can be appreciated from the ground. In this transept, too, is the Poets' Corner, among the most notable of all the Abbey shrines.

Of the crossing between these two transepts, or space under the tower, Mr. A. L. N. Russell in his book "Westminster Abbey" remarks that it is "of great ceremonial importance and its floor was originally eighteen inches above the

Photo]   [Fox

KNIGHTLY BANNERS IN A ROYAL SHRINE

The Coronation ceremony takes place in the older, central portion of Westminster Abbey, and so the framers of the sublime pageant are unable to make use of the magnificent Chapel of Henry VII. This photograph shows some of the banners hung above the stalls of the Knights of the Order of the Bath in the Chapel, and on page 318 is illustrated its temporary use as a drawing-office.

general floor level. For coronations, the throne was set up here [and still is—ED.] on a raised stage high enough for a man to ride under and surmounted by a canopy with silver bells at each corner." He adds : "One of the special characteristics of the Abbey as contrasted with other English churches is its tall and narrow proportion. The height of the vaulting is just 100 feet, nearly three times its span (35 feet), and this very tall and narrow proportion is noticeable in all parts of the church." The triforium, a long narrow gallery with unglazed windows, affords a dizzy view of the proceedings on the floor below, and this houses many spectators at a Coronation.

As a kind of semicircular design, behind St. Edward's chapel and the Sanctuary is the Ambulatory, around which are set six chapels—those of Islip, of St. John the Baptist, of St. Paul, led into from the north transept ; and of St. Benedict, St. Edmund and St. Nicholas, approached from the south transept.

Although Henry VII's chapel does not afford an actual background to any Coronation ceremony, it is a work of such historic value and architectural beauty that it cannot be dismissed in a line. Here the banners of the Knights of the Bath hang under the fan-vaulted ceiling with its heavy "drops". The chapel as a whole is a triumph of the Perpendicular style, which, as Mr. Russell, quoted above, points out, came to its fullest development in the three royal chapels at Westminster, Cambridge and Windsor. He adds, "essentially an English invention : a final chapter which England alone added to the history of Gothic. Fan vaulting, too, was entirely an English invention, so it is very appropriate that its greatest triumph should be the vault of Henry VII's chapel." In the chapel lie Henry VII, Elizabeth, Charles II, Anne and many other of England's monarchs in peace and watching, as it were, the crowning of the new King and Queen. The direct link is established and the tradition carved both in metal and in stone.

AGE-OLD SCENE OF THE CORONATION RITE

Thirteen centuries ago, if tradition may be believed, a little band of Saxon monks built a church in the marshes beside the Thames, just south of the old city of London. History takes up the tale with the foundation of the great church by Edward the Confessor, and through all the nine hundred years that have since elapsed Westminster Abbey has been the holiest shrine of our race. Above we see it in its everyday appearance : in page 320 is a photograph of the Abbey with the Coronation annexe in course of construction.

THE ROUTE FROM THE AIR

The Coronation procession of King George VI and Queen Elizabeth followed a longer route than had been taken by any of its predecessors. This photograph from the air shows the whole of the 6¼ miles of streets and parks that were traversed on the way to the Abbey and back. In the succeeding pages appear photographs of the more important points along the route.

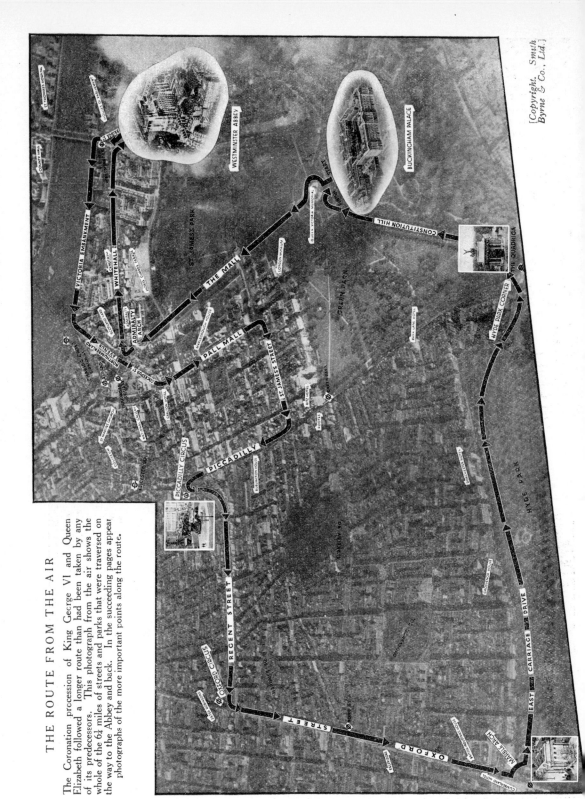

348

CHAPTER 29

THE ROUTE OF THE CORONATION PROCESSION

The six-mile route of the Coronation Procession lay through streets crowded with historic memories, past many famous buildings, along two of London's chief business thoroughfares and by three of its beautiful parks

WE begin at Buckingham Palace, starting point and journey's end of three Coronation processions planned in this century. Each time the State drive has been extended. The route arranged for King Edward VII in 1902 was short owing to his recent illness. In 1911 that for King George and Queen Mary was less than four miles. This year, on May 12th, the King and Queen drove over more than six miles of thoroughfare in the centre of royal London.

Though their starting point was the same, it wears a different aspect. The old east front of the Palace as designed by Edward Blore in Victorian days existed until 1912. Sir Aston Webb's reconstruction was completed in the following year. Before Queen Victoria's accession St. James's Palace was the official residence of the British sovereigns from the time of William and Mary. Queen Victoria chose BUCKINGHAM PALACE as her London home, and her Memorial dominates the view. It includes not only the vast monument opposite the railings, but also the semicircular gardens enclosed by colonnaded screen and wrought iron gates, the Mall and its termination at Whitehall in the handsome Admiralty Arch with triple archways.

Casual crowds gather daily at Buckingham Palace to watch the Changing of the Guard. London children mingle with visitors from the world over. They can also see this brief but colourful pageant when the Court is not in residence at the Palace,

in front of ST. JAMES'S PALACE, on the left of our route down the Mall.

Extending the length of THE MALL on our right, but temporarily hidden by the erection of Coronation seats, is the loveliness of St. James's Park. Anyone who remembers the fairy-like beauty of the celebrated view from the bridge over the lake when the park was floodlit during the Jubilee celebrations is glad that the effect was seen again on the evening of May 12th.

On the left we come to the Duke of York steps leading from the Mall to CARLTON HOUSE TERRACE. We pause to note how grandly the monumental column and statue at the top accord with the dignified architectural scheme of steps and terrace— finest remains of John Nash's Regency London. The monument is to Frederick Augustus, second son of George III, alluded to in a rhyme of the times beginning, "The brave old Duke of York, He had ten thousand men ; He marched them up a very high hill, And marched them down again." By the steps, on the west side, is the German Embassy.

At the end of the Mall is a block of Admiralty buildings including the residences of the First Sea Lord and the First Lord. Over the triple archway of the impressive ADMIRALTY ARCH are the rooms containing the Admiralty Library.

Through the central archway the route proceeds along the south side of TRAFALGAR SQUARE, built on the site of old Charing

Photo]   [Fox

BUCKINGHAM PALACE IN ITS SYLVAN SETTING

How imposing a pile Buckingham Palace is can be realized only when it is seen from the air. On Coronation Day the King and Queen emerged from the Palace by the King's Entrance seen on the further side of the Quadrangle. The procession passed out of the Quadrangle by the arch in the centre of the facade, through the middle gate of the forecourt, and to the right of the Queen Victoria Memorial. It returned down Constitution Hill, seen on the right of the photograph.

village. We get a fleeting impression of the National Gallery occupying the north side with satisfactory stateliness, and the graceful whiteness of ST. MARTIN'S-IN-THE-FIELDS, well known on account of its broadcast services; of the general pleasing result of mixed styles in SOUTH AFRICA HOUSE, of Portland stone, designed by Sir Herbert Baker with Italianate balustrades, Queen Anne windows and Georgian festoons of flowers, which tone down its modernity in a neighbourhood mainly built between 1830 and 1843 ; of the NELSON COLUMN, 145 feet high, surmounted by the statue of Trafalgar's victor, memorialized by the whole square; of Landseer's four bronze lions which guard it, their tameness of expression equalled by the actual tameness of the flocks of pigeons at home there.

In the roadway, before we turn down to Whitehall, is, by common consent, the finest statue to be found in London streets, the equestrian effigy of Charles I by the French sculptor, Hubert Le Sœur, with its beautifully decorated plinth. Between Trafalgar and Parliament Squares prac-

tically the whole Government is administered. In King Charles's day—and until 1698, when most of the building was destroyed by fire—the whole area we see on both sides of the connecting thoroughfare was the precincts of the Royal Palace of Whitehall. Some way down, on the left, is the beautiful BANQUETING HOUSE, built by Inigo Jones in 1619, all that remains of the Palace. It was the last scene of Charles's tragedy. On that snowy morning in January 1649, the King stepped out of the second upper window on to the scaffold

Also on the east side and before we come to the Banqueting House, now the Royal United Services Museum, is the WAR OFFICE, an imposing structure with Ionic pillars and four flanking towers, which extends to Whitehall Court. In the middle of the roadway is the equestrian statue of the Duke of Cambridge, suitably so placed as he was for nearly fifty years Commander-in-Chief of the British Army

On the west side of the route a modern note is struck by the neat little Whitehall

Theatre, erected in 1929. Further down is the HORSE GUARDS, dating from 1754, guardhouse of the Household Cavalry, a pleasing Palladian-style building chiefly associated in most people's minds with those living equestrian statues, the mounted sentries on either side of the entrance.

Between the Horse Guards and Downing Street we pass the Scottish Office, while in DOVER HOUSE are the Privy Council Office and the Treasury. On the east side of the route is GWYDYR HOUSE, recruiting office for the Royal Air Force, and MONTAGUE HOUSE, once the mansion of the Dukes of Buccleuch, now headquarters of the Minister of Labour. We glance up DOWNING STREET, on our right, noting No. 10, where the Prime Minister lives, and No. 11, official residence of the Chancellor of the Exchequer. The other side of the street forms part of the quadrangle of buildings erected in 1868–73 from the designs of Sir Gilbert Scott, including the Home Office, the India Office, Dominions Office and Foreign Office.

The dignified simplicity of the CENOTAPH makes it the most impressive architectural object in the thoroughfare. Designed by Sir Edwin Lutyens and erected in 1920 "to represent an Imperial Grave of all those citizens of the Empire, of every creed and rank, who gave their lives in the War", it is in the widest and truest sense a national memorial. Flowers are laid at its foot not only in the wreaths on Armistice Day, but throughout the year.

Out of Parliament Street the processional route follows the east and south sides of Parliament Square past that ancient part of the Houses of Parliament, WESTMINSTER HALL, the original structure of which dates from the reign of William Rufus. Erected in 1097, the Hall was the scene of the old Coronation banquets. It is connected in our thoughts with the Lying-in-State of King George V. Overshadowed by Westminster

Photo]   [Fox

LONDON'S GREAT PROCESSIONAL WAY

On emerging from Buckingham Palace the procession passed along the Mall, the great processional way which, with the Admiralty Arch, forms part of the Queen Victoria Memorial. Passing through the central arch, used only on State occasions, it reached the open space to the south of Trafalgar Square, which is officially known as Charing Cross, and thence turned down Whitehall.

Photo]   [Fox

NELSON'S QUARTER-DECK IN LONDON

Many thousands of people watched the Coronation procession as it touched the south-western corner of Trafalgar Square on its way to Westminster and proceeded along the south side on the return journey. In this photograph the south side and Cockspur Street are on the left. In the centre is Canada House, while on the right is the National Gallery.

Photo]   [Dixon-Scott

TO THE EMPIRE'S "GLORIOUS DEAD"

From Trafalgar Square the cavalcade of the Coronation passed down Whitehall, where stands the Empty Tomb erected in 1920 to commemorate the Empire's dead in the greatest of all wars. A tragic memory of another kind is suggested by the Banqueting Hall, before whose windows Charles I was executed in 1649. In this photograph it is the second building from the left.

Photo]   *[A. F. Kersting*

FROM WESTMINSTER TO THE CITY

This infra-red ray photograph shows with remarkable clarity the cities of London and Westminster, with the Abbey in the centre, standing out against the Houses of Parliament. In the distance St. Paul's Cathedral, set amidst the spires of many city churches, towers above the roofs. Just below St. Paul's the dome of Westminster Central Hall is seen, and to the left of it are the Foreign and India Offices and the imposing modern pile that houses the London Passenger Transport Board.

Abbey is little ST. MARGARET'S CHURCH, created the Dominions Parish Church in 1916, and also notable for the many society weddings which take place in it. And so to the west entrance of the ABBEY, which displays no fewer than seven centuries of English architecture—the main building erected by Henry III, the beautiful Henry VII's chapel, the twin towers erected from designs of Wren and his pupil Hawksmoor between 1713 and 1740, the north transept, remodelled by Sir Gilbert Scott and J. L. Pearson in 1890, the restorations carried out in 1921, paid for by public subscription, and the temporary annexe designed for the marshalling of the Coronation procession in 1937.

After the great traditional ceremony in the Abbey the homeward journey begins by the west and north sides of Parliament Square, passing the arch in Broad Sanctuary —which gives access to Dean's Yard and

WESTMINSTER SCHOOL—and the nineteenth-century memorial in granite and stone to men, educated at Westminster, who fell in various wars, Indian and Russian. On the left is to be seen the METHODIST CENTRAL HALL with its huge dome. On the north side of Broad Sanctuary is Westminster Hospital, established in 1719 and removed to its present site in 1834, first of the voluntary hospitals. There is a certain elegance about its neighbour, the neo-Renaissance building of the MIDDLESEX GUILDHALL, reconstructed in 1915. Opposite the north entrance of the Abbey is a copy of A. Saint-Gaudens' statue of Abraham Lincoln, made impressive by the placing of the figure in front of the large, vacant chair. During Coronation Week it was partly covered by the woodwork of a stand.

The Gothic spikiness of the vast MOTHER OF PARLIAMENTS now absorbs attention with

23

all its intricate detail, some part of which is usually under repair. Londoners are sentimentally attached to the clock tower, which houses Big Ben, but it never seems to accord harmoniously with the stately Victoria Tower at the other end.

On the left side of the approach to Westminster Bridge Thomas Thornycroft's group of Boadicea in her chariot with its pawing steeds attracts a glance. The route now turns to follow the VICTORIA EMBANKMENT. Through the bordering plane trees we see the massive pile of the LONDON COUNTY HALL across the river. Designed by the late Ralph Knott and E. Stone Collins, the tiled high-pitched roof, Ionic pillars and bowed peristyle give it a foreign, though decidedly distinguished, appearance.

Royal Empire Society

Turning from the Embankment at Charing Cross Underground station and the Playhouse Theatre, our way is along NORTHUMBERLAND AVENUE. This wide street has an air of Victorian solidity, though on the right is the new building of the ROYAL EMPIRE SOCIETY, opened in 1935 by the Duke of Windsor, then Prince of Wales. The London offices of the League of Nations are in Craven House.

Across the south side of Trafalgar Square, we proceed past Malaya House, the Malayan Information Agency, on the left, and Canada House on the right, at the corner of the Square and Cockspur Street. CANADA HOUSE, London headquarters of the Canadian Government, was opened in 1925. Its somewhat irrelevant classical features have been adversely criticized, but on the whole it harmonizes with its neighbours and achieves the important effect of dignity.

We now pass the CARLTON HOTEL, and beyond it arrive at WATERLOO PLACE and are in the midst of memorials. The largest is the Crimean, with statues of Lord Herbert of Lea and Florence Nightingale. Arctic and Antarctic expedition memorials are here. Opposite Sir John Franklin's is that to Captain Scott, sculptured by his widow.

In PALL MALL are the clubs for the erudite and serious-minded—the Athenaeum, Carlton and Reform. We pass the Royal Automobile Club, completed in 1911, the front of MARLBOROUGH HOUSE, and pause to admire the beautiful Tudor gateway of ST. JAMES'S PALACE. Turning up St. James's Street to Piccadilly we are still in clubland, for here are Boodle's, White's with the famous bow window, Brooks's, and the Thatched House.

As the route proceeds to Piccadilly Circus, we notice the grave building of BURLINGTON HOUSE, where the Royal Academy holds its summer exhibitions. Through the archway you can see the statue of Sir Joshua Reynolds, first president of the Academy, posed with his palette ready for work.

On the south side of Piccadilly are two beautiful buildings, one new and one old. The small Midland Bank, designed by Sir Edwin Lutyens in 1923, charms the eye and enhances the tranquillity of Sir Christopher Wren's ST. JAMES'S CHURCH.

London's Hub

We now arrive at PICCADILLY CIRCUS, hub of the West End, with all the traffic gyrating round Eros. Lightly poised above his fountain, he memorializes the philanthropic Lord Shaftesbury and was sculptured by Sir Alfred Gilbert. The route is on the west side and turns along Regent Street, passing the marble and ferroconcrete commercial palaces which have replaced Nash's stucco-fronted buildings. At OXFORD CIRCUS we proceed down OXFORD STREET to the Marble Arch.

Opposite Mount Royal, one of the newest blocks of luxury flats in London, is British Industries House, where window displays are arranged to promote the sale of British Empire products. We are now at MARBLE ARCH, and on the right are the impressive structures of the Cumberland Hotel and Regal Cinema. The Arch itself is fated no longer to fulfil the reason of its existence. Designed by John Nash, it began as an entrance to Buckingham Palace. It was to have been surmounted

Photos]

[Topical

THROUGH WEST END THOROUGHFARES

The return journey of the Royal procession was planned to pass along the most famous of London streets by way of Whitehall, Pall Mall, St. James's Street and Piccadilly, to Piccadilly Circus, seen in the top photograph. The route then turned left along Regent Street, the curving line of which is seen in the top left of the upper photograph. By this famous street Oxford Street was reached, and an air view of some of the great buildings of this thoroughfare is shown in the lower photograph

WESTERN TURNING-POINT OF THE PROCESSION

At the western extremity of Oxford Street the procession passed through the Marble Arch and then into Hyde Park. The photograph shows the Marble Arch on its island site. It was originally built as a gateway to Buckingham Palace, and afterwards became the north-east entrance to Hyde Park. The park boundary was set back a few years ago to make way for roundabout traffic, but the Arch remains in its original position.

by the equestrian statue of George IV which is now in Trafalgar Square. The classical style of the arch—somewhat after that of the Arch of Constantine in Rome—did not fit in with the scheme of the alterations to the Palace which were made for Queen Victoria. So in 1851, year of the Great Exhibition opened in HYDE PARK, the Marble Arch was removed to its present position, where, until 1908, it formed one of the entrances to the Park.

Its gates were opened for the Procession to pass through it, and the route then proceeds through the Park gates and along the East Carriage Drive. Near the Marble Arch end is the space where the Hyde Park orators expound their views on politics and reforms to audiences of varying sizes. On our left, across PARK LANE, we may notice the Dorchester and Grosvenor Hotels. Just inside Stanhope Gate is the Cavalry War Memorial—a St. George and the Dragon by Adrian Jones, M.V.O.

As we emerge by the triple gateway at Hyde Park Corner the great stone howitzer of the ARTILLERY MEMORIAL claims first attention. Though the gun itself is intentionally symbolic rather than representational, its sculptor, the late Charles Sargeant Jagger, had seen much active service. His carved reliefs and the bronze figures below it of gunners have the artistic verity of his actual experiences. In complete contrast is the Machine Gun Corps Memorial by F. Derwent Wood. His single bronze figure of David recalls Donatello's.

To the west is St. George's Hospital, founded in 1834, and soon to be rebuilt on its immensely valuable site. To the east we see the solemn grey building of APSLEY HOUSE, once the home of the great Duke of Wellington, whose equestrian statue in bronze by Sir Joseph Boehm faces it from the roadway. The Iron Duke is also memorialized by the triumphal arch which heads Constitution Hill and is crowned by the Quadriga, the large bronze group of "Peace" in her chariot, by Captain Adrian Jones. By way of CONSTITUTION HILL we follow the route to the Victoria Memorial Gardens and so arrive once more at our starting point, Buckingham Palace.

CHAPTER 30

THE PROCESSION WITHIN THE ABBEY
AND THE ORDER OF THE SERVICE

It may well be claimed that the Coronation Procession that moves from the West Door of the Abbey to the Theatre before the Altar is unsurpassed and unsurpassable. In it the history of a thousand years walks the stage with majestic tread

WHEN Westminster was a palace in fact as well as in name, the King on the eve of his Coronation proceeded thither in state from the Tower, heard evensong in the Abbey and then was served with specially prepared spiced wine, ceremonially bathed and put to bed.

In the morning he was bathed again, heard Mass, and was arrayed by the Lord Great Chamberlain in his royal robes. He then proceeded to Westminster Hall, where, seated on the King's Bench, he received the bishops and the Abbot of Westminster and his monks bearing the Regalia. The latter were placed on a table before the King and then distributed by him to the Officers of State charged to receive and carry them in the procession to the Abbey and during the ceremony.

This procession has been done away with since the Coronation of George IV in 1821—a fact which is to be regretted by those who might hope to have had a glimpse of the glittering cavalcade as it moved from the Hall along a raised platform to the Abbey. Nowadays the Abbey clergy collect the Regalia from the Jerusalem Chamber, and carry them on cushions of cloth-of-gold to the vestibule adjoining the west door of the Abbey. There they deposit their precious burdens until the royal procession is formed. Then each piece is borne before the King and Queen to the "theatre" by some noble or prelate.

This procession is in itself a pageant of incomparable magnificence. In the van walk the Chaplains in Ordinary, the Abbey prebendaries in their crimson copes, and the Dean, whose part in the ceremony is that played by the Abbot of medieval times.

Next the heraldic splendour of the feudal age is resurrected—pursuivants and heralds in resplendent emblazoned tabards, officers of the great orders of knighthood, standard-bearers, Knights of the Garter, Gentlemen-at-Arms, prelates of the Church and great Officers of State, noble bearers of the Regalia and clerics charged with the Bible, Chalice and Patina—and in their midst, cynosure of all eyes, the superbly royal figures of Their Majesties, the chief actors in this most imperial of ceremonies.

History on parade is an apt description of the procession, for in it are the great ones of the kingdom, men whose names are honoured throughout the Empire, men who hold offices of high-sounding fame that are links with the splendour of the Middle Ages. The heralds and knights, for instance, breathe the very spirit of chivalry. Note the medieval ring of their titles : Unicorn Pursuivant, Bluemantle, Portcullis, Rouge Dragon and Rouge Croix Pursuivants, Richmond Herald, Black Rod, and the Kings of Arms, Norroy, Ulster, Lyon and Clarenceux. The year is 1937, but men bearing these same titles walked in the

Coronation processions of the sovereigns of centuries ago.

The Order of the Garter, whose knights follow the Abbey clergy in the procession, was instituted by Edward III about 1349, and is held to be the most ancient and illustrious order of knighthood in the world. The "most ancient" Order of the Thistle was founded by James II in 1687 ; the "most honourable" Order of the Bath by George I in 1725 ; the "most illustrious" Order of St. Patrick by George III in 1788 ; the "most distinguished" Order of St. Michael and St. George by the Prince Regent, later George IV, in 1818 ; the "most exalted" Order of the Star of India and the "most eminent" Order of the Indian Empire by Queen Victoria in 1861 and 1877 respectively; and the "most excellent" Order of the British Empire by George V in 1917.

Accompanying the representatives of these knightly orders come the standard-

Photo]   [Keystone

HIS GRACE OF CANTERBURY

The Most Rev. Cosmo Gordon Lang has the unique distinction of having held the archiepiscopal see of York before his elevation to that of Canterbury. He is a Scotsman, and one of his younger brothers is a leading Presbyterian divine.

bearers, carrying the red banner of England, Scotland's orange and red and Ireland's blue and gold. Then come a host of dignitaries from amongst whom we may distinguish some of the most important.

Primate of All England

The archbishops may take the precedence, for they are the representatives of the religious power—of the Church that existed centuries before England became a single state. The first to carry Canterbury's archiepiscopal crosier was Augustine, sent to the Saxon kingdom of Kent by Pope Gregory I in A.D. 597. The Archbishop is the Primate of All England, and in processions and other State functions he takes precedence over all the nobility, temporal as well as spiritual, with the exception of Princes of the Blood Royal.

There have been in all ninety-six Archbishops of Canterbury since Augustine, and to look down the list is to be reminded of many of the most important and stirring events in our history. Archbishop Lang is the successor of Anselm and Lanfranc ; of Becket, whose place of martyrdom is still pointed out in his cathedral ; of Stephen Langton, who led the barons against King John ; of Cranmer, who perished at the stake, and Laud, who died on the scaffold ; Sancroft, who, much against his will, defied James II, and Davidson of our own day. Statesmen and scholars, men of the pen and sometimes of the sword, orators and administrators— they make a goodly show in the roll-call of the centuries.

His Grace of York, too, holds an office of time-honoured dignity. He is Primate of England—note the distinction between his title and that of his brother of Canterbury—and comes third in the table of precedence. The first Archbishop of York was enthroned in A.D. 627, when the city was the capital of the kingdom of Northumbria, and Archbishop Temple is the eighty-ninth successor of Paulinus.

By ancient custom—it was acknowledged as binding as far back as the reign of William the Conqueror—the Archbishop of

Canterbury is entrusted with the anointing, and it is he, too, who places the crown on the sovereign's head. Throughout the service he is the principal officiant, and it is from his hands that the royal pair receive the sacrament. The Archbishop of York is present, but his rôle is rather to watch than to act. At the Coronation of Edward VII Archbishop Maclagan claimed the right to perform the crowning of Queen Alexandra, and though no judgement on the matter was delivered by the Court of Claims, his request was granted by the King. In 1911, however, Queen Mary was crowned not by the then Archbishop of York (Dr. Lang, now Archbishop of Canterbury), but by Archbishop Davidson of Canterbury.

Only three of our kings have been crowned by prelates other than the Archbishops of Canterbury : Edward II, crowned by the Bishop of Winchester, as the Archbishop was abroad ; Elizabeth, crowned by Bishop Oglethorpe of Carlisle, as the see of Canterbury was vacant ; and William and Mary, crowned by Bishop Compton of London, as Sancroft refused to crown persons whom he, as a believer in the divine right of kings, could not but regard as usurpers.

Bishops and the Dean

Two other bishops always take part in the ceremony, their lordships of Durham and of Bath and Wells, who thus exercise a right conceded since the time of Richard I, nearly 750 years ago. Then the Dean and Chapter of Westminster Abbey are present, as the custodians of the sacred building itself, and as the successors of the abbots and monks of olden time. At each Coronation they prefer a claim to exercise certain functions (see page 271), and the Regalia are in their keeping from the time they leave the Tower to when they are returned thither. As already stated, on the eve of the Coronation the priceless objects are kept in the Jerusalem Chamber, the hall beside the Abbey which was formerly the Abbot's guest-room and is now part of the Deanery.

Photo]   [Keystone

PRIMATE OF ENGLAND

Son of a former Archbishop of Canterbury, the Most Rev. Dr. Temple, Archbishop of York (above) was Bishop of Manchester before his appointment to the see of the Northern Province in 1929. He is Primate of England, as compared with Cantuar's "All England".

So much for the ecclesiastics. Now amongst the laymen we turn to the chief of the temporal hierarchy of the realm—the Lord High Chancellor. He ranks immediately after the Archbishop of Canterbury and just before the Archbishop of York. Volumes have been written on his office— or, rather, offices. He is the Keeper of the Great Seal and the adviser-in-chief of the sovereign ; he is the Speaker of the House of Lords, where his seat is the famous Woolsack ; he is nowadays always a Cabinet Minister and the administrator of a vast patronage ; furthermore, he is a judge, not in one court only but several—the House of Lords, the Privy Council, the Court of Appeal and the Chancery Division of the High Court of Justice. Today the Lord Chancellor is always a lay lord, but in olden times he was generally a prince of the Church, for in those days the clerics were the best educated of the men about the king. It is more than 300 years, how-

Photos]   [Vandyk ; Elliott & Fry

DIGNITARIES OF THE ABBEY

In medieval times Westminster Abbey was ruled by an abbot. Then for fifteen years after the suppression of the monastic foundation in 1539 its head was a bishop. Since the reign of Elizabeth, however, it has been a deanery, and above (left) we see the present holder of the ancient office—the Very Rev. W. Foxley Norris, K.C.V.O., D.D. On the right is Canon F. L. Donaldson, perhaps the best-known of the Abbey's four Canons Residentiary

ever, since a bishop had the custody of the Great Seal and sat on the Woolsack.

The Lord Great Chamberlain is the holder of another venerable office, but that office has in the course of time lost most of its importance. In the twentieth century he is most in evidence at Coronations and other great ceremonies of State. As custodian of the Palace of Westminster he is responsible for the preliminary preparations, and in the actual proceedings he plays an honourable part. Thus in the Coronation it is he who touches the King's heels with the Spurs, hands him the Sword of State and girds it on, fastens the clasps of the royal robe and holds the crown while the King communicates.

His office was granted by Henry I to the family of de Vere, Earls of Oxford, and is now held in turn (see page 275), changing at each new reign, by Lords Ancaster, Cholmondeley and Lincolnshire and their heirs. Under George V the Lord Great Chamberlain was Lord Lewisham, grandson of the first Marquess of Lincolnshire ; Lord Cholmondeley held it during the short reign of Edward VIII, and the present holder is Lord Ancaster. By virtue of his office the Lord Great Chamberlain claims the right to enjoy certain privileges, etc., on the occasion of a Coronation (see page 272).

Next we may take note of the Lord High Constable. His is a high-sounding title, and he ranks seventh amongst the great Officers of State. Yet his post is a nominal one, and, indeed, is called out of abeyance only at Coronations. In medieval times his functions were numerous and important ; he was, for instance, commander of the royal forces and master of the King's Horse. In the reign of Henry VIII the office reverted to the Crown, on the attainder of the Duke of Buckingham, and it is now at His Majesty's disposal.

The Earl Marshal ranks after the Lord High Constable in the list of great Officers of State. Like the Constable, his main functions are in connexion with the Coronation, the arrangements for which—as for other State processions and ceremonies—are in his hands. There were Marshals of England in the reign of Henry I, and the first Earl Marshal was appointed as far back as 1386. The office was entailed on the male line of the Howard family in 1672, and the present Duke of Norfolk is, like his fathers, not only Earl of Arundel, Baron Maltravers, Earl of Surrey, Baron Fitz Alan, Clun and Oswaldestre, and Earl of Norfolk, but Earl Marshal and Hereditary Marshal and Chief Butler of England. The two batons crossed in saltire in His Grace's arms and the letters "E.M." after his signature are reminders of his tenure of this ancient office.

There is also, it may be mentioned, a Lord High Constable of Scotland, the office having been hereditary in the Hays family, earls of Erroll, since the fourteenth century. At each Coronation the Earl of Erroll has a place, and his claim has been already referred to (see page 271).

Another appointment made, as a rule, like that of Lord High Constable, only for the Coronation is that of Lord High Steward. He is the first of the great Officers of State, and he must not be confused with the Lord Steward, who is the first dignitary of the Court. On appointment he is given a white rod of office, and this is broken at the end of his period of service. The Lord High Steward has always been a nobleman of high degree, appointed for a brief space to supervise matters of domestic importance, and for centuries he has presided over the court which is set up to try a peer. Thus in 1901 the then Earl Russell was tried for bigamy before the High Steward's Court, composed of all the lords in Parliament and presided over by Lord Halsbury, created Lord High Steward for the purpose; and again in 1936 Lord de Clifford was charged with manslaughter before the Lord High Steward.

Scotland and Ireland have also High Stewards. In former times the Lord High Steward had a great part to play at Coronations, but nowadays even on these occasions he is but a picturesque survival.

Strictly speaking, there are nine great Officers of State, and five of these—the Lord High Steward, Lord High Chancellor, Lord Great Chamberlain, Lord High Constable and Earl Marshal—we have already discussed. There remain the Lord High

STATELY PROCESSION OF THE REGALIA

As is stated in page 357, in the Coronations of centuries ago the Royal Regalia were brought in state from the Tower to the Palace of Westminster and ceremonially distributed by the King to his attendant lords on the morning of the Coronation Day. On the last five occasions, however, the Regalia have been taken to Westminster Abbey, where they have rested overnight in the Jerusalem Chamber. Then early on the day of the ceremony they have been taken by the clergy to the retiring-room adjoining the West Door of the Abbey and placed on a table to await the coming of the Royal Procession. This photograph shows the clergy carrying the Regalia from the Jerusalem Chamber on the occasion of King George V's Coronation in 1911.

Treasurer, the Lord President of the Council, the Lord Privy Seal and the Lord High Admiral. The first and last are in commission, as we say; in other words, their functions are performed by a Board, whose chiefs are the First Lord of the Treasury (now generally the Prime Minister) and the First Lord of the Admiralty. Both are politicians, and so, too, are the Lord Privy Seal and the Lord President of the Council.

Neither the one nor the other is of any importance so far as the tenure of his office is concerned. The privy (private) seal was generally used in olden days as an authority for the Chancellor to affix the great seal or as a substitute for the latter in the sealing of documents of lesser importance. Nowadays the Lord Privy Seal has no seal in his custody, but is a Cabinet Minister entrusted as a rule with affairs of State which do not fall within the realm of any of the other Ministers. The Lord President of the Council—it is the Privy Council that is meant—is also a Cabinet Minister, and often he holds another portfolio. He presides over the meetings of the Privy Council—it meets very seldom, generally only on such great occasions as a royal accession or marriage.

Now we espy two high officers of the royal household. The Lord Steward, like the Lord High Steward, carries a white staff, but his appointment is a permanent one in the gift of the sovereign. He likewise presides at a court—the Board of Green Cloth, which is a committee of the royal household entrusted with the task of examining the household accounts and passing them for payment.

Duties of the Lord Chamberlain

Next to him in the Court is the Lord Chamberlain, who again must be distinguished from the Lord Great Chamberlain. He carries a white staff and a gold or jewelled key, to signify his domestic responsibilities. At Coronations and other great State ceremonies he makes the necessary arrangements and conducts the King to and from his carriage. He is, in other words, a kind of major-domo. Incidentally, he licenses all theatres in London, Westminster, Windsor and Brighton, and is also licenser of plays.

In addition to these great functionaries there is a host of minor dignitaries who by hereditary right or royal preference hold some office which may or may not be merely titular. Here we must pass them by, but in conclusion let us pay a meed of tribute to the representatives of the royal bodyguards that bring up the rear of the procession. Everyone knows the Yeomen of the Guard, the stately old soldiers who are to be seen walking beside the royal coach on State occasions; the Beefeaters of the Tower of London are an associated corps. The Yeomen are the oldest corps in the British service—they date from 1485—but not much younger is the bodyguard of the sovereign, the Honorable Corps of Gentlemen-at-Arms, instituted in 1509 by Henry VIII. They attend at royal drawing-rooms and levees, and are much in evidence at the Coronation.

Scottish Royal Bodyguard

The Royal Company of Archers, the king's bodyguard for Scotland, dates from 1676, though some claim for it an earlier origin. The Captain-General of the Company carries a gold stick—originally conferred by George IV—and this entitles him to march in the Coronation procession just behind the Gold Stick of England (who is a colonel of the Household Cavalry).

So they pass by, the sovereigns and the Princes of the Blood Royal, peers and prelates and gentlemen commoners, garbed in the gorgeous costumes of days gone by or in the brave show of Service uniforms.

No such procession could be staged now in any other country of the world. The Austria-Hungary of Francis Joseph might perhaps have emulated it, and Kaiser Wilhelm's Germany might have made the attempt. France has had nothing like it since the days of the last Napoleon or even of the Bourbons. Only in Britain are the links with the past so many and so unbroken. Only in Britain can the past live again and not be shamed by the glaring incongruities of the present.

THE CORONATION SERVICE
OF KING GEORGE VI AND QUEEN ELIZABETH

I
THE PREPARATION

In the morning upon the day of the Coronation early, care is to be taken that the Ampulla be filled with Oil and, together with the Spoon, be laid ready upon the Altar in the Abbey Church.

The Litany shall be sung as the Dean and Prebendaries and the Choir of Westminster proceed from the Altar to the West door of the Church.

The Archbishops and Bishops Assistant being already vested in their Copes, the procession shall be formed immediately outside of the West door of the Church, and shall wait till notice is given of the approach of their Majesties, and shall then begin to move into the Church.

II
THE ENTRANCE INTO THE CHURCH

The King and Queen, as soon as they enter at the West door of the Church, are to be received with the Anthem (Psalm cxxii, 1–3, 6, 7), to be sung by the choir of Westminster.

The King and Queen shall in the mean time pass up the body of the Church, into and through the Choir, and so up the stairs to the Theatre ; and having passed by their thrones, they shall make their humble adoration, and then kneeling at the faldstools set for them before their Chairs of Estate on the South side of the Altar, use some short private prayers ; and after, sit down in their chairs.

III
THE RECOGNITION

The King and Queen being so placed, the Archbishop, together with the Lord Chancellor, Lord Great Chamberlain, Lord High Constable, and Earl Marshal (Garter King of Arms preceding them) shall go to the East side of the Theatre, and after, shall go to the other three sides in this order, South, West, and North, and at every of the four sides the Archbishop shall with a loud voice speak to the People : and the King in the mean while, standing up by his chair, shall turn and shew himself unto the People at every of the four sides of the Theatre as the Archbishop is at every of them, the Archbishop saying :

SIRS, I here present unto you King GEORGE, your undoubted King : Wherefore all you who are come this day to do your homage and service, Are you willing to do the same ?

The People signify their willingness and joy, by loud and repeated acclamations, all with one voice crying out :

God save King George

Then the trumpets shall sound.

The Bible, Paten, and Chalice shall be brought by the Bishops who had borne them, and placed upon the Altar.

The Lords who carry in procession the Regalia, except those who carry the Swords, shall come near to the Altar, and present in order every one what he carries to the Archbishop, who shall deliver them to the Dean of Westminster, to be by him placed upon the Altar.

IV
THE OATH

Then shall the Archbishop go to the King, and standing before him, administer the Coronation Oath, first asking the King :

SIR, is your Majesty willing to take the Oath ?

And the King answering :

I am willing,

The Archbishop shall minister these questions ; and the King, having a book in his hands, shall answer each question severally as follows :

Archbishop. Will you solemnly promise and swear to govern the peoples of *Great Britain, Ireland, Canada, Australia, New Zealand*, and the Union of *South Africa*, of your Possessions and the other Territories to any of them belonging or pertaining, and of your Empire of *India*, according to their respective laws and customs ?

King. I solemnly promise so to do.

Archbishop. Will you to your power cause Law and Justice, in Mercy, to be executed in all your judgements ?

King. I will.

Archbishop. Will you to the utmost of your power maintain the Laws of God and the true profession of the Gospel ? Will you to the utmost of your power maintain in the *United Kingdom* the Protestant Reformed Religion established by law ? And will you maintain and preserve inviolably the settlement of the Church of *England*, and the doctrine, worship, discipline, and government thereof, as by law established in *England* ? And will you preserve unto the Bishops and Clergy of *England*, and to the Churches there committed to their charge, all such rights and privileges, as by law do or shall appertain to them, or any of them ?

King. All this I promise to do.

Then the King arising out of his chair, supported as before, and assisted by the Lord Great Chamberlain, the Sword of State being carried before him, shall go to the Altar, and there being uncovered, make his solemn Oath in the sight of all the people, to observe the premisses : laying his right The Bible *hand upon the Holy Gospel in the Great Bible* to be *(which was before carried in the Procession and* brought : *is now brought from the Altar by the Archbishop, and tendered to him as he kneels upon the steps), saying these words :*

THE things which I have here before promised, I will perform, and keep. So help me, God.

Then the King shall kiss the Book and sign the And a Silver *Oath.* Standish

The King having thus taken his Oath shall return again to his chair, and the Archbishop shall go to him and minister the Declaration prescribed by Act of Parliament, and His Majesty shall make, subscribe, and audibly repeat the same. This done, the Archbishop shall return to the Altar and begin the Communion Service.

V
THE BEGINNING OF THE COMMUNION SERVICE
THE INTROIT

LET my prayer come up into thy presence as the incense : and let the lifting up of my hands be as an evening sacrifice.

Then the Archbishop shall begin the Communion Service, saying :

The Lord be with you.

Answer. And with thy spirit.

Let us pray

O GOD, who providest for thy people by thy power, and rulest over them in love : Grant unto this thy servant GEORGE, our King, the Spirit of wisdom and government, that being devoted unto thee with all his heart, he may so wisely govern, that in his time thy Church and people may continue in safety and prosperity ; and that, persevering in good works unto the end, he may through thy mercy come to thine everlasting kingdom ; through Jesus Christ our Lord, who liveth and reigneth with thee and the Holy Ghost, ever one God, world without end. *Amen.*

THE EPISTLE

To be read by one of the Bishops : 1 S. Peter ii, 13–17.

THE GOSPEL

To be read by another Bishop, the King and Queen with the people standing : S. Matthew xxii, 15-22.

Then shall be sung the Nicene Creed, the King and Queen with the people standing, as before.

VI

THE ANOINTING

The Creed being ended, both the King and the Queen kneeling at their faldstools, the Archbishop shall begin the hymn, VENI CREATOR SPIRITUS, *and the choir shall sing it out.*

This being ended, the Archbishop shall say this prayer :

O LORD, Holy Father, who by anointing with Oil didst of old make and consecrate kings, priests, and prophets, to teach and govern thy people Israel : Bless and sanctify thy chosen servant GEORGE, who by our office and ministry is now to be anointed with this Oil [*here the Archbishop is to lay his hand upon the Ampulla*], and consecrated King : Strengthen him, O Lord, with the Holy Ghost the Comforter ; confirm and stablish him with thy free and princely Spirit, the Spirit of wisdom and government, the Spirit of counsel and ghostly strength, the Spirit of knowledge and true godliness, and fill him, O Lord, with the Spirit of thy holy fear, now and for ever. *Amen.*

This prayer being ended, the choir shall sing : 1 Kings i, 39, 40.

In the mean time, the King rising from his devotions, having been disrobed of his crimson robe by the Lord Great Chamberlain, and having taken off his Cap of State, shall go before the Altar, supported and attended as before.

The King shall sit down in King Edward's Chair (placed in the midst of the area over against the Altar, with a faldstool before it), wherein he is to be anointed. Four Knights of the Garter shall hold over him a rich pall of silk, or cloth of gold : The Dean of Westminster, taking the Ampulla and Spoon from off the Altar, shall hold them ready, pouring some of the holy Oil into the Spoon, and with it the Archbishop shall anoint the King in the form of a cross :

I. *On the palms of both the hands, saying :*

Be thy Hands anointed with holy Oil.

II. *On the breast, saying :*

Be thy Breast anointed with holy Oil.

III. *On the crown of the head, saying :*

BE thy Head anointed with holy Oil, as kings, priests, and prophets were anointed : And as Solomon was anointed king by Zadok the priest and Nathan the prophet, so be you anointed, blessed, and consecrated King over the Peoples, whom the Lord your God hath given you to rule and govern, In the Name of the Father, and of the Son, and of the Holy Ghost. *Amen.*

Then shall the Dean of Westminster lay the Ampulla and Spoon upon the Altar ; and the King kneeling down at the faldstool, the Archbishop standing shall say this Blessing over him :

O UR Lord Jesus Christ, the Son of God, who by his Father was anointed with the Oil of gladness above his fellows, by his holy Anointing pour down upon your Head and Heart the blessing of the Holy Ghost, and prosper the works of your Hands : that by the assistance of his heavenly grace you may preserve the people committed to your charge in wealth, peace, and godliness ; and after a long and glorious course of ruling a temporal kingdom wisely, justly, and religiously, you may at last be made partaker of an eternal kingdom, through Jesus Christ our Lord. *Amen.*

This prayer being ended, the King shall arise and sit down again in King Edward's Chair, while the Knights of the Garter give back the pall to the Lord Chamberlain ; whereupon the King again arising, the Dean of Westminster shall put upon his Majesty the Colobium Sindonis and the Supertunica or close pall of cloth of gold, together with a Girdle of the same. Then shall the King again sit down.

VII

THE PRESENTING OF THE SPURS AND SWORD, AND THE GIRDING AND OBLATION OF THE SAID SWORD

The Spurs shall be brought from the Altar by the Dean of Westminster, and delivered to the Lord Great Chamberlain ; who, kneeling down, shall touch his Majesty's heels therewith, and send them back to the Altar.

Then the Lord, who carries the Sword of State, delivering to the Lord Chamberlain the said Sword (which is thereupon deposited in the traverse in Saint Edward's Chapel) shall receive from the Lord Chamberlain, in lieu thereof, another Sword in a scabbard of purple velvet, provided for the King to be girt withal, which he shall deliver to the Archbishop ; and the Archbishop shall lay it on the Altar, saying the following prayer :

H EAR our prayers, O Lord, we beseech thee, and so direct and support thy servant King GEORGE, who is now to be girt with this Sword, that he may not bear it in vain ; but may use it as the minister of God for the terror and punishment of evildoers, and for the protection and encouragement of those that do well, through Jesus Christ our Lord. *Amen.*

Then shall the Archbishop take the Sword from off the Altar, and deliver it into the King's right hand, the Archbishop of York and the Bishops of London and Winchester and other Bishops assisting and going along with him ; and, the King holding it, the Archbishop shall say :

R ECEIVE this kingly Sword, brought now from the Altar of God, and delivered to you by the hands of us the Bishops and servants of God, though unworthy.

The King standing up, the Sword shall be girt about him by the Lord Great Chamberlain ; and then, the King sitting down, the Archbishop shall say :

W ITH this Sword do justice, stop the growth of iniquity, protect the holy Church of God, help and defend widows and orphans, restore the things that are gone to decay, maintain the things that are restored, punish and reform what is amiss, and confirm what is in good order : that doing these things you may be glorious in all virtue ; and so faithfully serve our Lord Jesus Christ in this life, that you may reign for ever with him in the life which is to come.

Then the King, rising up, shall ungird his Sword, and, going to the Altar, offer it there in the scabbard, and then return and sit down in King Edward's Chair: and the Peer, who first received the Sword, shall offer the price of it, namely, one hundred shillings, and having thus redeemed it, shall receive it from the Dean of Westminster, from off the Altar, and draw it out of the scabbard, and carry it naked before his Majesty during the rest of the solemnity.

Then the Bishops who have assisted during the offering shall return to their places.

VIII

THE INVESTING WITH THE ARMILL AND ROYAL ROBE, AND THE DELIVERY OF THE ORB

Then the King arising, the Armill and Robe Royal or Pall of cloth of gold shall be delivered by the Officer of the Great Wardrobe to the Dean of Westminster, and by him put upon the King, standing; the Lord Great Chamberlain fastening the clasps. Then shall the King sit down, and the Orb with the Cross shall be brought from the Altar by the Dean of Westminster, and delivered into the King's hand by the Archbishop, pronouncing this Blessing and exhortation:

RECEIVE this Imperial Robe, and Orb; and the Lord your God endue you with knowledge and wisdom, with majesty and with power from on high; the Lord embrace you with his mercy on every side; the Lord cloath you with the robe of righteousness, and with the garments of salvation. And when you see this Orb thus set under the Cross, remember that the whole world is subject to the Power and Empire of Christ our Redeemer.

Then shall the King deliver his Orb to the Dean of Westminster, to be by him laid on the Altar.

IX

THE INVESTITURE
PER ANNULUM ET BACULUM

Then the Keeper of the Jewel House shall deliver to the Archbishop the King's Ring, in which a table jewel is enchased: the Archbishop shall put it on the fourth finger of his Majesty's right hand, and say:

RECEIVE this Ring, the ensign of kingly dignity, and of defence of the Catholic Faith; and as you are this day solemnly invested in the government of an earthly kingdom, so may you be sealed with that Spirit of promise which is the earnest of an heavenly inheritance, and reign with him who is the blessed and only Potentate, to whom be glory for ever and ever. *Amen.*

Then shall the Dean of Westminster bring the Sceptre with the Cross and the Sceptre with the Dove to the Archbishop.

The Glove, presented by the Lord of the Manor of Worksop, being put on, the Archbishop shall deliver the Sceptre with the Cross into the King's right hand, saying:

RECEIVE the Royal Sceptre, the ensign of kingly power and justice.

And then shall he deliver the Sceptre with the Dove into the King's left hand, and say:

RECEIVE the Rod of equity and mercy: and God, from whom all holy desires, all good counsels, and all just works do proceed, direct and assist you in the administration and exercise of all those powers which he hath given you. Be so merciful that you be not too remiss; so execute justice that you forget not mercy. Punish the wicked, protect and cherish the just, and lead your people in the way wherein they should go.

The Lord of the Manor of Worksop may support his Majesty's right arm.

X

THE PUTTING ON OF THE CROWN

The Archbishop, standing before the Altar, shall take the Crown into his hands, and laying it again before S. Edward's *him upon the Altar, he shall say:* Crown

O GOD, the crown of the faithful: Bless we beseech thee and sanctify this thy servant GEORGE our King; and as thou *Here the King* dost this day set a Crown of pure gold *must be put in* upon his head, so enrich his royal heart *mind to bow his* with thine abundant grace, and crown *head* him with all princely virtues, through the King eternal Jesus Christ our Lord. *Amen.*

Then the King still sitting in King Edward's Chair, the Archbishop, assisted with other Bishops, shall come from the Altar: the Dean of Westminster shall bring the Crown, and the Archbishop taking it of him shall reverently put it upon the King's head. At the sight whereof the people, with loud and repeated shouts, shall cry:

God save the King

the Peers and the Kings of Arms shall put on their Coronets; and the trumpets shall sound, and by a signal given, the great guns at the Tower shall be shot off.

The acclamation ceasing, the Archbishop shall go on, and say:

GOD crown you with a crown of glory and righteousness, that by the ministry of this our benediction, having a right faith and manifold fruit of good works, you may obtain the crown of an everlasting kingdom by the gift of him whose kingdom endureth for ever. *Amen.*

Then shall the choir sing:

BE strong and play the man: keep the commandments of the Lord thy God, and walk in his ways.

XI

THE PRESENTING OF THE HOLY BIBLE

Then shall the Dean of Westminster take the Holy Bible from off the Altar, and deliver it to the Archbishop, who shall present it to the King, first saying these words to him:

OUR gracious King; we present you with this Book, the most valuable thing that this world affords. Here is wisdom; this is the royal Law; these are the lively Oracles of God.

Then shall the King deliver back the Bible to the Archbishop, who shall give it to the Dean of Westminster, to be reverently placed again upon the holy Altar; and the Archbishop of York and the Bishops shall return to their places.

XII

THE BENEDICTION

And now the King having been thus anointed and crowned, and having received all the ensigns of royalty, the Archbishop shall solemnly bless him: and the Archbishop of York and all the Bishops, with the rest of the Peers, shall follow every part of the Benediction with a loud and hearty Amen.

THE Lord bless you and keep you: and as he hath made you King over his people, so may he prosper you in this world, and make you partake of his eternal felicity in the world to come. *Amen.*

THE Lord give you fruitful lands and healthful seasons; victorious fleets and armies, and a quiet Empire; a faithful Senate, wise and upright counsellors and magistrates, a loyal nobility, and a dutiful gentry ; a pious and learned and useful clergy ; an honest, peaceable, and obedient commonalty. *Amen.*

Then shall the Archbishop turn to the people, and say :

AND the same Lord God Almighty grant, that the Clergy and Nobles assembled here for this great and solemn service, and together with them all the people of the land, fearing God, and honouring the King, may by the merciful superintendency of the divine Providence, and the vigilant care of our gracious Sovereign, continually enjoy peace, plenty, and prosperity ; through Jesus Christ our Lord, to whom, with the eternal Father, and God the Holy Ghost, be glory in the Church, world without end. *Amen.*

XIII

THE INTHRONIZATION

Then shall the King go to his Throne, and be lifted up into it by the Archbishops and Bishops, and other Peers of the Kingdom ; and being Inthronized, or placed therein, all the Great Officers, those that bear the Swords and the Sceptres, and the Nobles who carried the other Regalia, shall stand round about the steps of the Throne ; and the Archbishop standing before the King, shall say :

STAND firm, and hold fast from hence - forth the seat and state of royal and imperial dignity, which is this day delivered unto you, in the Name and by the authority of Almighty God, and by the hands of us the Bishops and servants of God, though unworthy : And as you see us to approach nearer to God's Altar, so vouchsafe the more graciously to continue to us your royal favour and protection. And the Lord God Almighty, whose ministers we are, and the stewards of his mysteries, establish your Throne in righteousness, that it may stand fast for ever—more, like as the sun before him, and as the faithful witness in heaven. *Amen.*

XIV

THE HOMAGE

The Exhortation being ended, all the Princes and Peers then present shall do their Homage publicly and solemnly unto the King.

The Archbishop first shall kneel down before his Majesty's knees, and the rest of the Bishops shall kneel in their places : and they shall do their Homage together, for the shortening of the ceremony, the Archbishop saying :

I   Cosmo Archbishop of **Canterbury** [*and so every one of the rest, I N. Bishop of N., repeating the rest audibly after the Archbishop*] will be faithful and true, and faith and truth will bear unto you our Sovereign Lord, and your heirs Kings of **Great Britain, Ireland,** and the British Dominions beyond the Seas, Defenders of the Faith, and Emperors of India. And I will do, and truly acknowledge, the service of the lands which I claim to hold of you, as in right of the Church. So help me God.

Then shall the Archbishop kiss the King's left cheek.

Then the Duke of Gloucester, taking off his Coronet, shall kneel down before his Majesty's knees, the rest of the Princes of the Blood Royal, being Peers of the Realm, kneeling in their places, taking off their Coronets, and pronouncing the words of Homage after him, the Duke of Gloucester saying :

I   N. Prince, or Duke, &c., of N. do become your liege man of life and limb, and of earthly worship ; and faith and truth I will bear unto you, to live and die, against all manner of folks. So help me God.

Then shall the Princes of the Blood Royal, being Peers of the Realm, arising severally touch the Crown on his Majesty's head and kiss his Majesty's left cheek. After which the other Peers of the Realm, who are then in their seats, shall kneel down, put off their Coronets, and do their Homage, the Dukes first by themselves, and so the Marquesses, the Earls, the Viscounts, and the Barons, severally in their places, the first of each Order kneeling before his Majesty, and the others of his Order who are near his Majesty also kneeling in their places, and all of his Order saying after him :

I   N. Duke, or Earl, &c., of N. do become your liege man of life and limb, and of earthly worship ; and faith and truth I will bear unto you, to live and die, against all manner of folks. So help me God.

The Peers having done their Homage, the first of each Order, putting off his Coronet, shall singly ascend the throne, and stretching forth his hand, touch the Crown on his Majesty's head, as promising by that ceremony for himself and his Order to be ever ready to support it with all their power ; and then shall he kiss the King's cheek.

While the Princes and Peers are thus doing their Homage, the King, if he thinks good, shall deliver his Sceptre, with the Cross and the Sceptre or Rod with the Dove, to some one near to the Blood Royal, or to the Lords that carried them in the procession, or to any other that he pleaseth to assign, to hold them by him.

And the Bishops that support the King in the procession may also ease him, by supporting the Crown, as there shall be occasion. At the same time the choir shall sing anthems.

[*Anthems by Christopher Tye, Henry Purcell, Orlando Gibbons, William Boyce, George Dyson, and Samuel Sebastian Wesley were sung.*]

When the Homage is ended, the drums shall beat, and the trumpets sound, and all the people shout, crying out :

God save King George
Long live King George
May the King live for ever

The solemnity of the King's Coronation being thus ended, the Archbishop shall leave the King in his throne and go to the Altar.

XV

THE QUEEN'S CORONATION

The Queen shall arise and go to the steps of the Altar, supported by two Bishops, and there kneel down, whilst the Archbishop saith the following prayer :

ALMIGHTY GOD, the fountain of all goodness : Give ear, we beseech thee, to our prayers, and multiply thy blessings upon this thy servant ELIZABETH, whom in thy Name, with all humble devotion, we consecrate our Queen ; defend her evermore from all dangers, ghostly and bodily ; make her a great example of virtue and piety, and a blessing to the kingdom ; through Jesus Christ our Lord, who liveth and reigneth with thee, O Father, in the unity of the Holy Spirit, world without end. *Amen.*

This prayer being ended, the Queen shall arise and come to the place of her anointing : which is to be at a faldstool set for that purpose before the Altar, between the steps and King Edward's Chair. There shall she kneel down, and four Peeresses, appointed for that service, holding a rich pall of cloth of gold over her, the Archbishop shall pour the holy Oil upon the crown of her head, saying these words :

IN the Name of the Father, and of the Son, and of the Holy Ghost : Let the anointing with this Oil increase your honour, and the grace of God's Holy Spirit establish you, for ever and ever. *Amen.*

Then shall the Archbishop receive from the Keeper of the Jewel House the Queen's Ring, and put it upon the fourth finger of her right hand, saying :

RECEIVE this Ring, the seal of a sincere faith ; and God, to whom belongeth all power and dignity, prosper you in this your honour, and grant you therein long to continue, fearing him always, and always doing such things as shall please him, through Jesus Christ our Lord. *Amen.*

Then the Archbishop shall take the Crown from off the Altar into his hands, and reverently set it upon the Queen's head, saying :

RECEIVE the Crown of glory, honour, and joy : And God, the crown of the faithful, who by our Episcopal hands (though unworthy) doth this day set a crown of pure gold upon your head, enrich your royal heart with his abundant grace, and crown you with all princely virtues in this life, and with everlasting gladness in the life that is to come, through Jesus Christ our Lord. *Amen.*

The Queen being crowned all the Peeresses shall put on their Coronets.

Then shall the Archbishop put the Sceptre into the Queen's right hand, and the Ivory Rod with the Dove into her left hand ; and say this prayer :

O LORD, the giver of all perfection : Grant unto this thy servant ELIZABETH our Queen, that by the powerful and mild influence of her piety and virtue, she may adorn the high dignity which she hath obtained, through Jesus Christ our Lord. *Amen.*

The Queen being thus anointed, and crowned, and having received all her ornaments, shall arise and go from the Altar, supported by her two Bishops, and so up to the Theatre. And as she passeth by the King on his throne, she shall bow herself reverently to his Majesty, and then be conducted to her own throne, and without any further ceremony take her place in it.

XVI

THE COMMUNION

Then shall the organ play and the choir sing the Offertory.

O HEARKEN thou unto the voice of my calling, my King and my God : for unto thee will I make my prayer.

In the mean while the King and Queen shall deliver their Sceptres to the Lords who had previously borne them, and descend from their thrones, supported and attended as before ; and go to the steps of the Altar, where, taking off their Crowns, which they shall deliver to the Lord Great Chamberlain and other appointed Officer to hold, they shall kneel down.

And first the King shall offer Bread and Wine for the Communion, which being brought out of Saint Edward's Chapel, and delivered into his hands (the Bread upon the Paten by the Bishop that read the Epistle, and the Wine in the Chalice by the Bishop that read the Gospel), shall by the Archbishop be received from the King, and reverently placed upon the Altar, and decently covered with a fair linen cloth, the Archbishop first saying this prayer :

BLESS, O Lord, we beseech thee, these thy gifts, and sanctify them unto this holy use, that by them we may be made partakers of the Body and Blood of thine only-begotten Son Jesus Christ, and fed unto everlasting life of soul and body : And that thy servant King GEORGE may be enabled to the discharge of his weighty office, whereunto of thy great goodness thou hast called and appointed him. Grant this, O Lord, for Jesus Christ's sake, our only Mediator and Advocate. *Amen.*

Then the King kneeling, as before, shall make his Oblation, offering a Pall or Altar-cloth delivered by the Officer of the Great Wardrobe to the Lord Great Chamberlain, and by him, kneeling, to his Majesty, and an Ingot or Wedge of Gold of a pound weight, which the Treasurer of the Household shall deliver to the Lord Great Chamberlain, and he to his Majesty ; and the Archbishop coming to him, shall receive and place them upon the Altar.

The Queen also at the same time shall make her Oblation of a Pall or Altar-cloth, and a Mark weight of Gold, in like manner as the King.

Then shall the King and Queen return to their chairs, and kneel down at their faldstools, and the Archbishop shall say the Prayer for the Church Militant.

[Now comes the Service of Holy Communion.]

When the Archbishops, and Dean of Westminster, with the Bishops Assistants (namely, those who have read the Epistle and the Gospel), have communicated in both kinds, the King and Queen shall advance to the steps of the Altar and kneel down, and the Archbishop shall administer the Bread, and the Dean of Westminster the Cup, to them.

[After the actual Communion]

The King and Queen shall then put on their Crowns, and repair to their Thrones, there taking the Sceptres in their hands again.

Then shall the Archbishop go on to the Post-Communion, he and all the people saying the Lord's Prayer.

[Then follows the Prayer of Oblation, the singing of the Gloria, and the Benediction by the Archbishop.]

XVII

Then shall the choir sing Te Deum Laudamus.

XVIII

THE RECESS

In the mean time, the King attended and accompanied as before, the four Swords being carried before him, shall descend from his throne crowned, and, carrying his Sceptre and Rod in his hands, go into the area eastward of the Theatre, and pass on through the door on the South side of the Altar into Saint Edward's Chapel ; and as they pass by the Altar, the rest of the Regalia, lying upon it, are to be delivered by the Dean of Westminster to the Lords that carried them in the procession, and so they shall proceed in state into the Chapel. The Queen at the same time descending, shall go in like manner into the same Chapel at the door on the North side of the Altar ; bearing her Sceptre in her right hand, and her Ivory Rod in her left.

The King and Queen being come into the Chapel, the King, standing before the Altar, shall deliver the Sceptre with the Dove to the Archbishop, who shall lay it upon the Altar there. And the golden Spurs and Saint Edward's Staff are to be given into the hands of the Dean of Westminster, and by him laid there also.

The King shall then be disrobed of his Royal Robe of State, and arrayed in his Robe of purple velvet, and wearing his Imperial Crown shall then receive in his left hand the Orb from the Archbishop.

Then their Majesties shall proceed through the Choir to the West door of the Church, in the same way as they came, wearing their Crowns : the King bearing in his right hand the Sceptre with the Cross, and in his left the Orb ; the Queen bearing in her right hand her Sceptre with the Cross, and in her left the Ivory Rod with the Dove ; all Peers wearing their Coronets.

Photo]   *[Fox*

CROWNED WITH THE CROWN OF HIS FATHERS

This historic photograph, taken in Westminster Abbey on the Coronation Day of George VI, shows the supreme moment of the Service, when the Archbishop of Canterbury placed St. Edward's Crown on the head of the young King, who is seated in King Edward's Chair and holding the Royal Sceptre with the Dove in his left hand. Behind the Archbishop stands the Dean of Westminster holding the Bible which was later presented to the King.

CHAPTER 31

SPLENDOURS OF CORONATION DAY
AN EYE–WITNESS ACCOUNT

To the millions who glimpsed its extraordinary pageantry and the enormously great multitude who "listened-in" to the broadcasts of the processions and the ceremony in Westminster Abbey, May 12th, 1937, must be a day ever to be held in undying remembrance. Here we have some impressions penned within a few minutes of the great events

WHEN dawn broke on the day King George VI was crowned at Westminster a thin mist shrouded the expectant city. The banners and flags hung limp from their poles, and the glorious colours of the decorations were but dimly seen. In the parks, where thousands had spent the hours of the night, moisture dripped from the trees on the forms scattered about the grass in grotesque attitudes, and the route was lined by huddled figures, macintoshed or swathed in coats or newspapers. Overhead the skies were grey and lowering, though fortunately the rain kept off for the time.

For millions in London, in Britain, that night there was no sleep.

Trains packed to the guards'-vans rushed through the dark from all the great cities, and the lights of a myriad motor-coaches and cars sprayed the roads of the countryside for a hundred miles and more around the metropolis. Through the streets, usually so quiet at that early hour, the invaders marched on foot or rushed in taxis, all impelled by the same desire to obtain as good a place as possible on the processional way.

By two o'clock in the morning many of the best places of vantage were well-nigh filled. Trafalgar Square was a mist-strewn sea of heads, the Mall was lined by a dense throng, and before the Palace an uncountable multitude filled every inch of pavement and watched with unrelenting gaze the blinded windows where the prime movers in the great drama were sleeping.

Piccadilly Circus was as lively as on a Boat-race night, the kerbs of Whitehall and Parliament Square were littered with sleepers, and family parties partook of an early breakfast of tea and sandwiches beneath the magnificent decorations of the great shops in Oxford Street and Regent Street.

At dawn the stream became a torrent. The sleepers in the parks, wakened by stumbling feet, stretched their limbs and danced and sang. Hyde Park had been a dormitory for fifty thousand men and women and children, but each minute that passed saw hundreds streaming in at every gate.

Barrier after barrier was shut by the watchful police, but still the mighty multitude grew and grew. The roads, long cleared of traffic, were lined by "specials" and soldiery, and as each detachment took up its post it was given a friendly cheer of greeting. Boy Scouts were much in evidence, and the ambulance men and girls were already busy about their work of mercy.

So the hours passed, and with full daylight the mist passed too. Now the millions were keyed into a state of high expectancy and when at last the first of the processions moved away from the Palace it passed between a packed mass of ebullient humanity.

The first cheers came, appropriately enough, for an Indian contingent—magnificent men, garbed in brilliant uniforms of red and gold, purple and green and blue, riding magnificent mounts. Then the cheers broke out afresh when the cavalry escorts of Dominion troops rode past—Royal Canadian Mounted Police, Aussies and Anzacs, and South Africans. And none cheered so loudly or so long as the veterans of the Great War, whose hearts were warmed by seeing once again the jaunty hats of their old-time comrades.

On the stroke of time the first of the processions began to leave the courtyard of the Palace. Car after car passed in procession—too quickly for the crowd's taste, who would gladly have looked long at the distinguished men and women who were carried past on their way to the Abbey. Almost all the States of the world were represented in the cavalcade, from the great United States to tiny San Marino. Princess Juliana of Holland was rapturously received, and the dusky Sultan of Zanzibar was given a cheer. So they passed, and for a space the roadway was left to the mounted police and military stewards.

Half an hour went by. And now the premiers of the British Commonwealth drove past, led by Mr. Baldwin and his wife, who were given a particularly cordial, even affectionate, reception.

"Not long to wait now!" Amid a sea

Photo]   [L.N.A.

SOME OF THE MILLIONS WHO WAITED TO CHEER

More than three million people—so it is estimated—lined the route of the Coronation Procession of George VI. Many of them took up their positions overnight, as shown in this photograph (right) of the crowd at midnight beneath Nelson's Column in Trafalgar Square. Left is a picture taken in the Square a few hours later ; note the large number of box periscopes in use—a device not yet invented when King George V was crowned.

Photo] [Fox

ENTERING LONDON'S PROCESSIONAL WAY

The Mall has seen many splendid spectacles, but never one to surpass the Coronation Procession of King George VI and Queen Elizabeth. Fifty thousand people greeted the cavalcade as it swept round the Victoria Memorial and headed east for the Admiralty Arch. On each side were erected huge stands for spectators, and the banners of red and blue were as dignified as impressive.

of fluttering handkerchiefs the little Princesses passed by, as fairy princesses ought to do, in a glittering coach of glass and gold. Then a great roar of cheering greeted the departure of Queen Mary from Marlborough House.

And now it is ten-thirty. A deep hush comes upon the people, for all are thinking of the royal pair who are now just about to leave the Palace to embark upon their Coronation journey.

Suddenly the hush is broken, and almost at that moment a ray of sunshine pierces the ashen canopy overhead. Preceded by a glittering array of trumpeters and guards, the soon-to-be-crowned sovereigns of the British Commonwealth emerge from the Palace gates and set out on their triumphal progress to the Abbey.

The roar of cheers is incessant. The waves of acclamation rebound from the ancient coach as it rumbles past the memorial to Queen Victoria of blessed memory, down the royal way of the Mall, through the Admiralty Arch and past Trafalgar Square

—packed to capacity and more than capacity, with thousands massed on every wall and roof in the vicinity—and so swinging down Whitehall to Parliament Square and the Abbey doors. And thus we come to the Abbey itself, so long closed to the outer world.

Though a pale and silvery sunshine bathed its walls, hardly a ray penetrated into the building itself, for most of the windows were closed against the light of day. The grey dignity of the glorious fane gave place on Coronation Day to splendid pageantry. The interior of the Abbey was transformed into a symphony in blue and silver. The walls were hung with draperies, and, to accommodate the vast throng of those who had been bidden to the ceremony, tier upon tier of seats had been built up reaching almost to the clerestory.

But if the windows shut out the light of day a myriad of ingeniously concealed lights supplemented the ordinary illumination of the Abbey, and during the ceremony

Photos]   *[Keystone ; Fox*

THEIR MAJESTIES GO TO THEIR CROWNING

The glass sides of the State Coach in which the King and Queen travelled to and from Westminster Abbey enabled the host of sightseers to gratify their dearest wish—to see their Sovereigns in the flesh. That the spectacle was a wonderful one—so wonderful as to be almost incredible—is apparent from these photographs, taken as the coach bearing Their Majesties emerged from the Admiralty Arch into Trafalgar Square   The King wears the Cap of Maintenance.

itself showed the latter's colour and splendour as they have never been seen before. But the symphony of grey and silver into which the Abbey had been transformed in preparation for the Coronation underwent yet another change, for in the early hours of May 12th the seven thousand spectators the King had bidden to attend upon his crowning began to arrive in the Abbey.

From six o'clock onwards the seats had been filling up. Some 300 gold-staff officers marshal the guests to their appointed seats. Everything goes in a quiet and orderly fashion. No one is hurried, no one is flustered: everyone has arrived betimes. And so, slowly, the Abbey fills.

The King has forgotten no one. Within the walls of the Abbey are those who are there by ancient right, Royal Princes, Ambassadors and Ministers of foreign States, peers and peeresses. But there are humbler guests too. Among that great congregation are working men and women who have come at the King's wish, war widows and the mothers of men who gave their lives in the war.

The Abbey had been transformed once with the work of months. It is transformed again in a few hours by the gorgeous array of those who form this vast congregation.

Even before the pageantry of the royal procession begins the scene is one of kaleidoscopic colour. The peers in the South transept with their purple robes, the peeresses in the North transept with their glittering tiaras, the many-hued uniforms of the foreign representatives: costumes and uniforms build up a mass of glittering colour that forms a setting of living jewels for the scene that is to follow.

At half past nine the doors of the Abbey are shut. All those except the members of the Royal Family who are to witness the ceremony are in their places, from peer to pit-boy, and by the special wish of the King a pit-boy had his place in that great assemblage, a fine token of the interest that His Majesty has in the humblest of his subjects.

For two hours there is an expectant hush ;

Photo] [P.N.A.

DRAWING NEAR TO THE ABBEY

On Coronation Day King George and his Queen moved through the streets in the famous State Coach, drawn by eight Windsor Greys and escorted by Royal Footmen and Yeomen of the Guard. This photograph shows the cavalcade approaching the Abbey entrance.

a subdued murmur, that sense of anticipation that seems to electrify such an assembly on such an occasion. The time of waiting passes quickly. The tiers of seats have been filled up, and then when the lesser people have taken their places there come to seats in the choir the representatives of foreign powers. There is Princess Juliana, future Queen of Holland, with her newly wed husband, Prince Bernhard, Prince and Princess Chichibu of Japan, the Count of Flanders representing the King of the Belgians, sixty of them all told, representing the world literally from China to Peru.

In the meantime, too, the royal gallery has been filling up. Of all the seven thousand or more who fill the Abbey only about 500 actually see the crowning of the King, but the occupants of the royal gallery see every incident of the great

Photos]　　　　　　　　　　　　　　　　　　　　　　　　　[Fox

BEFORE THE ANOINTING AND CROWNING

After proceeding up the body of the Abbey from the west door, the King and Queen passed to their Chairs of Estate placed on the south side of the altar. Behind them is the royal box, in which are (left to right) the Earl and Countess of Strathmore (parents of the Queen), the Duchess of Kent, the Duchess of Gloucester, the Queen of Norway, Queen Mary, Princess Elizabeth, Princess Margaret Rose and the Princess Royal—a nearer view of some of whom is seen above. Left of the King are the Marquess of Zetland and the Earl of Cork bearing Swords of State.

Photo]

[Fox

HOMAGE TO THE NEWLY CROWNED KING

The photograph above shows a peer paying homage to the King after he had been crowned and enthroned. Formerly each peer paid homage separately, but at the coronation of George VI only the premier peer of each order rendered homage. He acted for the other peers of his own rank who, with coronets doffed, repeated the oath of allegiance to the King.

ceremony. Altogether eighteen members of the Royal Family were present, but the moment that those assembled in the Abbey awaited with the keenest anticipation was that when Queen Mary should enter. She had broken precedent in attending her son's Coronation, but she broke it with that true appreciation of the feeling of the people that has made her so much-loved a figure in English life.

At twenty minutes to eleven she entered the Abbey, accompanied by her sister-in-law the Queen of Norway. The great congregation rose and Queen Mary in a golden gown beneath her purple robes was escorted up the nave by the heralds to her place in the royal gallery, and was received there by the Duchess of Gloucester. Her progress up the nave was deeply impressive and no more stately or gracious figure was seen on that day.

Eleven o'clock approaches, the hour of the King's arrival. A hush falls on the great congregation; even the whispered conversations that had been carried on

before die down. All eyes are turned towards the west door of the Abbey, through which first of all the Queen's procession will come. Even through the walls of the Abbey the clock of Big Ben is heard striking eleven o'clock, and within a minute or two a roar of cheers is heard: the King and Queen are here. Another pause, but this time a shorter one. Their Majesties have entered the Annexe on the west front of the Abbey where are the robing-rooms in which they assume the robes worn during the first part of the ceremony, and where the great officers of the household take charge of the Regalia which they are to carry in the procession up the nave to the theatre.

Carefully guarded through the night, the Regalia now lies on a table covered with cloth of gold in the middle of which is St. Edward's Crown, with which the King is presently to be crowned, on a crimson cushion. First the Queen's procession is formed, and soon after a quarter past eleven Her Majesty entered the Abbey. Pale,

Photo]
[Fox

THE ARCHBISHOP CROWNS THE QUEEN

The coronation of the Queen is a much simpler ceremony than that of the coronation of the King. After the crowning of the King she is anointed on the head, a ring is placed on her finger, and the crown is placed on her head by the Archbishop of Canterbury. The photograph above shows the Archbishop in the act of placing the crown on the head of Queen Elizabeth.

grave and obviously impressed by the solemnity of the occasion, the Queen passed to her place before the high altar, there to await the coming of the King. As the Queen passed up the nave she was greeted according to custom by the boys of Westminster School with cries of *"Vivat, vivat Regina"*. A few minutes later the King's procession entered through the West door, long, stately, impressive, it is correctly called the "Great Proceeding". The Abbey Beadle leads it and then come the King's Chaplains, the Domestic Chaplains and the clergy of Westminster Abbey; then follow the officers of the Orders of Chivalry, the Standard Bearers and the peers carrying the Regalia, and last the King in his crimson robe of state, his train borne by eight pages, with the Bishop of Bath and Wells walking on his left and the Bishop of Durham on his right.

As the King, a regal but, for his age, a slim and almost boyish figure walked up the nave to the theatre with measured and dignified steps, the scholars of Westminster hailed him as they had hailed the Queen, *"Vivat, vivat Rex"*, but this time their cry was blended with the fanfare of trumpets, and to all who saw and heard the Coronation ceremony those fanfares, which recurred from time to time, echoing from the roof, will remain one of the ineffaceable musical memories of the day.

Arrived before the altar the King took his place on the Chair of Estate on the right of that which the Queen already occupied. Then the great ceremony began with the presentation of the King to his people by the Archbishop of Canterbury. From the "theatre" the King showed himself four times to the people, North, South, East and West, while the Archbishop in ringing tones cried: "Sirs, I here present unto you King George, your undoubted King:

IN ALL THE POMP OF IMPERIAL MAJESTY

At the close of the Coronation Service the newly crowned King returned in procession down the nave to the west door. The spectacle was superb in its arrangement and composition. His Majesty, arrayed in his robe of purple velvet, wearing the Imperial Crown and carrying the Orb and Sceptre, passed between the ranks of the brilliant assembly. Attending him were the lords spiritual and temporal who, by time-honoured custom, have parts in the ancient ceremony.

Wherefore all you who are come this day to do your homage and service, Are you willing to do the same ?'' To be answered by the boys of Westminster School with a cry of "Ay, God Save the King", and after each presentation by the Archbishop the State trumpeters sounded their silvery fanfare.

Thereafter the King took the Coronation Oath, and in this a significant change was made since the Coronation of King George V. On the previous day General Smuts had pointed out that the King was the first King to be "King of Kingdoms", and on Coronation Day His Majesty swore to govern not only Great Britain but Ireland, Canada, Australia, New Zealand and South Africa and his other Possessions and Territories and the Empire of India "according to their respective laws and customs".

Now came the culminating scene of the great ceremony. The King left his Chair of Estate and passed to the Chair of St. Edward. Everyone who has ever been inside Westminster Abbey has seen the Coronation Chair, a rough wooden chair, on which vandals have carved their initials and beneath the wooden seat of which is the Stone of Destiny on which every sovereign since Edward I has been crowned. Now, at this solemn moment, the King takes his place on that chair for the anointing and the actual crowning.

The Solemn Act of Crowning

As he sat in King Edward's Chair, four Knights of the Garter held a silken canopy above his head while the Archbishop of Canterbury anointed him with oil from the ampulla. There followed the presenting of the spurs, the girding of the sword and those other ceremonies that precede the actual crowning.

Then came the putting on of the crown. That culminating act of the Coronation was performed by the Archbishop of Canterbury with impressive dignity. It is the privilege of the Dean of Westminster to give St. Edward's Crown into the hands of the Archbishop, and the rubric of the Coronation service prescribes that the Archbishop shall reverently place the crown on the King's head. In the Coronation Chair the King sat with the Sceptre and Orb in his hands while the Archbishop held the crown high above his head, and then after a moment's pause lowered it slowly on to his head amid cries of "God Save the King". At the moment the King was crowned the peers and heralds with a simultaneous uplifting of the arms placed their coronets on their heads. One last ceremony remained to be gone through before the whole act of Coronation was concluded—the inthronization, when the King was led by the Archbishop, other bishops and peers to the throne upon the dais which hitherto had remained vacant.

Homage to Their Liege Lord

The King is crowned, and it remains only for his subjects to do him homage as he sits upon his throne : first the Archbishop of Canterbury, then the Duke of Gloucester on behalf of the Princes of the Blood Royal, and so on through each degree of the peerage. Once each peer did separate homage, but this ceremony has been dispensed with, the first of each order of the peerage only kneeling before the King and repeating the words of homage.

Throughout the ceremony Her Majesty had sat in her Chair of Estate watching every detail of the ceremony. Her eyes were always upon the King, following him with solicitous appreciation throughout the long and trying ceremonial through which he had gone. The Coronation of the Queen was, in comparison, a brief ceremony. By the Archbishop of Canterbury the Queen was anointed, the ring was placed on her finger and the delicate crown of platinum and diamonds was placed on her head. Finally, the King and Queen took Communion together and the *Te Deum* brought the service to a close.

No hitch marred it. The King's voice rang strong and sincerely when he made the responses and took the Oath. There was no sign of hesitancy, only such pauses as a man may make when he weighs the solemn words he is called upon to speak before he utters them.

SETTING OFF FOR THE TRIUMPHAL PROGRESS

The Coronation Service is over, and the royal procession has returned through the Abbey nave to the Annexe (specially built for the occasion and shown on the left of the photograph). The just-crowned King and Queen have entered the coach and are about to set out on the four mile journey through the streets of their capital to Buckingham Palace.

CHAPTER 32

THE PEOPLE ACCLAIM THEIR MAJESTIES

When the newly crowned King George and Queen Elizabeth emerged from the Abbey on the day of their Coronation they were met with a tremendous demonstration of loyalty—and of something more. During that historic drive millions of their subjects made it plain that they had taken their new sovereigns to their hearts

AFTER a short respite in the Abbey, during which the procession was reformed, the signal to start was given. At 2.15 p.m. the Royal Standard was broken over the Annexe, and the carriages drew up before the entrance. Some time beforehand the head of the procession had been formed up at Hanover Street, and in a moment or two, under a darkening sky, the great return journey to Buckingham Palace began.

At the moment the King left the Abbey the eight ringers in the tower began a complete peal of 5,040 changes, which took three and a half hours. During the ceremony they had rung "rounds", followed, at the moment the crown was placed on the King's head, by the crashes of bells technically known as a "fire".

Such was the length of the procession that when the State Coach left the Annexe, the leading troops had already reached Oxford Circus. Never can such a triumphal progress have been seen in the streets of London, despite the centuries of history of which those same streets have been witnesses. The cheering must have been heard miles away.

But of all the cheering which greeted them in full-throated, spontaneous outbursts along the line of route, none can have touched the hearts of Their Majesties more than that which came frantically from the lips of the 40,000 children representing 877 schools assembled along the Embankment

between Westminster Bridge and Embankment Place.

With their lunches in shopping-bags or school satchels, they had waited with all the eagerness of childhood for that passage of a fairy coach which was to make this day for ever remembered in their lives. The time did not hang heavy on their hands, for while they were waiting for the great moment to come they saw part of the procession as it passed down the Embankment to its forming-up point. For them, as was only right, there was no rushing and scrambling, special sections being allotted to the 877 schools represented.

A great feature of the day was the widespread use of periscopes, in which street-hawkers did a lively trade. Some were patriotically decorated in red, white and blue, others were sixpenny plain, and there were even home-made ones formed by the simple process of fixing a mirror to the end of a walking-stick or umbrella. In the latter case we witnessed the paradoxical sight of their owners turning their backs on the procession they had come to see, that they might view it the better.

To the crowds, among whom were vast numbers who had never seen soldiers in anything save their khaki field dress, a striking feature of the procession was the variety of full-dress uniforms. The infantry wore for the first time their new blue uniforms, but the most outstanding were those of the cavalry units : the steel breastplates of the Household Cavalry ; the bearskins and red tunics of the Royal Scots Greys ; the flat-topped, plumed hats and coloured facings of the Lancers ; while even more gorgeous were the splendid uniforms of the Indian contingent, the King's Indian Orderly Officers and his Indian A.D.C.s.

Apart from the coach containing the King and Queen, it is difficult to say which portion of this great procession drew the greatest measure of applause from a crowd which welcomed everything with frantic cheers. One thing is certain : an added warmth was noticeable in the acclamations which greeted the regal figure of Queen Mary as she drove part in a glass coach in which were seated with her the young Princesses Elizabeth and Margaret.

To pass away the time during their long vigil the crowd sang their favourite songs.

Probably the finest piece of community singing heard during the day was the whole-hearted rendering of "Old Soldiers Never Die" by the body of ex-Service men stationed at Hyde Park Corner. It was surpassed only by their cheering as the State Coach passed under the arch at the top of Constitution Hill.

What a lot there was to look at ! One pair of eyes seemed totally inadequate to cope with the swiftly moving pageant : the King's bargemaster and watermen ; the King's marshalmen with shakos on their heads ; the Yeomen of the Guard in their picturesque Tudor garb ; the Burmese soldiers, with their unusual head-gear ; the magnificent "Mounties" in scarlet tunics and stetsons, the finest horsemen in the world ; the "Aussies" and 'Anzacs", bringing back memories of twenty years ago ; the swarthy, bearded Indians ; bronzed South Africans ; repre-

Photo]   *[L.N.A.*

TURNING POINT ON THE PROCESSIONAL ROUTE

This striking photograph of the procession turning round the Royal Artillery Memorial at Hyde Park Corner, shows a detachment of the Royal Canadian Mounted Police, or "Mounties", as they are popularly called, in their scarlet tunics and wide brimmed stetson hats. On the left can be seen the stand erected in front of St. George's Hospital and in the background the southern entrance to Hyde Park, Apsley Gate.

A RIGHT ROYAL KING

Enthusiasm knew no bounds as our young King, wearing his Imperial Crown, drove back to his palace after the Coronation. All who saw the youthful monarch marvelled at his royal mien and demeanour.

sentatives of the Home services—infantry, cavalry of the line, "K" battery of the R.H.A., the five regiments of Guards, the Royal Marines, the Royal Air Force, the Royal Tank Corps and many others.

Then there was the carriage procession of Prime Ministers, colonial rulers and representatives of India and Burma, in the passage of which Mr. Baldwin was singled out for a specially hearty burst of cheering. These carriages were accompanied by mounted escorts of lancers, dragoons, and cavalry units from India, Australia, Canada and New Zealand, as well as an escort of Metropolitan Mounted Police. There were four divisions of the Sovereign's escort of Life Guards, and riding beside the Royal State Coach were the Master of the Horse, Gold and Silver Sticks in Waiting, the Field Marshal commanding the troops and the Field Officer in Brigade Waiting; behind the coach the King's standard was borne by the Regimental Corporal-Major of the Life Guards. Following the standard rode

HOME AGAIN AFTER THE CORONATION

After their long journey through the streets of London, the royal cavalcade arrived back at Buckingham Palace just after four-o'clock. By then the weather, which had been lowering all day, had taken a turn for the worse, but the falling rain was unable to damp the tremendous enthusiasm of the many thousands who had waited so long and so patiently to greet their newly crowned sovereigns in the crowded streets from Westminster through Piccadilly, Oxford Street and Hyde Park to the Palace.

the Duke of Gloucester in scarlet and plumed hat, the Duke of Kent in naval uniform, Lord Louis Mountbatten, the Earl of Athlone and the Earl of Harewood.

But the high light of this colourful pageant, the final glorious moment for which the crowds had waited patiently for hours, was the passage of the Coach of State itself, resplendent in gold, drawn by four pairs of Windsor Greys, with four scarlet-coated riders, and inside it the new-crowned King of England and his Consort, both of them wearing their crowns, and bowing graciously to the deafening acclamations of their subjects.

In spite of the fitful rain the densely packed crowds were in no wise discouraged and shouted their welcome as the cavalcade went on through Piccadilly Circus, Regent Street, Oxford Street, Hyde Park and Constitution Hill and so back to Buckingham Palace.

It was five minutes past four when the royal coach turned into the quadrangle of Buckingham Palace, after a two-hour drive among Their Majesties' loyal subjects, every yard of which had been made amid a mighty roar of welcome.

Half an hour later the King and Queen, still crowned and robed, with Queen Mary and other members of the Royal Family, appeared on the balcony of the palace. The spontaneous tribute the royal pair received from the thousands massed in front of the railings, coupled with the continuous acclamations they had received on their Coronation progress through their capital, must have assured them not only of the homage and loyalty of their subjects, but also of the deep affection unreservedly bestowed upon them from the hearts of their people.

At 7.20 p.m. that same evening, an all-world relay, representing the homage and devotion of the assembled peoples of the Empire, was broadcast by the B.B.C. Among the bearers of messages of goodwill from their people were Lt.-General Sir Reginald Hildyard, Governor of Bermuda ; the vice-chairman of the Newfoundland

Photo　　　　　　　　　　　　　　　　　　　　　　　　　　　　　　　[*B.I.P.P.A.*

CROWNED AND ACCLAIMED BY THE PEOPLE

Half an hour after the Royal Coach returned to the Palace and to the accompaniment of vociferous cheers from the tens of thousands massed in front of the Palace railings, the King and Queen, still robed and with their crowns, appeared on the balcony in company with Queen Mary and the Princesses Elizabeth and Margaret, to acknowledge their people's greeting.

Commission of Government, Mr. W. R. Howley; the Prime Minister of Canada, the Rt. Hon. W. L. Mackenzie King; the Rt. Hon. M. J. Savage, Prime Minister of New Zealand; the Rt. Hon. J. A. Lyons, Prime Minister of Australia; the chief Minister of Burma; the Viceroy of India; the Prime Minister of Southern Rhodesia, the Hon. G. M. Huggins; General Hertzog, Prime Minister of the Union of South Africa, and the Rt. Hon. Stanley Baldwin, Prime Minister of the United Kingdom.

And then, fitting climax to an historic day, at eight o'clock the King, speaking from Buckingham Palace, broadcast his first message to his Empire, his myriad peoples throughout the world. It is given below.

The King's Broadcast Message to The Empire

*I*T is with a very full heart that I speak to you tonight. Never before has a newly crowned King been able to talk to all his peoples in their own homes on the day of his Coronation. Never has the ceremony itself had so wide a significance, for the Dominions are now free and equal partners with this ancient Kingdom, and I felt this morning that the whole Empire was in very truth gathered within the walls of Westminster Abbey.

I REJOICE that I can now speak to you all, wherever you may be, greeting old friends in distant lands and, as I hope, new friends in those parts where it has not yet been my good fortune to go. In this personal way the Queen and I wish health and happiness to you all, and we do not forget at this time of celebration those who are living under the shadow of sickness or distress. The example of courage and good citizenship is always before us, and to them I would send a special message of sympathy and good cheer.

I CANNOT find words with which to thank you for your love and loyalty to the Queen and myself. Your good will in the streets today, your countless messages from overseas and from every quarter of these islands, have filled our hearts to overflowing. I will only say this: If, in the coming years, I can show my gratitude in service to you, that is the way above all others that I would choose.

To many millions the Crown is the symbol of unity. By the grace of God and by the will of the free peoples of the British Commonwealth, I have assumed that Crown. In me, as your King, is vested for a time the duty of maintaining its honour and integrity.

*T*HIS is, indeed, a grave and constant responsibility, but it gave me confidence to see your representatives around me in the Abbey and to know that you, too, were enabled to join in that infinitely beautiful ceremonial. Its outward forms come down from distant times, but its inner meaning and message are always new; for the highest of distinctions is the service of others, and to the ministry of Kingship I have in your hearing dedicated myself, with the Queen at my side, in words of the deepest solemnity. We will, God helping us, faithfully discharge our trust.

*T*HOSE of you who are children now will, I hope, retain memories of a day of carefree happiness such as I still have of the day of my Grandfather's Coronation. In years to come some of you will travel from one part of the Commonwealth to another, and moving thus within the family circle will meet others whose thoughts are coloured by the same memories, whose hearts are united in devotion to our common heritage.

You will learn, I hope, how much our free association means to us, how much our friendship with each other and with all the nations upon earth can help the cause of peace and progress.

*T*HE Queen and I will always keep in our hearts the inspiration of this day. May we ever be worthy of the goodwill which, I am proud to think, surrounds us at the outset of my reign. I thank you from my heart, and may God bless you all.

GOD SAVE THE KING